TYPE THEORY
AND
FUNCTIONAL
PROGRAMMING

INTERNATIONAL COMPUTER SCIENCE SERIES

Consulting editors   **A D McGettrick**   University of Strathclyde

                  J van Leeuwen   University of Utrecht

SELECTED TITLES IN THE SERIES

Functional Programming *A J Field and P G Harrison*

Comparative Programming Languages *L B Wilson and R G Clark*

Distributed Systems: Concepts and Design *G Coulouris and J Dollimore*

Software Prototyping, Formal Methods and VDM *S Hekmatpour and D Ince*

An Introduction to Functional Programming through Lambda Calculus
  G Michaelson

Clausal Form Logic: An Introduction to the Logic of Computer Reasoning
  T Richards

Software Engineering (3rd Edn) *I Sommerville*

Programming in Ada (3rd Edn) *J G P Barnes*

Elements of Functional Programming *C Reade*

Interactive Computer Graphics: Functional, Procedural and Device-Level
  Methods *P Burger and D Gillies*

Common Lisp Programming for Artificial Intelligence *T Hasemer and
  J Domingue*

Program Derivation: The Development of Programs from Specifications
  R G Dromey

Object-Oriented Programming with Simula *B Kirkerud*

Programming for Artificial Intelligence: Methods, Tools and Applications
  W Kreutzer and B J McKenzie

Parallel Processing: Principles and Practice *E V Krishnamurthy*

Real Time Systems and Their Programming Languages *A Burns and A Wellings*

Prolog Programming for Artificial Intelligence (2nd Edn) *I Bratko*

Introduction to Expert Systems (2nd Edn) *P Jackson*

Logic For Computer Science *S Reeves and M Clarke*

Computer Architecture *M De Blasi*

The Programming Process: an Introduction using VDM and Pascal *J T Latham,
  V J Bush and I D Cottam*

Handbook of Algorithms and Data Structures in Pascal and C (2nd Edn)
  G H Gonnet and R Baeza-Yates

Data Models, Database Languages and Database Management Systems
  G Vossen

TYPE THEORY
AND
FUNCTIONAL
PROGRAMMING

Simon Thompson

University of Kent at Canterbury

ADDISON-WESLEY
PUBLISHING
COMPANY

Wokingham, England · Reading, Massachusetts · Menlo Park, California · New York
Don Mills, Ontario · Amsterdam · Bonn · Sydney · Singapore
Tokyo · Madrid · San Juan · Milan · Paris · Mexico City · Seoul · Taipei

©1991 Addison-Wesley Publishers Ltd.
©1991 Addison-Wesley Publishing Company Inc.

The programs in this book have been included for their instructional value. They have been tested with care but are not guaranteed for any particular purpose. The publisher does not offer any warranties or representations, nor does it accept any liabilities with respect to the programs.

Many of the designations used by manufacturers and sellers to distinguish their products are claimed as trademarks. Addison-Wesley has made every attempt to supply trademark information about manufacturers and their products mentioned in this book. A list of the trademark designations and their owners appears on p. xvi.

Cover designed by Crayon Design of Henley-on-Thames
Using an illustration of 'The Spirit of the Snake' by E. Paolozzi reproduced by courtesy of the Trustees of the Victoria and Albert Museum
and printed by The Riverside Printing Co. (Reading) Ltd.
Printed in Great Britain by T. J. Press (Padstow) Ltd, Cornwall.

First printed in 1991.

British Library Cataloguing in Publication Data

Thompson, Simon
    Type theory and functional programming.
    I. Title
    005.1

    ISBN 0-201-41667-0

Library of Congress Cataloging-in-Publication Data

Thompson, Simon.
    Type theory and functional programming / Simon Thompson.
       p.   cm.
    Includes bibliography references (p.   ) and index.
    ISBN 0-201-41667-0
      1. Functional programming (Computer science) 2. Type theory.
    I. Title.   II. Title: Type theory and functional programming.
    QA76.62.T46   1991
    511'.3–dc20   91–12295
                                        CIP

To my parents

Preface

Constructive type theory has been a topic of research interest to computer scientists, mathematicians, logicians and philosophers for a number of years. For computer scientists it provides a framework which brings together logic and programming languages in a most elegant and fertile way: program development and verification can proceed within a single system. Viewed in a different way, type theory is a functional programming language with some novel features, such as the totality of all its functions, its expressive type system allowing functions whose result type depends upon the value of its input, and sophisticated modules and abstract types whose interfaces can contain logical assertions as well as signature information. A third point of view emphasizes that programs (or functions) can be extracted from proofs in a logic.

Up until now most of the material on type theory has only appeared in proceedings of conferences and in research papers, so it seems appropriate to try to set down the current state of development in a form accessible to interested final-year undergraduates, graduate students, research workers and teachers in computer science and related fields – hence this book.

The book can be thought of as giving both a first *and* a second course in type theory. We begin with introductory material on logic and functional programming, and follow this by presenting the system of type theory itself, together with many examples. As well as this we go further, looking at the system from a mathematical perspective, thus elucidating a number of its important properties. Then we take a critical look at the profusion of suggestions in the literature about why and how type theory could be augmented. In doing this we are aiming at a moving target; it must be the case that further developments will have been made before the book reaches the press. Nonetheless, such a survey can give the reader a much more developed sense of the potential of type theory, as well as giving the background of what is to come.

Outline

It seems in order to give an overview of the book. Each chapter begins with a more detailed introduction, so we shall be brief here. We follow this with a guide on how the book might be approached.

The first three chapters survey the three fields upon which type theory depends: logic, the λ-calculus and functional programming and constructive mathematics. The surveys are short, establishing terminology, notation and a general context for the discussion; pointers to the relevant literature and in particular to more detailed introductions are provided. In the second chapter we discuss some issues in the λ-calculus and functional programming which suggest analogous questions in type theory.

The fourth chapter forms the focus of the book. We give the formal system for type theory, developing examples of both programs and proofs as we go along. These tend to be short, illustrating the construct just introduced – Chapter 6 contains many more examples.

The system of type theory is complex, and in the chapter which follows we explore a number of different aspects of the theory. We prove certain results *about* it (rather than *using* it) including the important facts that programs are terminating and that evaluation is deterministic. Other topics examined include the variety of equality relations in the system, the addition of types (or 'universes') of types and some more technical points.

Much of our understanding of a complex formal system must derive from our using it. Chapter 6 covers a variety of examples and larger case studies. From the functional programming point of view, we choose to stress the differences between the system and more traditional languages. After a lengthy discussion of recursion, we look at the impact of the quantified types, especially in the light of the universes mentioned above. We also take the opportunity to demonstrate how programs can be extracted from constructive proofs, and one way that imperative programs can be seen as arising. We conclude with a survey of examples in the relevant literature.

As an aside it is worth saying that for any *formal* system, we can really only understand its precise details after attempting to *implement* it. The combination of symbolic and natural language used by mathematicians is surprisingly suggestive, yet ambiguous, and it is only the discipline of having to implement a system which makes us look at some aspects of it. In the case of TT, it was only through writing an implementation in the functional programming language Miranda that the author came to understand the distinctive role of assumptions in TT, for instance.

The system is expressive, as witnessed by the previous chapter, but are programs given in their most natural or efficient form? There is a host of proposals of how to augment the system, and we look at these in Chapter 7. Crucial to them is the incorporation of a class of subset types, in which the *witnessing* information contained in a type such as $(\exists x : A) . B(x)$ is suppressed. As well as describing the subset type, we lay out the arguments for its addition to type theory, and conclude that it is not as necessary as has been thought. Other proposals include quotient (or equivalence class) types, and ways in which general recursion can be added to the system without its losing its properties such as termination. A particularly elegant proposal for the addition of co-inductive types, such as infinite streams, without losing these properties, is examined.

Chapter 8 examines the foundations of the system: how it compares with other systems for constructive mathematics, how models of it are formed and used and how certain of the rules, the closure rules, may be seen as being generated from the introduction rules, which state what are the canonical members of each type. We end the book with a survey of related systems, implemented or not, and some concluding remarks.

Bibliographic information is collected at the end of the book, together with a table of the rules of the various systems.

We have used standard terminology whenever we were able, but when a subject is of current research interest this is not always possible.

Using the book

In the hope of making this a self-contained introduction, we have included Chapters 1 and 2, which discuss natural deduction logic and the λ-calculus – these chapters survey the fields and provide an introduction to the notation and terminology we shall use later. The core of the text is Chapter 4, which is the introduction to type theory.

Readers who are familiar with natural deduction logic and the λ-calculus could begin with the brief introduction to constructive mathematics provided by Chapter 3, and then turn to Chapter 4. Here we lay out type theory as both a logic and a functional programming system, giving small examples as we go. The chapters which follow are more or less loosely coupled.

Someone keen to see applications of type theory can turn to Chapter 6, which contains examples and larger case studies; only occasionally will readers need to need to refer back to topics in Chapter 5.

Another option on concluding Chapter 4 is to move straight on to Chapter 5, where the system is examined from various mathematical perspectives, and an number of important results on the consistency, expressibility and determinacy are proved. Chapter 8 should be seen as a continuation of this, as it explores topics of a foundational nature.

Chapter 7 is perhaps best read after the examples of Chapter 6, and digesting the deliberations of Chapter 5.

In each chapter exercises are included. These range from the routine to the challenging. Not many programming projects are included as it is expected that readers will to be able to think of suitable projects for themselves – the world is full of potential applications, after all.

Acknowledgements

The genesis of this book was a set of notes prepared for a lecture series on type theory given to the Theoretical Computer Science seminar at the University of Kent, and subsequently at the Federal University of Pernambuco, Recife, Brazil. Thanks are due to colleagues from both institutions; I am especially grateful to David Turner and Allan Grimley for both encouragement and stimulating discussions on the topic of type theory. I should also thank colleagues at UFPE, and the Brazilian National Research Council, CNPq, for making my visit to Brazil possible.

In its various forms the text has received detailed commment and criticism from a number of people, including Martin Henson, John Hughes, Nic McPhee, Jerry Mead and various anonymous reviewers. Thanks to them the manuscript has been much improved, though needless to say, I alone will accept responsibility for any infelicities or errors which remain.

The text itself was prepared using the LaTeX document preparation system; in this respect Tim Hopkins and Ian Utting have put up with numerous queries of varying complexity with unfailing good humour – thanks to both of them. Duncan Langford and Richard Jones have given me much appreciated advice on using the Macintosh.

The editorial and production staff at Addison-Wesley have been most helpful; in particular Simon Plumtree and Stephen Bishop have given me exactly the right mixture of editorial assistance and direction. Thanks also to the TeX experts at CUP for getting the manuscript into its final polished shape.

The most important acknowledgements are to Jane and Alice: Jane has supported me through all stages of the book, giving me encouragement when it was needed and coping so well with having to share me with this enterprise over the last year; without her I am sure the book would not have been completed. Alice is a joy, and makes me realise how much more there is to life than type theory.

Contents

Trademark notice

LISP Machine™ is a trademark of LISP Machine Incorporated.
Miranda™ is a trademark of Research Software Limited.

Introduction

Types are types and propositions are propositions; types come from programming languages, and propositions from logic, and they seem to have no relation to each other. We shall see that if we make certain assumptions about both logic and programming, then we can define a system which is *simultaneously* a logic and a programming language, and in which propositions and types are *identical*. This is the system of *constructive type theory*, based primarily on the work of the Swedish logician and philosopher, Per Martin-Löf. In this introduction we examine the background in both logic and computing before going on to look at constructive type theory and its applications.

Correct programming

The problem of correctness is ever-present in computing: a program is written with a particular specification in view and run on the assumption that it meets that specification. As is all too familiar, this assumption is unjustified: in most cases the program does *not* perform as it should. How should the problem be tackled? Testing cannot ensure the absence of errors; only a formal proof of correctness can guarantee that a program meets its specification. If we take a naïve view of this process, we develop the program and then, *post hoc*, give a proof that it meets a specification. If we do this the possibility exists that the program developed does not perform as it ought; we should instead try to develop the program in such a way that it *must* behave according to specification.

A useful analogy here is with the types in a programming language. If we use a typed language, we are prevented by the rules of syntax from forming an expression which will lead to a type error when the program is executed. We could *prove* that a similar program in an untyped language shares this property, but we would have to do this for each program developed, whilst in the typed language it is guaranteed in every case.

Our aim, then, is to design a language in which correctness is guaranteed. We look in particular for a *functional programming language* with

1

this property, as semantically the properties of these languages are the most straightforward, with a program simply being a value of a particular explicit type, rather than a state transformer.

How will the new language differ from the languages with which we are familiar?

- The type system will have to be more powerful. This is because we will express a specification by means of a statement of the form

  $$p : P$$

  which is how we write 'the value p has the type P'. The language of types in current programming languages can express the domain and range of a function, say, but cannot express the constraint that for every input value (of numeric type), the result is the positive square root of the value.

- If the language allows general recursion, then every type contains at least one value, defined by the equation $x = x$. This mirrors the observation that a non-terminating program meets every specification if we are only concerned with partial correctness. If we require total correctness we will need to design a language which only permits the definition of *total* functions and fully defined objects. At the same time we must make sure that the language is expressive enough to be usable practically.

To summarize, from the programming side, we are interested in developing a language in which correctness is guaranteed just as type-correctness is guaranteed in most contemporary languages. In particular, we are looking for a system of types within which we can express logical specifications.

Constructive logic

Classical logic is accepted as the standard foundation of mathematics. At its basis is a truth-functional semantics which asserts that every proposition is true or false, so making valid assertions such as $A \lor \neg A$, $\neg\neg A \Rightarrow A$ and

$$\neg\forall x.\neg P(x) \Rightarrow \exists x.P(x)$$

which can be given the gloss

> If it is contradictory for no object x to have the property $P(x)$, then there is an object x with the property $P(x)$

This is a principle of indirect proof, which has formed a cornerstone of modern mathematics since it was first used by Hilbert in his proof of the basis theorem about 100 years ago. The problem with the principle is that it asserts the existence of an object without giving any indication of what the object is. It is a *non-constructive* method of proof, in other words. We can give a different, constructive, rendering of mathematics, based on the work of Brouwer, Heyting, Bishop and many others, in which every statement has computational content; in the light of the discussion above it is necessary to reject classical logic and to look for modes of reasoning which permit only constructive derivations.

To explain exactly what can be derived constructively, we take a different foundational perspective. Instead of giving a classical, truth-functional, explanation of what is valid, we will explain what it means for a particular object p to be a proof of the proposition P. Our logic is *proof-functional* rather than truth-functional.

The crucial explanation is for the existential quantifier. An assertion that $\exists z.P(z)$ can only be deduced if we can produce an a with the property $P(a)$. A proof of $\exists z.P(z)$ will therefore be a *pair*, (a, p), consisting of an object a and a proof that a does in fact have the property P. A universal statement $\forall z.Q(z)$ can be deduced only if there is a function taking any object a to a proof that $Q(a)$. If we put these two explanations together, a constructive proof of the statement

$$\forall x.\exists y.R(x, y)$$

can be seen to require that there is a function, f say, taking any a to a value so that

$$R(a, f\ a)$$

Here we see that a constructive proof has computational content, in the shape of a function which gives an explicit *witness* value $f\ a$ for each a.

The other proof conditions are as follows. A proof of the conjunction $A \wedge B$ can be seen as a *pair* of proofs, (p, q), with p a proof of A and q of B. A proof of the implication $A \Rightarrow B$ can be seen as a proof transformation: given a proof of A, we can produce a proof of B from it. A proof of the disjunction $A \vee B$ is either a proof of A or a proof of B, together with an indication of which (A or B). The negation $\neg A$ is defined to be the implication $A \Rightarrow \perp$, where $\perp$ is the absurd or false proposition, which has no proof but from which we can infer anything. A proof of $\neg A$ is thus a function taking a proof of A to a proof of absurdity.

Given these explanations, it is easy to see that the law of the excluded middle will *not* be valid, as for a general A we cannot say that either A or $\neg A$ is provable. Similarly, the law of indirect proof will not be valid.

Having given the background from both computing and logic, we turn to examining the link between the two.

The Curry–Howard isomorphism

The central theme of this book is that we can see propositions and types as the same, the *propositions-as-types* notion, also known as the *Curry–Howard* isomorphism, after two of the (many) logicians who observed the correspondence.

We have seen that for our constructive logic, validity is explained by describing the circumstances under which 'p is a proof of the proposition P'. To see P as a type, we think of it as the type of its proofs. It is then apparent that familiar constructs in logic and programming correspond to each other. We shall write

$$p : P$$

to mean, interchangeably, 'p is of type P' and 'p is a proof of proposition P'.

The proofs of $A \wedge B$ are pairs (a, b) with a from A and b from B – the conjunction forms the *cartesian product* of the propositions as types. Proofs of $A \Rightarrow B$ are functions from A to B, which is lucky as we use the same notation for implication and the function space. The type $A \vee B$ is the *disjoint union* or *sum* of the types A and B, the absurd proposition, $\perp$, which has no proofs, is the empty type, and so on.

The correspondence works in the other direction too, though it is slightly more artificial. We can see the type of natural numbers N as expressing the proposition 'there are natural numbers', which has the (constructive!) proofs $0, 1, 2, \ldots$.

One elegant aspect of the system is in the characterization of inductive types such as the natural numbers and lists. Functional programmers will be familiar with the idea that functions defined by recursion have their properties proved by induction; in this system the principles of induction and recursion are *identical*.

The dual view of the system as a logic and a programming language can enrich both aspects. As a logic, we can see that all the facilities of a functional programming language are at our disposal in defining functions which witness certain properties and so forth. As a programming language, we gain various novel features, and in particular the quantified types give us dependent function and sum types. The dependent function space $(\forall x : A) \cdot B(x)$ generalizes the standard function space, as the type of the result $B(a)$ depends on the value $a : A$. This kind of dependence is usually not available in type systems. One example of its use is in defining array operations parametrized on the dimension of the array, rather than on the type of the array elements. Dependent sum types $(\exists x : A) \cdot B(x)$ can be used to represent modules and abstract data types amongst other things.

More radically, we have the possibility of combining verification and programming, as types can be used to represent propositions. As an example consider the existential type again. We can think of the elements of $(\exists x : A).B(x)$ as objects a of type A with the logical property $B(a)$, witnessed by the proof $b:B(a)$. We can give a third interpretation to $p:P$, in the case that P is an existential proposition:

$$(a,b) \; : \; (\exists x:A).B(x)$$

can be read thus:

a of type A meets the *specification* $B(x)$, as proved by $b:B(a)$

This fulfills the promise made in the introduction to logic that we would give a system of types strong enough to express specifications. In our case the logic is an extension of many-sorted, first-order predicate logic, which is certainly sufficient to express all practical requirements. The system here integrates the process of program development and proof: to show that a program meets a specification we provide the program/proof pair.

As an aside, note that it is misleading to read $p:P$ as saying 'p meets specification P' when P is an arbitrary proposition, an interpretation which seems to be suggested by much of the literature on type theory. This is because such statements include simple *typings* such as

$$plus \; : \; N \Rightarrow N \Rightarrow N$$

in which case the right-hand side is a woeful underspecification of addition! The specification statement is an existential proposition, and objects of that type include an explicit *witness* to the object having the required property: in other words we can only state that a program meets its specification when we have a proof of correctness for it.

We mentioned that one motivation for re-interpreting mathematics in a constructive form was to extract algorithms from proofs. A proof of a statement such as

$$\forall x. \exists y. \, R(x,y)$$

contains a description of an *algorithm* taking any x into a y so that $R(x,y)$. The logic we described makes explicit the proof terms. On the other hand it is instead possible to suppress explicit mention of the proof objects, and to *extract* algorithms from more succinct derivations of logical theorems, taking us from proofs to programs. This idea has been used with much success in the Nuprl system developed at Cornell University, and indeed in other projects.

Background

Our exposition of type theory and its applications will make continual reference to the fields of functional programming and constructivism. Separate introductions to these topics are provided by the introduction to Chapter 2 and by Chapter 3 respectively. The interested reader may care to refer to these now.

Section 9.2 contains some concluding remarks.

Chapter 1
Introduction to Logic

1.1   Propositional logic   1.2   Predicate logic

This chapter constitutes a short introduction to formal logic, which will establish notation and terminology used throughout the book. We assume that the reader is already familiar with the basics of logic, as discussed in the texts [Lemmon, 1965; Hodges, 1977] for example.

Logic is the science of argument. The purposes of formalization of logical systems are manifold.

- The formalization gives a clear characterization of the valid proofs in the system, against which we can judge individual arguments, so sharpening our understanding of informal reasoning.

- If the arguments are themselves about formal systems, as is the case when we verify the correctness of computer programs, the argument itself should be written in a form which can be checked for correctness. This can only be done if the argument is formalized, and correctness can be checked mechanically. Informal evidence for the latter requirement is provided by *Principia Mathematica* [Russell and Whitehead, 1910] which contains numerous formal proofs; unfortunately, many of the proofs are incorrect, a fact which all too easily escapes the human proof-reader's eye.

- As well as looking at the correctness or otherwise of individual proofs in a formal theory, we can study its properties as a whole. For example, we can investigate its expressive strength, relative to other theories, or to some sort of meaning or *semantics* for it. This work, which is predominantly mathematical in nature, is called mathematical logic, more details of which can be found in [Mendelson, 1987] amongst others.

7

As we said earlier, our aim is to provide a formal system in which arguments for the validity of particular sentences can be expressed. There are a number of different styles of logical system – here we look at natural deduction systems for first propositional and then predicate logic.

1.1   Propositional logic

Propositional logic formalizes arguments which involve the **connectives** such as 'and', 'or', 'not', 'implies' and so on. Using these connectives we build complex propositions starting from the propositional variables or atomic propositions.

Definition 1.1

Our syntax is given formally by stating that a **formula** is either

- a **propositional variable** $X_0, X_1, X_2, \ldots$, or
- a **compound** formula of the form

$$(A \wedge B) \quad (A \Rightarrow B) \quad (A \vee B)$$

$$\perp \quad (A \Leftrightarrow B) \quad (\neg A)$$

where A and B are formulas.

The compound formulas above are intended to represent the following informal combinations

A and B   A implies B   A or B

False   A if and only if B   not A

We shall adopt the convention that capital italic letters A, B,... stand for arbitrary formulas. (In more formal terms these are variables in the meta-language which is used to discuss the object language introduced by the syntax definition above.) We shall also omit parentheses from formulas when no ambiguity can result.

There are two parts to the description of a logical system. We have just introduced the language in which the assertions or **propositions** are written; we must now describe what are the valid arguments. The valid arguments are called the **proofs** or **derivations** of the system.

The general form of an argument is to infer a conclusion on the basis of some (or possibly no) assumptions. Larger derivations are built up inductively from smaller ones by the application of **deduction rules**. The simplest derivations are introduced by the rule of assumptions, which states that any formula A can be derived from the assumption of A itself.

Assumption rule
The proof

$$A$$

is a proof of the formula A from the assumption A.

More complex derivations are built by combining simpler ones. The first example of a rule which builds a composite derivation is the rule of conjunction introduction. Derivations of the two halves of the conjunction are combined by this rule to give a derivation of the conjunction itself.

∧ introduction
From proofs of A and B we can infer $A \wedge B$ by the rule of conjunction introduction. The rule is written

$$\frac{A \quad B}{A \wedge B}(\wedge I)$$

The assumptions upon which the proof of $A \wedge B$ depends are those of the proofs of A and B combined.

A simple proof can be built from the two rules we have seen so far:

$$\frac{\dfrac{A \quad B}{(A \wedge B)}(\wedge I) \quad \dfrac{A \quad C}{(A \wedge C)}(\wedge I)}{((A \wedge B) \wedge (A \wedge C))}(\wedge I)$$

At the leaves of the tree which represents the proof we find the assumptions, A, appearing twice, and B and C appearing once. Applying the introduction rule for conjunction three times, we have inferred the conjunction from its constituent parts.

The rule above was called the ∧ *introduction* rule, since it shows how a formula whose top-level connective is a conjunction can be introduced. The rule states that we can introduce a conjunction when we have proofs of its two component halves. Conversely, we have a rule which states what we can infer on the basis of a conjunction; in other words it tells us when we can *eliminate* a conjunction.

∧ elimination
From a proof of $A \wedge B$ we can infer both A and B by the rules of conjunction elimination. The rules are written

$$\frac{A \wedge B}{A}(\wedge E_1) \qquad \frac{A \wedge B}{B}(\wedge E_2)$$

The assumptions upon which the proofs of A and B depend are those of the proof of $A \wedge B$.

We have another example which combines the use of the rules of introduction and elimination. From the assumption $(A \wedge B) \wedge C$ we have

$$\cfrac{\cfrac{(A \wedge B) \wedge C}{A \wedge B}(\wedge E_1)}{A}(\wedge E_1)$$

and

$$\cfrac{\cfrac{\cfrac{(A \wedge B) \wedge C}{A \wedge B}(\wedge E_1)}{B}(\wedge E_2) \quad \cfrac{(A \wedge B) \wedge C}{C}(\wedge E_2)}{B \wedge C}(\wedge I)$$

Putting these proofs together we have

$$\cfrac{\begin{array}{cc} (A \wedge B) \wedge C & (A \wedge B) \wedge C \\ \vdots & \vdots \\ A & B \wedge C \end{array}}{A \wedge (B \wedge C)}(\wedge I)$$

This proof exhibits the associativity of the conjunction operation, a fact with which we are familiar. Note that the single assumption upon which the proof depends is the formula $(A \wedge B) \wedge C$, with the assumption appearing at three different points in the proof.

There is another way in which we can read the elimination rules. Note that the introduction rule states that we can infer $A \wedge B$ from A and B. The elimination rules state that this is (essentially) the *only* way we can infer it, since it states that if we can prove $A \wedge B$ then we can prove each of the component formulas.

In giving the rules for implication, $\Rightarrow$, we first take an informal look at what the connective is meant to mean. We think of $A \Rightarrow B$ as expressing A implies B or that we can deduce B from A. In other words we would like to conclude $A \Rightarrow B$ when we have a deduction of B *assuming* A. What are the assumptions upon which this new proof of $A \Rightarrow B$ depends? All those on which the proof of B depends, *except* the assumption A itself. The reason that we no longer depend upon A is that A has become the hypothesis in the formula $A \Rightarrow B$ – this expresses through a formula of the logic that we can deduce B from A.

This is reinforced by the elimination rule for $\Rightarrow$ which states that given proofs of A and $A \Rightarrow B$, we can infer B. Now we state the rules.

⇒ introduction

From a proof of the formula B, which may depend upon the assumption A amongst others, we can infer the formula $A \Rightarrow B$ from the same set of assumptions *with A removed*. We write this thus

$$\begin{array}{c} [A] \\ \vdots \\ \dfrac{B}{A \Rightarrow B}(\Rightarrow I) \end{array}$$

where the square brackets around the A indicate that all occurrences of the assumption A in the proof of B are to be discharged. It should be stressed that the proof of the formula B *need not* contain the assumption A for this rule to be applied. We shall see an example of this in the proof of

$$B \Rightarrow (A \Rightarrow B)$$

which appears later in this section.

In a substantial proof there will be many occurrences of rules which discharge assumptions. In order to make the link between the discharged assumption and the instance of the rule discharging it, we use labels, as in the schematic

$$\begin{array}{c} [A]^1 \\ \vdots \\ \dfrac{B}{A \Rightarrow B}(\Rightarrow I)_1 \end{array}$$

We shall see further examples of the use of labels after seeing the rule for implication elimination.

⇒ elimination

From proofs of the formulas A and $A \Rightarrow B$ we can infer the formula B. The assumptions upon which the proof of B depends are those of the proofs of A and $A \Rightarrow B$ combined. The rule is written

$$\frac{A \quad A \Rightarrow B}{B}(\Rightarrow E)$$

Now we can consider a more complicated example,

$$\frac{\dfrac{A \quad B}{A \wedge B}(\wedge I) \quad (A \wedge B) \Rightarrow C}{C}(\Rightarrow E)$$

We can discharge the three assumptions B, A and $(A \wedge B) \Rightarrow C$ in turn, giving first

$$\cfrac{\cfrac{A \quad [B]^1}{A \wedge B}(\wedge I) \quad (A \wedge B) \Rightarrow C}{\cfrac{C}{B \Rightarrow C}(\Rightarrow I)_1}(\Rightarrow E)$$

and finally

$$\cfrac{\cfrac{\cfrac{[A]^2 \quad [B]^1}{A \wedge B}(\wedge I) \quad [(A \wedge B) \Rightarrow C]^3}{\cfrac{\cfrac{C}{B \Rightarrow C}(\Rightarrow I)_1}{A \Rightarrow (B \Rightarrow C)}(\Rightarrow I)_2}(\Rightarrow E)}{((A \wedge B) \Rightarrow C) \Rightarrow (A \Rightarrow (B \Rightarrow C))}(\Rightarrow I)_3$$

In this example, we see how a deduction can be free of assumptions. As the deduction proceeds, we eliminate all the assumptions we have introduced. Other formulas we can derive in this way include $A \Rightarrow A$, derived thus:

$$\frac{[A]}{A \Rightarrow A}(\Rightarrow I)$$

and the formula $B \Rightarrow (A \Rightarrow B)$, 'if B is true then it is a consequence of any formula A', which is deduced as follows. First observe that in describing the introduction rule, we said that the deduction of B from A *may* involve the assumption A. It is not forced to, and we can infer $A \Rightarrow B$ from a proof of B *not* involving A. In proving $B \Rightarrow (A \Rightarrow B)$ we first introduce the assumption B, then discharge the assumption A, and finally discharge the assumption B. It is written thus

$$\cfrac{\cfrac{[B]^2}{A \Rightarrow B}(\Rightarrow I)_1}{B \Rightarrow (A \Rightarrow B)}(\Rightarrow I)_2$$

Note that there is no occurrence of an assumption labelled 1 – this indicates that the discharge of A is trivial, as we discussed above.

The third connective we consider is the disjunction operator, the formula $A \vee B$ meaning A *or* B. How can we introduce a disjunction? When one of the disjuncts is valid.

$\vee$ introduction
We can introduce $A \vee B$ if we have either a proof of A or a proof of B. The assumptions of the proof of $A \vee B$ are those of the proof of A or B. We

write the rules thus:

$$\frac{A}{A \vee B}(\vee I_1) \qquad \frac{B}{A \vee B}(\vee I_2)$$

Suppose we know that a particular formula C is a consequence of A and is a consequence of B – it should then be a consequence of $A \vee B$. This gives the law of $\vee$ elimination.

$\vee$ elimination
If we have a proof of $A \vee B$, a proof of C from A (that is a proof of C which might have A amongst its assumptions) and a proof of C from B then we can infer C. The assumption of A in the first proof of C and the assumption of B in the second are discharged. This is written:

$$\frac{A \vee B \qquad \begin{matrix}[A]\\ \vdots\\ C\end{matrix} \qquad \begin{matrix}[B]\\ \vdots\\ C\end{matrix}}{C}(\vee E)$$

A further example is given by the following derivation in which we see discharge of assumptions due to both $(\Rightarrow I)$ and $(\vee E)$. We look at a proof in which we have a disjunctive assumption $A \vee B$. The elimination rule is one way to use the assumption: we prove a result assuming A and then assuming B; from these proofs we get a proof from $A \vee B$. Suppose that we also assume $(A \Rightarrow C) \wedge (B \Rightarrow C)$; now

$$\frac{A \qquad \dfrac{(A \Rightarrow C) \wedge (B \Rightarrow C)}{(A \Rightarrow C)}(\wedge E_1)}{C}(\Rightarrow E)$$

and in an analogous way we have the result from the assumption B,

$$\frac{B \qquad \dfrac{(A \Rightarrow C) \wedge (B \Rightarrow C)}{(B \Rightarrow C)}(\wedge E_2)}{C}(\Rightarrow E)$$

Using disjunction elimination, we have

$$\frac{A \vee B \qquad \begin{matrix}[A]^1\\ (A \Rightarrow C) \wedge (B \Rightarrow C)\\ \vdots\\ C\end{matrix} \qquad \begin{matrix}[B]^1\\ (A \Rightarrow C) \wedge (B \Rightarrow C)\\ \vdots\\ C\end{matrix}}{C}(\vee E)_1$$

and now we discharge the remaining assumptions to give

$$[A \vee B]^2 \, , \; [(A \Rightarrow C) \wedge (B \Rightarrow C)]^3$$

$$\vdots$$

$$\cfrac{\cfrac{C}{((A \vee B) \Rightarrow C)} \; (\Rightarrow I)_2}{((A \Rightarrow C) \wedge (B \Rightarrow C)) \Rightarrow ((A \vee B) \Rightarrow C)} \; (\Rightarrow I)_3$$

The final connective we introduce is 'absurdity', or 'the false proposition', $\perp$, using which we can define negation. How is $\perp$ characterized? The fact that $\perp$ means contradiction or absurdity suggests that there is no way of introducing the proposition and so no introduction rule. How do we eliminate $\perp$? If it occurs, then we have absurdity, implying everything. This rule is sometimes known under the Latin '*ex falso quodlibet*'.

$\perp$ elimination
From a proof of $\perp$ we can infer any formula A. The assumptions of the latter proof are those of the former. This is written thus:

$$\frac{\perp}{A}(\perp E)$$

We define the **negation** of A, $\neg A$ by

$$\neg A \equiv_{df} (A \Rightarrow \perp)$$

We can show that the standard introduction and elimination rules for $\neg$ which follow

$$\begin{array}{cc} [A] & [A] \\ \vdots & \vdots \\ B & \neg B \end{array}$$
$$\frac{}{\neg A}(\neg I) \qquad \frac{A \quad \neg A}{B}(\neg E)$$

can be derived from the definition and the rules given above. In a similar way we define the **bi-implication**, $A \Leftrightarrow B$, by

$$(A \Leftrightarrow B) \equiv_{df} (A \Rightarrow B) \wedge (B \Rightarrow A)$$

and we can derive rules for $A \Leftrightarrow B$ from this.

Exercises

1.1   Give a proof of the transitivity of implication, by showing that we can derive $A \Rightarrow C$ from the assumptions $A \Rightarrow B$ and $B \Rightarrow C$.

1.2 Give a proof of $((A \vee B) \Rightarrow C) \Rightarrow ((A \Rightarrow C) \wedge (B \Rightarrow C))$.

1.3 Give a proof of $(A \Rightarrow (B \Rightarrow C)) \Rightarrow ((A \wedge B) \Rightarrow C)$.

1.4 Give proofs of $(A \Rightarrow B) \Rightarrow (\neg B \Rightarrow \neg A)$ and $A \Rightarrow \neg\neg A$.

1.5 From the assumption $(B \vee C)$ prove $\neg(\neg A \wedge \neg B)$.

1.6 Give derivations of the rules ($\neg$I) and ($\neg$E) given above. In other words

- show that from proofs of B and $\neg B$ from the assumption A among others, we can find a proof of $\neg A$ without the assumption A, and

- show that from proofs of A and $\neg A$ we can find a proof of any proposition B.

The system introduced above is *intuitionistic*, or constructive. Such systems form the main focus of this book, but it is worth remarking on the means by which we extend the system to a *classical* one. Classical logic is based on a truth-functional theory of meaning, in which every proposition is considered to be either true or false. This means that it is a general truth that for every proposition A, $A \vee \neg A$ is true – the law of the excluded middle. To put this in the form of the rules above, we have a rule with no hypotheses:

$$\frac{}{A \vee \neg A}(EM)$$

Alternative rules which characterize classical logic (as an extension of the intuitionistic logic above) are the rule of double negation

$$\frac{\neg\neg A}{A}(DN)$$

and the (classical) rule of proof by contradiction

$$\frac{\begin{array}{cc} [\neg A] & [\neg A] \\ \vdots & \vdots \\ B & \neg B \end{array}}{A}(CC)$$

Exercises

1.7 Show that the three characterizations of classical logic (as an extension of the intuitionistic system) above are equivalent.

1.8 Using one of the classical systems, give a derivation of the formula $((A \Rightarrow B) \Rightarrow A) \Rightarrow A$, which is known as Pierce's law.

1.2   Predicate logic

In this section we look at predicate logic, that is the logic of properties or *predicates*. In our exploration of propositional logic, the simplest propositions were 'atomic' or unanalysed. Here we build a system in which the propositions are built up from statements to the effect that certain objects have certain properties, or that certain objects are equal.

Syntactically, our language will have two categories, formulas and *terms*.

Definition 1.2

Terms are intended to denote objects, and have one of the forms below.

Individual variables, or simply **variables,** $v_0, v_1, v_2, \ldots$. We shall write $x, y, z, u, v, \ldots$ for arbitrary individual variables in the following exposition.

Individual constants $c_0, c_1, c_2, \ldots$. We shall use $a, b, c, \ldots$ for arbitrary constants below.

Composite terms. These are formed by *applying function symbols to other terms.* Each function symbol has an **arity**, $1,2,\ldots$; an n-ary function symbol $f_{n,m}$ takes n argument terms $t_1, \ldots, t_n$ in forming the term

$$f_{n,m}(t_1, \ldots, t_n)$$

We shall use $f, g, h, \ldots$ to denote arbitrary function symbols in what follows.

We shall use $s, t, t_1, \ldots$ as a notation for arbitrary terms.

Note that we can think of constants as 0-ary function symbols, if we so wish, and also that the variables we have introduced here are intended to stand for *objects*, and *not* for propositions as did our propositional variables above. Our propositions are formed as follows.

Definition 1.3

Propositions have three forms:

Atomic formulas are of two forms. The first is

$$P_{n,m}(t_1, \ldots, t_n)$$

where $P_{n,m}$ is an n-ary **predicate symbol** and $t_1, \ldots, t_n$ are terms. This formula is intended to express the fact that the relation represented by predicate symbol $P_{n,m}$ holds for the sequence of values denoted by $t_1, \ldots, t_n$. We shall use $P, Q, R, \ldots$ for arbitrary predicate symbols.

Equality is taken to be a primitive of the system, so another class of formulas are the equalities

$$t_1 = t_2$$

where t_1 and t_2 are terms.

Propositional combinations are combinations of formulas under the propositional connectives $\vee, \wedge, \Rightarrow, \Leftrightarrow, \neg$.

Quantified formulas are formulas such as

$$\forall x.A \qquad \exists x.B$$

where as in the propositional case we use $A, B, \ldots$ for arbitrary formulas, as well as using x for an arbitrary variable.

The quantifiers $\forall$ – for all – and $\exists$ – there exists – are intended to express the assertions that a particular formula holds *for all* objects and *for some* object, respectively. (Hence the name 'quantifier'; quantified formulas express the quantity of objects with a particular property.)

To reinforce the intuitive interpretation of the quantifiers, we now look at their use in expressing various properties. In each particular case, there will be an intended domain of application of the quantifiers, so that 'for all' will mean 'for all fish', 'for all real numbers' and so on. We assume for these examples that our domain of discourse is the natural numbers, so that the quantifiers will range over $0, 1, 2, \ldots$. Moreover, we assume that the (infix) predicate symbol $<$ is chosen so that $x < y$ expresses

y is greater than x

Suppose first that f is a function. We say that a value is in the range of f if it is the value of f at some argument. How can we state in logical terms that m is the *maximum* value in the range? First we say that m is in the range

$$\exists i.(f(i) = m)$$

and then that m is greater than or equal to every element in the range

$$\forall j.(f(j) \leq m)$$

The complete property is expressed by the conjunction of the formulas:

$$\exists i.(f(i) = m) \wedge \forall j.(f(j) \leq m)$$

A second example shows that the *order* in which we write different quantifiers is significant. What does

$$\forall x.\exists y.(x < y)$$

express intuitively? For every x, there is a y greater than x. Clearly this is true, as given a particular x we can choose y to be $x + 1$. The ys asserted to exist can, and in general will, be *different* for different xs – y can be thought of as a function of x, in fact. On the other hand

$$\exists y.\forall x.(x < y)$$

asserts that there is a single number y with the property that

$$\forall x.(x < y)$$

That is, this y is greater than every number (including itself!), clearly a falsehood.

Exercises

1.9   With the same interpretation for the predicate $x < y$ as above, express the property that 'between every distinct pair of numbers there is a number'.

1.10 How would you express the following properties of the function f (from natural numbers to natural numbers, for example)
f is a one-to-one function
f is an onto function
the function f respects the relation $<$?

1.2.1 Variables and substitution

Before we supply the rules for the quantifiers, we have to consider the rôle of variables, and in particular those which are involved in quantified formulas. Remember that when we define a procedure in a programming language such as Pascal, the formal parameters have a special property: they are 'dummies' in the sense that all the occurrences of a formal parameter can be replaced by any other variable, so long as that variable is not already 'in use' in the program. Quantified variables have a similar property. For instance, the formula

$$\forall x.\forall y.(P(x, y) \Rightarrow P(y, x))$$

expresses exactly the same property as

$$\forall w.\forall q.(P(w, q) \Rightarrow P(q, w))$$

Now we introduce some terminology.

Definition 1.4

An occurrence of a variable x within a sub-formula $\forall x.A$ or $\exists x.A$ is **bound**; all other occurrences are **free**. We say that a variable x occurs free in a formula A if *some* occurrence of x is free in A. A variable x is bound by the syntactically **innermost** enclosing quantifier $\forall x$ or $\exists x$, if one exists, just as in any block-structured programming language.

The same variable may occur both bound and free in a single formula. For example, the second occurrence of x is bound in

$$\forall y.(x > y \wedge \forall x.(P(x) \Rightarrow P(y)) \wedge Q(y, x))$$

whilst the first and third occurrences are free.

In what follows we will need to **substitute** arbitrary terms, t say, for variables x in formulas A. If the formula A is without quantifiers, we simply replace every occurrence of x by t but, in general, we only replace the *free* occurrences of x by t – the bound variable x is a dummy, used to express a universal or an existential property, not a property of the object named x.

There is a problem with the definition of substitution, which has not always been defined correctly by even the most respected of logicians! The term t may contain variables, and these may become bound by the quantifiers in A. This is called **variable capture**. Consider the particular example of

$$\exists y.(y > x)$$

This asserts that for x we can find a value of y so that $x < y$ holds. Suppose that we substitute the term $y + 1$ for x. We obtain the expression

$$\exists y.(y > y + 1)$$

('+' is an infix function symbol – an addition to the notation which we shall use for clarity). The y in the term $y + 1$ which we have substituted has been *captured* by the $\exists y$ quantifier. The name of the quantified variable was meant to be a dummy; because of this we should ensure that we change its name before performing the substitution to avoid the capture of variables.

In the example we would first substitute a *new* variable, z say, for the bound variable y, thus:

$$\exists z.(z > x)$$

and after that we would perform the substitution of $y + 1$ for x,

$$\exists z.(z > y + 1)$$

We shall use the notation $A[t/x]$ for the formula A with the term t substituted for x. The definition is by induction over the syntactic structure of the formula A. First we define substitution of t for x within a term s, for which we use the notation $s[t/x]$. In the definition we also use '$\equiv$' for 'is identical with'.

Definition 1.5

The **substitution** $s[t/x]$ is defined thus:

- $x[t/x] \equiv_{df} t$ and for a variable $y \not\equiv x$, $y[t/x] \equiv_{df} y$.
- For composite terms,

$$(f_{n,m}(t_1, \ldots, t_n))[t/x] \equiv_{df} f_{n,m}(t_1[t/x], \ldots, t_n[t/x])$$

Definition 1.6

The **substitution** $A[t/x]$ is defined as follows:

- For atomic formulas,

$$(P_{n,m}(t_1, \ldots, t_n))[t/x] \equiv_{df} P_{n,m}(t_1[t/x], \ldots, t_n[t/x])$$

$$(t_1 = t_2)[t/x] \equiv_{df} (t_1[t/x] = t_2[t/x])$$

- Substitution commutes with propositional combinations, so that

$$(A \wedge B)[t/x] \equiv_{df} (A[t/x] \wedge B[t/x])$$

  and so on.
- If $A \equiv \forall x.B$ then $A[t/x] \equiv_{df} A$. If $y \not\equiv x$, and $A \equiv \forall y.B$ then
  - if y does not appear in t, $A[t/x] \equiv_{df} \forall y.(B[t/x])$;
  - if y does appear in t,

  $$A[t/x] \equiv_{df} \forall z.(B[z/y][t/x])$$

  where z is a variable which does not appear in t or B. (Note that we have an infinite collection of variables, so that we can always find such a z.)

- Substitution into $A \equiv \exists x.B$ is defined in an analogous way to $\forall x.B$.
- In general, it is easy to see that if x is not free in A then $A[t/x]$ is A.

We shall use the notation above for substitution, but also on occasions use a more informal notation for substitution. If we use the notation $A(t)$ we intend this to mean $A[t/x]$ where the variable x should be understood from the context. Note that in writing $A(x)$, say, we mean neither that x occurs in the formula A nor that it is the only variable occurring in A if it occurs; it is simply used to indicate sufficient contextual information.

Throughout the book we shall identify formulas which are the same after change of bound variables.

Exercises

1.11 Identify the free and bound variables in the formula

$$\forall x.(x < y \wedge \forall z.(y > z \Rightarrow \exists x.(x > z)))$$

and show to which quantifier each bound variable is bound.

1.12 Suppose we want to rename as y the variable x in the formula

$$\forall z.\exists y.(z < y \wedge y < x)$$

Explain how you would change names of bound variables to avoid variable capture by one of the quantifiers.

1.2.2   Quantifier rules

The rules for the quantifiers will explain how we are to introduce and eliminate quantified formulas. In order to find out how to do this we look at the ways in which we use variables. There are two distinct modes of use, which we now explain.

First, we use variables in stating theorems. We intend free variables to be *arbitrary* values, such as in the trigonometrical formula

$$sin^2 x + cos^2 x = 1$$

and indeed we could equally well make the formal statement

$$\forall x.(sin^2 x + cos^2 x = 1)$$

This is a general phenomenon; if x is arbitrary then we should be able to make the inference

$$\frac{A}{\forall x.A}$$

This will be our rule for introducing ∀, once we have decided what we mean by 'arbitrary'.

On the other hand, in the process of proving a theorem we may use variables in a different way. If we make an *assumption* with a free x, $x > 0$ say, and then prove a result such as

$$\forall z.(z \leq x \lor z \geq 0)$$

then this result is *not* true for all x. (Try $x = -1$!). This is precisely because the x is not arbitrary – we have assumed something about it: that it is greater than zero. In other words, we can say that x is arbitrary if and only if x does not appear free in any of the assumptions of the proof of the result.

We can now state formally our introduction rule for the universal quantifier.

∀ introduction

For any formula A, which may or may not involve the free variable x, we can from a proof of A infer $\forall x.A$ if x is arbitrary, that is if x does not occur free in any of the assumptions of the proof of $A(x)$. This is called the **side condition** of the rule.

$$\frac{A}{\forall x.A}(\forall I)$$

The assumptions of the proof derived are the same as those of the proof of A. Note that the formula A may or may not involve the free variable x, and may involve free variables other than x.

The elimination rule for ∀ is easier to state. It says that a universally quantified formula is true for an arbitrary object, and so is true of any term. We express this by substituting the term for the quantified variable.

∀ elimination

From a proof of $\forall x.A(x)$ we can infer $A(t)$ for any term t.

$$\frac{\forall x.A(x)}{A(t)}(\forall E)$$

With our notation for substitution as above, we would write

$$\frac{\forall x.A}{A[t/x]}(\forall E)$$

Now we turn to the existential quantifier. There is a certain *duality* between the two quantifiers and we find it reflected in the rules. The simpler of the rules to state is the existential introduction rule: it states that if we can prove a substitution instance of a formula, then we can infer the existentially quantified statement.

∃ introduction

If for a particular term t we can prove $A(t)$ then clearly we have demonstrated that there is some object for which A is provable.

$$\frac{A(t)}{\exists x.A(x)}(\exists I)$$

Alternatively, we write

$$\frac{A[t/x]}{\exists x.A}(\exists I)$$

In order to frame the existential elimination rule we have to decide what we are able to deduce on the basis of $\exists x.A$. Let us return to the informal discussion we started on page 22. We looked there at an argument which had an assumption of the form

$$x > 0$$

What is the force of such an assumption? It is to assume the *existence* of an object greater than zero, and to name it x. Now, suppose that on the basis of this we can prove some B which does not mention x; if we also know that the existential assumption is indeed valid, that is we know that

$$\exists x.(x > 0)$$

then we can infer B outright, discharging the assumption.

∃ elimination

$$\frac{\exists x.A \quad \overset{\displaystyle [A]}{\underset{\displaystyle B}{\vdots}}}{B}(\exists E)$$

where x is not free in B or any of the assumptions of the proof of B, except for A itself, in which it may be free. (This stipulation is the *side condition* for the application of the rule.) The assumption A is discharged by the application of this rule, so that the assumptions of the resulting proof are those of the proof of $\exists x.A$ together with all those from the proof of B apart from A.

Thinking of the rule in programming terms, we can think of it as introducing a temporary (or 'local') name x for the object asserted to exist by the formula $\exists x.A$.

Returning to our informal discussion a second time, we can perhaps see more clearly a duality between the two quantifiers and their treatment of formulas with free variables.

- The formula A involving the free variable x has *universal* content when x is arbitrary, that is when it occurs in the conclusion of an argument (and *not* in the assumptions).
- The formula A has *existential* content when it occurs as an assumption, giving a name to the object assumed to have the property A.

We can give another informal reading of the quantifiers. $\forall$ and $\exists$ behave like a large (in fact *infinite*) conjunction and disjunction:

$$\forall x.A(x) \equiv A(a) \wedge A(b) \wedge \ldots$$

$$\exists x.A(x) \equiv A(a) \vee A(b) \vee \ldots$$

if the objects in the domain of discourse are $a, b, \ldots$. We can see the rules for $\forall$ elimination and $\exists$ introduction agree with this analogy immediately, and in fact the same is true of the other rules. To introduce $C \wedge D$ we have to have proofs of C and D. To introduce

$$A(a) \wedge A(b) \wedge \ldots$$

we need proofs for $A(a), A(b), \ldots$ and so on. In other words, we need a proof for *arbitrary* x, which is exactly what the rule states. The rule for elimination of $\vee$ suggests the following for existential elimination:

$$\frac{\exists x.A(x) \quad \begin{matrix} [A(a)] \\ \vdots \\ B \end{matrix} \quad \begin{matrix} [A(b)] \\ \vdots \\ B \end{matrix} \quad \ldots}{B}$$

We obtain our rule by replacing all the individual proofs of B from $A(a)$, $A(b)$ and so forth by a proof from $A(x)$ for an arbitrary x.

1.2.3   Examples

Now we put these rules to some use in a series of examples. For the first example we assume

$$\theta \equiv_{df} \forall x.(P(x) \Rightarrow Q(x))$$

$$\exists x.P(x)$$

and try to prove that

$$\exists x.Q(x)$$

Informally the inference is clear, but what do we do in our system? We have a universal assumption, θ, and the rule of universal elimination tells us that we can use any instance

$$P(x) \Rightarrow P(x)$$

of θ in our proof. If we adopt a *backwards* reading of the rule of existential elimination, then we see how to use an existential assumption.

> To use an existential assumption $\exists x.P(x)$, use the instance $P(x)$ and finally discharge this using the rule $(\exists E)$.

Proceeding thus we have

$$P(x) \quad \dfrac{\dfrac{\forall x.(P(x) \Rightarrow Q(x))}{(P(x) \Rightarrow Q(x))}(\forall E)}{Q(x)}(\Rightarrow E)$$

From this we can infer $\exists x.Q(x)$ (even though x is free in one of the assumptions – there are no restrictions on the rule $(\exists I)$), and finally by existential elimination we have:

$$\exists x.P(x) \quad \dfrac{\dfrac{[P(x)]^1 \quad \dfrac{\dfrac{\forall x.(P(x) \Rightarrow Q(x))}{(P(x) \Rightarrow Q(x))}(\forall E)}{Q(x)}(\Rightarrow E)}{\exists x.Q(x)}(\exists I)}{\exists x.Q(x)}(\exists E)_1$$

For our second example, suppose we make the assumption that every object is either an apple or a banana:

$$\forall x.(A(x) \lor B(x))$$

and that both apples and bananas are tasty:

$$\forall x.(A(x) \Rightarrow T(x))$$

$$\forall x.(B(x) \Rightarrow T(x))$$

We will show that everything is tasty, $\forall x.T(x)$. Applying the universal elimination rule three times we have

$$(A(y) \lor B(y))$$

$$(A(y) \Rightarrow T(y))$$

$$(B(y) \Rightarrow T(y))$$

and then we can infer $T(y)$ on the basis of the second of these and the assumption $A(y)$, using $(\Rightarrow E)$.

$$\dfrac{A(y) \quad \dfrac{\forall x.(A(x) \Rightarrow T(x))}{(A(y) \Rightarrow T(y))}(\forall E)}{T(y)}(\Rightarrow E)$$

We can similarly infer $T(y)$ from $B(y)$ and the universal statement, and are then in a position to apply $(\vee E)$. (In the diagram which follows the hypotheses of the central proof are listed vertically.)

$$\dfrac{\dfrac{\forall x.(A(x) \vee B(x))}{(A(y) \vee B(y))}(\forall E) \qquad \begin{array}{c} [A(y)]^1 \\ \forall x.(A(x) \Rightarrow T(x)) \\ \vdots \\ T(y) \end{array} \qquad \begin{array}{c} [B(y)]^1 \\ \dots \\ \vdots \\ T(y) \end{array}}{T(y)}(\vee E)_1$$

$\forall$ introduction is then applied, giving

$$\dfrac{\vdots}{\forall x.T(x)}(\forall I)$$

Our final example concerns the proof of

$$\exists y.\forall x.A(x,y) \Rightarrow \forall x.\exists y.A(x,y)$$

The reader might like to refer back to the discussion on page 17. Remembering the rule of implication introduction, it is sufficient to prove

$$\forall x.\exists y.A(x,y)$$

on the assumption of

$$\exists y.\forall x.A(x,y)$$

We have an existential assumption, so stripping off the quantifier we can by the rule $(\exists E)$ use instead the assumption

$$\forall x.A(x,y)$$

Using $(\forall E)$ we have

$$\frac{\forall x.A(x,y)}{A(x,y)}(\forall E)$$

and by $(\exists I)$

$$\frac{\vdots}{\exists y.A(x,y)}(\exists I)$$

Now, we can deduce

$$\frac{\vdots}{\forall x.\exists y.A(x,y)}(\forall I)$$

using $(\forall I)$, since x is not free in the assumptions (and therefore arbitrary). We complete the proof with applications of $(\exists E)$ and $(\Rightarrow I)$:

$$\cfrac{[\exists y.\forall x.A(x,y)]^2 \qquad \cfrac{\cfrac{\cfrac{[\forall x.A(x,y)]^1}{A(x,y)}(\forall E)}{\exists y.A(x,y)}(\exists I)}{\forall x.\exists y.A(x,y)}(\forall I)}{\cfrac{\forall x.\exists y.A(x,y)}{\exists y.\forall x.A(x,y) \Rightarrow \forall x.\exists y.A(x,y)}(\Rightarrow I)_2}(\exists E)_1$$

Exercises

1.13 Explain how the side conditions in the proof rules prevent the construction of a proof of

$$\forall x.\exists y.A(x,y) \Rightarrow \exists y.\forall x.A(x,y)$$

analogous to the proof of

$$\exists y.\forall x.A(x,y) \Rightarrow \forall x.\exists y.A(x,y)$$

above.

1.14 Assuming that the variable x is not free in B, prove that the following formulas are equivalent, that is each can be proved on the assumption of the other:

$$\forall x.(A(x) \Rightarrow B)$$

$$((\exists x.A(x)) \Rightarrow B)$$

1.15 Using the previous exercise, or otherwise, argue that the following formulas are equivalent:

$$\neg(\exists x.A(x)) \qquad \forall x.\neg A(x)$$

and show that

$$\exists x.\neg A(x) \Rightarrow \neg\forall x.A(x)$$

Would you expect the converse of the final result to be provable?

Chapter 2
Functional Programming and
λ-Calculi

Type theory has aspects of both a logic and a functional programming language. We have seen a brief introduction to logic in Chapter 1; here we first survey current practice in functional programming and then look at a number of λ-calculi, which are formal theories of functions. The λ-calculus was invented in the 1930s by Church as a notation for functions, with the aim of developing a foundation for mathematics. As with much of the work of that time, the original aim was not met, but the subject itself has become an object of study in its own right. Interest in the λ-calculus has grown again in the last two decades as it has found a role in the foundations of computing science, in particular through its model theory, which underpins much of denotational semantics. The theory usually studied is the *untyped* λ-calculus, and we look at this first. We are lucky to have the encyclopaedic [Barendregt, 1984] to refer to for proofs, bibliographic and historical information and so forth. Any important result in the untyped λ-calculus is to be found there, together with (at least!) one proof of it.

Running through our material, we first look at variable binding and substitution, which are central to the λ-calculus. Variables are bound when a function is formed by abstraction, and when a function is applied, the formal parameters are replaced by their actual counterparts by substitution. We then look at the relations of evaluation, or reduction, '$\rightarrow$' and convertibility '$\leftrightarrow$', the latter of which represents a form of equality over the λ-expressions. We discuss these from a general standpoint, which will form a foundation for similar discussions for type theory. In particular we look at the determinacy of computation (the Church–Rosser property) and termination properties of evaluation, or as they are more commonly known, the *normalization* properties of expressions. We draw a distinction between different kinds of reduction rule – the computation and equivalence rules – which again we will carry through into the body of the book. After a short look at the expressiveness of the untyped system, we turn to an examination of typed theories, which more closely reflect current functional programming practice. We highlight the difference between the typed and untyped by showing that the former is strongly normalizing – all evaluation sequences are finite, meaning that, in particular, every program terminates. We give a proof of this theorem, which forms a model for other results of this sort in its proof by induction over types and its formulation of a strong induction hypothesis, a method first introduced by William Tait. Augmenting the type structure with product types and natural numbers, we finish by returning to the discussion of computation and equivalence rules in the context of a typed language.

The survey [Huet, 1990b] gives a useful overview of typed λ-calculi.

2.1   Functional programming

The functional style of programming has been growing in popularity over the last 30 years, from its beginnings in early dialects of LISP, to the present day and the availability of a number of production-quality languages such as Haskell, Hope, Miranda, and Standard ML (SML) amongst others [Hudak and Wadler, 1990; Burstall *et al.*, 1980; Turner, 1985; Harper, 1986]. Although there are differences between them, there is a wide degree of consensus about the forms of the systems, which provide the following.

First-class functions: Functions may be passed as arguments to and returned as results of other functions; they may form components of composite data structures and so on. An example is the `map` function. It takes a function, `f` say, as argument, returning the function which takes a list, `x` say, as argument and returns the list resulting from applying `f` to every item in `x`.

Strong type systems: The language contains distinctions between different values, classing similar values into types. The typing of values restricts the application of operators and data constructors, so that errors in which, for example, two boolean values are added will not be permitted. Moreover, and this is what is meant by the adjective 'strong', no run-time errors can arise through type mismatches.

Polymorphic types: A potential objection to strong typing runs thus: in an untyped language we can re-use the same code for the identity function over every type; after all it simply returns its argument. Similarly we can re-use the code to reverse a linked list over structurally similar lists (which only differ in the type of entry at each node) as the code is independent of the contents. We can accommodate this kind of genericity and retain strong typing if we use the Hindley–Milner type system [Milner, 1978], or other sorts of polymorphic types. The type of the identity function becomes * -> *, where * is a type variable, indicating that the type of the function is a functional type, in which the domain and range types are the same. This means that it can be used on booleans, returning a boolean, on numeric functions returning a numeric function, and so on.

Algebraic types: Lists, trees, and other types can be defined directly by recursive definitions, rather than through pointer types. The mechanism of algebraic types generalizes enumerated types, (variant) records, certain sorts of pointer type definitions, and also permits type definitions (such as those of lists) to be parametrized over types (such as the type of their contents). Pattern matching is usually the means by which case analyses and selections of components are performed.

Modularity: The languages provide systems of modules of varying degrees of complexity by means of which large systems can be developed more easily.

One area in which there are differences is in the mechanism of evaluation. The SML system incorporates *strict* evaluation, under which scheme arguments of functions are evaluated before the instantiated function body, and components of data types are fully evaluated on object formation. On the other hand, Miranda and Haskell adopt *lazy* evaluation, under which function arguments and data type components are only evaluated when this becomes necessary, if at all. This permits a distinctive style of programming based on infinite and partially defined data structures. There are advantages of each system, and indeed there are hybrids such as Hope+ [Perry, 1989] which combine the two.

This is not the place to give a complete introduction to functional programming. There is a growing number of good introductory textbooks on the subject [Bird and Wadler, 1988; Reade, 1989; Wikström, 1987], as well as books looking at the foundations of the subject [Huet, 1990a] and at current research directions [Peyton Jones, 1987; Turner, 1990]. We shall look at the topics described above as we develop our system of type theory; first, though, we investigate the lambda calculus, which is both a precursor of current functional programming languages, having been developed in the 1930s, and an abstract version of them.

In what follows we use the phrase 'languages such as Miranda' – it is meant to encompass all the languages discussed above rather than simply Miranda.

2.2   The untyped λ-calculus

The original version of the λ-calculus was developed by Church, and studied by a number of his contemporaries including Turing, Curry and Kleene. It provides a skeletal functional programming language in which every object is considered to be a function. (An alternative view of this, propounded by [Scott, 1980] amongst others, is of a typed theory containing a type which is isomorphic with its function space.) The syntax could not be simpler.

Definition 2.1

There are three kinds of λ-**expressions** (we use $e, f, e_1, e_2, \ldots$ for arbitrary λ-expressions). They are:

Individual variables or simply *variables*, $v_0, v_1, v_2, \ldots$.. We shall write $x, y, z, u, v, \ldots$ for arbitrary individual variables in the following.

Applications $(e_1 e_2)$. This is intended to represent the application of expression e_1 to e_2.

Abstractions $(\lambda x . e)$. This is intended to represent the function which returns the value e when given formal parameter x.

The notation above can become heavy with parentheses, so we introduce the following syntactic conventions.

Definition 2.2

The syntax of the system is made more readable by the following **syntactic conventions:**

C1   Application binds more tightly than abstraction, so that $\lambda x . xy$ means $\lambda x . (xy)$ and not $(\lambda x . x)y$.

C2   Application associates to the left, implying that xyz denotes $(xy)z$ and not $x(yz)$.

C3 $\lambda x_1 . \lambda x_2 . \ldots \lambda x_n . e$ means $\lambda x_1 . (\lambda x_2 . \ldots (\lambda x_n . e))$

The crux of the calculus is the mechanism of λ-abstraction. The expression

$$\lambda x . e$$

is the general form that functions take in the system. To specify a function we say what is its formal parameter, here x, and what is its result, here e. In a functional language such as Miranda we give these definitions by equations which name the functions, such as

```
f x = e
```

and in mathematical texts we might well talk about the function f given by

$$f(x) = e$$

In the λ-calculus we have an anonymous notation for the function which introduces the function without giving it a name (such as f). The parameter x is a *formal* parameter and so we would expect that the function

$$\lambda x . \lambda y . xy$$

would be indistinguishable from

$$\lambda u . \lambda v . uv$$

for instance. Formally, as we saw in the chapter on logic, such variables x are called bound, the λ being the binding construct.

How do we associate actual parameters with the formals? We form applications

$$(\lambda x . e_1) e_2$$

To evaluate these applications, we pass the parameter: we substitute the actual parameter for the formal, which we denote

$$e_1[e_2/x]$$

As for the binding constructs of logic, the quantifiers, we have to be careful about how we define substitution, which we do, after saying formally what it means to be bound and free.

Definition 2.3

An occurrence of a variable x within a sub-expression $\lambda x . e$ is **bound**; all other occurrences are **free**. The occurrence of x in $\lambda x.$ is the **binding** occurrence which introduces the variable – other occurrences are called **applied**. We say that a variable x occurs free in an expression f if *some* occurrence of x is free in f. A variable x is bound by the syntactically *innermost* enclosing λ, if one exists, just as in any block-structured programming language. An expression is **closed** if it contains no free variables; otherwise it is **open**.

The same variable may occur both bound and free in an expression. For example, the first applied occurrence of x in

$$(\lambda x . \lambda y . yx)((\lambda z . zx)x)$$

is bound, but the second and third applied occurrences are free.

Definition 2.4

The **substitution** of f for the free occurrences of x in e, written $e[f/x]$, is defined thus.

- $x[f/x] \equiv_{df} f$ and for a variable $y \not\equiv x$, $y[f/x] \equiv_{df} y$.
- For applications, we substitute into the two parts:

$$(e_1\ e_2)[t/x] \equiv_{df} (e_1[t/x]\ e_2[t/x])$$

- If $e \equiv \lambda x . g$ then $e[f/x] \equiv_{df} e$. If y is a variable distinct from x, and $e \equiv \lambda y . g$ then

    - if y does not appear free in f, $e[f/x] \equiv_{df} \lambda y . g[f/x]$.
    - if y does appear free in f,

    $$e[f/x] \equiv_{df} \lambda z . (g[z/y][f/x])$$

    where z is a variable which does not appear in f or g. (Note that we have an infinite collection of variables, so that we can always find such a z.)

- In general, it is easy to see that if x is not free in e then $e[f/x]$ is e.

Convention on expression equivalence: We shall not distinguish between expressions which are equivalent up to change of bound variable names in what follows. (As an aside, this convention, which is easy to state, and indeed for us to follow, is surprisingly difficult to implement.)

As we said, we evaluate expressions by passing parameters in function applications. We formalize this by the following *reduction* or *computation* rules.

Definition 2.5

The rule of **β-reduction** states that, for all x, e and f, we can reduce the application

$$(\lambda x . e)f \rightarrow_\beta e[f/x]$$

Definition 2.6

A sub-expression of a lambda expression of the form $(\lambda x . e)f$ is called a **(β-)redex**. We write $g \rightarrow_\beta g'$ if g' results from applying β-reduction to a redex within g. Alternatively we can say that if $e \rightarrow_\beta e'$ then

$$(fe) \rightarrow_\beta (fe')$$

$$(eg) \rightarrow_\beta (e'g)$$

$$\lambda y . e \rightarrow_\beta \lambda y . e'$$

Definition 2.7

We write $e \twoheadrightarrow f$ if there is a sequence of zero or more reductions so that

$$e \equiv e_0 \rightarrow_\beta \cdots \rightarrow_\beta e_n \equiv f$$

giving a sequence of reduction steps. We call such an f a **reduct** of e.

In the section which follows we look further at the reduction relation $\twoheadrightarrow$. One point is worthy of note before we do that. We have only introduced one-argument functions into our theory; is this a restriction? It is not, as we can represent a two-argument function by a function which takes its arguments one at a time. The addition function, for example, would be represented by

$$\lambda x . \lambda y . (x + y)$$

where we assume (purely for illustrative purposes) that the language contains the $+$ operator. This form of representation is known as the *curried* form in honour of Haskell B. Curry, and has the property that it is sensible to pass to it one of its arguments only. In this case, for instance,

$$(\lambda x . \lambda y . (x + y)) \, 4$$

is the function which adds four to its argument.

Exercise

2.1   Investigate the reduction behaviour of the following terms:

$$(\lambda x . x)((\lambda y . (\lambda z . z))(\lambda x . x))$$

$$(\lambda x . xxx)(\lambda x . xxx)$$

2.3   Evaluation

The reduction relation, $\twoheadrightarrow$, of the previous section embodies what it is for one expression to reduce to another by a number of elementary computation steps. We can ask a number of fundamental questions about this relation.

It is somewhat artificial to examine evaluation in the context of the untyped λ-calculus, since all we have in this context are functions, and we do not usually consider functions to be objects which can be evaluated themselves; rather we work in typed systems and print only the results of evaluating expressions of *ground type*, such as numbers, pairs of booleans and so forth. Nonetheless we can both establish some terminology and begin discussions here, even if we will have more to say later.

First, if the relation describes evaluation, what is it that expressions evaluate *to*? There are a number of answers to this.

Definition 2.8

Normal form: An expression is in normal form if it contains no redexes.

Head normal form: All expressions of the form

$$\lambda x_1 \ldots \lambda x_n . y e_1 \ldots e_m$$

where y is a variable, $e_1, \ldots, e_m$ are arbitrary expressions and n and m are greater than or equal to zero, are in head normal form.

Weak head normal form: All expressions which are either λ-abstractions or of the form

$$y e_1 \ldots e_m$$

where y is a variable, $e_1, \ldots, e_m$ are arbitrary expressions and m is greater than or equal to zero, are in weak head normal form.

Definition 2.9

We say that e' is a **normal form** (head normal form, and so forth) of e if $e \twoheadrightarrow e'$ and e' is in normal form (head normal form, and so forth).

The three definitions above are given in inclusion order: normal forms are head normal forms which are themselves weak head normal forms. Neither of the converses holds; $\lambda x . (x((\lambda x . xx)(\lambda x . xx)))$ is in head normal form but not in normal form (and indeed has no normal form) whilst $\lambda y . ((\lambda x . xx)(\lambda x . xx))$ is a weak head normal form with no head normal form. Both these examples use the term

$$\Omega \equiv_{df} (\lambda x . xx)(\lambda x . xx)$$

which has the property that $\Omega \rightarrow_\beta \Omega$ and only to Ω, thus proving that it has no normal form; indeed it has no weak head normal form. Whatever the notion of answer, an attempt to evaluate Ω results in an undefined answer, since computation fails to terminate.

It is clear why we can think of a normal form as being the result of a computation, but how do the other definitions arise? It might at first be thought that any expression without a normal form is in some sense equivalent to Ω in being undefined, but the position is not so simple. A crucial example is the function

$$F \equiv_{df} \lambda f . ((\lambda x . f(xx))(\lambda x . f(xx)))$$

which has the following properties. It has no normal form, so computation of it fails to terminate, yet when applied to an argument f it returns a *fixed point* of the function f, that is an object with the property

$$(F\ f) \longrightarrow f\ (F\ f)$$

In many cases the computation of the application will terminate – consider the case that f is a constant function whose value is a normal form. We can characterize the property of F as being able to yield an answer (normal form) in *some* context, even though it has no normal form itself. Wadsworth has shown that it is precisely those functions which have a head normal form, so in evaluating functions it seems more sensible only to compute to head normal form, if we wish computations on 'meaningful' objects to terminate. More details on this analysis can be found in the useful discussion of Section 2 of [Barendregt, 1984]. Not every functional expression has a head normal form, the simplest case being $\lambda x.\Omega$.

In evaluating functional expressions we might choose to halt evaluation as soon as a functional form $\lambda x.e$ is reached – this gives rise to the notion of weak head normal form which has recently been discussed in [Peyton Jones, 1987; Abramsky, 1990].

The context for this discussion about termination, the untyped λ-calculus, is somewhat artificial since it contains no true printable values such as numbers or characters. We therefore defer discussion of the form that results (or canonical values) take until Section 2.11.

Whichever notion we choose, we can see that there are expressions whose evaluation fails to terminate. No sequence of reductions starting from Ω ends in a weak head normal form.

Another problem is of determinacy: do different sequences of reductions give the same final value if they terminate? An important result here is the Church–Rosser theorem.

Theorem 2.10 (Church–Rosser)

For all e, f and g, if $e \longrightarrow f$ and $e \longrightarrow g$ then there exists h such that $f \longrightarrow h$ and $g \longrightarrow h$.

A proof of the Church–Rosser theorem is found in [Barendregt, 1984]. The proofs use a form of induction over the syntactic structure of terms, usually called structural induction.

Definition 2.11

The method of **structural induction** states that to prove the result $P(e)$ for all λ-expressions e it is sufficient

- to prove $P(x)$ for all variables x,
- to prove $P(e\ f)$ assuming that $P(e)$ and $P(f)$ hold,

- to prove $P(\lambda x \,.\, e)$ assuming that $P(e)$ holds.

The Church–Rosser theorem has the following important corollary.

Theorem 2.12

If a term has a normal form then it is unique.

Proofs of these results can be found in the encyclopaedic [Barendregt, 1984]. Note that neither head normal forms nor weak head normal forms of expressions are unique.

The result on unique normal forms tells us that terminating reduction sequences all end in the same normal form. There are expressions with normal forms which have non-terminating reduction sequences, an example being

$$(\lambda x \,.\, \lambda y \,.\, y)\,\Omega$$

The whole expression forms a redex which reduces to $\lambda y \,.\, y$, in normal form. If we choose repeatedly to reduce the redex Ω we have a non-terminating reduction sequence. Can we always find a terminating sequence if one exists?

Definition 2.13

If an expression contains more than one redex, then we say that the **leftmost-outermost** redex is that found by searching the parse tree top-down, going down the left-hand subtree of a non-redex application before the right. In other words we make a preorder traversal of the parse tree looking for the first node which is a redex.

In the following expressions the leftmost-outermost redex is marked by a brace, with the others marked by a bar.

$$\underbrace{(\lambda x \,.\, xx)(\overline{(\lambda y \,.\, y)(\lambda z \,.\, z)})}$$

$$((\lambda w \,.\, w)(\lambda x \,.\, xx))(\overline{(\lambda y \,.\, y)(\lambda z \,.\, z)})$$

$$((\lambda w \,.\, w)(\underbrace{\overline{(\lambda x \,.\, xx)(\lambda x \,.\, x)}}))(\overline{(\lambda y \,.\, y)(\lambda z \,.\, z)})$$

Theorem 2.14 (normalization)

The reduction sequence formed by choosing for reduction at each stage the leftmost-outermost redex will result in a normal form, head normal form or weak head normal form if any exists.

Proofs of the normalization theorem can be found in [Barendregt, 1984].

The **strategy** of choosing the leftmost-outermost redex at each stage corresponds to the **lazy** evaluation mechanism, although the latter is optimized to avoid duplication of evaluation caused by duplication of redexes. The **strict** or applicative order discipline will not always lead to termination, even when this is possible: arguments may not terminate even if their values are not needed for the evaluation of the expression as a whole.

There is a second basic rule of reduction, called η-reduction.

Definition 2.15 (η-reduction)

For all x and e, if x is not free in e then we can perform the following reduction.

$$\lambda x \,.\, (ex) \to_\eta e$$

It is not clear that this is strictly a rule of *computation*. The expressions on the two sides of the reduction symbol have the same computational behaviour on all arguments, since

$$(\lambda x \,.\, (ex)) \, y \to_\beta e \, y$$

for arbitrary y. The rule identifies certain (terms for) functions which have the same behaviour, yet which are represented in different ways. In a context in which we distinguish printable values from others, the beta rule will be sufficient, *computationally*, to ensure the same results from the application of η-equivalent functions.

We generally consider η-reduction as an adjunct to β-reduction, and we define their joint transitive closure in the obvious way. We can prove a Church–Rosser theorem for this relation (see, again, [Barendregt, 1984] for details).

It seems more appropriate to read the η rule as symmetrical, equating its two sides. We look at this idea in the next section.

Exercises

2.2   Show that if we write I for $\lambda x \,.\, x$ then

$$\lambda x \,.\, x(II) \qquad \lambda x \,.\, xI$$

are both head normal forms of $\lambda x \,.\, (Ix)(II)$

2.3   Prove Theorem 2.12 from Theorem 2.10.

2.4   By showing that the leftmost-outermost reduction sequence is infinite, argue that the following expressions fail to have normal form:

$$\Omega \qquad (\lambda f \,.\, ((\lambda x \,.\, f(xx))(\lambda x \,.\, f(xx))))(\lambda x \,.\, \lambda y \,.\, x)$$

2.4   Convertibility

Our introduction to the λ-calculus has focused so far on the computation relations $\to_\beta$, $\twoheadrightarrow$ and $\to_\eta$. We can also ask the more general question of which expressions have the same computational behaviour. This section introduces a number of **convertibility** relations, that is equivalence relations which are also substitutive: equivalent expressions substituted into equivalent contexts are equivalent.

The relations '$\to_\beta$' and '$\to_\eta$' are asymmetrical: the left-hand side is (in some sense) simplified in transition to the right-hand side. The relations generate two convertibility relations, $\leftrightarrow\!\!\!\twoheadrightarrow$ and $\leftrightarrow\!\!\!\twoheadrightarrow_{\beta\eta}$:

Definition 2.16

'$\leftrightarrow\!\!\!\twoheadrightarrow$' is the smallest equivalence relation extending '$\twoheadrightarrow$' Explicitly, $e \leftrightarrow\!\!\!\twoheadrightarrow f$ if and only if there is a sequence $e_0, \cdots, e_n$ with $n \geq 0$ $e \equiv e_0, e_n \equiv f$ and for each i, $0 \leq i < n$, $e_i \twoheadrightarrow e_{i+1}$ or $e_{i+1} \twoheadrightarrow e_i$.

A similar relation based on β and η reduction together is called $\beta\eta$-convertibility.

As a consequence of the Church–Rosser theorems, two expressions e and f will be ($\beta\eta$-)convertible if and only if there exists a common ($\beta\eta$-)reduct of e and f. If one of them has a normal form then the other has the same.

Two functions with normal forms are convertible if and only if they have the *same* normal form; in particular we fail to identify

$$\lambda y.(\lambda x.(yx)) \qquad \lambda y.y$$

Applied to an argument z, the functions give equivalent results, as they β-reduce to

$$(\lambda x.(zx)) \qquad z$$

which themselves have the same behaviour as functions. It is for this reason that $\beta\eta$-convertibility is defined. $\beta\eta$-convertibility is the smallest substitutive equivalence relation R extending $\leftrightarrow\!\!\!\twoheadrightarrow$ which is *extensional*, meaning that if $(f\,y)\,R\,(g\,y)$ for y a variable, then $f\,R\,g$. This result is again found in the encyclopaedic [Barendregt, 1984].

The convertibility relations are not necessary to explain the computational behaviour of λ-expressions; they are used when we reason about the behaviour of expressions; in particular they can tell us which functions have the same behaviour, and which transformations (of one expression into another) are permissible. We shall return to this topic in Section 2.11, after discussing typed λ-calculi.

Exercise

2.5 Show that if e has the form $\lambda y \,.\, e'$ where x is not free in e' then

$$(\lambda x \,.\, ex) \rightarrow_\beta e$$

2.5   Expressiveness

The untyped λ-calculus is a simple theory of (pure) functions, yet computationally it is as strong as other fundamental theories of computation. It is Turing complete, exhibiting an equivalence with Turing computability. One half of this equivalence consists in showing that objects such as the natural numbers, booleans and so forth can be represented as λ-terms, and that recursive functions can be defined over them. Yet again, Barendregt provides a suitable reference for this material. One representation of the natural numbers is as the iterators, n being represented by

$$\lambda f \,.\, \lambda x \,.\, \underbrace{f \, (f \, \ldots \, f \, (f \, x) \ldots)}_{n}$$

which are in normal form. To derive recursive functions, with definitions such as

$$f \, x \equiv_{df} \, \ldots f \, \ldots$$

which can be written

$$f \equiv_{df} \lambda x. \ldots f \ldots$$

we need to be able to solve equations of the form

$$f \equiv_{df} R \, f$$

where R is a λ-term. In fact we can define operations, F, called **fixed point combinators** which solve these equations thus:

$$F \, R \twoheadrightarrow R \, (F \, R)$$

Two examples are the expressions:

$$\theta\theta \quad \text{where} \quad \theta \equiv_{df} \lambda a \,.\, \lambda b \,.\, (b(aab)))$$

$$F \equiv_{df} \lambda f \,.\, ((\lambda x \,.\, f(xx))(\lambda x \,.\, f(xx)))$$

Each of these expressions has a head normal form, but neither has a normal form. This is a general property of fixed point combinators, since

$$\lambda x \,.\, (F\,x) \quad \rightarrow_\beta \quad \lambda x \,.\, (x\,(F\,x))$$
$$\rightarrow_\beta \quad \lambda x \,.\, (x\,(x\,(F\,x)))$$
$$\rightarrow_\beta \quad \dots$$

and F has a normal form if and only if $\lambda x\,.\,(F\,x)$ has. This is an interesting point: here we have meaningful functions which cannot be represented by expressions in normal form, showing that the class of meaningful expressions extends beyond those with normal form.

2.6   Typed λ-calculus

The untyped λ-calculus is powerful, containing as it does the fixed point combinators, representatives of all the common base types and their combinations under standard type forming operations. The disadvantage of this power is the fact that our programs can continually break the stipulations of our conceptual type system, which permits only numbers to be added and so forth.

Another aspect of the system is the presence of non-termination: we have seen that not every term has even a weak head normal form. Any attempt to evaluate Ω results in a non-terminating computation. Ω does not have a legitimate type in any type system, except those which include a reflexive type C isomorphic to its function space $(C \Rightarrow C)$. Terms with the computational behaviour of Ω are introduced by a fixed point combinator:

$$F\,(\lambda x\,.\,x) \quad \rightarrow_\beta \quad (\lambda x\,.\,x)\,(F\,(\lambda x\,.\,x))$$
$$\rightarrow_\beta \quad (F\,(\lambda x\,.\,x))$$
$$\rightarrow_\beta \quad \dots$$

and the existence of such a combinator does not contradict the type discipline, despite the fact that the definitions of the previous section are not typeable, containing as they do applications of objects to themselves.

We now examine a number of typed λ-calculi of differing expressive strengths which will culminate in the system of constructive type theory itself.

In this chapter we are able to develop separately first the types and then the terms of the theory. We begin by defining a system with function types (and a number of base types), progressively adding further types and objects.

Definition 2.17

Given a set B of base types, we form the set S of **simple types** closing under the rule of function type formation. This states that if σ and τ are types then so is $(\sigma \Rightarrow \tau)$. We assume that '$\Rightarrow$' is right associative, and omit parentheses accordingly.

In typed lambda calculi each λ-expression (or term; we use these interchangeably) has a type. We shall write

$e : \tau$

for 'e is a λ-expression of type τ'. We specify the type of each defined λ-expression below.

Definition 2.18

The **expressions** of the typed λ-calculus have three forms.

Individual variables or *variables*, $v_{\tau,0}, v_{\tau,1}, v_{\tau,2}, \ldots$, for each type τ.

$v_{\tau,i} : \tau$

We shall write $x_\tau, y_\tau, z_\tau, \ldots$, with or without type subscripts for arbitrary individual variables in what follows.

Applications. If $e_1 : (\sigma \Rightarrow \tau)$ and $e_2 : \sigma$ then

$(e_1\, e_2) : \tau$

We can only form an application when the type of the argument is the same as the type of the domain of the function.

Abstractions. If $x : \sigma$ and $e : \tau$ then

$(\lambda x_\sigma . e) \; : \; (\sigma \Rightarrow \tau)$

The type of an abstraction is a function type, whose domain is the type of the formal parameter and whose range is the type of the function body (or result).

Many notions defined in the untyped case carry over to here. These include the substitution mechanism, β- and η-reduction and convertibility and the notions of canonical element: normal form, head normal form etcetera. It is easy to see that convertible expressions must be of the same type.

Many results carry over too. The Church–Rosser theorems for β- and $\beta\eta$-reduction have the same proofs. Given a variable x_σ, we are unable to form the application $x_\sigma x_\sigma$ and thus unable to define Ω and the fixed point combinators we saw above. This is no accident, as we can prove the following theorem.

Theorem 2.19 (strong normalization)

Every reduction sequence terminates.

This important result is proved in the next section, and also in [Fortune *et al.*, 1983]. Clearly the system is less expressive than the untyped calculus; precise details are also found in [Fortune *et al.*, 1983].

We can present the calculus in a slightly different form, closer to the practice in programming languages. Instead of there being an infinite class of variables for each type we can simply take one (infinite) class of variables. When we use a variable we assume it is associated with a type: we call this a *type assumption* but it might be more familiar as a *declaration* in a language such as Pascal. We then assign types to expressions in the **type context** of a number of type assumptions. We shall write $\Gamma, \ldots$ for such contexts, using $\Gamma, x : \tau$ for the context Γ with the type assumption $x : \tau$ added. We assume throughout that all contexts Γ are **consistent** in containing at most one occurrence of each variable – we can give *any* expression a type using the appropriate inconsistent context. Writing

$$\Gamma \vdash e : \tau$$

for 'e has the type τ in the context Γ', the syntax rules become as follows.

Definition 2.20

Individual variables. For any context Γ,

$$\Gamma, x : \tau \vdash x : \tau$$

Applications. If

$$\Gamma \vdash e_1 : (\sigma \Rightarrow \tau)$$

and

$$\Gamma \vdash e_2 : \sigma$$

then

$$\Gamma \vdash (e_1\, e_2) : \tau$$

As before, we can only form an application when the type of the argument is the same as the type of the domain of the function.

Abstractions. If

$$\Gamma, x : \sigma \vdash e : \tau$$

then

$$\Gamma \vdash (\lambda x_\sigma . e) : (\sigma \Rightarrow \tau)$$

The type of an abstraction is a function type, whose domain is the type of the formal parameter and whose range is the type of the function body (or result).

The rule giving the type of an abstraction has one unusual aspect. The assumption that $x : \sigma$ is used in typing the body of the function, e, but is not needed to give a type to the function itself. Why is this? In general the variable x will appear free in the expression e – we cannot type an expression containing a free variable without knowing the type for the variable, and this is given by the assumption. On the other hand, in $(\lambda x_\sigma . e)$ x is bound and associated with the type σ it is assumed to have in the expression e, which is the scope of that particular declaration of the variable x.

Exercises

2.6 Show that

$$\lambda x . \lambda y . \lambda z . (xz)(yz) : (\sigma \Rightarrow \tau \Rightarrow \rho) \Rightarrow (\sigma \Rightarrow \tau) \Rightarrow (\sigma \Rightarrow \rho)$$

2.7 Explain why $\lambda x . xx$ and the fixed point combinator F are not terms of the typed λ-calculus.

2.7   Strong normalization

This section introduces a result which is important both in itself and because of its method of proof. This method, introduced in [Tait, 1967] and known as the **reducibility** method, is a general means of proof for systems which are typed. It involves an induction over the complexity of the types, rather than over syntactic complexity, which we saw was the major method of proof for untyped systems.

Theorem 2.21 (strong normalization)

For all expressions e of the simply typed λ-calculus, all reduction sequences beginning with e are finite.

How should the proof proceed? One method we cannot use is a straightforward structural induction, as a proof using this alone would carry over to the untyped case, where we know that not even the terms with normal form are strongly normalizing. The method we use will involve an induction over the structure of types.

Definition 2.22

The method of **induction over types** states that to prove the result $P(\tau)$ for all types τ it is sufficient

- to prove $P(\sigma)$ for all base types $\sigma \in B$ – this is called the base case;
- to prove $P(\sigma \Rightarrow \tau)$ assuming that $P(\sigma)$ and $P(\tau)$ hold – this is called the induction step.

As is common in proofs by induction, in order to prove a property $R(e)$ of every expression e we in fact prove a strengthening R' of R. This is because the obvious induction hypothesis will not be strong enough to work at the induction step. This is the case with the property 'e is **strongly normalizing**' which we abbreviate 'e is SN': two terms e and e' may be strongly normalizing without it being clear that the application $(e\,e')$ is so. (It *will* of course be strongly normalizing by the proof we construct, but that begs the question of how we establish it.)

Definition 2.23

We say that an expression e of type τ is **stable**, written $e \in \|\tau\|$

- if e is of base type and e is SN, or
- if e is of type $\sigma \Rightarrow \tau$ and for all e' in $\|\sigma\|$, $(e\,e') \in \|\tau\|$

Stability is designed to be preserved by application, so that it is easier to see that it will be carried through that case of the induction. Note also that we use the type system in an essential way in this definition: we define stability for a function type in terms of stability for its domain and range types.

Before we begin the proof of the theorem, we note the following properties of the class of strongly normalizing terms.

Lemma 2.24

If x is a variable then

(a) $x \in SN$,

(b) if $e_1, \ldots, e_k \in SN$ then $xe_1 \ldots e_k \in SN$,

(c) if $ex \in SN$ then $e \in SN$,

(d) if $e \in SN$ then $(\lambda x\,.\,e) \in SN$.

Proof:

(a) This is obvious, as the variable contains no redex.

(b) Any reduction sequence from $xe_1 \ldots e_k$ will have the form

$$xe_1 \ldots e_k \to_\beta \ldots \to_\beta xf_1 \ldots f_k \to_\beta xg_1 \ldots g_k \to_\beta \ldots$$

where at each stage for exactly one index j, $f_j \to_\beta g_j$ and for the others, $f_i \equiv g_i$. This means that if there is an infinite reduction sequence from $xe_1 \ldots e_k$ then there must be one from one of the e_is, a contradiction to their being SN.

(c) A reduction sequence from ex will have either the form

$$ex \to_\beta e_1 x \to_\beta e_2 x \to_\beta \ldots \to_\beta e_n x \to_\beta \ldots$$

or the form

$$ex \to_\beta e_1 x \to_\beta \ldots \to_\beta (\lambda y . f) \, x \to_\beta f[x/y] \to_\beta f_1[x/y] \to_\beta f_2[x/y] \to_\beta \ldots$$

where

$$\lambda y . f \to_\beta \lambda y . f_1 \to_\beta \lambda y . f_2 \to_\beta \ldots$$

is a reduction sequence continuing $e \to_\beta e_1 \to_\beta \ldots$. In either case an infinite sequence starting at ex gives rise to one starting at e.

(d) A reduction sequence starting at $\lambda x . e$ will have the form

$$\lambda y . e \to_\beta \lambda y . e_1 \to_\beta \lambda y . e_2 \to_\beta \ldots$$

where

$$e \to_\beta e_1 \to_\beta e_2 \to_\beta \ldots$$

and so an infinite sequence starting at $\lambda y . e$ gives rise to another starting at e. $\qquad\qquad\square$

The proof of the theorem itself is based on two further lemmas. In the first we show that stable objects are strongly normalizing (at the same time showing that variables are stable), and in the second we show that all objects are stable.

Lemma 2.25

(a) If $e \in \|\tau\|$ then $e \in SN$.

(b) If $xe_1 \ldots e_n : \tau$ and $e_1, \ldots, e_n \in SN$ then $xe_1 \ldots e_n \in \|\tau\|$.

(c) If $x : \tau$ then $x \in \|\tau\|$.

Proof: We prove (a), (b) and (c) by a simultaneous induction over the type τ.

Base case: τ is a base type. The property (a) is true by definition of stability for a base type.

For (b), if $e_1, \ldots, e_n \in SN$ then by Lemma 2.24, part (b), $xe_1 \ldots e_k$ will be strongly normalizing, and since τ is a base type, the expression is stable.

Finally, to prove (c) observe that any variable is strongly normalizing and therefore stable if it is of base type.

Induction step: We assume that τ is the type $(\sigma \Rightarrow \rho)$ and that the results (a), (b) and (c) hold for the types σ, ρ.

To prove (a) we assume that $e \in \|\tau\|$. We have to prove that e is SN. Take x of type σ. By (c) for σ, x is stable, and so by the definition of stability for e, ex will be stable. ex is of type ρ and so by (a) for ρ, ex is SN. Using Lemma 2.24, part (c), e is therefore SN.

Now we show (b). To prove that $xe_1 \ldots e_n \in \|\tau\|$ we need to show that $xe_1 \ldots e_n f$ is in $\|\rho\|$, if $f \in \|\sigma\|$. By hypothesis $e_1, \ldots, e_n \in SN$ and by (a) for σ, f is also SN. The expression $xe_1 \ldots e_n f$ is of type ρ and so by (b) for ρ,

$$xe_1 \ldots e_n f \in \|\rho\|$$

as required.

Finally, we show (c). Suppose that f in $\|\sigma\|$. By (a) for σ, f is SN, and since the expression (xf) has type ρ, by (b) for ρ, (xf) is in $\|\rho\|$, so x is stable. □

Our task now is to show that all expressions are stable. We aim to do this by structural induction over the expressions. We know that variables are stable by the previous result, and we prove easily that application preserves stability: indeed this was a motivation of the definition. The case of λ-abstraction is more tricky. We aim to prove that $\lambda x . f$ is stable, assuming f is, and so we have to prove that for all stable g of the appropriate type,

$$(\lambda x . f) g$$

is stable. This expression reduces to $f[g/x]$. We need to deduce the stability of the former from that of the latter. In fact we need to prove a generalization of this to get the induction to work, which readers can see for themselves by trying a direct proof. The generalization is clause (b) of the next lemma.

Before we state the lemma, we give another definition.

Definition 2.26

An **s-instance** e' of an expression e is a substitution instance

$$e' \equiv e[g_1/x_1, \ldots, g_r/x_r]$$

where the g_i are stable expressions.

Lemma 2.27

(a) If e and f are stable then so is (ef).

(b) For all $k \geq 0$, if $f[g/x]h_1 \ldots h_k \in \|\tau\|$ and $g \in SN$ then

$$(\lambda x . f)gh_1 \ldots h_k \in \|\tau\|$$

(c) All s-instances e' of expressions e are stable.

Proof: We prove the clauses one at a time.

(a) If $e \in \|\sigma \Rightarrow \tau\|$ and $f \in \|\sigma\|$ then by definition of stability for the function space, $(ef) \in \|\tau\|$, in other words (ef) is stable.

(b) This we prove by induction over the type τ.

Base case: Suppose first that τ is of base type. We need to prove that $(\lambda x . f)gh_1 \ldots h_k$ is strongly normalizing assuming that $f[g/x]h_1 \ldots h_k$ and g are.

Consider the general form of a reduction sequence starting from

$$(\lambda x . f)gh_1 \ldots h_k$$

Redexes will either be contained in f, g and $h_1, \ldots h_k$ or consist of the head redex $(\lambda x . f)g$. All sequences will take either the form

$$
\begin{aligned}
(\lambda x . f)gh_1 \ldots h_k \quad &\twoheadrightarrow \quad (\lambda x . f')g'h_1' \ldots h_k' \\
&\rightarrow_\beta \quad f'[g'/x]h_1' \ldots h_k' \\
&\rightarrow_\beta \quad \ldots
\end{aligned}
$$

or the form

$$
\begin{aligned}
(\lambda x . f)gh_1 \ldots h_k \quad &\twoheadrightarrow \quad (\lambda x . f')g'h_1' \ldots h_k' \\
&\rightarrow_\beta \quad \ldots
\end{aligned}
$$

in which the top-level redex is not reduced in subsequent computation. In the first case, since

$$f[g/x]h_1 \ldots h_k \twoheadrightarrow f'[g'/x]h_1' \ldots h_k'$$

the sequence must be finite, as $f[g/x]h_1 \ldots h_k$ is strongly normalizing. In the second case, can we have an infinite reduction sequence without ever reducing the top-level redex? A sequence of this form will consist of a number of parallel sequences, for f, g and $h_1, \ldots, h_k$. Such a sequence can be factored into two separate sequences, one starting with g and the other containing no g reductions. The sequence of g reductions will be finite, as g is SN, and the other sequence will be finite as it can be transformed into a corresponding sequence of reductions of the term $f[g/x]h_1 \ldots h_k$ in which no g reductions take place. Any such sequence must also be finite, so the expression $(\lambda x . f)gh_1 \ldots h_k$ is SN.

Induction step: Suppose that τ is the functional type $(\sigma \Rightarrow \rho)$. To show that $(\lambda x . f)gh_1 \ldots h_k \in \|\tau\|$ we need to show that

$$(\lambda x . f)gh_1 \ldots h_k h \in \|\rho\|$$

for every h in $\|\sigma\|$. Now, since $f[g/x]h_1 \ldots h_k \in \|\tau\|$,

$$f[g/x]h_1 \ldots h_k h \in \|\rho\|$$

and so by (b) for the type ρ, we have $(\lambda x . f)gh_1 \ldots h_k h \in \|\rho\|$ as required. This completes the proof of (b).

(c) We prove (c) by structural induction over the expressions e. There are three cases.

Case: variables. For variables x, either x' will be the stable expression g, when the substitution has the form $[\ldots, g/x, \ldots]$, or when x is not the target of a substitution, x' is x which is stable by Lemma 2.25, part (c).

Case: application. If e has the form $(e_1 e_2)$ then an s-instance of e will have the form $(e_1' e_2')$ where e_i' is an s-instance of e_i. By induction, each of e_i' is stable, and by Lemma 2.27, part (a), the application $(e_1' e_2')$ is stable.

Case: abstraction. Suppose that e has the form $\lambda x . f$. We need to show that every substitution instance of this is stable. These instances have the form $\lambda x . f'$ where f' is a substitution instance of f. Now, how do we prove the stability of $\lambda x . f'$? We have to show that

$$(\lambda x . f') \, g$$

is stable for stable g. By Lemma 2.25, part (a), g is SN, so applying Lemma 2.27, part (b) with $k = 0$ it is sufficient to show that $f'[g/x]$ is stable. This is also an s-instance of f and by induction it is stable. This completes the proof of this case, part (c) of the proof and therefore the proof itself.   □

Proof (Theorem 2.21): By part (c) of Lemma 2.27, every expression is stable (as it is the trivial substitution instance of itself), and by Lemma 2.25(a), all stable expressions are strongly normalizing.   □

2.8   Further type constructors: the product

The simply typed λ-calculus could not be simpler: we have only some unspecified base types, carrying no operations, and a single form of type construction, the function space. We can extend the system in two different ways, adding both new base types and new constructors. First we look at type constructors.

Familiar type constructors include the product type and the disjoint sum (or disjoint union). In Pascal these together are embodied in the variant record type. The addition of these is standard; we review briefly the addition of the product type to the simply typed λ-calculus now.

- To the definition of types we add the third clause that $\sigma \times \tau$ is a type if σ and τ are.

- We add two clauses to the definition of expressions:

  Pairs: If $x:\sigma$ and $y:\tau$ then

  $$(x, y) \; : \; \sigma \times \tau$$

  The pair (x, y) is a member of the product type.

  Projections: If $p \; : \; \sigma \times \tau$ then *fst* $p:\sigma$ and *snd* $p:\tau$. The operations *fst* and *snd* project a pair onto its components.

- To the rules of computation we add the rules

  $$fst\,(p, q) \to p \qquad snd\,(p, q) \to q$$

  which show that *fst* and *snd* do indeed behave as projection operations, and we ask also that reduction is preserved by pairing, so that if

  $$p \to p'$$

  then

  $$(p, q) \to (p', q) \qquad (q, p) \to (q, p')$$

- To the rules we can also add

  $$(fst\,p,\,snd\,p) \to p$$

  for p of product type. This implies the *extensionality* rule that an element of a product type is characterized by its components, since if

  $$fst\,p \leftrightarrow\!\!\!\rightarrow fst\,q \qquad snd\,p \leftrightarrow\!\!\!\rightarrow snd\,q$$

  then

  $$p \leftrightarrow\!\!\!\rightarrow (fst\,p,\,snd\,p) \leftrightarrow\!\!\!\rightarrow (fst\,q,\,snd\,q) \leftrightarrow\!\!\!\rightarrow q$$

We have added the operations *fst* and *snd* as primitives. Alternatively we could think of them as constants, belonging to particular types. For this to work here we need to add a collection of constants, one for each product type, thus:

$$fst_{\sigma,\tau} \; : \; (\sigma \times \tau) \Rightarrow \sigma$$

$$snd_{\sigma,\tau} \; : \; (\sigma \times \tau) \Rightarrow \tau$$

Our notation is made unwieldy by this addition; common practice in such situations is to omit the type subscripts from these constants – in any expression generated by the rules above we can deduce the type of each instance from the context.

A second alternative is to add two constants, but to allow each of them to have many types. *fst* would have the type $(\sigma \times \tau) \Rightarrow \sigma$ for *all* the types σ and τ. This is the idea of *polymorphism* which we mentioned in our introduction to functional programming on page 30. To make this introduction in a disciplined way we need to strengthen the type system to allow polymorphic types – a further extension of the calculus. The literature on polymorphism is extensive: [Milner, 1978; Reynolds, 1990].

A second distinction, touched upon in Section 2.4, was the distinction between β- and η-reduction. We have a similar distinction between the two rules

$$fst\,(p,q) \rightarrow p \qquad snd\,(p,q) \rightarrow q$$

and the rule

$$(fst\,p, snd\,p) \rightarrow p$$

We shall call rules of the first sort **computation rules** and those of the latter kind **equivalence rules**, as their main purpose is to develop a convertibility relation. A common distinction between the two pairs derives from an examination of the types of the objects they relate: the computation rules relate objects of *arbitrary* type:

$$(\lambda x \,.\, e)f \twoheadrightarrow e[f/x]$$

$$fst\,(p,q) \rightarrow p$$

where e and p are of arbitrary type. On the other hand, the equivalence rules relate elements of *restricted* type. In the case of η reduction

$$\lambda x \,.\, (ex) \rightarrow_{\eta} e$$

for the left-hand side to be a term of the typed calculus, e must be of a function type. Similarly, in

$$(fst\ p, snd\ p) \rightarrow p$$

for *fst p* and *snd p* to be well formed, p must be of product type. We will take up this discussion further below, after adding a base type.

Exercise

2.8 Show that

$$\lambda x . \lambda y . \lambda z . (x\ (y, z)) \ : \ ((\sigma \times \tau) \Rightarrow \rho) \Rightarrow (\sigma \Rightarrow \tau \Rightarrow \rho)$$

and that

$$\lambda x . \lambda y . (x\ (fst\ y)\ (snd\ y)) \ : \ (\sigma \Rightarrow \tau \Rightarrow \rho) \Rightarrow ((\sigma \times \tau) \Rightarrow \rho)$$

2.9 Base types: natural numbers

Computations are usually performed over concrete types, such as numbers, booleans, characters and so forth. Here we look at how the natural numbers can be added to the typed λ-calculi above.

- We add the type N to our set of base types (we may have $B = \{N\}$).
- To the syntax of expressions we add two clauses

Numbers: 0 is of type N, and if $n:N$ then $succ\ n:N$.
Primitive recursion: For all types τ, if

$$e_0:\tau \qquad f:(N \Rightarrow \tau \Rightarrow \tau)$$

then

$$Prec\ e_0\ f \ : \ N \Rightarrow \tau$$

Prec is called the **primitive recursor**, and the term above is intended to be the primitive recursive function F defined by the equations

$$F\ 0 \equiv_{df} e_0$$

$$F\ (n+1) \equiv_{df} f\ n\ (F\ n)$$

To ensure the term does represent the function we add the following computation rules for *Prec*.

- The reduction rules for *Prec* are

$$Prec\ e_0\ f\ 0 \to e_0$$

$$Prec\ e_0\ f\ (succ\ n) \to f\ n\ (Prec\ e_0\ f\ n)$$

- We can also define equivalence rules for *Prec*. Given a function

$$h\ :\ N \Rightarrow \tau$$

we can give a definition of a function taking exactly the same values as *h* by primitive recursion thus:

$$F\ 0\ \equiv_{df}\ h\ 0$$

$$F\ (n+1)\ \equiv_{df}\ f\ n\ (F\ n)$$

where

$$f\ n\ m\ \equiv_{df}\ h\ (n+1)$$

h and the function just defined take the same values at every numeral 0, *succ* 0, *succ* (*succ* 0) and so on: we state that the two functions are themselves equivalent by adding the reduction rule:

$$Prec\ (h\ 0)\ (\lambda n\,.\,\lambda m\,.\,h\ (succ\ n))\ \to\ h$$

for *h* of type $N \Rightarrow \tau$. Again, it is worth noting that the types of the objects related by this rule are not completely arbitrary: they are functions over the domain *N*.

We can extend the strong normalization result of Section 2.7 to a system containing product types and a base type of natural numbers. We retain the notion that expressions of type *N* are stable if and only if they are strongly normalizing, and add the clause that pairs *p* are stable if and only if their components *fst p* and *snd p* are. It is not hard to show that all stable objects are strongly normalizing; we then have to show that all objects are stable.

To do this we need an auxiliary result analogous to Lemma 2.27, part (b), stating that if all the expressions accessible by a single reduction from the expression *Prec e₀ f t* are stable, then so is the expression itself. We prove this by a type induction.

Given this result, the proof of stability of all terms proceeds by a structural induction, with an auxiliary induction over the natural numbers in the proof that

$$Prec\ e_0\ f\ t$$

is stable for stable e_0, f and t.

Details of this proof can be found in [Tait, 1967; Girard *et al.*, 1989; Troelstra, 1973].

Exercise

2.9 Give primitive recursive definitions of addition and multiplication.

2.10   General recursion

A further step is to add an operator R for general recursion. This should have the property that

$$R f \rightarrow f(R f)$$

so that $(R\, f)$ is a fixed point of the functional term f. This is a much stronger notion than primitive recursion (which is definable in terms of R and a number of primitive operations – details can be found in [Cutland, 1981]) and introduces non-terminating computations. In general, any recursively defined object will have at least one non-terminating reduction sequence,

$$
\begin{aligned}
R f \;&\rightarrow\; f(R f) \\
&\rightarrow\; f(f(R f)) \\
&\rightarrow\; \ldots \\
&\rightarrow\; f^n(R f) \\
&\rightarrow\; \ldots
\end{aligned}
$$

and some have all such sequences non-terminating:

$$
\begin{aligned}
R(\lambda x . x) \;&\rightarrow\; (\lambda x . x)(R(\lambda x . x)) \\
&\rightarrow\; R(\lambda x . x) \\
&\rightarrow\; \ldots
\end{aligned}
$$

We can see that although there are many fixed points of the identity function, computationally we have the 'least defined', which simply loops forever.

The semantic explanation of general recursion in the definition of objects and types has led to the development of denotational semantics, which was initiated by the work of Scott and Strachey in the late 1960s. The values computed by general recursive functions are members of domains, which reify the ideas of approximation and limit by which we can give an informal explanation of recursion. More details can be found in the excellent [Schmidt, 1986].

In type theory we adopt a different approach, keeping to systems in which normalization, at least in some form, is assured.

2.11   Evaluation revisited

This section allows us to round off earlier discussions, in Sections 2.3, 2.4 and 2.8, about evaluation, the various kinds of (head,...) normal form and computation and equivalence rules.

In a (typed) functional programming language such as Miranda, we can ask for the system to evaluate expressions of any type. If the object is a function, the result of the evaluation is simply the message

    <function>

This reflects the fact that we can print no representation of the function *qua* transformation, but only in some *intensional* way by a normal form for its code.

In addition to this, the ultimate values computed by programs will be finite – as finite beings we cannot wait an infinite time for a complete print-out, however close we feel we come sometimes! We would therefore argue that the values which we seek as final results of programs are non-functional.

Definition 2.28

The **order** of a type is defined thus, writing $\partial(\tau)$ for the order of τ:

$$
\begin{aligned}
\partial(\tau) &= 0 \quad \text{if } \tau \in B \\
\partial(\tau \times \sigma) &= max(\partial(\tau), \partial(\sigma)) \\
\partial(\tau \Rightarrow \sigma) &= max(\partial(\tau) + 1, \partial(\sigma))
\end{aligned}
$$

Definition 2.29

The terms we evaluate are not only zeroth order, that is of **ground** type, they also have the second property of being closed, containing as they do no free variables. The results will thus be closed (β-)normal forms of zeroth-order type. It is these that we call the **printable** values.

In our example λ-calculus, the closed normal forms in N are

$0, \ succ\,0, \ succ\,(succ\,0), \ldots$

in other words are 0 and $succ\,n$ where n itself is in normal form.

For a pair of ground types, $(\tau \times \sigma)$, the closed normal forms will be

$$(t, s)$$

where t, s are closed normal forms of type τ and σ.

How do we prove that these are the only closed normal forms at these types? We consider the (notationally) simpler case omitting product types. An induction over the structure of numerical terms suffices:

- A variable is not closed.
- 0 is a normal form.
- $succ\ t$: we argue by induction for t.
- $(f\ e)$ where f is of functional type. Closed terms of this type have three forms

  - $\lambda x\,.\,t$ or $Prec\ t_1\ t_2$. If f has either of these forms, we have a contradiction, since $(f\ e)$ will form a redex (by induction for e in the case of $Prec$).
  - $(g\ h)$ where g is an application. First we expand g fully as an application, writing the term as

    $$g_1\ g_2\ \ldots\ g_k\ h$$

    Each of the g_i is closed, and g_1 must be of function type. Also g_1 is not an application so $g_1\ g_2$ must be a redex in contradiction to f (that is $g\ h$), being in normal form

A similar argument establishes the result when product types are added. What is important to note here is that we have no redexes for the equivalence rules here: we have reached a normal form excluding such redexes without applying the reduction rules. Clearly this depends upon our twin assumptions of

Closure: This excludes terms of the form

$$(fst\ p, snd\ p)$$

where p is a variable of type $N \times N$, say.

Printable types: This excludes the obvious η-redexes, such as

$$\lambda x\,.\,\lambda y\,.\,(xy)$$

which can occur within *closed* terms of functional type.

We therefore feel justified in making the distinction between the two kinds of rules which we called computation and equivalence rules above. The computation rules suffice for the evaluation of particular terms, whilst the equivalence rules are used when reasoning about the general behaviour of functions (applied to terms which may contain variables).

Chapter 3
Constructive Mathematics

The aim of this brief chapter is to introduce the major issues underlying the conflict between 'constructive' and 'classical' mathematics, but it cannot hope to be anything other than an *hors d'oeuvre* to the substantial and lengthy dialogue between the two schools of thought which continues to this day.

Luckily, there are other sources. Bishop gives a rousing call to the constructive approach in the prologue to [Bishop and Bridges, 1985], which is followed by a closely argued 'Constructivist Manifesto' in the first chapter. Indeed the whole book is proof of the viability of the constructivism, developing as it does substantial portions of analysis from such a standpoint. It contains a bibliography of further work in the field.

An invaluable historical account of the basis of the conflict as well as subsequent activity in the field can be found in the historical appendix of [Beeson, 1985]. The first part of [Beeson, 1985], entitled 'Practice and Philosophy of Constructive Mathematics', also gives a most capable summary of both the scope and the foundations of constructive mathematics. [Dummett, 1977] is also a good introduction, looking in detail at the philosophy of intuitionism, and the recent survey [Troelstra and van Dalen, 1988] also serves its purpose well.

Bishop identifies constructivism with realism, contrasting it with the idealism of classical mathematics. He also says that it gives mathematical statements 'empirical content', as opposed to the purely 'pragmatic' nature of parts of classical mathematics, and sums up the programme of [Bishop and Bridges, 1985] thus 'to give numerical [that is *computational*] meaning to as much as possible of classical abstract analysis'.

A constructive treatment of mathematics has a number of interlinked aspects. We look at these in turn now.

3.1   Existence and logic

What constitutes a proof of *existence* of an object with certain properties? A mathematician will learn as a first-year undergraduate that to prove $\exists x.P(x)$ it is sufficient to prove that $\forall x.\neg P(x)$ is contradictory. The constructivist would argue that all this proof establishes is the contradiction: the proof of existence *must* supply a t and show that $P(t)$ is provable. Proofs of existential statements abound in mathematics: the fundamental theorem of algebra states that a polynomial of degree n has n complex roots; the intermediate value theorem asserts that continuous functions which change sign over a compact real interval have a zero in that interval, just to take two examples.

Sanction for proof by contradiction is given by the law of the excluded middle

$$A \vee \neg A$$

which states in particular that

$$\exists x.P(x) \vee \neg \exists x.P(x)$$

If $\forall x.\neg P(x)$, which is equivalent to $\neg \exists x.P(x)$, is contradictory, then we must accept $\exists x.P(x)$. Our view of existence thus leads us to reject one of the classical logical laws, which are themselves justified by an idealistic view of truth: every statement is seen as true or false, independently of any evidence either way. If we are to take the strong view of existence, we will have to modify in a radical way our view of logic and particularly our view of disjunction and existential quantification.

Bishop gives the interesting example that the classical theorem that every bounded non-empty set of reals has a least upper bound, upon which results like the intermediate value theorem depend, not only seems to depend for its proof upon non-constructive reasoning, it *implies* certain cases of the law of the excluded middle which are not constructively valid. Consider the set of reals $\{r_n \mid n \in N\}$ defined by

$$
\begin{aligned}
r_n \quad &\equiv_{df} \quad 1 \quad \textbf{if } P(n) \\
&\equiv_{df} \quad 0 \quad \textbf{if not}
\end{aligned}
$$

The least upper bound of this set is 1 if and only if $\exists x.P(x)$; we can certainly tell whether the upper bound is 1 or not, so

$$\exists x.P(x) \vee \neg \exists x.P(x)$$

As a consequence of this, not only will a constructive mathematics depend upon a different logic, but also it will not consist of the same results. One interesting effect of constructivizing is that classically equivalent results often split into a number of constructively *inequivalent* results, one or more of which *can* be shown to be valid by constructive means.

The constructive view of logic concentrates on what it means to prove or to demonstrate convincingly the validity of a statement, rather than concentrating on the abstract truth conditions which constitute the semantic foundation of classical logic. We examine these **proof conditions** now.

To prove a conjunction $A \wedge B$ we should prove both A and B; to prove $A \vee B$ we should prove one of A, B, and know which of the two we have proved. Under this interpretation, the law of the excluded middle is not valid, as we have no means of going from an assertion to a proof of either it or its negation. On the other hand, with this strong interpretation, we can extract computationally meaningful information from a proof of $A \vee B$, as it allows us to decide which of A or B is proved, and to extract the information contained in the proof of whichever of the two statements we have.

How might an implication $A \Rightarrow B$ be given a constructive proof? The proof should *transform* the information in a proof of A into similar information for B, in other words we give a function taking proofs of A into proofs of B. A proof of a universally quantified formula $\forall x.P(x)$ is also a transformation, taking an arbitrary a into a proof of the formula $P(a)$. We shall have more to say about the exact nature of functions in the section to come.

Rather than thinking of negation as a primitive operation, we can define the negation of a formula $\neg A$ to be an implication,

$$A \Rightarrow \perp$$

where $\perp$ is the absurd proposition, which has no proof. A proof of a negated formula has no computational content, and the classical tautology $\neg\neg A \Rightarrow A$ will not be valid – take the example where A is an existential statement.

Finally, to give a proof of an existential statement $\exists x.P(x)$ we have to give two things. First we have to give a *witness*, a say, for which $P(a)$ is provable. The second thing we have to supply is, of course, the proof of $P(a)$. Now, given this explanation, we can see that a constructive proof of

$$\exists x.P(x) \vee \neg\exists x.P(x)$$

constitutes a demonstration of the *limited principle of omniscience*. It gives a decision procedure for the predicates $P(x)$ over the natural numbers, say, and can be used to decide the truth or otherwise of the Goldbach conjecture, as well as giving a solution to the halting problem. It therefore seems not to be valid constructively, or at least no constructive demonstration of its validity has so far been given!

Given the explanation of the logic above, we can see that we have to abandon many classical principles, such as

$$\neg\neg A \Rightarrow A, \neg(\neg A \wedge \neg B) \Rightarrow (A \vee B), \neg\forall x.\neg P(x) \Rightarrow \exists x.P(x)$$

and so on.

We shall see in the section to come that as well as modifying our logic we have to modify our view of mathematical objects.

3.2   Mathematical objects

The nature of objects in classical mathematics is simple: *everything is a set*. The pair of objects a and b 'is' the set $\{\{a\}, \{a, b\}\}$ and the number 4 'is' the set consisting of

$$\emptyset \,,\, \{\emptyset\} \,,\, \{\emptyset, \{\emptyset\}\} \,,\, \{\emptyset, \{\emptyset\}, \{\emptyset, \{\emptyset\}\}\}$$

Functions are represented by sets of pairs constituting their graph, so that the successor function on the natural numbers is

$$\{(0,1), (1,2), (2,3), \ldots\}$$

which is itself shorthand for

$$\{\{\{\emptyset\}, \{\emptyset, \{\emptyset\}\}\} \,,\, \{\{\{\emptyset\}\}, \{\{\emptyset\}, \{\emptyset, \{\emptyset\}\}\}\} \ldots\}$$

Objects like this are infinite, and an arbitrary function graph will be **infinitary**, that is it will have no finite description. Such objects fail to have computational content: given the finitary nature of computation, it is impossible completely to specify such an object to an algorithm. This is an example of a fundamental tenet of constructive mathematics:

Every object in constructive mathematics is either *finite*, such as natural or rational numbers, or has a *finitary* description, such as the rule

$$\lambda x \,.\, x + 1$$

which describes the successor function over the natural numbers.

The real numbers provide an interesting example: we can supply a description of such a number by a sequence of approximations, $(a_n)_n$ say. This sequence is finitary if we can write down an algorithm or rule which allows us to compute the transformation

$$n \mapsto a_n$$

for all n. (We shall return to the example of the reals below.)

A second aspect of the set theoretic representation is the loss of distinction between objects of different conceptual type. A pair is a set, a number is a set, a function is a set, and so on. We are quite justified in forming a set such as

$$(3,4) \cup 0 \cup succ$$

although its significance is less than crystal clear! This does not reflect usual mathematical practice, in which the *a priori* distinctions between numbers, functions and so on are respected. In other words, the objects of mathematics are quite naturally thought of as having *types* rather than all having the trivial type 'set'. We summarize this in the slogan:

Constructive mathematics is naturally typed.

One obvious consequence of this is that quantification in a constructive setting will always be typed.

If we accept that a typed system is appropriate, what exactly do we mean by saying that 'object a has type A'? To understand what this means, we must explain type by type what are the objects of that type, and what it means for two objects of the type to be equal. For instance, for the type of functions, $A \Rightarrow B$, we might say that objects of the type are (total) algorithms taking objects of A to objects of B, and that two algorithms are deemed equal if they give the same results on every input (the *extensional* equality on the function space).

Each object a should be given in such a way that we can decide whether it is a member of the type A or not. Consider an example. Suppose that we say that the real numbers consist of the class of sequences $(a_n)_n$ which are convergent, that is which satisfy

$$\forall n.\exists m.\forall i \geq m.\forall j \geq m \, . \, |a_i - a_j| < 1/n$$

When presenting such a sequence it is not sufficient to give the sequence, it must be presented with the **witness** that it has the property required. In this case the witnessing information will be a modulus of convergence function μ together with a *proof* that

$$\forall n.\forall i \geq \mu(n).\forall j \geq \mu(n) \, . \, |a_i - a_j| < 1/n$$

This is an example of the general principle:

Principle of complete presentation. Objects in constructive mathematics are completely presented, in the sense that if an object a is supposed to have type A then a should contain sufficient *witnessing* information so that the assertion can be verified.

This is a principle to which Bishop adheres in principle but, to smooth the presentation of the results, he adopts a policy of systematic suppression of the evidence, invoking it only when it is necessary. This schizophrenic attitude will also pervade the systems we shall introduce.

There is a relationship between this view and the classical. The constructive model of objects such as the reals can be seen as related to the classical; witnessing evidence which can always be provided by a non-constructive existence proof in the classical setting is incorporated into the object itself by the constructivist.

A final area of note is *equality* over infinite objects such as the reals. For the natural numbers, we can judge whether two objects are equal or not, simply by examining their form. For the reals, we are not interested so much in the syntactic form of two numbers as their respective *limits*. Two reals $(a_n)_n$, $(b_n)_n$ (we suppress the evidence!) have the same limit, and so are deemed equal, if

$$\forall n.\exists m.\forall i \geq m.\forall j \geq m \; . \; |a_i - b_j| < 1/n$$

We cannot expect that for an arbitrary pair of reals that we can decide whether $a = b$ or $a \neq b$, as one consequence of this is the limited principle of omniscience. A final precept which is useful here is

> negative assertions should be replaced by positive assertions whenever possible.

In this context we replace '$\neq$' by a notion of 'apartness'. Two real numbers $(a_n)_n$, $(b_n)_n$ are **separated**, $a\#b$, if

$$\exists n.\exists m.\forall i \geq m.\forall j \geq m \; . \; |a_i - b_j| > 1/n$$

This is a strong enough notion to replace the classically equivalent inequality. We shall return to the topic of the real numbers in Section 7.6.

3.3   Formalizing constructive mathematics

The reader should not conclude from the foregoing discussion that there is a 'Golden Road' to the formalization of constructive mathematics. The type theory which we explore below represents one important school of many, and we should say something about them now. [Beeson, 1985] provides a very useful survey addressing precisely this topic, and we refer the reader to this for more detailed primary references. The text covers theories such as intuitionistic set theory (IZF), Feferman's theories of operations and classes [Feferman, 1979], as well as various formalized theories of rules, all of which have been proposed as foundations for a treatment of constructive mathematics.

One area which is overlooked in this study is the link between *category theory* and logic, the topic of [Lambek and Scott, 1986]. This link has a number of threads, including the relationship between the λ-calculus and cartesian closed categories, and the category-theoretic models of intuitionistic type theory provided by toposes. The interested reader will want to follow up the primary references in [Lambek and Scott, 1986].

3.4   Conclusion

We have seen that constructive mathematics is based on principles quite different from classical mathematics, with the idealistic aspects of the latter replaced by a finitary system with computational content. Objects such as functions are given by rules, and the validity of an assertion is guaranteed by a proof from which we can extract relevant computational information, rather than on idealist semantic principles. We lose some theorems, such as

Theorem 3.1 (intermediate value theorem – classical)

Suppose that f is continuous on $[0,1]$ with $f(0) < 0$ and $f(1) > 0$, then there is an $r \in [0,1]$ with $f(r) = 0$.

All is not lost, and we can prove the weaker

Theorem 3.2 (intermediate value theorem – constructive)

Suppose that f is continuous on $[0,1]$ with $f(0) < 0$ and $f(1) > 0$, then for all $\varepsilon > 0$ there is an $r \in [0,1]$ with $|f(r)| < \varepsilon$.

The constructive version states that we can get arbitrarily close to the root, and of course, that is all we could expect to do, from a computational point of view. In this respect, we have in the latter theorem a truer picture of our 'empirical' capabilities.

For other examples, and more cogent pleading of the constructivist case, we would heartily recommend the opening passages of [Bishop and Bridges, 1985]. Indeed, the whole book will repay detailed study. We now pass on to looking at our formal system for type theory.

Chapter 4
Introduction to Type Theory

This chapter forms the focus of the book, drawing together the three themes of logic, functional programming and constructive mathematics into a single system, which we investigate, develop and criticize in the chapters to come. The short discussion of constructive mathematics introduced the idea that proofs should have computational content; we saw that, to achieve this goal, the underlying logic of the system needed to be changed to one in which we only assert the validity of a proposition when we have a *proof* of the proposition. Because of this, the system we define is different from those of the first chapter, deriving as it does statements of the form

> p is a proof of the proposition P

which we write thus:

> $p : P$

Central to type theory is the duality between propositions and types, proofs and elements: a proof of a proposition T can be seen as a member of the type T, and conversely. Ideas which come from one side of the divide can be re-interpreted on the other, enriching both fields. We first present type theory as a logical system, and then re-interpret the derivation rules as rules for program construction in a typed functional language, with $p : P$ read as

p is a member of the type P

The chapter begins with an informal examination of what it means for something to be a proof of a formula of propositional logic. Before introducing the formal system itself, we look at the general form that the rules will take, and establish some important terminology which will distinguish between the formal proof objects, such as p above, and derivations of the statements, or *judgements*, like $p : P$.

With each connective or type forming operation we associate four kinds of rule. The familiar rules of introduction and elimination describe how certain propositions can be proved. From the programming point of view they assert the existence of certain objects of certain types; in other words, they specify the syntax of a programming language. To describe a language we need to supply not only the syntax but also to explain how to *evaluate* or *run* programs written in the language. The *computation* rules explain this, with

$e_1 \ \rightarrow \ e_2$

denoting 'e_1 reduces to e_2 in one step of computation'; their logical interpretation is a description of how proof objects may be simplified. We also give a *formation* rule which embodies the syntax of the connective: this presentation of the syntax together with the rules of the system is one of the distinctive features of type theory, and it is necessary because of the interdependence in the definitions of types and values.

The formal presentation of the logical rules for propositional calculus is followed by a number of examples, in which we see standard functions such as composition serving as proofs of familiar statements such as

$$(A \Rightarrow B) \Rightarrow (B \Rightarrow C) \Rightarrow (A \Rightarrow C)$$

After this we introduce the logical notions of universal and existential quantifiers which, when given a programming interpretation, define dependent function spaces and modules, amongst other things.

Programming is dependent on the presence of data types such as the booleans, the finite types and the natural numbers, which are introduced next. The one and zero element types are also representatives of the logical statements *Truth* and *Falsity*, truth having the trivial proof, and falsity having none. Infinite data types are characterized by principles of definition by recursion and proof by induction; as we cannot define every case of a function or examine every case in a proof, we need these indirect methods. The two methods go hand in hand, as we define an object by recursion and then prove any property of the object by induction. One of the most elegant aspects of the type theoretic approach is that the two are identical – a proof by induction is nothing other than a proof object defined using recursion.

This recursive characterization carries over to other types, and we look at binary trees as an example of a general well-founded type.

The primitive propositions introduced thus far are the types *bool*, N and so on. The assertion of the identity

$$a =_A b$$

of two values a and b of type A forms a fundamental atomic proposition, or type. Here we can see the interdependence between the definitions of types and values in the language: $a =_A b$ is a type of the language if a and b are values of type A.

There is another relation linking items, generated by '$\to$': two expressions are convertible if a sequence of forwards or backwards reductions using '$\to$' leads from the first to the second: as each step leads from equals to equals, convertible expressions are deemed to be equal internally, so that we can use the relation '$=$' to reason about the computational behaviour of programs. This means that our system gives an *integrated* treatment of programming and verification: we can prove a program correct, or develop it from a specification, in the *same* system in which the program is written.

4.1   Propositional logic: an informal view

Our first view of the material is an *informal* account of what it is to have a proof of a proposition built using the connectives $\wedge, \Rightarrow, \vee$ and $\bot$. Recall that we use the notation $p : P$ for 'p is a proof (or demonstration) of the proposition P'.

Looking at the connectives in turn, we have the following.

$A \wedge B$ A proof of $A \wedge B$ will be a pair of proofs p and q, $p : A$ and $q : B$. The reasons for this should be obvious. In order to demonstrate that $A \wedge B$ is valid we have to be able to demonstrate the validity of both A and B separately, and from a proof of the conjunction we can extract proofs of the component propositions. (It is interesting to observe that this property will hold for classical systems as well as for constructive ones.)

$A \Rightarrow B$ A proof of $A \Rightarrow B$ consists of a method or function which *transforms* any proof of A into a proof of B. Clearly, then, given proofs a of A and f of $A \Rightarrow B$ we can derive a proof of B by *applying* the proof transformer f to a.

$A \vee B$ A proof of $A \vee B$ will either be a proof of A or be a proof of B, *together with* an indication of which formula the proof proves. This is quite different from the classical reading of $\vee$. A classical logician can assert (or prove, depending upon the particular system) the proposition $A \vee \neg A$ as a general result. However, there are cases in which it is clear that we can prove neither the proposition A nor its negation $\neg A$. Note that from a constructive proof of $A \vee B$ we can read off a proof of one of A, B and moreover know which it proves. This is *not* the case for the classical disjunction; witness the classically valid $A \vee \neg A$.

$\perp$ There is no proof of the *contradictory* proposition $\perp$.

Definition 4.1

Implicit in these descriptions is a description of proofs of $\neg A$ and $A \Leftrightarrow B$, since we choose to define them by

$$\neg A \equiv_{df} A \Rightarrow \perp$$

$$A \Leftrightarrow B \equiv_{df} (A \Rightarrow B) \wedge (B \Rightarrow A)$$

We see that a proof of $\neg A$ is a function which transforms proofs of A into proofs of $\perp$. A proof of $A \Leftrightarrow B$ is a pair of functions, one transforming proofs of A into proofs of B, and the other taking proofs of B to proofs of A.

To give a flavour of the approach, let us develop a proof of the proposition

$$(A \wedge B) \Rightarrow (B \wedge A)$$

This proof will be a function, taking proofs of $A \wedge B$ to proofs of $B \wedge A$. Suppose we are given a proof p of $A \wedge B$ – we know that it consists of two halves, $p_1 : A$ and $p_2 : B$. Given these component parts we can build the proof of $B \wedge A$: it is simply (p_2, p_1). If we write *fst* and *snd* for the functions which extract the first and second components, then the proof of the implication takes the form

$$\lambda p.(snd\ p, fst\ p)$$

A second example is provided by a proof of

$$(((A \vee B) \Rightarrow C) \wedge A) \Rightarrow C$$

Our proof will again be a function, taking a proof of

$$((A \vee B) \Rightarrow C) \wedge A \qquad\qquad (4.1)$$

into a proof of C. What does a proof of the expression 4.1 look like? It is a pair of proofs, the first, q say, is of

$$(A \vee B) \Rightarrow C$$

and the second, r say, of A. Now, from a proof of A we can build a proof of $A \vee B$, simply by labelling it as a proof of the left-hand formula, *inl r*. Now, q is a proof of $(A \vee B) \Rightarrow C$ and so is a function from proofs of $A \vee B$ to proofs of C. We can therefore apply it to the proof *inl r* to get a proof of C, as required. The full proof can be written

$$\lambda(q, r).q(inl\ r)$$

where we use a lambda abstraction over a *pattern* to indicate that the argument will be a pair.

Clearly, if we are to build more complex proofs along these lines then we must give a formal notation for these proofs, and for the way that we derive the proof objects.

4.2   Judgements, proofs and derivations

Recall the form that our logic took in Chapter 1. There we gave rules which took the form of the example which follows:

$$\frac{A \quad B}{A \wedge B}(\wedge I)$$

The rule above should be read, in full,

if A is valid and B is valid then $A \wedge B$ is valid

or more generally under a set Γ of assumptions,

if A is valid assuming Γ and B is valid assuming Γ then $A \wedge B$ is valid assuming Γ

Schematically, it should be written

$$\frac{A\ is\ valid \quad B\ is\ valid}{(A \wedge B)\ is\ valid}(\wedge I)$$

The rules tell us how one **judgement**, $(A \wedge B)$ *is valid*, can be inferred from a number of others.

The system of rules we introduce here is similar, except that the form of the judgements is different. Our constructive approach to mathematics means that we are not interested in validity alone, but in *explicit* demonstrations or proofs of propositions. The judgements we introduce therefore have the form '$p : P$' which should be read 'the object p is a proof of the proposition P'.

The rule to introduce conjunctions, according to the explanation in the previous section, will be

$$\frac{p \; : \; A \quad q \; : \; B}{(p,q) \; : \; (A \wedge B)}(\wedge I)$$

The rules are to be used just as were the logical rules in Chapter 1, to produce **derivations** of judgements: a rule is applied to derivations of the judgements above the line to produce a derivation of the judgement below the line. Note that this is a change of terminology from the earlier chapter; there we used rules to give proofs of judgements – here we use rules to derive judgements which themselves contain proof objects or constructions. To re-iterate, proofs and propositions form the object language; derivations are the means by which we infer judgements concerning the object language. Derivations are built inductively by applying the deduction rules. If we now introduce the rules for conjunction elimination, we will be able to look at an example which we examined informally a little earlier:

$$\frac{r \; : \; (A \wedge B)}{fst \; r \; : \; A}(\wedge E_1) \qquad \frac{r \; : \; (A \wedge B)}{snd \; r \; : \; B}(\wedge E_2)$$

Here we see a derivation of the judgement $(snd \; r, fst \; r) \; : \; (B \wedge A)$

$$\frac{\dfrac{r \; : \; (A \wedge B)}{snd \; r \; : \; B}(\wedge E_2) \quad \dfrac{r \; : \; (A \wedge B)}{fst \; r \; : \; A}(\wedge E_1)}{(snd \; r, fst \; r) \; : \; (B \wedge A)}(\wedge I)$$

The proof object derived is the pair $(snd \; r, fst \; r)$ which is shown to prove $(B \wedge A)$ assuming that r is a proof of $(A \wedge B)$.

As in our earlier treatment of logic, derivations can be based on assumptions, and these assumptions can be discharged by certain of the rules. We will use the same notation for discharge as we did earlier.

Note that, as there is no possibility of ambiguity, we have used the same names for the proof rules, $(\wedge I)$, $(\wedge E)$ and so on, as we did in the chapter covering logic.

Some of our rules will involve another judgement, which asserts that a particular sequence of symbols is a formula:

A is a formula

For conjunction, for instance, we write

$$\frac{A\ is\ a\ formula \quad B\ is\ a\ formula}{(A \wedge B)\ is\ a\ formula}(\wedge F)$$

Rules of this sort are called **formation** rules as they explain the circumstances under which a particular formula can be formed. In other words, they are the rules of syntax for the language of propositions. We might think it simpler to state the rules quite separately (by means of BNF for example), but we shall see later, in Section 4.10, that some formulas are only well formed if certain judgements are derivable, linking syntax and derivations inextricably.

For each connective we shall specify four different kinds of rules. Each will have introduction and elimination rules, which are used to introduce and eliminate formulas involving the particular connective. As we discussed above, we shall also have the formation rule. Finally, each connective will have **computation** rules which tell us how proofs of formulas involving that connective can be *simplified*. This is a new idea, and we look at a brief example of it now. Recall the way that we treated $\wedge$ in the previous section. If p was a proof of A and q a proof of B, then (p, q) is a proof of $A \wedge B$. Now, given such a proof we can extract proofs of A and B by applying *fst* and *snd*. All that these do is to extract the first and second components of the pair, so we want to say that

$$fst\ (p, q)\ \rightarrow\ p \qquad snd\ (p, q)\ \rightarrow\ q$$

and it is this *computational* information about the operations *fst* and *snd* which appears in the computation rules. The symbol '$\rightarrow$' is read 'reduces to' (and should be compared with the reduction symbol of the lambda calculus from Section 2.2.) We use the symbol $\twoheadrightarrow$ for the closure of this relation; see Section 4.11.

4.3 The rules for propositional calculus

We first give the rules for the $\wedge$ connective, as we set them out above.

Formation rule for $\wedge$

$$\frac{A\ is\ a\ formula \quad B\ is\ a\ formula}{(A \wedge B)\ is\ a\ formula}(\wedge F)$$

Introduction rule for ∧

$$\frac{p \,:\, A \quad q \,:\, B}{(p,q) \,:\, (A \wedge B)}(\wedge I)$$

Elimination rules for ∧

$$\frac{r \,:\, (A \wedge B)}{\mathit{fst}\ r \,:\, A}(\wedge E_1) \qquad \frac{r \,:\, (A \wedge B)}{\mathit{snd}\ r \,:\, B}(\wedge E_2)$$

Computation rules for ∧

$$\mathit{fst}\ (p,q) \ \rightarrow\ p \qquad \mathit{snd}\ (p,q) \ \rightarrow\ q$$

These are simply the rules we introduced informally in our discussion above.

Recall that we characterized proofs of the conjunction as pairs of proofs. We can read the introduction and elimination rules as expressing precisely this. The introduction rule states that all pairs of proofs *are* proofs of the conjunction, but leaves open the possibility of other kinds of proofs. The elimination rule excludes any other sort of proof of the conjunction, since it states that we can extract two component proofs from any proof of the pair. In other words we can read the elimination rule as a 'closure' rule. This duality will be true for all introduction–elimination pairs. We take a formal look at the duality in Section 8.4.

The next set of rules concerns implication. The formation rule is standard.

Formation rule for ⇒

$$\frac{A \text{ is a formula} \quad B \text{ is a formula}}{(A \Rightarrow B) \text{ is a formula}}(\Rightarrow F)$$

Recall that we *discharged* an assumption in a proof when we introduced the connective. A proof of an implication is a function transforming an arbitrary proof of A into a proof of B. We form that transformation by building a proof e of B *assuming* that we have an (arbitrary) proof, x say, of A. The function itself is formed by lambda abstraction over the variable, giving $(\lambda x : A)\,.\,e$. This expression is independent of the variable x, since this is bound, reflecting the discharge of the assumption $x : A$.

Introduction rule for ⇒

$$\frac{\begin{array}{c}[x : A]\\ \vdots\\ e \,:\, B\end{array}}{(\lambda x : A)\,.\,e \,:\, (A \Rightarrow B)}(\Rightarrow I)$$

The notation $[x : A]$ is used to record the fact that the assumption $x : A$ which will in general appear in the derivation of $e : B$ is *discharged* from the derivation of $(\lambda x : A).e : (A \Rightarrow B)$ which results from applying the rule to the given derivation of $e : B$.

In the dual case, we eliminate an implication by supplying a proof of the hypothesis. The proof of the implication is *applied* to the proof of the hypothesis to give a proof of the consequent, recalling the description of proofs of $A \Rightarrow B$ above. The elimination rule can also be read as saying that all proofs of $A \Rightarrow B$ are functions, since they can all be applied (to proofs of the right 'type', A).

Elimination rule for $\Rightarrow$

$$\frac{q : (A \Rightarrow B) \quad a : A}{(q\,a) : B}(\Rightarrow E)$$

Finally, what happens if we apply the proof $(\lambda x : A).e$ of $A \Rightarrow B$ to the proof $a : A$? Recall that e was a proof of B, on the assumption that x was a proof of A. Now, we have such a proof, a, and so we get a proof of B by replacing x by a throughout e. We have

Computation rule for $\Rightarrow$

$$((\lambda x : A).e)\,a \;\rightarrow\; e[a/x]$$

where the notation $e[a/x]$ means the expression e in which every *free* occurrence of x is replaced by a, and where this is done in such a way as to avoid free variables becoming bound (exactly as we stipulated in Section 2.2).

What are the rules for disjunction, $\vee$? We have straightforward formation and introduction rules.

Formation rule for $\vee$

$$\frac{A \text{ is a formula} \quad B \text{ is a formula}}{(A \vee B) \text{ is a formula}}(\vee F)$$

Introduction rules for $\vee$

$$\frac{q : A}{inl\,q : (A \vee B)}(\vee I_1) \qquad \frac{r : B}{inr\,r : (A \vee B)}(\vee I_2)$$

The operator *inl* registers the fact that the proof available is for the left-hand disjunct, and *inr* registers that it is for the right, as in general we may not be able to differentiate between the two different kinds of proofs without these 'tags' to distinguish between them.

The elimination rule for $\vee$ in Chapter 1 was rather more complex, involving the discharge of two premises – we present a slight variant of it here, but we can see that it has exactly the same motivation as our earlier rule.

Elimination rule for ∨

$$\frac{p \,:\, (A \vee B) \quad f \,:\, (A \Rightarrow C) \quad g \,:\, (B \Rightarrow C)}{cases\ p\ f\ g \ :\ C}(\vee E)$$

cases p f g is a proof of C which is built from a proof p of $A \vee B$ and from proofs $f \,:\, (A \Rightarrow C)$ and $g \,:\, (B \Rightarrow C)$. How does it work? The proof p comes either from a proof q of A, and has the form *inl q*, or from a proof r of B, and has the form *inr r*. In the first case we get a proof of C by applying f to q, and in the second by applying g to r. Hence the name '*cases*' and the computation rules:

Computation rules for ∨

$$cases\ (inl\ q)\ f\ g \ \rightarrow \ f\ q$$

$$cases\ (inr\ r)\ f\ g \ \rightarrow \ g\ r$$

Each elimination rule has a major premiss, containing the connective to be eliminated. The remainder are known as minor premisses. The rule corresponding directly to the rule in Chapter 1 has as its two minor premisses proofs of C from assumptions $x : A$ and $y : B$. As these two assumptions are to be discharged the *cases* operation will have to bind the variables x and y, just as the variable in the assumption is bound in an $(\Rightarrow I)$ by the lambda. This variant of the rule is given in Section 5.3.

Finally, what rules do we associate with absurdity, $\bot$? First we have the formation rule:

Formation rule for ⊥

$$\frac{}{\bot\ is\ a\ formula}(\bot F)$$

We have **no** introduction rule associated with $\bot$, as we know of no way of forming proofs of the absurd proposition. We can eliminate it freely, thus:

Elimination rule for ⊥

$$\frac{p \,:\, \bot}{abort_A\ p \ :\ A}(\bot E)$$

This rule says that if we can prove absurdity (with p), then the proof $abort_A\ p$ proves A. This is the second half of our characterization of $\bot$ as absurdity. Not only do we give no method by which $\bot$ can be introduced, but in order to show that we did not simply *forget* to give these rules we say that given any such proof our system must crash, and prove everything, the rule of *ex falso quodlibet*. There are no computation rules associated with such an object – it simply registers the fact that the object is proved directly from absurdity.

The rule for implication introduction discharges an assumption of the form $x:A$ where x is a variable. How do these assumptions become parts of derivations? In order for an assumption $x:A$ to be sensible, we need A to be a formula. This is a sufficient condition too, so we have

Rule of assumption

$$\frac{A \; is \; a \; formula}{x:A}(AS)$$

We make the implicit (informal!) assumption that our sets of assumptions will always be consistent: we will not assume that any variable is a proof of more than one formula. We elaborate on the details of this in the chapter to come.

This rule is unusual, in that it shows that our assumptions do not appear at the leaves of derivations, but rather only after a derivation that the expression which follows the colon is indeed a formula.

In many of our examples we shall relax this constraint, omitting the derivation of '*A is a formula*'; this will only be done when the derivation is trivial, or we simply assume, *informally*, that the derivation has been performed prior to the derivation at issue.

This completes our exposition of the propositional part of type theory – in the next section we get to the heart of our exposition, and tie the link between functional programming (as represented by the lambda calculus) and logic.

Exercises

4.1   Show that conjunction is associative by deriving a proof of the formula

$$(A \wedge B) \wedge C \Rightarrow A \wedge (B \wedge C)$$

4.2   Show that the formula $(\neg A \vee B) \Rightarrow (A \Rightarrow B)$ is valid by exhibiting a proof object for it. Do you expect the converse, $(A \Rightarrow B) \Rightarrow (\neg A \vee B)$, to be provable?

4.3   Show that from the assumption $x:(A \vee \neg A)$ you can derive a proof object for the formula $(\neg\neg A \Rightarrow A)$. Show that you can find a proof object for the converse, $(A \Rightarrow \neg\neg A)$, without this assumption.

4.4   Show that from the assumptions $x:((A \wedge B) \Rightarrow C)$ and $y:A$ you can derive a proof of $B \Rightarrow C$. What is the formula which results from the discharge of the two assumptions, and what proof object of this formula is given by your construction?

4.4   The Curry–Howard isomorphism

This section forms the heart of our development of type theory. In it we look at a remarkable correspondence, or *isomorphism*, linking the typed lambda calculus and constructive logic. It has become known as the Curry–Howard isomorphism, in tribute to Haskell B. Curry and W. Howard who were among those first to observe it [Curry and Feys, 1958; Howard, 1980]. Others include Scott, Lauchli and Martin-Löf himself. Under the isomorphism, types correspond to propositions and members of those types, such as pairs, functions and so on, to proofs. We were prepared for such a coincidence by the development of constructive logic in the last section, because the proofs we introduced there were familiar objects such as pairs and functions. In the sections and chapters which follow, we shall see the extent of this correspondence, and the degree to which it can illuminate our understanding of both logic and programming. This section illustrates the core of the isomorphism by giving a re-interpretation of the rules of logic above as rules of program formation. The rules are then seen to explain

> formation rule   what the types of the system are,

> introduction and   which expressions are members of
> elimination rules   which types, and

> computation rule   how these objects can be reduced to simpler
> forms, that is how we can *evaluate* expressions.

Another way of looking at the rules is to say that the formation rules explain the types of the language and that the introduction and elimination rules explain the typing rules for expressions (and so explain how type checking for the system should proceed) – together these describe the *static* part of a traditional language, with the computation rules explaining the *dynamics* of its behaviour. We shall see in Section 4.10 that the distinction between the static and the dynamic becomes blurred in the full system, as type checking and computation become inextricably linked.

We now run through the rules connective by connective, changing the judgement '*is a formula*' to '*is a type*' to reflect our different orientation.

Formation rule for $\wedge$

$$\frac{A \; is \; a \; type \quad B \; is \; a \; type}{(A \wedge B) \; is \; a \; type}(\wedge F)$$

Introduction rule for $\wedge$

$$\frac{p \; : \; A \quad q \; : \; B}{(p, q) \; : \; (A \wedge B)}(\wedge I)$$

Elimination rules for ∧

$$\frac{r \,:\, (A \wedge B)}{fst\ r \,:\, A}(\wedge E_1) \qquad \frac{r \,:\, (A \wedge B)}{snd\ r \,:\, B}(\wedge E_2)$$

Computation rules for ∧

$$fst\ (p,q) \ \rightarrow\ p \qquad snd\ (p,q) \ \rightarrow\ q$$

Read as a type, $A \wedge B$ is the *product* of the two types, whose formation is permitted by the formation rule. The introduction rule tells us that members of the type include pairs (p,q) of objects, where p is taken from the first type and q is taken from the second. The elimination rule states that from an object of the product type we can extract objects of the two component types, and the computation rule shows that the objects thus extracted are indeed the two components of the pair. These two rules therefore state that all objects of the product type are pairs.

Alternatively, we can read the elimination rules as giving the type of the two *projection* operators which take us from the product type to the two components. The computation rules give the computational definitions of these operators. In terms of traditional programming languages, the product type is usually called a *record* type. Nearly every modern programming language features a record type.

As we suggested above, we can think of members of $A \Rightarrow B$ as functions from A to B. This is perhaps not surprising, as not only do we already see proofs of implications as functions, but also the arrow notation is suggestive in itself. Just to re-iterate the rules,

Formation rule for ⇒

$$\frac{A\ is\ a\ type \quad B\ is\ a\ type}{(A \Rightarrow B)\ is\ a\ type}(\Rightarrow F)$$

Introduction rule for ⇒

$$
\begin{array}{c}
[x:A] \\
\vdots \\
\dfrac{e \,:\, B}{(\lambda x:A)\,.\,e \,:\, (A \Rightarrow B)}(\Rightarrow I)
\end{array}
$$

This rule discharges the assumption $x:A$.

This is the rule which introduces a *lambda abstraction*, or function, as we explained in Chapter 2. It is by a use of the lambda symbol that we form functions. We have modified the notation slightly so that the expression includes the type of the domain of the function formed. The rule which gives the type of function *applications* is

Elimination rule for $\Rightarrow$

$$\frac{q \,:\, (A \Rightarrow B) \quad a \,:\, A}{(q\,a) \,:\, B}(\Rightarrow E)$$

Finally, with the following rule we see our justification of the phrase 'computation rule':

Computation rule for $\Rightarrow$

$$((\lambda x \,{:}\, A)\,.\,e)\,a \;\;\rightarrow\;\; e[a/x]$$

This is precisely the rule of β-reduction, by which an actual parameter is substituted for the formal parameter.

Two notes on notation

- The notation we have given for functions is complete, in that it carries the type of the hypothesis (or domain); it is unwieldy, however. In most cases we shall indicate the type by a subscript, thus:

  $$\lambda x_A \,.\, e$$

  and in situations where there is no danger of ambiguity, we shall simply write

  $$\lambda x \,.\, e$$

- As is traditional, we shall assume that function application is left associative and that '$\Rightarrow$' is right associative, meaning that

  $$f\,g\,x$$

  abbreviates $(f\,g)\,x$ and that

  $$A \Rightarrow B \Rightarrow C$$

  abbreviates $A \Rightarrow (B \Rightarrow C)$.

What type operation does $\vee$ correspond to? Again, we should re-examine the rules for the operator:

Formation rule for $\vee$

$$\frac{A \text{ is a type} \quad B \text{ is a type}}{(A \vee B) \text{ is a type}}(\vee F)$$

Introduction rules for ∨

$$\frac{q \; : \; A}{inl \; q \; : \; (A \vee B)}(\vee I_1) \qquad \frac{r \; : \; B}{inr \; r \; : \; (A \vee B)}(\vee I_2)$$

Given a member q of A we have a corresponding member of $A \vee B$, namely *inl q*. Similarly, if r is in B then *inr r* is in $A \vee B$. This introduction rule tells us that among the members of the type $A \vee B$ are the members of A and B, labelled according to their origin. As previously, the elimination rule will ensure that *only* these objects are members of the type. This kind of type is often known as a *disjoint union* of the two types A and B. Such a construction appears in Pascal in the variant record construction, where a particular record type can contain different kinds of record, according to the value of a tag field. Pascal does not handle this construction very happily, and it can lead to run-time type errors. In handling a variable of variant record type the user is allowed to treat its contents as though they are of one particular variant, rather than having to deal with all the possible variants. As the particular variant that a value will have cannot be predicted at compile time, errors can result.

Is there a type-secure way of dealing with such disjoint unions? Yes, and it is given by the *cases* operator, specified in the elimination rule

Elimination rule for ∨

$$\frac{p \; : \; (A \vee B) \quad f \; : \; (A \Rightarrow C) \quad g \; : \; (B \Rightarrow C)}{cases \; p \; f \; g \; : \; C}(\vee E)$$

cases p f g is a member of C which is built from a member p of $A \vee B$, and from functions $f \; : \; (A \Rightarrow C)$ and $g \; : \; (B \Rightarrow C)$.

What is the effect of this case statement? We know that the object p should either be a (tagged) member of A, and have the form *inl q* or will be a (tagged) member of B, having the form *inr r*. The functions f and g are sufficient to give us a member of C *in either case* – in the first case we get a member of C by applying f to q, and in the second by applying g to r. This computational information is expressed by

Computation rules for ∨

$$cases \; (inl \; q) \; f \; g \; \rightarrow \; f \; q$$

$$cases \; (inr \; r) \; f \; g \; \rightarrow \; g \; r$$

The last rules we gave were for the type ⊥, the absurd proposition. We characterized this as a formula without proofs so, under our other view, it is a *type without members*, the *empty* type.

Formation rule for ⊥

$$\frac{}{\bot \ is \ a \ type}(\bot F)$$

Elimination rule for ⊥

$$\frac{p \ : \ \bot}{abort_A \ p \ : \ A}(\bot E)$$

This rule says that if we can find a member p of the empty type then our program should abort – we express this by saying that for any A at all, the object $abort_A \ p$ is a member of A.

The final rule we saw was the rule of assumption; in order for the assumption that x is a member of A to make sense, A must be a type.

Rule of assumption

$$\frac{A \ is \ a \ type}{x:A}(AS)$$

As we said earlier, in many of our examples we shall omit the derivation of 'A is a type', assuming that it has already been performed. Nonetheless, the system does not make sense without this condition.

That completes our second reading of the rules, and shows that they can equally well be read as

- rules for the types and objects of a typed functional programming system and as

- rules for the propositions and proofs of a logic.

We shall explore the correspondence further in the coming sections, seeing some of the ramifications of the correspondence in propositional logic, and also how extensions to both the logic and the functional language have their analogues. Finally we shall explore the consequences of this correspondence for programming methodology. Note also that we have not yet introduced any dependent types – we do this with the identity or I types of Section 4.10.

Exercises

4.5   Given a function of type $A \Rightarrow (B \Rightarrow C)$ how would you define a function of type $(A \wedge B) \Rightarrow C$ from it? How would you do the reverse?

4.6   Show that from objects $x:A$ and $y:(B \vee C)$ you can derive an object of type $(A \wedge B) \vee (A \wedge C)$.

4.7 Show how to define a function of type

$$(A \wedge B) \Rightarrow (C \wedge D)$$

from functions $f : A \Rightarrow C$ and $g : B \Rightarrow D$.

4.5   Some examples

In this section we look at a number of examples of derivations within type theory. We can see how these form both proofs of propositions and objects of particular type, depending on our particular point of view. We assume throughout this section that we have already derived the various type hypotheses, A *is a type* and so forth.

4.5.1   The identity function; A implies itself

One of the simplest functions we know is the identity function, $\lambda x_A . x$. How does it appear in our system?

Assuming $x : A$ allows us to deduce that $x : A$. Using the rule for $\Rightarrow$ introduction we have that

$$\frac{[x : A]}{\lambda x_A . x \; : \; (A \Rightarrow A)}(\Rightarrow I)$$

giving us that the identity function has type $A \Rightarrow A$ if its parameter has type A. At the same time we have shown that the identity function is a proof of the implication $A \Rightarrow A$.

4.5.2   The transitivity of implication; function composition

Here we show that given $A \Rightarrow B$ and $B \Rightarrow C$ we can deduce that $A \Rightarrow C$, in other words that implication is transitive. We first examined this as an exercise in Chapter 1 – here we build an explicit proof object. We assume that

$$a : (A \Rightarrow B) \quad b : (B \Rightarrow C)$$

and we make a third assumption, $x : A$, which will be discharged during the proof.

$$\frac{\dfrac{x : A \quad a : (A \Rightarrow B)}{(a \, x) : B}(\Rightarrow E) \quad b : (B \Rightarrow C)}{(b \, (a \, x)) : C}(\Rightarrow E)$$

This gives an element of C, depending upon the element x of A. We now abstract over this to give

$$\cfrac{\cfrac{[x:A]^1 \quad a:(A \Rightarrow B)}{(a\,x):B}(\Rightarrow E) \quad b:(B \Rightarrow C)}{\cfrac{(b\,(a\,x)):C}{\lambda x_A.(b\,(a\,x)) : (A \Rightarrow C)}(\Rightarrow I)_1}(\Rightarrow E)$$

We have on the last line a derivation of a function of type $A \Rightarrow C$, as was required.

The function derived here is the composition of the functions b and a. If we abstract over these, we form the composition function

$$\lambda a_{(A \Rightarrow B)} . \lambda b_{(B \Rightarrow C)} . \lambda x_A . (b\,(a\,x))$$

which has type

$$(A \Rightarrow B) \Rightarrow (B \Rightarrow C) \Rightarrow (A \Rightarrow C)$$

Note that we have assumed that the '$\Rightarrow$' is right associative in writing the type above.

A standard result in logic is

$$(A \Rightarrow B) \Rightarrow (\neg B \Rightarrow \neg A)$$

Recall that we defined $\neg A$ to be $A \Rightarrow \bot$, so expanding the definitions we have

$$(A \Rightarrow B) \Rightarrow ((B \Rightarrow \bot) \Rightarrow (A \Rightarrow \bot))$$

It is precisely the composition operator which gives this proof.

4.5.3   Different proofs. . .

In general, types have more than one element and a proposition can be proved in more than one way. Taking a simple example,

$$\lambda x_{(A \wedge A)} . x : ((A \wedge A) \Rightarrow (A \wedge A))$$

as we have seen above. Also,

$$\cfrac{\cfrac{[x:(A \wedge A)]^1}{snd\ x\ :\ A}(\wedge E_2) \quad \cfrac{[x:(A \wedge A)]^1}{fst\ x\ :\ A}(\wedge E_1)}{\cfrac{(snd\ x, fst\ x)\ :\ (A \wedge A)}{\lambda x_{(A \wedge A)} . (snd\ x, fst\ x)\ :\ ((A \wedge A) \Rightarrow (A \wedge A))}(\Rightarrow I)_1}(\wedge I)$$

This proof is not the same as the earlier one: it swaps the two halves of the proof of $A \wedge A$ about, rather than leaving them alone as is done by the identity function.

4.5.4 ... and different derivations

Note also that different derivations can give rise to the same proof object, if we apply the computation rules to the derived object. If we name the composition function

$$comp \equiv_{df} \lambda f_{((A \wedge A) \Rightarrow (A \wedge A))} \cdot \lambda g_{((A \wedge A) \Rightarrow (A \wedge A))} \cdot \lambda x_{(A \wedge A)} \cdot (g\,(f\,x))$$

and the swap function

$$swap \equiv_{df} \lambda x_{(A \wedge A)} \cdot (snd\,x, fst\,x)$$

then it is not hard to find a derivation of

$$comp\,swap\,swap\,(a_1, a_2) \; : \; (A \wedge A)$$

if we assume that $a_1 : A$ and $a_2 : A$. Since the expression is an iterated application of functions, the derivation will consist of a series of implication eliminations. (Note that we have used our assumption that function application is left associative here.)

Applying the computation rules we have

$$
\begin{array}{lll}
comp\,swap\,swap\,(a_1, a_2) & & \\
\equiv_{df} & (\lambda f . \lambda g . \lambda x . (g\,(f\,x)))\,swap\,swap\,(a_1, a_2) & \\
\rightarrow & (\lambda g . \lambda x . (g\,(swap\,x)))\,swap\,(a_1, a_2) & \text{by } (C \Rightarrow) \\
\rightarrow & (\lambda x . (swap\,(swap\,x)))\,(a_1, a_2) & \text{by } (C \Rightarrow) \\
\rightarrow & (swap\,(swap\,(a_1, a_2))) & \text{by } (C \Rightarrow) \\
\equiv_{df} & (swap\,((\lambda x . (snd\,x, fst\,x))\,(a_1, a_2))) & \\
\rightarrow & swap\,(snd\,(a_1, a_2), fst\,(a_1, a_2)) & \text{by } (C \Rightarrow) \\
\rightarrow & swap\,(a_2, a_1) & \text{by } (C \wedge) \\
\equiv_{df} & \lambda x . (snd\,x, fst\,x)\,(a_2, a_1) & \\
\rightarrow & (snd\,(a_2, a_1), fst\,(a_2, a_1)) & \text{by } (C \Rightarrow) \\
\rightarrow & (a_1, a_2) & \text{by } (C \wedge)
\end{array}
$$

There is a much simpler derivation of $(a_1, a_2) : (A \wedge A)$ from the two assumptions; we simply use $(\wedge I)$. We shall return to the discussion of which proof objects are to be considered to be the same in Section 4.11.

4.5.5   Conjunction and disjunction

Let us consider one relationship between conjunction and disjunction now. We first look at a proof of an earlier exercise from page 15.

$$((A \vee B) \Rightarrow C) \Rightarrow ((A \Rightarrow C) \wedge (B \Rightarrow C))$$

First we show how to prove $A \Rightarrow C$ from $(A \vee B) \Rightarrow C$:

$$\cfrac{\cfrac{\dfrac{[x:A]^1}{inl\ x\ :\ A \vee B}(\vee I_1) \quad y\ :\ (A \vee B) \Rightarrow C}{(y\,(inl\ x))\ :\ C}(\Rightarrow E)}{\lambda x_A\,.(y\,(inl\ x))\ :\ A \Rightarrow C}(\Rightarrow I)_1$$

Similarly we prove $B \Rightarrow C$ from $(A \vee B) \Rightarrow C$:

$$\cfrac{\begin{array}{c} y\ :\ (A \vee B) \Rightarrow C \\[4pt] \vdots \end{array}}{\lambda w_B\,.(y\,(inr\ w))\ :\ B \Rightarrow C}$$

Finally we can put the proofs together,

$$\cfrac{\vdots \quad \vdots}{(\ \lambda x_A\,.(y\,(inl\ x))\,,\ \lambda w_B\,.(y\,(inr\ w))\,)\ :\ ((A \Rightarrow C) \wedge (B \Rightarrow C))}(\wedge I)$$

and if lastly we abstract over the variable y we obtain an object of the requisite type.

Now we look at a converse to the last result, constructing a proof of

$$(A \vee B) \Rightarrow C$$

on the basis of the assumption

$$p\ :\ (A \Rightarrow C) \wedge (B \Rightarrow C)$$

The proof is simpler than the version we saw in the first chapter of the book, on page 13. This is because in the form we saw there we would have to make the *cases* operator into a *binding* operator – here we choose to perform the bindings (of the hypothetical proofs of A and B) prior to the invocation of the cases operator.

$$\cfrac{z\ :\ (A \vee B) \quad (fst\ p)\ :\ (A \Rightarrow C) \quad (snd\ p)\ :\ (B \Rightarrow C)}{cases\ z\,(fst\ p)\,(snd\ p)\ :\ C}(\vee E)$$

This is a straightforward application of the rule of disjunction elimination, which we follow with two abstractions, first over z and then over p.

$$\frac{\overline{\lambda z.\,(cases\ z\ (fst\ p)\ (snd\ p))\ :\ (A \vee B) \Rightarrow C}^{\;\vdots}\ (\Rightarrow I)}{\begin{array}{c}\lambda p.\lambda z.\,(cases\ z\ (fst\ p)\ (snd\ p))\ :\\ ((A \Rightarrow C) \wedge (B \Rightarrow C)) \Rightarrow ((A \vee B) \Rightarrow C)\end{array}}(\Rightarrow I)$$

This completes the required derivation.

We defined the negation operator in terms of implication and absurdity. If we replace the C above with $\bot$ we can see that we have proved the equivalence of the two propositions

$$\neg(A \vee B) \quad (\neg A \wedge \neg B)$$

which is one of the de Morgan laws of classical boolean algebra. The other states the equivalence of

$$\neg(A \wedge B) \quad (\neg A \vee \neg B)$$

Only one half of this is valid constructively, the implication

$$(\neg A \vee \neg B) \Rightarrow \neg(A \wedge B)$$

We can see why it is implausible that the converse is valid constructively. We would need to extract a proof of $(\neg A \vee \neg B)$ from a proof of $\neg(A \wedge B)$. To find a proof of a disjunction we need to be able to prove one of the disjuncts, but there is no way of seeing which of $\neg A$ and $\neg B$ is valid given an arbitrary proof of $\neg(A \wedge B)$.

Exercises

4.8 Show that the following formulas are valid, by giving a proof object for each of them.

$$A \Rightarrow \neg\neg A$$

$$(B \vee C) \Rightarrow \neg(\neg B \wedge \neg C)$$

$$(A \Rightarrow B) \Rightarrow ((A \Rightarrow C) \Rightarrow (A \Rightarrow (B \wedge C)))$$

4.9 Show that the following formulas are equivalent, by proving each assuming the other. Can you think of what is going on in terms of the functions involved here?

$$(A \wedge B) \Rightarrow C \quad A \Rightarrow (B \Rightarrow C)$$

4.10 Show that the de Morgan formula

$$(\neg A \vee \neg B) \Rightarrow \neg(A \wedge B)$$

is valid by giving an object of type

$$((A \Rightarrow C) \vee (B \Rightarrow C)) \Rightarrow ((A \wedge B) \Rightarrow C)$$

4.11 Giving appropriate types to the variables a, b and c, give derivations of the following judgements.

$$\lambda a.\lambda b.a \quad : \quad A \Rightarrow (B \Rightarrow A)$$

and

$$\lambda a.\lambda b.\lambda c.(ac)(bc) \quad : \quad (A \Rightarrow (B \Rightarrow C)) \Rightarrow ((A \Rightarrow B) \Rightarrow (A \Rightarrow C))$$

4.6   Quantifiers

In this section we introduce the rules which govern the behaviour of the universal and existential quantifiers in constructive type theory. The differences between classical and constructive logic are most apparent when investigating the meaning of '$\exists$', the *existential* quantifier. To assert

$$\exists x.P$$

constructively, we need to have some object x so that

$$P$$

is valid. Because our language is typed, we shall only concern ourselves with typed or *bounded* quantifications, of the form

$$(\exists x : A).P$$

where A is a type, the quantifiers being labelled with their domain of discourse. A proof of an existential statement $(\exists x : A).P$ consists of two items. These are the *witness* of the property, $w : A$, together with a proof that P holds of the witness, that is that $P[w/x]$ holds. Recall that the notation $P[w/x]$ was introduced in Chapter 1 for the substitution of the term w for the variable x in the formula P.

How do we explain the universal quantifier? A proof of

$$(\forall x : A).P$$

should express the fact that $P[a/x]$ is valid for every a in A. A proof will therefore be a transformation or function which takes us from any a in A to a proof of $P[a/x]$.

As for the propositional connectives, our rules are of four kinds. We start by giving the rules for the universal quantifier.

Formation rule for $\forall$

$$[x:A]$$
$$\vdots$$

$$\frac{A \text{ is a formula} \quad P \text{ is a formula}}{(\forall x:A).P \text{ is a formula}}(\forall F)$$

This shows a rather more subtle formation rule than we have seen so far. There are two hypotheses:

- the first is that A is a formula, or type;
- the second, that P is a formula, on the assumption that x is a variable of type A.

This is an analogue, at the level of types, of the rule of λ-abstraction, in which the typing of the expression forming the body of the function depends upon the hypothesis which types the bound variable. We have not yet seen how to build type expressions (or propositions) which depend upon free variables; these result from our introducing the atomic propositions of the system, including equality in Section 4.10, and through reflection principles which are consequences of the introduction of universes (see Section 5.9).

If we can prove P by a proof p which may depend upon the assumption of the existence of a variable, x say, of type A, then we are entitled to assert the universal generalization, abstracting over the variable x, as long as x is not free in any other of the assumptions upon which the proof depends. This is just the condition of being arbitrary which we discussed in our introduction to logic earlier. Note also that formally any remaining occurrence of x in the assumptions would be a 'dangling reference' to an object outside its scope, as it were.

Introduction rule for $\forall$

If in a proof p of P no assumptions other than $x:A$ contain x free, then we can infer the universal generalization of P by means of the lambda abstraction of p over x. This abstraction discharges the assumption x.

$$[x:A]$$
$$\vdots$$

$$\frac{p : P}{(\lambda x:A).p \; : \; (\forall x:A).P}(\forall I)$$

As is to be expected, when we eliminate a universal quantifier, we go to a particular instance:

Elimination rule for ∀

$$\frac{a \; : \; A \quad f \; : \; (\forall x : A) . P}{f \, a \; : \; P[a/x]} (\forall E)$$

Now, we have seen that our two rules respectively form parametric proofs of universal generalizations and apply such proofs to individual elements of A. The result of such an application should be the substitution of a for x in the parametric proof:

Computation rule for ∀

$$((\lambda x : A) . p) \, a \;\; \rightarrow \;\; p[a/x]$$

It is interesting to see that we have naturally thought of some formulas as formulas, P being an example, and others, such as A, as types. Thus the dual interpretations can be mixed. Note also that the rules are similar to those for the connective '$\Rightarrow$'. Indeed if the formula P is replaced by B which does not involve the variable x, we have exactly the rules as stated on page 75, because we shall not need to use the assumption that $x : A$ in the proof of 'B is a formula' if B has already been established to be a formula.

As a type, we also have a generalization of the function space. This is one in which the type of the result, $P[a/x]$, depends upon the value of the argument a in A. This is not permitted in almost all the type systems of existing programming languages, because apparently it would break the static nature of the type system which allows type checking to proceed separately from program execution. In this case, the situation is different; even though the static and dynamic are mixed, we avoid the risk of non-termination. We will say more about applications of the dependent function space, as the universally quantified type has become known, in Section 6.3.

Another important use of the dependent product type is in representing forms of *type polymorphism*. This arises when we have types whose members are themselves types, such types often being known as *universes*.

Now we turn to the existential quantifier. The formation rule is the exact analogue of the rule for the universal quantifier.

Formation rule for ∃

$$[x : A]$$
$$\vdots$$
$$\frac{A \; is \; a \; formula \quad P \; is \; a \; formula}{(\exists x : A) . P \; is \; a \; formula} (\exists F)$$

We can introduce an existential quantifier when we have an object with the appropriate property:

Introduction rule for ∃

$$\frac{a : A \quad p : P[a/x]}{(a, p) \ : \ (\exists x : A) . P}(\exists I)$$

The precise formulation of the rule of existential elimination is complicated. The most straightforward version from the point of view of the *type* $(\exists x : A).P$ is to view it as a type of pairs. The obvious elimination rules are those which project a pair onto its first and second components.

Elimination rules for ∃ (projections)

$$\frac{p \ : \ (\exists x : A) . P}{Fst \ p \ : \ A}(\exists E_1') \qquad \frac{p \ : \ (\exists x : A) . P}{Snd \ p \ : \ P[Fst \ p/x]}(\exists E_2')$$

This rule is unusual in mentioning a proof, in this case p, on the right-hand side of a 'colon' judgement. We look at variants of the rule in Section 5.3.

The computation rules for *Fst* and *Snd* generalize the rules for conjunction.

Computation rules for ∃

$$Fst \ (p, q) \ \rightarrow \ p \qquad Snd \ (p, q) \ \rightarrow \ q$$

If the formula P does not contain the variable x free, then the rules outlined here can be seen to be the same (modulo trivial syntactic changes) to those for the conjunction. If we wish, we can read $A \wedge B$ as a syntactic shorthand for $(\exists x : A) . B$ in the case that B does not depend on x.

How do we interpret $(\exists x : A) . P$ as a type? There are a number of readings, which we shall explore at some length below. These include the following.

- A generalization of the binary product type, in which the type of the second component $P[a/x]$ depends upon the value of the first, a.

- An (infinitary) sum type. We can think of the type as the union of the types $P[a/x]$ for all a in A, in which objects in the type $P[a/x]$ are paired with the 'tag' a indicating from which of the summands the element comes. This interpretation gives rise to the nomenclature 'dependent sum type' which is used for the type.

- A subset of the type A, consisting of those elements a which have the property P. In keeping with the constructivist philosophy, we pair each object a with the evidence $p : P[a/x]$ that it belongs to the subset.

- A type of modules, each of which provides an implementation (of type A) of the specification P, together with evidence that the implementation meets the specification.

We shall look at these interpretations further in Section 6.3.

We have yet to see how to form formulas with free variables; we will have to wait until we consider the equality type and universes below. Before we do that we look at some example proofs using the quantifiers and then investigate 'base' types such as booleans and natural numbers.

4.6.1 Some example proofs

In this section we present three examples of the use of the quantifier rules.

First we examine a standard result from the logic of the universal quantifier. Let us assume that

$$r \; : \; (\forall x : A) . (B \Rightarrow C)$$

and that

$$p \; : \; (\forall x : A) . B$$

(Recall that in general the variable x will be free in B and C.) We aim to prove the formula $(\forall x : A) . C$, that is to construct an element of this type. First, instantiating both hypotheses using the assumption $x : A$ we have

$$\frac{x : A \quad r \; : \; (\forall x : A) . (B \Rightarrow C)}{r \, x \; : \; B \Rightarrow C} (\forall E)$$

and

$$\frac{x : A \quad p \; : \; (\forall x : A) . B}{p \, x \; : \; B} (\forall E)$$

Putting the two together, eliminating the implication and eliminating the assumption $x : A$ by a $\forall$ introduction, we have

$$\cfrac{\cfrac{\begin{array}{c} [x : A]^1 \\ r \; : \; (\forall x : A) . (B \Rightarrow C) \\ \vdots \\ r \, x \; : \; B \Rightarrow C \end{array} \qquad \begin{array}{c} [x : A]^1 \\ p \; : \; (\forall x : A) . B \\ \vdots \\ p \, x \; : \; B \end{array}}{(r \, x)(p \, x) \; : \; C} (\Rightarrow E)}{(\lambda x : A) . ((r \, x)(p \, x)) \; : \; (\forall x : A) . C} (\forall I)_1$$

In the proof above the assumptions of the two hypothetical proofs are listed one above the other, rather than next to each other; this makes the representation of the derivation easier to read. If we now abstract over both the hypotheses (and omit the typings on the variables) we have

$$\lambda r.\lambda p.\lambda x.(r\ x)(p\ x)$$

which is of type

$$(\forall x:A).(B \Rightarrow C) \Rightarrow (\forall x:A).B \Rightarrow (\forall x:A).C$$

if we choose to omit the type annotations on the variables. This function is familiar to functional programmers as the S combinator, as well as proving the formula

$$(A \Rightarrow (B \Rightarrow C)) \Rightarrow (A \Rightarrow B) \Rightarrow (A \Rightarrow C)$$

in the case that B and C do not involve the variable x.

Next we prove the equivalence between the following pair of formulas

$$((\exists x:X).P) \Rightarrow Q \qquad (\forall x:X).(P \Rightarrow Q)$$

in the case that x is not free in Q. (It is not valid in general — think of the case when P and Q are the same.) Reading the rule $(\forall I)$ backwards, we see that to find an object of type $(\forall x:X).(P \Rightarrow Q)$ it is sufficient to find an object in $(P \Rightarrow Q)$ assuming we have an x in X. To find an object of type $(P \Rightarrow Q)$ it is enough to find an object of type Q assuming an object of type P (as well as the object of type X we assumed earlier). Building the proof tree backwards we have

$$\frac{\dfrac{??\ :\ Q}{\lambda p_P.??\ :\ (P \Rightarrow Q)}(\Rightarrow I)}{\lambda x_X.\lambda p_P.??\ :\ (\forall x:X).(P \Rightarrow Q)}(\forall I)$$

There are constraints on the form of proof of ?? here. We can only introduce a universal quantifier or an implication abstracting over the variable y, say, in the case that y is free only in the assumption discharged. How are we to infer Q? Proceeding from the assumptions we have

$$\frac{x:X \quad p:P}{(x,p)\ :\ (\exists x:X).P}(\exists I)$$

and then by *modus ponens*, we have

$$\frac{\dfrac{x:X \quad p:P}{(x,p)\ :\ (\exists x:X).P}(\exists I) \quad e\ :\ ((\exists x:X).P) \Rightarrow Q}{e\ (x,p)\ :\ Q}(\Rightarrow E)$$

Putting the parts together, and replacing the unknown terms ?? with actual values, we have

$$\dfrac{\dfrac{[x:X]^2 \quad [p:P]^1}{(x,p) \;:\; (\exists x:X).P}(\exists I) \quad e:((\exists x:X).P) \Rightarrow Q}{\dfrac{\dfrac{e\,(x,p) \;:\; Q}{\lambda p_P.(e\,(x,p)) \;:\; (P \Rightarrow Q)}(\Rightarrow I)_1}{\lambda x_X.\lambda p_P.(e\,(x,p)) \;:\; (\forall x:X).(P \Rightarrow Q)}(\forall I)_2}}(\Rightarrow E)$$

The first abstraction, over p, is legitimate as p is free in none of the other assumptions, and the second is OK as there is only one active assumption at this stage. Note, however, that we cannot discharge the assumptions in the opposite order, since x will in general be free in P and thus in the assumption $p : P$.

How does the converse proof proceed?

To find a proof of an implication, we proceed with an assumption of the antecedent formula, in this case $p : (\exists x:X).P$, and try to find $?? : Q$. Proceeding forward from the assumption p, we have

$$\dfrac{p \;:\; (\exists x:X).P}{Snd\ p \;:\; P[Fst\ p/x]}(\exists E'_2)$$

Using the other assumption, which is $e : (\forall x:X).(P \Rightarrow Q)$, we can match the hypothesis of this implication with $P[Fst\ p/x]$ by universal elimination

$$\dfrac{\dfrac{p \;:\; (\exists x:X).P}{Fst\ p \;:\; X}(\exists E'_1) \quad e \;:\; (\forall x:X).(P \Rightarrow Q)}{(e(Fst\ p)) \;:\; P[Fst\ p/x] \Rightarrow Q}(\forall E)$$

Note that in the conclusion we have Q and not $Q[Fst\ p/x]$, since we have assumed that x is not free in Q, and we noted that $Q[t/x] \equiv Q$ (for any t) in such a case. We now apply implication elimination, and complete as above.

$$\dfrac{\dfrac{[p \;:\; (\exists x:X).P]^1 \qquad \begin{array}{c}[p \;:\; (\exists x:X).P]^1 \\ e \;:\; (\forall x:X).(P \Rightarrow Q)\end{array}}{\vdots \qquad\qquad \vdots}}{}$$

$$\dfrac{\dfrac{Snd\ p \;:\; P[Fst\ p/x] \qquad (e(Fst\ p)) \;:\; P[Fst\ p/x] \Rightarrow Q}{(e(Fst\ p))(Snd\ p) \;:\; Q}(\Rightarrow E)}{\lambda p.((e(Fst\ p))(Snd\ p)) \;:\; ((\exists x:X).P) \Rightarrow Q}(\Rightarrow I)_1$$

Is there a functional interpretation of the equivalence we have seen above? If we consider the case in which P does not contain x free, we have the types

$$(X \wedge P) \Rightarrow Q \qquad X \Rightarrow (P \Rightarrow Q)$$

These two function spaces give two different representations of binary functions. In the first, the function takes a *pair* of arguments, of type $(X \wedge P)$, to a result of type Q. The other representation, which is often called the *curried* form in honour of Haskell B. Curry, the λ-calculus pioneer, makes the function higher order. By this we mean that on being passed an argument of type X, the function returns a function of type $(P \Rightarrow Q)$ which expects an argument of type P, the second half of the pair. (We often call the first representation the *uncurried* form, in contrast to the latter.)

The pair of functions we derived above can be seen to map from one function representation to another:

$$\lambda x_X . \lambda p_P . (e\,(x,p))$$

takes separately the two arguments x and p, forms a pair from them, and applies the uncurried function e to the result. Conversely,

$$\lambda p . ((e(Fst\ p))(Snd\ p))$$

takes a pair p as argument, and splits the pair into its components $Fst\ p$ and $Snd\ p$, and applies the curried function e to the two halves one at a time.

The functions perform a similar function in the general case that P depends upon x, and we deal with dependent sum and product types.

Exercises

4.12 Give a derivation of a proof object of the formula

$$(\exists x : X) . \neg P \Rightarrow \neg(\forall x : X) . P$$

Would you expect the reverse implication to be derivable?

4.13 Show that the formulas $(\forall x : X) . \neg P$ and $\neg(\exists x : X) . P$ are equivalent by deriving two functions mapping each into the other.

4.14 Derive an object of type

$$(\forall x : X) . (A \Rightarrow B) \Rightarrow ((\exists x : X) . A \Rightarrow (\exists x : X) . B)$$

What is this formula in the case that A and B are independent of the variable x?

4.15 Derive an object of type

$$(\exists y : Y) . (\forall x : X) . P \Rightarrow (\forall x : X) . (\exists y : Y) . P$$

where in general P will contain x and y free. Under what circumstances can you derive an object of the converse type?

$$(\forall x : X) . (\exists y : Y) . P \Rightarrow (\exists y : Y) . (\forall x : X) . P$$

Can you give a simpler reading of the formula in cases when P does not contain both x and y free?

4.7   Base types

The material in the chapter so far has had different emphases. The propositional part of the system can be viewed as both a logic and a typed λ-calculus; the quantifiers are logical constructs, but have a natural programming interpretation. Now we introduce some base types, whose origins lie in programming, but we shall see that they have a logical interpretation too.

In this and subsequent sections we introduce a number of familiar types: the booleans as an example of a finite type, finite types in general, with the special case of the one-element type, the natural numbers, and finally trees as an example of an algebraic type.

4.7.1   Booleans

The system we are building here is one in which propositions, or formulas, are identified with types, and vice versa. Amongst these propositions are the propositions $\bot$, or 'false', $\top$, or 'true' (which we introduce below), and combinations of the propositions using logical connectives such as $\wedge$ and $\vee$. Each of these propositions is a type: the collection of proofs of that proposition.

Consider the case in which we want to return one of two results *conditional* on some property. We need, informally, to be able to ask the question and to receive the answer *Yes* or the answer *No*, so we need a particular type which contains these two values. We call this the type *bool* of boolean values and for the sake of tradition call the two values *True* and *False*. The type *bool* is simply a finite type containing two values. The rôle of the type is computational: we can build the expression *if ... then ... else ...* (where the condition is a boolean expression) in our language, allowing case switches in computations. The value of *if b then e else f* is e if b evaluates to *True*, otherwise it is f.

To recap, *True* and *False* are values of the type *bool*, whilst $\bot$ and $\top$ are the false and true propositions. Readers may be familiar with similar distinctions between boolean values and propositions from program verification. Languages such as Pascal contain a boolean type – if we reason about these programs we use an external logical language to construct statements *about* the language, we are not constructing expressions of type *bool* which are expressions *of* the language.

We should also note that these definitions form a *template* for the definition of any type with a finite set of members.

Formation rule for *bool*

$$\frac{}{bool\ is\ a\ type}(bool\ F)$$

Introduction rules for *bool*

$$\frac{}{True\ :\ bool}(bool\ I_1)\qquad\frac{}{False\ :\ bool}(bool\ I_2)$$

The two rules above require no explanation. We eliminate a *bool*ean value by a two-way case switch, conventionally called a *conditional expression*. In the case of defining a finite type with n elements, we shall introduce an n-way switch instead.

Elimination rule for *bool*

$$\frac{tr\ :\ bool\quad c\ :\ C[True/x]\quad d\ :\ C[False/x]}{if\ tr\ then\ c\ else\ d\ \ :\ C[tr/x]}(bool\ E)$$

This is stronger than the conventional case switch, as the type of the result can depend upon the value of the boolean. This of course depends upon our being able to define types C which contain free variables, which we can think of as *families* of types; we have not yet done so, but will do in due course. For the present, we can just consider the simplified form:

$$\frac{tr\ :\ bool\quad c\ :\ C\quad d\ :\ C}{if\ tr\ then\ c\ else\ d\ \ :\ C}(bool\ E)$$

We embody the case switching mechanism in the following rules. The '*then*' or '*else*' case is selected, according to the value of the boolean:

Computation rules for *bool*

$$if\ True\ then\ c\ else\ d\ \rightarrow\ c$$

$$if\ False\ then\ c\ else\ d\ \rightarrow\ d$$

Consider the example

$$if\ tr\ then\ False\ else\ True$$

This has the type *bool* if we assume that $tr : bool$. Now, by $\Rightarrow$ introduction,

$$\lambda tr_{bool} \,.\, (if\ tr\ then\ False\ else\ True)\ :\ (bool \Rightarrow bool)$$

and this is the (classical) negation operator on the boolean type. Similarly,

$$\lambda x_{(bool \wedge bool)} \,.\, (if\ (fst\ x)\ then\ (snd\ x)\ else\ False)$$

which has type

$$(bool \wedge bool) \Rightarrow bool$$

is the (classical) conjunction operation on *bool*. We leave it as an exercise for the reader to identify the other boolean operations.

Again, we should note the distinction between these functions over the boolean type, which represent the classical boolean operations, and the connectives $\wedge$, $\vee$, and so forth which form propositions from other propositions, or alternatively, which are type constructors forming types from other types.

Exercises

4.16 Define functions which behave as the disjunction ('or') and material implication ('implies') operations over the boolean type.

4.17 Define the function

$$equiv\ :\ bool \Rightarrow bool \Rightarrow bool$$

so that $equiv\ b_1\ b_2$ is *True* if and only if b_1 and b_2 are equal. This is an *equality function* on the boolean type and also represents the 'if and only if' connective.

4.7.2   Finite types

For n a natural number, the type N_n has n elements,

$$1_n\ ,\ 2_n\ ,\ \ldots\ ,\ n_n$$

the subscript showing the type from which the element comes. We have already seen a two-element type, *bool*, where we identify 1_2 with *True* and 2_2 with *False*.

The formation and introduction rules are as follows:

Formation rule for N_n

$$\frac{}{N_n\ is\ a\ type}(N_n F)$$

Introduction rules for N_n

$$\frac{}{1_n \; : \; N_n}(N_n I) \quad \ldots \quad \frac{}{n_n \; : \; N_n}(N_n I)$$

We eliminate an element of an n-element type by an n-way case switch.

Elimination rule for N_n

$$\frac{e:N_n \quad c_1:C[c_1/x] \; \ldots \; c_n:C[c_n/x]}{cases_n \, e \, c_1 \ldots c_n \; : \; C[e/x]}(N_n E)$$

The computation rules choose the appropriate case from the choice.

Computation rules for N_n

$$cases_n \, 1_n \, c_1 \ldots c_n \; \rightarrow \; c_1$$
$$cases_n \, 2_n \, c_1 \ldots c_n \; \rightarrow \; c_2$$
$$\ldots$$
$$cases_n \, n_n \, c_1 \ldots c_n \; \rightarrow \; c_n$$

Exercises

4.18 Explain how to define the equality function

$$equal_n \; : \; N_n \Rightarrow N_n \Rightarrow bool$$

4.19 The successor and predecessor of m_n are $(m + 1)_n$ and $(m - 1)_n$, except for the predecessor of 0_n, which is n_n, and the successor of n_n, which is 0_n. Give formal definitions of the functions $succ_n$ and $pred_n$ of type $N_n \Rightarrow N_n$ and prove that for all values of m_n

$$succ \, (pred \, m_n) \twoheadrightarrow m_n$$

4.7.3 $\top$ and $\bot$

If we have a one-element type, the rules may be specialized. We express the results in a slightly different syntax, replacing N_1 by $\top$, 1_1 by $Triv$ and $cases_1$ by $case$. We obtain the following rules.

Formation rule for $\top$

$$\frac{}{\top \; is \; a \; type}(\top F)$$

Introduction rule for $\top$

$$\frac{}{Triv \, : \, \top}(\top I)$$

Elimination rule for $\top$

$$\frac{x:\top \quad c:C(Triv)}{case \; x \, c \; : \; C(x)}(\top E)$$

Computation rule for $\top$

$$case \; x \, c \; \rightarrow \; c$$

The one-element type, $\top$, has a logical interpretation. Just as the false proposition 'falsity' (which should not be confused with the object *False* of type *bool*) was represented by the empty type, so the true proposition is represented by the one-element type. Why one element? The intuition is that the proposition is valid for obvious reasons, so there is only one *trivial* proof *Triv* of it.

The rules can also be interpreted in the case that $n = 0$, yielding the rules for $\bot$.

Exercise

4.20 Show that in the case $n = 0$ the rules for N_n reduce to those for $\bot$.

4.8   The natural numbers

We have already seen the natural numbers as a base type of our λ-calculus in Chapter 2.

Formation rule for N

$$\frac{}{N \; is \; a \; type}(NF)$$

Natural numbers are either zero or a successor.

Introduction rules for N

$$\frac{}{0 \, : \, N}(NI_1) \qquad \frac{n \, : \, N}{(succ \; n) \, : \, N}(NI_2)$$

We eliminate natural numbers by means of definition by primitive recursion. Modifying the rule we saw earlier, we have

Elimination rule for N (special case)

$$\frac{n \,:\, N \quad c \,:\, C \quad f \,:\, (N \Rightarrow C \Rightarrow C)}{prim \; n \; c \; f \;\; : \;\; C}(NE)$$

If we discharge the assumption that $n : N$, then

$$\frac{c \,:\, C \qquad f \,:\, (N \Rightarrow C \Rightarrow C)}{\lambda n_N \,.(prim \; n \; c \; f) \;\; : \;\; (N \Rightarrow C)}$$

which is the familiar rule for primitive recursion which we saw in Section 2.9. Why is the rule we have presented above a special case? To answer this we turn to our logical view of the type.

The proof principle which goes along with primitive recursion is ('mathematical') induction. Suppose that we wanted to show that, for example, all the factorials of natural numbers are strictly positive. This assertion takes the form

$$(\forall n : N)(fac \; n > 0) \;\; \equiv_{df} \;\; (\forall n : N)C(n)$$

What do we have to do to prove this? First of all we show that $C(0)$ is valid, that is we supply some c with

$$c \,:\, C(0)$$

and then we show that $C(n+1)$ is valid, *assuming* that $C(n)$ is. In this case we supply some

$$f' \,:\, ``C(n) \Rightarrow C(n+1)"$$

In fact, the f' can be slightly more general,

$$f \,:\, ``N \Rightarrow C(n) \Rightarrow C(n+1)"$$

Note that we have enclosed the types in inverted commas – they are not part of our system. We can make them so, using the *dependent type* constructor:

$$f \,:\, (\forall n : N)(C(n) \Rightarrow C(succ \; n))$$

Given these we produce the proof:

Elimination rule for N (general case)

$$\frac{n \,:\, N \quad c \,:\, C[0/x] \quad f \,:\, (\forall n{:}N)\,.(C[n/x] \Rightarrow C[succ \; n/x])}{prim \; n \; c \; f \;\; : \;\; C[n/x]}(NE)$$

Again, if we discharge the assumption $n : N$, we have

$$\frac{c \; : \; C[0/x] \quad f \; : \; (\forall n \!:\! N).(C[n/x] \Rightarrow C[succ \; n/x])}{\lambda n_N \, . \, (prim \; n \; c \; f) \; \; : \; \; (\forall n \!:\! N).\,C[n/x]}$$

which is the familiar proof of the universal statement.

The computation rule is exactly the same in the two cases. Thinking of a computation of a recursive function we inspect the argument and then *unfold* the definition according to whether we are at the base case or not.

Computation rules for N

$$prim \; 0 \; c \; f \quad \rightarrow \quad c$$
$$prim \; (succ \; n) \; c \; f \quad \rightarrow \quad f \; n \; (prim \; n \; c \; f)$$

What do the rules mean in the logical case? They tell us how to build a proof for any particular natural number that we might supply. This is, of course, how we justify the rule in the first place. Using $C(k)$ for $C[k/x]$, we argue that $C(2)$ is valid thus: '$C(0)$ is valid outright, and by the inductive case for $n = 0$, $C(0) \Rightarrow C(1)$ and applying *modus ponens*, we have $C(1)$. In a similar way, we have $C(1) \Rightarrow C(2)$, and so we can get $C(2)$.'

This rule is one of the high points of type theory. Intuitively, we can appreciate that there is an affinity between the rules for primitive recursion and mathematical induction. Functions introduced by primitive recursion have their properties proved by mathematical induction. What is so elegant here, with our identification of propositions and types, is that they are *exactly* the same rule.

Let us consider some examples. The successor function is defined to be

$$(\lambda x : N)(succ \; x)$$

For the purposes of illustration, without recommending this as an efficient algorithm, we now examine the behaviour of a successor function defined by primitive recursion:

$$addone \; 0 \;\; = \;\; 1$$
$$addone \; (n + 1) \;\; = \;\; (addone \; n) + 1$$

which is formalized thus:

$$addone \equiv_{df} \lambda x_N \, . \, (prim \; x \; (succ \; 0) \; f)$$

where

$$f \equiv_{df} \lambda n_N \, . \, (\lambda y_N \, . \, (succ \; y))$$

What happens when we apply *addone* to the formal representative of 2, that is *succ* (*succ* 0)?

$$((\lambda x : N)(prim \; x(succ \; 0)f)) \; (succ \; (succ \; 0))$$
$$\rightarrow \quad (prim \; (succ \; (succ \; 0)) \; (succ \; 0) \; f)$$
$$\rightarrow \quad f \; (succ \; 0)(prim \; (succ \; 0) \; (succ \; 0) \; f)$$
$$\equiv \quad ((\lambda n : N)(\lambda y : y)(succ \; y)) \; (succ \; 0) \; (prim \; (succ \; 0) \; (succ \; 0) \; f)$$
$$\rightarrow \quad succ(prim \; (succ \; 0) \; (succ \; 0) \; f)$$

By a similar process we see that

$$prim \; (succ \; 0) \; (succ \; 0) \; f \; \twoheadrightarrow \; (succ \; (succ \; 0))$$

and so finally we see that

$$addone(succ \; (succ \; 0)) \; \twoheadrightarrow \; (succ \; (succ \; (succ \; 0)))$$

where '$\twoheadrightarrow$' is generated from $\rightarrow$ *à la* Definition 2.7. We shall look at the successor function again when we come to look at equality, and in particular equality of functions.

Note that, to make the definition above readable, we used the device of naming it, *addone*, and giving explicit recursion equations for it. This helps us to read these definitions, and it is quite possible for an implementation either to decide whether a particular set of recursion equations constitutes a definition by primitive recursion, or to provide a 'pretty printed' version of any primitive recursive definition. We shall continue to give these equational versions of functions defined in this and similar ways. We shall also use '$(n + 1)$' instead of '$(succ \; n)$' whenever this can cause no confusion.

Primitive recursion is a powerful method of definition. We can define addition thus:

$$add \; m \; 0 \quad = \quad m$$
$$add \; m \; (n + 1) \quad = \quad succ \; (add \; m \; n)$$

so formally we say

$$add \equiv_{df} \lambda m \, . \, \lambda n \, . \, prim \; n \; m \; (\lambda p \, . \, \lambda q \, . \, (succ \; q))$$

In a similar way

$$mult \; m \; 0 \quad = \quad 0$$
$$mult \; m \; (n + 1) \quad = \quad add \; m \; (mult \; m \; n)$$

which may be rendered formally thus:

$$mult \equiv_{df} \lambda m \,.\, \lambda n \,.\, prim \; n \; 0 \; (\lambda p \,.\, \lambda q \,.\, (add \; m \; q))$$

There are standard expositions about what can be defined by primitive recursion over the natural numbers, a good reference being [Cutland, 1981]. Among the functions are the following: the usual arithmetic operations; bounded search, providing search within a finite range for an object with a property defined by a primitive recursive function with *boolean* values; definition by course-of-values recursion; and so forth. We shall look again at the various forms of recursion available within the system later; see Sections 4.9 and 5.10 as well as 6.1.

The functions we see above are *first order* in that their arguments are numbers. It is well known that there are limits to the expressibility of first-order primitive recursion. Ackermann gave a graphic example of this with his 'fast-growing' function, which is proved to be non-(first-order) primitive recursive in [Péter, 1967]. The system here is more powerful, since arguments can be higher order, and here we give a version of the Ackermann function. The two-argument version of the function is given by the recursion equations

$$
\begin{aligned}
ack \; 0 \; n &= n + 1 \\
ack \; (m + 1) \; 0 &= 1 \\
ack \; (m + 1) \; (n + 1) &= ack \; m \; (ack \; (m + 1) \; n)
\end{aligned}
$$

We can take a higher-order view of this, defining the functions thus:

$$
\begin{aligned}
ack \; 0 &= succ \\
ack \; (m + 1) &= iter \; (ack \; m)
\end{aligned}
$$

where the function *iter*, of type

$$(N \Rightarrow N) \Rightarrow (N \Rightarrow N)$$

iterates its argument, having the definition

$$
\begin{aligned}
iter \; f \; 0 &= 1 \\
iter \; f \; (n + 1) &= f \; (iter \; f \; n)
\end{aligned}
$$

This function is given by the term

$$\lambda f_{(N \Rightarrow N)} \,.\, \lambda n_N \,.\, prim \; n \; 1 \; (\lambda p \,.\, \lambda q \,.\, (f \; q))$$

which we shall call *iter*, and the Ackermann function itself will be given by

$$\lambda n_N \,.\, (prim \; n \; succ \; \lambda p \,.\, \lambda g \,.\, (iter \; g))$$

There is a limit to the expressibility of primitive recursion, even at higher orders. All functions defined by primitive recursion are total, and so there are intuitively computable functions which are not primitive recursive. Among these are the functions which code an interpreter for the process of computation of primitive recursive functions. We return to the issue of expressibility below.

We are not in a position to give any non-trivial examples of proof by induction as we still have not defined any predicates which contain free variables, a situation which we remedy in due course (in Section 4.10, in fact).

Exercises

4.21 Define the equality function

$$equal_N \ : \ N \Rightarrow N \Rightarrow bool$$

4.22 Define the function geq of type

$$geq \ : \ N \Rightarrow N \Rightarrow bool$$

so that $geq \ n \ m$ is $True$ if and only if n is greater than or equal to m.

[*Hint:* the best way to do this is to define the functions $geq \ n$ by induction, that is to define $geq \ 0$ outright (by induction) and to define $geq \ (n+1)$ using $geq \ n$.]

4.23 Using geq or otherwise show how to define the bounded search function

$$search \ : \ (N \Rightarrow bool) \Rightarrow N \Rightarrow N$$

so that $search \ p \ n$ is the smallest l less than n so that $(p \ l)$ is $True$, and which is n if no such l exists.

4.24 Give a formal definition of the function $sumf$ given by

$$sumf \ f \ n \ m \equiv_{df} \sum_{i=n}^{m} (f \ i)$$

What is its type? What type has the partial application

$$sumf \ id$$

where $id \ x \equiv_{df} x$ is the identity function?

4.9   Well-founded types – trees

In this section we look at an example of how to incorporate recursive data types such as lists and trees into the system. The mechanism is similar to the Miranda algebraic type mechanism. Martin-Löf has proposed a general scheme to achieve this; we examine it in full generality in the following chapter.

We call the types *well founded* as they are types over which we can define objects by recursion and prove properties by induction, as we did for the natural numbers; informally, for this to be possible we need to be sure that when we make a recursive definition (or an inductive proof) we never encounter an infinite sequence of simplifications, as in the simplification from $(n + 1)$ to n. If we have one of these infinite sequences, then the function will be defined on none of the values in that sequence, as each value depends upon an earlier value; there is no *foundation* to the sequence or the recursion, in other words.

We shall again see that the principles of induction and recursion are embodied by exactly the same rule.

Miranda type definitions for booleans and natural numbers might be given by

```
bool ::= True | False
nat  ::= Zero | Succ nat
```

The example of a general algebraic type which we shall take here is a type of numerical trees, defined by

```
tree ::= Null |
         Bnode nat tree tree
```

As we mentioned above, accompanying a definition like this we have the two principles of *proof by structural induction* and *definition by primitive recursion*.

Definition 4.2

Structural induction states that in order to prove P(t) for every tree, t, it is sufficient to prove it outright for Null,

```
P(Null)
```

and to prove

```
P(Bnode n u v)
```

assuming P(u) and P(v), that is assuming the validity of the result for the immediate *predecessors* u and v of the node (Bnode n u v).

Compare this with the principle of induction over the natural numbers; we prove the result outright at 0, and prove it at $(n + 1)$ assuming it is valid at the (immediate) predecessor n.

Definition 4.3

Primitive recursion is a principle of definition for functions. In order to define a (total) function

```
f : tree -> P
```

we need only supply a starting value,

```
a : P
```

which will be the value of **f Null** and a means of defining

```
f (Bnode n u v)
```

in terms of the previous values (**f u**) and (**f v**), the subtrees **u** and **v** and the entry at the node, **n**. We shall represent this as a function

```
F : nat -> tree -> tree -> P -> P -> P
```

so that

```
f (Bnode n u v) = F n u v (f u) (f v)
```

In other words we define the value of (**f t**) in terms of the values of **f** on the *predecessors* of **t**, together with the components of the node itself. This is similar to the principle of primitive recursion over the natural numbers, N, where we specify outright the value at 0 and specify how the value at $(n + 1)$ is computed from the value at n, together with n itself.

As we might expect from what we have seen above, in a constructive setting the principles of proof and definition are *identical*. The proofs required by structural induction will be objects

```
a : P(Null)
```

and F of 'type'

```
(n:nat)->(u:tree)->(v:tree)->P(u)->P(v)->P(Bnode n u v)
```

The preceding type is enclosed in inverted commas as it is not a Miranda type. In type theory this kind of type, in which the type of the result depends upon the value of an argument, is represented using the dependent function space, thus:

$$F \; : \; (\forall n : N)(\forall u : tree)(\forall v : tree)(P(u) \Rightarrow P(v) \Rightarrow P(Bnode \; n \; u \; v))$$

Let us now look at the explicit form taken by the rules for trees. Formation is simple.

Formation rule for *tree*

$$\frac{}{tree \; is \; a \; type}(tree \; F)$$

There are two kinds of tree: a null node and a non-null node with two immediate predecessors, a **binary** node, hence *Bnode*.

Introduction rules for *tree*

$$\frac{}{Null \; : \; tree}(tree \; I_1) \qquad \frac{n:N \quad u:tree \quad v:tree}{(Bnode \; n \; u \; v):tree}(tree \; I_2)$$

Induction and recursion are embodied by the elimination rule.

Elimination rule for *tree*

$$\frac{\begin{array}{l} t:tree \\ c:C[Null/x] \\ f: \; (\forall n:N).(\forall u:tree).(\forall v:tree). \\ \qquad (C[u/x] \Rightarrow C[v/x] \Rightarrow C[(Bnode \; n \; u \; v)/x]) \end{array}}{trec \; t \; c \; f \; : \; C[t/x]}(tree \; E)$$

To make the rule above more readable, we have listed the three hypotheses vertically instead of in a horizontal line. We shall do this where presentation is thus improved.

There are two computation rules for the recursion operator *trec*; the first eliminates a *Null* tree and the second a non-null *Bnode* tree.

Computation rules for *tree*

$$trec \; Null \; c \; f \quad \rightarrow \quad c$$
$$trec \; (Bnode \; n \; u \; v) \; c \; f \quad \rightarrow \quad f \; n \; u \; v \; (trec \; u \; c \; f) \; (trec \; v \; c \; f)$$

As an example, we can present the function which sums the contents of a tree. It is defined thus

$$sum_t \; Null \quad = \quad 0$$
$$sum_t \; (Bnode \; n \; u \; v) \quad = \quad n + (sum_t \; u) + (sum_t \; v)$$

If we define

$$f \equiv_{df} \lambda n \, . \, \lambda t_1 \, . \, \lambda t_2 \, . \, \lambda s_1 \, . \, \lambda s_2 \, . \, (n + s_1 + s_2)$$

then

$$\lambda t_{tree} \cdot (trec\ t\ 0\ f)$$

defines the sum_t function formally.

It behoves us to fit this kind of construction into a uniform framework. Martin-Löf has done this, and indeed given an infinitary generalization of the construction; we postpone this until we have given an account of the equality type.

Exercises

4.25 Define the function which returns the left subtree of a tree if it has one, and the $Null$ tree if not.

4.26 Define the equality function over trees.

4.27 We say that a tree $(Bnode\ n\ u\ v)$ is ordered if and only if all objects in u are smaller than or equal to n, all objects in v are greater than or equal to n and the trees u and v are themselves ordered. The tree $Null$ is ordered. Define a function

$$ordered\ :\ tree \Rightarrow bool$$

which returns $True$ if and only if its argument is ordered. You can assume that the function

$$leq\ :\ N \Rightarrow N \Rightarrow bool$$

represents the ordering relation over N. How might you define this by primitive recursion?

4.28 Define functions $insert$ and $delete$ of type

$$N \Rightarrow tree \Rightarrow tree$$

which, respectively, insert an object into an ordered tree, preserving the order of the tree, and delete an object, if present, from the tree, preserving the ordered property. (If in either case the tree argument is not ordered, it is not specified how the function should behave.)

4.10   Equality

We have introduced a number of type constructors or logical operations which can bind variables which are free in formulas, but as yet we have no formulas containing free variables; we have no primitive predicates, in other words. We remedy that deficiency here, introducing the equality proposition. To assert that

a and b are equal elements of the type A

we write either

$$a =_A b$$

or to remind us forcibly that this is a proposition or *type* of the system we sometimes use Martin-Löf's notation of

$$I(A, a, b)$$

instead of using the (often overused) equality symbol '='.

The I types have a drastic effect on the behaviour of the system, both formally and intuitively. We shall see why as we introduce the type and look at examples which use it.

We now introduce the rules governing the I-proposition. First the formation rule. If a and b are both elements of the type A, then $I(A, a, b)$ is a type.

Formation rule for I

$$\frac{A \; is \; a \; type \quad a:A \quad b:A}{I(A, a, b) \; is \; a \; type}(IF)$$

This is different from the type (or formula) formation rules we have seen so far. These take the form

$$\frac{\ldots \; is \; a \; type \quad \ldots \; is \; a \; type}{\ldots \; is \; a \; type}(\ldots F)$$

which means that, with these rules alone, we can say what are the formulas or types of the system independently of which elements occupy those types. The rule of I formation breaks this rule, since a necessary condition for $I(A, a, b)$ to be a type is that $a:A$. This means that the rules generating the formulas are inextricably mixed up with the rules for derivations, which explains our decision not to express the syntax of formulas (or types) separately.

Now, the presence of an element in the type $I(A, a, b)$ will indicate that the objects a and b are taken to be equal. When can we conclude that? The object a is equivalent to itself, so

Introduction rule for I

$$\frac{a:A}{r(a) \; : \; I(A, a, a)}(II)$$

We can derive rules which look stronger than this, a subject we defer until the next section.

What is the content of this rule, and more to the point, what is the structure of $r(a)$? This object has no internal structure, and at first sight this seems to render it useless. However, its mere presence can allow us to do things which would not be possible without it – we shall amplify this after we have considered the elimination and computation rules, and especially in our case studies.

The essence of equality is that

equals can be substituted for equals

and this is known as Leibnitz's law, after the logician who coined it. Suppose that we have some proof p of a proposition P involving a, and also that we know that $c : I(A, a, b)$. We should be able to infer the proposition P' resulting from us replacing *some* of the occurrences of a in P by b. To capture the idea of substituting for *some* of the occurrences we think of P as the formula

$$C[a/x, a/y]$$

in which a replaces two free variables x and y. In the result of our substitution we replace the occurrences of y by b, thus

$$C[a/x, b/y]$$

We can of course replace *all* the occurrences of a by making sure that x is not free in C. We shall use also the informal notation $C(a, b)$ for $C[a/x, b/y]$ when no confusion can result. There is one extra refinement in our rule – we allow the formula C to mention the equality proof object r too.

Elimination rule for I

$$\frac{c : I(A, a, b) \quad d : C(a, a, r(a))}{J(c, d) : C(a, b, c)} (IE)$$

Theorem 4.4

Leibnitz's law is derivable.

Proof: Take

$$C(a, b, c) \equiv_{df} P(b)$$

and suppose that

$$d : P(a)$$

that is

$$d \; : \; C(a, a, r(a))$$

Assuming that $c \; : \; I(A, a, b)$, we can conclude that

$$J(c, d) \; : \; P(b)$$

as desired.   □

How do we eliminate the J operator? If we eliminate an $r(a)$ we simply return the object d.

Computation rule for I

$$J(r(a), d) \; \to \; d$$

Let us consider some further properties of equality. The introduction rule means that equality is reflexive. If $a : A$ then the type $I(A, a, a)$ is inhabited by $r(a)$.

Theorem 4.5

Equality is symmetric.

Proof: We want to prove

$$I(A, b, a)$$

on the basis of

$$I(A, a, b)$$

so we have to show that the former has an element on the basis of having an element of the latter. Let

$$C(a, b, c) \equiv_{df} I(A, b, a)$$

now, as

$$C(a, a, r(a)) \equiv I(A, a, a)$$

and as we have

$$r(a) \; : \; I(A, a, a)$$

we can apply the I elimination rule,

$$\frac{z : I(A, a, b) \quad r(a) : I(A, a, a)}{J(z, r(a)) : I(A, b, a)} (IE)$$

which gives the result we desire.   □

Finally we show that it is transitive, making it an equivalence relation.

Theorem 4.6

Equality is transitive.

Proof: Choose

$$C(b, c, r) \equiv_{df} I(A, a, c)$$

then substituting c for b in $C(b, b, r)$ takes us from $I(A, a, b)$ to $I(A, a, c)$. Formally,

$$\frac{z : I(A, b, c) \quad w : I(A, a, b)}{J(z, w) : I(A, a, c)} (IE)$$

ending the proof.   □

4.10.1   Equality over base types

When we first talked about the different sorts of rules, we observed that it was the elimination rules which specified that all the elements of a type had the form introduced by the introduction rules. We now show this formally, by proving that

$$(\forall x : bool) . (x =_{bool} True \lor x =_{bool} False)$$

is inhabited. Recall the rule for $bool$ elimination:

$$\frac{tr : bool \quad c : C[True/x] \quad d : C[False/x]}{if \ tr \ then \ c \ else \ d \ : C[tr/x]} (bool \ E)$$

Suppose we assume that $x : bool$, and take the formula C to be

$$(x =_{bool} True \lor x =_{bool} False)$$

Now, $r(True) : True =_{bool} True$ so that

$$(c \equiv_{df} \ ) \quad inl \ r(True) \ : C[True/x]$$

and similarly

$$(d \equiv_{df})\quad inr\,r(False)\ :\ C[False/x]$$

By the elimination rule we have

$$if\ x\ then\ c\ else\ d\ \ :\ C$$

and so

$$\lambda x\ .\ if\ x\ then\ c\ else\ d\ \ :\ (\forall x : bool)\,.\,(x =_{bool} True \vee x =_{bool} False)$$

In a similar way, we can show that for the natural numbers, every number is either zero or a successor, in other words that the type

$$(\forall x : N)\,.\,(x =_N 0 \vee (\exists y : N)\,.\,(x =_N succ\ y))$$

is inhabited.

Exercise

4.29 Prove the result above for the natural numbers. Formulate and prove a similar result for the type *tree* of trees of natural numbers.

4.10.2 Inequalities

Nothing we have specified in the system so far prevents there being a single element at each type. In order to make the system non-trivial we can add an axiom to the effect that

$$ax\ :\ \neg(True =_{bool} False)$$

so that *True* and *False* are distinct. This is sufficient to imply the non-triviality of other types; we can show that 0 is not the successor of any natural number using a definition by primitive recursion of the function

$$f\,0\ \ \equiv_{df}\ \ True$$
$$f\,(n+1)\ \ \equiv_{df}\ \ False$$

This proof follows a further discussion of convertibility and equality in the next section.

4.10.3   Dependent types

With the introduction of the equality predicate we are able to define non-trivial dependent types. A simple example is a family of types over a boolean variable x which is N when that variable is $True$ and $bool$ when the variable is $False$. Using the type constructors, we can represent the type by

$$(x = True \wedge N) \vee (x = False \wedge bool)$$

Elements of this type are either

$$inl(r, n)$$

with $r:(x = True)$ and $n:N$, or

$$inr(r, b)$$

with $r:(x = False)$ and $b:bool$. An alternative representation of this type is given by

$$(x = True \Rightarrow N) \wedge (x = False \Rightarrow bool)$$

whose members consist of pairs of functions (f, g) with

$$f \; : \; ((x = True) \Rightarrow N)$$

and

$$g \; : \; ((x = False) \Rightarrow bool)$$

In Section 5.9 we shall see a more direct means of defining dependent types.

From programming, an interesting example is the predecessor function over the natural numbers. Only the positive natural numbers, $(n+1)$, have a predecessor, n. In traditional programming languages, we usually give the predecessor an arbitrary value, such as 0, at 0. In our language we can represent its type thus:

$$(\forall x:N) . ((x \neq_N 0) \Rightarrow N)$$

where we use $x \neq_N 0$ as an abbreviation for $\neg(x =_N 0)$.

To define the function we need to find an element of

$$(x \neq_N 0) \Rightarrow N$$

for each x in N. We do this by primitive recursion, and so first we have to find an element of

$$(0 \neq_N 0) \Rightarrow N$$

Now, we have $r(0) : (0 =_N 0)$. Suppose we have $z : (0 \neq_N 0)$. The application of z to $r(0)$ is in $\bot$, since $0 \neq_N 0$ is an abbreviation of

$$(0 =_N 0) \Rightarrow \bot$$

From this we can construct $abort_N(z\ r(0)) : N$, giving the element in the case of 0. This trivial element simply reflects the fact that at zero we have no true predecessor.

In the induction step, we have to define the predecessor of the element $(n + 1)$ from the predecessor of n and n itself. We simply choose the latter. Putting these together into a formal deduction and writing C for $(x \neq_N 0) \Rightarrow N$, we have first for the two cases

$$\frac{\dfrac{\dfrac{r(0):(0 =_N 0) \quad [z:(0 \neq_N 0)]^1}{(z\ r(0)):\bot}(\Rightarrow E)}{abort_N(z\ r(0)):N}(\bot E)}{\lambda z\ .\ abort_N(z\ r(0)) \ : \ C[0/x]}(\Rightarrow I)_1$$

and

$$\frac{\dfrac{\dfrac{[n:N]^1}{\lambda q\ .\ n \ : \ C[succ\ n/x]}(\Rightarrow I)}{\lambda p\ .\ \lambda q\ .\ n \ : \ (C[n/x] \Rightarrow C[succ\ n/x])}(\Rightarrow I)}{\lambda n\ .\ \lambda p\ .\ \lambda q\ .\ n \ : \ (\forall n:N)\ .\ (C[n/x] \Rightarrow C[succ\ n/x])}(\Rightarrow I)_1$$

We put these together using the N elimination rule, which introduces a primitive recursion term, in the standard way. The predecessor function is defined by

$$pred \equiv_{df} \lambda n\ .\ prim\ n\ f\ g$$

where

$$f \equiv_{df} \lambda z\ .\ abort_N(z\ r(0))$$

and

$$g \equiv_{df} \lambda n\ .\ \lambda p\ .\ \lambda q\ .\ n$$

4.10.4 Equality over the I-types

What is the general form of elements of an I-type? For each $a:A$, the type $I(A, a, a)$ has the element $r(a)$, but are there any other elements? We can use the rule (IE) to show that they are all equal. Suppose that $a:A$, then

$$r(a):I(A, a, a)$$

and by the rule of I-formation,

$$r(r(a)) \ : \ I(I(A, a, a), r(a), r(a))$$

Suppose we also have

$$p:I(A, a, a)$$

by the rule (IE) we can replace occurrences of $r(a)$ by p. If we replace the second occurrence only, we have

$$J(p, r(r(a))) \ : \ I(I(A, a, a), r(a), p)$$

showing that all elements of an I-type can be proved to be equal.

Exercise

4.30 The functions *insert* and *delete* defined in Exercise 4.28 are designed to be applied to ordered trees. Redefine them so that they are defined *only over ordered trees*, in a similar way to the restricted type of the predecessor function above.

4.11 Convertibility

In this section we examine the rules of computation together with the relation of equivalence or *convertibility* generated by them.

The rules of our system have two quite distinct forms and purposes. The formation, introduction and elimination rules describe how derivations of judgements are constructed. If we are simply interested in finding out from the logical point of view which propositions have proofs, or are *inhabited*, then this category of rule would seem to suffice. This would be the case if we were to omit the equality rules, but in the full system the derivability of equality propositions is closely linked with the computability rules through the convertibility relation and the rules of substitution.

On the other hand, if we read the rules as those of a programming language, then the first three kinds of rules express only the *syntax* of the language, specifying as they do which expressions have which type. In programming the process of execution or evaluation is central, and it is this that the rules express. We might ask what it is in logic that corresponds to evaluation? It is the idea of *simplification* of proof objects. For example, suppose we choose the following (partial) proof for A: 'Given proofs $a : A$ and $b : B$, build the proof (a, b) of $A \wedge B$, then construct a proof of A by taking the first component.' This is the proof *fst* (a, b) and the proof object we have constructed can be reduced simply to the object a.

4.11.1   Definitions; convertibility and equality

First we give some definitions which generalize those of the simply typed λ-calculus.

Definition 4.7

We call a sub-expression f of an expression e a **free sub-expression** of the expression e if none of the free variables in f is bound within e.

A free sub-expression of an expression e is exactly the kind of sub-expression of an expression which could arise by substitution into e – sub-expressions which contain variables bound within e *cannot* arise thus.

Definition 4.8

The rules for computation $\rightarrow$ have been introduced construct by construct above. We call a sub-expression of an expression a **redex** if it matches one of the left-hand sides of these rules. We extend the relation $\rightarrow$ so that we write $e_1 \rightarrow e_2$ when a *free* sub-expression f_1 of e_1 is a redex, and e_2 results from e_1 by replacing f_1 with the corresponding right-hand side, or **reduct**.

Note that this is more restrictive than the definition of reduction we had earlier, since the reduction can take place within a variable-binding operator such as $\lambda x \ldots$ only when the expression reduced has nothing bound by the lambda – in other words it does not contain x free. This restriction is reasonable for the sorts of reasons we discussed in Chapter 2, and makes the reduction relation more amenable to analysis.

Definition 4.9

We define the reflexive, transitive closure of $\rightarrow$, the **reduction** relation $\twoheadrightarrow$, as follows. $e \twoheadrightarrow f$ if and only if there is a sequence of terms $e_0, \ldots, e_n$ so that

$$e \equiv e_0 \rightarrow \cdots \rightarrow e_n \equiv f$$

Definition 4.10

The relation of **convertibility**,' $\leftrightarrow$ ', is the smallest equivalence relation extending ' $\rightarrow$ '. Explicitly, $e \leftrightarrow f$ if and only if there is a sequence $e_0, \ldots, e_n$ with $e \equiv e_0$, $e_n \equiv f$ so that for each i, $e_i \rightarrow e_{i+1}$ or $e_{i+1} \rightarrow e_i$.

Because type expressions (or formulas) can contain embedded object (or proof) expressions we extend the convertibility relation to type expressions in the obvious way.

As we argued when we looked at the simply typed λ-calculus, we can see the relation $\leftrightarrow$ as a relation of equivalence. The rules of computation replace terms with other terms which mean the same thing, according to our intuitive idea of what the rules are intended to capture. This thus means that two interconvertible terms have the same intended meaning, so that they should be interchangeable as far as the judgements of the system are concerned. We express this by means of the following rules of substitution, which licence substitutions of interconvertible object and type expressions.

Substitution rules

$$\frac{a \leftrightarrow b \quad B(a) \; is \; a \; type}{B(b) \; is \; a \; type}(S_1) \qquad \frac{a \leftrightarrow b \quad p(a):B(a)}{p(b):B(b)}(S_2)$$

$$\frac{A \leftrightarrow B \quad A \; is \; a \; type}{B \; is \; a \; type}(S_3) \qquad \frac{A \leftrightarrow B \quad p:A}{p:B}(S_4)$$

(In writing these rules we have used our informal notation for substitution. The reader may be happier to replace $B(a)$ by $B[a/x]$ and so on.)

There are two corresponding rules which permit substitution for a free variable. They can be derived from the rules above.

$$\frac{[x:A]}{\begin{array}{c} \vdots \\ a:A \quad B \; is \; a \; type \end{array}}{B[a/x] \; is \; a \; type}(S_5) \qquad \frac{[x:A]}{\begin{array}{c} \vdots \\ a:A \quad b:B \end{array}}{b[a/x]:B[a/x]}(S_6)$$

There is one other point we should emphasize about substitution and assumptions. If we make a substitution of a, say, for a free variable x in a derivation, then we should substitute a for any occurrence of x in the assumptions other than in the assumption on x itself.

On the basis of the substitution rules we can give a strengthened version of the rule of equality introduction. From $a : A$ we can derive $I(A, a, a)$. If $a \leftrightarrow b$ then we can substitute b for the second occurrence of a in $I(A, a, a)$, giving $I(A, a, b)$. We write this

Introduction rule for I

$$\frac{a \leftrightarrow b \quad a:A \quad b:A}{r(a):I(A,a,b)}(II')$$

This makes plain that interconvertible expressions are not only equal according to a relation of convertibility *external* to the system, but also can be proved equal (by the trivial proof object $r(a)$).

   With this strengthening of the equality proposition we can reason about the computational behaviour of expressions inside the system. We give an example in the next subsection.

4.11.2   An example – adding one

In this subsection we show that two methods of adding one over the natural numbers have the same result for all arguments. We shall be slightly informal in our syntax, but this is only done to make the exposition more readable; nothing significant is being omitted. Recall our definition of *addone* from page 102.

$$addone \equiv_{df} \lambda x.\, prim\; x\; 1\; succ'$$

where we write 1 for $succ\, 0$ and $succ'$ for $\lambda y.\lambda z.succ\, z$. Our aim is to prove that

$$addone\; x =_N succ\; x$$

is inhabited for every x in N. We do this by induction, of course, and we begin by looking at the base case.

$$succ\, 0$$

is in normal form

$$addone\; 0$$
$$\equiv \quad (\lambda x.prim\; x\; 1\; succ')\, 0$$
$$\rightarrow \quad prim\; 0\; 1\; succ'$$
$$\rightarrow \quad 1$$
$$\equiv \quad succ\, 0$$

so that the expressions $succ\, 0$ and *addone* 0 are interconvertible, and so by (II') the type ($addone\; 0 =_N succ\, 0$) is inhabited, establishing the base case.

Now assuming that

$$z : addone\ x =_N succ\ x \tag{4.2}$$

we want to show that the type

$$addone\ (succ\ x) =_N succ\ (succ\ x) \tag{4.3}$$

is inhabited. Note that

$$\begin{array}{ll} addone\ (succ\ x) & \\ \quad\equiv & (\lambda x.prim\ x\ 1\ succ')\ (succ\ x) \\ \quad\to & prim\ (succ\ x)\ 1\ succ') \\ \quad\to & succ'\ x\ (prim\ x\ 1\ succ') \\ \quad\twoheadrightarrow & succ(prim\ x\ 1\ succ') \end{array}$$

By (II') we can conclude that the following type is inhabited:

$$addone\ (succ\ x) =_N succ\ (addone\ x)$$

In order, therefore, to conclude that Equation 4.3 is inhabited, it will be sufficient to conclude that the following type is inhabited:

$$succ\ (addone\ x) =_N succ\ (succ\ x)$$

and to use the transitivity of equality, which we derived in the previous section. In order to do that, we apply the I elimination rule to allow us to conclude

$$succ\ (addone\ x) =_N succ\ (succ\ x)$$

on the basis of the assumption 4.2 and a substitution of *succ* x for the second occurrence of *addone* x in

$$succ\ (addone\ x) =_N succ\ (addone\ x)$$

Let us lay this out as a derivation in which we elide some information, such as the element part of the r identity witnesses, and the precise object derived by the transitivity (derived) rule, and in which we abbreviate the function names *addone* and *succ* by their initial letters.

$$\dfrac{\begin{array}{c} a\,(s\,x) \twoheadleftarrow\!\!\twoheadrightarrow s\,(a\,x) \\ \vdots \\ r : (a\,(s\,x) =_N s\,(a\,x)) \end{array} \quad \begin{array}{c} z : (a\,x =_N s\,x) \\ \vdots \\ J(z,r) : (s\,(a\,x) =_N s\,(s\,x)) \end{array}}{\cdots : (a\,(s\,x) =_N s\,(s\,x))}\,(I\ trans)$$

We have shown that the two functions take the same values at every point in their (common) domain. Can we conclude that they are equal, that is can we conclude that

$$\lambda x.(succ\ x) =_{N \Rightarrow N} \lambda x.(addone\ x) \tag{4.4}$$

is inhabited? The answer is no, since the two terms are obviously not themselves convertible. We can, of course, assert the universal generalization of the equality statement for the applications,

$$(\forall x : N)(succ\ x =_N addone\ x)$$

and indeed that was precisely what the induction proof established. It is interesting that we *cannot* within the system as it stands infer that Equation 4.4 holds. We shall discuss what we can do about this further in Section 5.8.

4.11.3   An example – natural number equality

Here we show that not all natural numbers are equal. First, we prove the simpler result that zero is not equal to a successor. Let us define a function which is *True* on 0 and *False* off it, by recursion, thus:

$$\cfrac{[n:N]^1 \quad True:bool \quad \cfrac{\cdots}{\lambda n.\lambda b.False \ : \ (N \Rightarrow bool \Rightarrow bool)}(\Rightarrow I)}{\cfrac{prim\ n\ True\ f\ :\ bool}{\lambda n_N.(prim\ n\ True\ f)\ :\ (N \Rightarrow bool)}(\Rightarrow I)_1}(NE)$$

where we write f for $\lambda n.\lambda b.False$.

Now, if we write

$$discrim \equiv_{df} \lambda n_N.(prim\ n\ True\ f)$$

then we can see that

$$
\begin{aligned}
discrim\ 0 \quad &\equiv \quad \lambda n_N.(prim\ n\ True\ f)\ 0 \\
&\longrightarrow \quad prim\ 0\ True\ f \\
&\longrightarrow \quad True
\end{aligned}
$$

and

$$
\begin{aligned}
discrim\ (succ\ n) \quad &\equiv \quad \lambda n_N.(prim\ n\ True\ f)\ (succ\ n) \\
&\longrightarrow \quad prim\ (succ\ n)\ True\ f \\
&\longrightarrow \quad f\ n\ (prim\ n\ True\ f)
\end{aligned}
$$

$$\equiv \quad (\lambda n . \lambda b . False) \, n \, (prim \; n \; True \; f)$$
$$\rightarrow \quad (\lambda b . False) \, (prim \; n \; True \; f)$$
$$\rightarrow \quad False$$

so that by (II') the types

$$(discrim \; 0 = True)$$

and

$$(discrim \; (succ \; n) = False)$$

will be inhabited. Now, if $(0 = (succ \; n))$ is also inhabited, we have by substitution that

$$(discrim \; 0 = discrim \; (succ \; n))$$

will be inhabited. Using the transitivity and symmetry of equality, we can show that $(True = False)$ is inhabited, which leads to $\perp$ by our axiom (ax) to the effect that the booleans are distinct.

Using the predecessor function from Section 4.10.3 we can also show that the formula

$$((succ \; n) =_N (succ \; m)) \Rightarrow (n =_N m)$$

is valid. (Its converse is valid by the substitution rules.) We investigate the application

$$pred \, (succ \; n) \; : \; ((succ \; n) \neq_N 0) \Rightarrow N$$

By the above, we have for all n, the type $((succ \; n) \neq_N 0)$ is inhabited, by t_{sn}, say. Then,

$$pred \, (succ \; n) \, t_{sn} \; : \; N$$

How does this behave under reduction?

$$pred \, (succ \; n) \, t_{sn} \; : \; N \quad \equiv \quad (\lambda n . prim \; n \; f \; g) \, (succ \; n) \, t_{sn}$$
$$\rightarrow \quad (prim \, (succ \; n) \, f \; g) \, t_{sn}$$
$$\rightarrow \quad g \, n \, (prim \; n \; f \; g) \, t_{sn}$$
$$\equiv \quad (\lambda n . \lambda p . \lambda q . n) \, n \, (prim \; n \; f \; g) \, t_{sn}$$
$$\rightarrow \quad (\lambda p . \lambda q . n) \, (prim \; n \; f \; g) \, t_{sn}$$
$$\rightarrow \quad (\lambda q . n) \, t_{sn}$$
$$\rightarrow \quad n$$

If we know that n and m have equal successors, then by the above calculation and the substitutivity of equality, we have the equality of m and n themselves.

To recap, we have shown that the successor function is 1–1 and that zero is not a successor. These are standard properties of the natural numbers which we have proved using primitive recursion over the natural numbers, together with the fact that the two booleans are distinct.

This short discussion of conversion completes our exposition of the core system of type theory, together with some small examples of the system in use. In the chapter which follows we shall step back from the system and survey some alternative formulations of rules; look at some of the properties of the system; examine the various identity relations in the theory; and so on.

Exercises

4.31 Show that

$$\lambda x . ((\lambda y . y)x) \;\rightarrow\; \lambda x . x$$

but argue that we cannot generate $\lambda x . ((\lambda y . y)x)$ by substituting $(\lambda y . y)x$ for z in $\lambda x . z$.

4.32 Show that the substitution rules which follow are derivable from the other rules of the system.

$$
\begin{array}{cc}
[x:A] & [x:A] \\
\vdots & \vdots \\
\dfrac{a:A \quad B \text{ is a type}}{B[a/x] \text{ is a type}} & \dfrac{a:A \quad b:B}{b[a/x]:B[a/x]}
\end{array}
$$

We say that a rule is derivable if whenever we can derive the hypotheses of a rule then we can derive the conclusions of the corresponding instance of the rule, with the appropriate hypotheses discharged.

4.33 Formulate a characterization of equality on *tree* similar to that on N formulated above.

4.34 Formulate and prove the results that the *insert* and *delete* functions defined on page 109 preserve the ordering of their tree arguments.

4.35 Formulate and prove that result that the factorial of any natural number is greater than zero.

This concludes our introduction to type theory. We shall call the system introduced here TT_0, and in the next chapter we explore some of the properties of the system, after clarifying some of the more technical points of the presentation. In fact, the system TT_0 is defined in full in Section 5.3, where we give a generalization of the elimination rules for disjunction ($\lor$) and the existential quantifier ($\exists$).

Chapter 5
Exploring Type Theory

The last chapter was taken up with the introduction of the system of type theory TT_0. It is a complicated system, with many of its aspects deserving of further study – this we do here.

As type theory is a formal system, it is amenable to study as an object in its own right. In Section 5.4 we show that from some derivations, such as $a:A$, we can deduce others, such as A *is a type*. Following that, we show that the derivable types of objects are unique, and that the substitution rules can be derived.

An important aspect of type theory is its computational behaviour, and we study this for two systems related to TT_0. We introduced the basic questions in our earlier introduction to the λ-calculus – here we ask them of the system of type theory. First we give (in Section 5.5) a *strong normalization* result for the system TT_0^*, which unfortunately fails to have the Church–Rosser property. We then present TT_0^c which was first introduced by Martin-Löf in [Martin-Löf, 1975b]. This differs from TT_0 in the way in which abstraction is performed. After explaining the abstraction mechanism and showing that TT_0^c is an extension of TT_0, we prove a normalization theorem for it. From the proof we obtain a number of important corollaries, including the Church–Rosser property for TT_0^c and the decidability of '$\leftrightarrow$' and of judgements in general. It is interesting to note that the precise form of λ-abstraction in TT_0^c is very close to the way in which it is performed in modern 'compiled' implementations of functional programming languages [Peyton Jones, 1987].

We begin the chapter by looking at some more technical aspects of the system which merit more attention than they received in the introduction. These include the precise role played by assumptions and ways in which terms can be made more readable by naming and abbreviation. Naming is a fundamental part of any programming language; we look at how our programs and proofs can be made more comprehensible by judicious abbreviations. The version of disjunction elimination given in the last chapter was simplified somewhat; here we give the general version. We also give a variant formulation of the existential elimination rule, as well as mentioning a weaker version, which is more akin to the traditional rule of the first-order predicate calculus.

Our introduction to the system involves the use of four different notions of equality: definitional equality is as close as we get to literal identity: two expressions being definitionally equal if they are identical up to change of bound variables after all definitions have been expanded out. Convertibility is external to the system, with the I type giving an internal representation of it as a proposition, so allowing it to be combined into complex propositions. Lastly, there are equality functions, which return values in the type *bool* when given two elements of a particular type; these are used in computations, giving the conditional expressions familiar to programmers. In Sections 5.7 and 5.8 we compare these different relations, and then examine how a truly extensional equality can be added to the system without destroying its admirable formal properties.

The system TT_0 can be augmented in a number of ways; we look at two means of strengthening it in Sections 5.9 and 5.10. The notion of a type of types is inconsistent, roughly because it allows the impredicative definition of classes in terms of themselves, *à la* Russell's paradox, but we show how a sequence of 'universes' of types can be added in a coherent way. Then we give the general mechanism by which well-founded types are defined, incidentally giving the rules for lists as well.

We conclude the chapter with a second look at the Curry–Howard isomorphism, particularly at the treatment of assumptions and the process of proof normalization, both cases where the isomorphism seem less than one hundred per cent happy.

5.1   Assumptions

The derivations we construct using the rules of type theory depend in general upon collections of assumptions. In this section we look at the precise form that these collections take, together with consistency criteria that they should obey, and re-examine the rules and tighten up their statement in some cases.

A useful exercise for anyone interested in a formal system is to make an implementation of it. Many of the issues discussed here became apparent to the author while writing an implementation of type theory in the functional programming language Miranda. It is easy in a written presentation simply to overlook aspects of a system without which an implementation is impossible; mathematical notation is a powerful tool, not least because it admits ambiguity, and also because an imaginative reader is used to filling gaps in an exposition in the obvious way. (The utility and breadth of the adjective 'similarly' cannot be overestimated!)

An important reference here is [Troelstra, 1987] which addresses a number of lower-level but nonetheless important aspects of Martin-Löf's systems of type theory.

A first peculiarity of the system is that the assumptions do not appear at the leaves of a derivation. In order to make the assumption $x : A$ we have to establish that A is itself a type, the assumption only appearing below this derivation.

The assumptions of a derivation do not simply form a set: there is an ordering of dependency between them, as the types in some assumptions may depend upon variables introduced by others. To see an example of this, we might reconsider the proof of the symmetry of equality. Suppose we have derived

A is a type

then we may make the assumptions

$a : A \qquad b : A$

Then we can conclude that

$a =_A b$

is a type, and so introduce a variable

$x \; : \; (a =_A b)$

whose type contains the variables a and b introduced by other assumptions. This is written as a derivation thus:

$$\cfrac{A \text{ is a type} \qquad \cfrac{\begin{array}{c}\vdots\\A \text{ is a type}\end{array}}{a : A}(AS) \qquad \cfrac{\begin{array}{c}\vdots\\A \text{ is a type}\end{array}}{b : A}(AS)}{\cfrac{I(A, a, b) \text{ is a type}}{x : I(A, a, b)}(IF)}(AS)$$

These prior assumptions appear above the assumption $x \; : \; (a =_A b)$ in the derivation tree. The I elimination rule allows us to conclude that

$$\frac{x : I(A,a,b) \quad r(a):I(A,a,a)}{J(x,r(a)):I(A,b,a)}(IE)$$

We can then discharge the assumptions, $a:A$, $b:A$ and $x \; : \; (a =_A b)$, but *not in any order.*

> We may only discharge an assumption $a : A$ if the variable a does not appear free in any other assumption.

The reason for this is clear. If, for example, we first discharge the assumption $a:A$, we have an expression $\lambda a \,.\, J(x,r(a))$ which contains the variable x free. We expect subsequently to bind that variable, forming a product over the type of x – but what *is* that type? It is $I(A,a,b)$, but the a in the type is bound within the expression $\lambda a \,.\, J(x,r(a))$ (and in the type of that expression $(\forall a : A)\,.\,I(A,b,a)$). We have a use of the variable a outside its scope, in the terminology of computer science, and such a use is meaningless. To avoid that, we make the stipulation above. In this particular example, we must therefore discharge the assumption on x, before discharging either of the assumptions on a and b.

We now present the derivation after discharge of the assumptions x and b.

$$\frac{\dfrac{[x:I(A,a,b)]^1 \qquad \dfrac{A \text{ is a type}, \; a:A}{\vdots} \; r(a):I(A,a,a)}{\dfrac{J(x,r(a)):I(A,b,a)}{(\lambda x:I(A,a,b))\,.\,J(x,r(a)) \; : \; I(A,a,b) \Rightarrow I(A,b,a)}(\Rightarrow I)_1}}{(\lambda b:A)\,.\,(\lambda x:I(A,a,b))\,.\,J(x,r(a)) \; : \; (\forall b:A)\,.\,(I(A,a,b) \Rightarrow I(A,b,a))}(\forall I)_2$$

There is an interesting aspect to this proof as we see it now. The assumption $a:A$ appears in two places in the derivation, and this is what happens in the general case. If we are to have multiple assumptions about the same variable, how should they be treated? We ask that when there are multiple assumptions then they should be *consistent*: all assumptions about the variable a should assume that it has the same type (up to change of bound variable names in types). While constructing a derivation we should enforce this requirement at every occurrence of a rule with more than one hypothesis, as each derivation of a hypothesis will contain assumptions, in general.

Returning to the derivation, discharging the assumption a will discharge every assumption in the tree, giving the closed derivation.

A *is a type* , $[a:A]^3$, $[b:A]^2$ A *is a type* , $[a:A]^3$

$$\vdots \qquad\qquad\qquad\qquad \vdots$$

$$\cfrac{\cfrac{\cfrac{\cfrac{[x:I(A,a,b)]^1 \qquad r(a):I(A,a,a)}{J(x,r(a)):I(A,b,a)}(IE)}{(\lambda x:I(A,a,b)).J(x,r(a))\ :\ I(A,a,b)\Rightarrow I(A,b,a)}(\Rightarrow I)_1}{(\lambda b:A).(\lambda x:I(A,a,b)).J(x,r(a))\ :\ (\forall b:A).(I(A,a,b)\Rightarrow I(A,b,a))}(\forall I)_2}{\begin{array}{c}(\lambda a:A).(\lambda b:A).(\lambda x:I(A,a,b)).J(x,r(a))\ :\\ (\forall a:A).(\forall b:A).(I(A,a,b)\Rightarrow I(A,b,a))\end{array}}(\forall I)_3$$

Another point to observe is that when we discharge an assumption a : A we discharge *every* occurrence of that assumption (above the node of discharge). Failure so to do leaves an occurrence of a variable outside its scope. Note that we have *not* necessarily discharged every assumption of the formula A (in other words every variable of type A), only those named a.

An alternative presentation of the theory gives an explicit listing of the undischarged assumptions at every node.

Definition 5.1

A list of one or more assumptions

$$x_1:A_1,\ldots,x_n:A_n$$

is known as a **context**, if it satisfies the following conditions.

- x_i may only appear free in assumptions $x_j:A_j$ for $j>i$.
- A_{j+1} *is a type* should be a consequence of $x_1:A_1,\ldots,x_j:A_j$ for each $0<j<n$.
- The variables x_j are distinct.

If we write $\Gamma,\Gamma',\ldots$ for contexts, and $\Gamma\vdash J$ for a judgement together with its assumption list, then we can explain the circumstances in which a derivation is consistent.

Definition 5.2

Two contexts Γ, Γ' are **consistent** if and only if for every variable x, if x appears in both contexts, it is assumed to have the same type in each.

A derivation d is **consistent** if

- In an application of a rule taking, for example, the form

$$\frac{\Gamma\vdash J \quad \Gamma'\vdash J'}{\Gamma''\vdash J''}$$

the contexts Γ and Γ' must be consistent, and the list Γ'' which results from merging the contexts is itself a context.

- We may only discharge an assumption $x_j : A_j$ from a context Γ if x_j does not occur free in any assumption $x_k : A_k$ $(k > j)$ of Γ.

The rules above may best be understood by realizing that the linear ordering of the assumptions in a valid context is simply an (arbitrary) extension of the partial ordering on the assumptions induced by their position in a derivation tree constructed according to the restrictions we outlined above, and which we summarize now.

- We may only discharge an assumption $x : A$ if the variable x appears free in the (types of) no other assumptions.

- In applying a rule with at least two hypotheses, the assumptions should be consistent: a variable x must be assumed to have the same type, up to change of bound variable names, in all the derivations of the hypotheses.

We might ask whether we could relax the restriction on consistency of assumptions to their types being convertible, rather than the same. In fact by the rules of substitution this is no stronger; see the exercises below. Note, however, that to perform the test for convertibility as part of the process of derivation construction would require that convertibility was decidable.

Exercises

5.1 Show that if we have derivations of $p : P$ and $q : Q$ from the assumptions $x : A$ and $x : A'$ respectively, then we can construct derivations of $P \vee Q$ from either $x : A$ or $x : A'$.

5.2 From a logical point of view, do we ever require two or more assumptions $x : A, y : A, \ldots$ of the same formula A? From the programming side, why do we need them?

5.3 Give a version of the derivation of the symmetry of equality above in which the contexts are made explicit at each point.

5.4 What is the effect on the system of relaxing the consistency condition?

5.2   Naming and abbreviations

In order to make the expressions and derivations of the system more readable, we allow expressions to be named and allow certain forms of abbreviation in derivations, judgements and expressions.

5.2.1   Naming

The pure system, just like the pure λ-calculus, is a calculus of expressions *without names*. In using a system like this, we need some primitive notion of naming expressions, to make them both more readable and more abbreviated. We say, simply, that

$$name \equiv_{df} expression$$

when we want to use the name *name* as a shorthand for the expression *expression*, the two being treated as identical. We call $\equiv_{df}$ the **definitional equality** symbol. We do not permit recursive namings, or the use of a name before its definition, thereby avoiding indirect mutual recursions; we just require a shorthand.

To make sum types more readable we allow the renaming of the injection functions *inl* and *inr*, so we might say

$$numOrBool \equiv_{df} num\ N + boo\ bool$$

with the intention that objects of this type look like *num n* and *boo b* where $n:N$ and $b:bool$. We can extend this notation to *n*-ary sums, if we represent them in some standard form – a left-associated form, say. We shall also use the *n*-tuple notation for iterated products when this is appropriate.

Again, disallowing recursive definitions, we shall sometimes write

$$f\ x \equiv_{df} e$$

instead of a definition

$$f \equiv_{df} \lambda x_A\ .\ e$$

An elegant form of definition in Miranda uses pattern matching. For a simple case analysis over the type *numOrBool* we use the operator *cases*, with

$$c \equiv_{df} \lambda p\ .\ cases\ p\ g\ h\ :\ (A \vee B) \Rightarrow C$$

if $g:A \Rightarrow C$ and $h:B \Rightarrow C$. Suppose that

$$g\ n \equiv_{df} e$$

$$h\ b \equiv_{df} f$$

then we can write the definition of *c* directly thus:

$$c\,(num\ n)\ \ \equiv_{df}\ \ e$$
$$c\,(boo\ b)\ \ \equiv_{df}\ \ f$$

An example is provided by

$$toNum\,(num\;n) \quad \equiv_{df} \quad n$$
$$toNum\,(boo\;b) \quad \equiv_{df} \quad if\;b\;then\;1\;else\;0$$

which is shorthand for the definition

$$toNum \equiv_{df} \lambda p\,.\,(cases\;p\,(\lambda n\,.\,n)\,(\lambda b\,.\,if\;b\;then\;1\;else\;0\,))$$

We can allow constrained forms of recursion, too, as long as they conform to the recursion operation over the type in question. Over the natural numbers, we allow definitions such as

$$fac\,0 \quad \equiv_{df} \quad 1$$
$$fac\,(succ\;n) \quad \equiv_{df} \quad mult\,(succ\;n)\,(fac\;n)$$

In the first clause we permit no recursive call. In the second we can call only $fac\,n$ and n itself. This corresponds to the formal definition

$$fac \equiv_{df} \lambda n\,.\,(prim\;n\;1\,(\lambda p,q\,.\,(mult\,(succ\;p)\;q)))$$

Of course, in all these abbreviations, we assume that the derivations of the hypotheses of the appropriate rule, like (NE) here, have been derived. In this case, we assume that we can already derive $1:N$ and that $(mult\,(succ\;p)\;q):N$ assuming that $p,q\;:\;N$.

We shall look at a system based on naming of abstractions in Section 5.5.3.

5.2.2   Abbreviations

There are various places in the system where we can abbreviate derivations without problems. In any situation where the same judgement forms more than one hypothesis of a rule we may supply a single derivation of that judgement. Examples are

$$\frac{A\;is\;a\;type \quad A\;is\;a\;type}{A \wedge A\;is\;a\;type}(\wedge F) \qquad \frac{a:A \quad a:A}{(a,a):A \wedge A}(\wedge I)$$

and the common case

$$\frac{A\;is\;a\;type \quad a:A \quad a:A}{I(A,a,a)\;is\;a\;type}(IF)$$

Often the same derivation will appear as two or more sub-derivations of a particular derivation. For instance, in any case where we use the number

$2 \equiv_{df} (succ\,(succ\,0))$, its use will be prefaced by the derivation

$$\cfrac{\cfrac{\cfrac{}{0\,:\,N}(NI_1)}{(succ\,0):N}(NI_2)}{(succ\,(succ\,0)):N}(NI_2)$$

which establishes that it is a term of type N. We shall omit these repeated derivations, for brevity.

Any system for functional programming based upon type theory will need to include the naming mechanisms above as an absolute minimum. With naming come a number of other issues, such as equality between types. We do not intend to look at these issues any further here. We intend to discuss the relevance of the system and further naming issues as we proceed.

Exercises

5.5 Suggest naming conventions for functions defined over the algebraic type *tree* introduced in the previous chapter.

5.6 Explain the naming conventions used in the definition

$$
\begin{aligned}
merge\,x\,[\,] &\equiv_{df} && x && \\
merge\,[\,]\,y &\equiv_{df} && y && \\
merge\,(a::x)\,(b::y) &\equiv_{df} && a::(merge\,x\,(b::y)) && \text{if } a < b \\
&\equiv_{df} && a::(merge\,x\,y) && \text{if } a = b \\
&\equiv_{df} && b::(merge\,(a::x)\,y) && \text{if } a > b
\end{aligned}
$$

5.3 Revising the rules

For pedagogical reasons we have simplified or modified some of the rules of type theory in the introduction of Chapter 4; here we give the rules in their full generality and look at alternative versions of them.

5.3.1 Variable binding operators and disjunction

In our original exposition we choose to incorporate a single binding operation, the λ for function formation by lambda abstraction. In Martin-Löf's system [Martin-Löf, 1985] there are a number of binding operators. As an example we shall consider $\vee$ elimination, and go back to the form we saw in Chapter 1. There we had the rule

$$\frac{(A \vee B) \quad \overset{[A]}{\underset{\vdots}{C}} \quad \overset{[B]}{\underset{\vdots}{C}}}{C} (\vee E)$$

in which we produced a proof of C from two hypothetical proofs of C, the first based on the assumption A and the second on the assumption B. These assumptions are discharged (from their respective sub-proofs) in the proof thus formed. In the version we gave above, we supplied instead proofs of the formulas $A \Rightarrow C$ and $B \Rightarrow C$: these correspond to the hypothetical proofs through the rules of $(\Rightarrow I)$ and $(\Rightarrow E)$. The alternative type-theoretic rule has the form

$$\frac{p:(A \vee B) \quad \overset{[x:A]}{\underset{\vdots}{u:C}} \quad \overset{[y:B]}{\underset{\vdots}{v:C}}}{vcases'_{x,y} \, p \, u \, v \, : \, C} (\vee E')$$

The operator $vcases'_{x,y}$ binds the variable x in its second argument and y in its third. How does this new operator behave computationally?

Computation rules for $vcases'$

$$vcases'_{x,y} \, (inl \, a) \, u \, v \; \longrightarrow \; u[a/x]$$

$$vcases'_{x,y} \, (inr \, b) \, u \, v \; \longrightarrow \; v[b/y]$$

It seems clear that the rules $(\vee E)$, $(\vee E')$ are in some sense equivalent, and moreover give rise to the same computational behaviour. Can we make this precise?

Any formula derived by $(\vee E)$ can be derived by using $(\vee E')$ and vice versa. For suppose we have $f : (A \Rightarrow C)$ and $g : (B \Rightarrow C)$; we can form hypothetical proofs, based on the assumptions $x : A$ and $y : B$ respectively, thus:

$$f \, x : C$$

$$g \, y : C$$

we then form a proof

$$vcases'_{x,y} \, p \, (f \, x) \, (g \, y) \; : \; C$$

Now consider the computational behaviour of this:

$$vcases'_{x,y} \, (inl \, a) \, (f \, x) \, (g \, y) \; \rightarrow \; (f \, x)[a/x] \equiv f \, a$$

$$vcases'_{x,y} \, (inr \, b) \, (f \, x) \, (g \, y) \; \rightarrow \; (g \, y)[b/y] \equiv g \, b$$

so that not only is derivability preserved, but also the computational behaviour, in the sense that for every closed term p of the sum type, the expression $vcases'_{x,y} \, p \, (f \, x) \, (g \, y)$ behaves in exactly the same way as *cases p f g*. It is an exercise for the reader to prove the converse of this result.

In a similar vein, there is a form of the rule of existential elimination which introduces a variable binding operator. We look at this in Section 5.3.3.

Exercise

5.7 Show that the rule $(\vee E')$ can be derived from the rule $(\vee E)$ in a way which preserves computational behaviour as above.

5.3.2   Generalizing $\vee$

One reason for presenting the rule for $\vee$ as we did in the previous section is that in this form it naturally suggests a generalization. The type C can be a type family, dependent upon a variable z of type $A \vee B$. Stated in this form, we have

$$\frac{p:(A \vee B) \quad u:C[inl \, x/z] \quad v:C[inr \, y/z]}{vcases''_{x,y} \, p \, u \, v \; : \; C[p/z]}(\vee E'')$$

$$[x:A] \qquad\qquad [y:B]$$
$$\vdots \qquad\qquad \vdots$$

In the second hypothesis we have an object x of type A, from which we form the object *inl x* of type $A \vee B$; this is substituted for the variable z in the formula C as this case covers those elements from the left-hand summand. In the third hypothesis we have $y:B$, giving *inr y* $: A \vee B$. In the result, the object p of type $A \vee B$ is substituted for the variable z. The rule of computation is exactly the same as the rule for *vcases'*. The operator $vcases''_{x,y}$ binds occurrences of the variables x and y.

We can, in fact, give a version of this rule in which the operator is not binding, but it involves our using the quantifiers; this is the reason we deferred its introduction originally. It is

$$\frac{p:(A \vee B) \quad q:(\forall x:A).C[inl\ x/z] \quad r:(\forall y:B).C[inr\ y/z]}{cases^\dagger\ p\ q\ r\ :\ C[p/z]}(\vee E^\dagger)$$

The computation rule for $cases^\dagger$ is the same as for $cases$ – a generalization of type need not alter the dynamic behaviour of an operator.

How is this generalization useful? The operator $cases$ can be seen as a way of combining functions f and g with domains A and B and common codomain C into a single function on the sum domain $A \vee B$. The generalized operator will do the same for *dependent* functions for which the type of the result depends upon the value of the input. The families which are the result types of the dependent functions must fit together in the appropriate way: we ensure this by asking that each is a specialization to a family over A, that is $C[inl\ x/z]$, or over B ($C[inr\ y/z]$) of a family C over $A \vee B$.

From the logical point of view, we have a way of lifting proofs of universal results over A and B separately into universal results over $A \vee B$. We might, for example, choose to represent the **integers** by the sum $N \vee N$, or using a more suggestive notation

$$integers \equiv_{df} poszro\ N + neg\ N$$

(We think of $neg\ n$ as representing $-(n+1)$.) We would then be able to prove results for the integers by means of twin inductions over the non-negative and the negative integers. If we define the factorial of an integer by

$$
\begin{aligned}
fac\ 0 \quad &\equiv_{df} \quad 1 \\
fac\ (succ\ n) \quad &\equiv_{df} \quad mult\ (succ\ n)\ (fac\ n) \\
fac\ -1 \quad &\equiv_{df} \quad 1 \\
fac\ (-(succ\ n)) \quad &\equiv_{df} \quad mult\ (succ\ n)\ (fac\ (-n))
\end{aligned}
$$

a proof that for all integers p, $fac\ p > 0$, would take the form suggested above.

Exercises

5.8   Expand the definition of factorial given above, and using the expanded definition give a proof that $fac\ p$ is positive for all integers p.

5.9   Give a definition of subtraction over the integers, and prove for all a and b that

$$(a+b) - b = a$$

5.3.3 The existential quantifier

The existential elimination rule we stated in Chapter 1 discharged an assumption. In its type-theoretic form, we have

Elimination rule for $\exists$

$$[x:A; y:B]$$
$$\vdots$$

$$\frac{p \ : \ (\exists x:A) . B \qquad c:C}{Cases_{x,y} \ p \ c \ : \ C} (\exists E')$$

Computation rule for $\exists$

$$Cases_{x,y} \ (a, b) \ c \ \rightarrow \ c[a/x, b/y]$$

How are these justified? An arbitrary object of type $(\exists x:A) . B$ will be a pair (x, y) with $x:A$ and $y:B$ (which in general contains x free). If we can construct an object c in C assuming the existence of the components x and y, we can build an object of that type from an object p of type $(\exists x:A) . B$, replacing the assumptions x and y by the two components of p. The object thus formed we call $Cases_{x,y} \ p \ c$, and this operator binds the variables x and y in c.

When $Cases_{x,y}$ is applied to a pair (a, b), we substitute the components for the appropriate component variables, x and y, which explains the computation rule.

As with the rule for $\vee$ elimination, we can ask the question of whether the type C can in fact be variable, and indeed it can. We derive the rule

Elimination rule for $\exists$

$$[x:A; y:B]$$
$$\vdots$$

$$\frac{p:(\exists x:A) . B \qquad c:C[(x, y)/z]}{Cases_{x,y} \ p \ c \ : \ C[p/z]} (\exists E)$$

In the hypothesis, the type of c depends upon the pair (x, y), the arbitrary member of the existential type. In the conclusion we substitute the actual value p for this arbitrary one. The computation rule is unchanged.

How are the various rules for existential elimination related? From the rule $(\exists E')$ we can derive the term Fst thus: make $c \equiv_{df} x$ and $C \equiv_{df} A$; we then have

$$Cases_{x,y} \ p \ x \ : \ A$$

if $p : (\exists x : A) . B$. Moreover,

$$Cases_{x,y} \ (a,b) \ x \ \rightarrow \ x[a/x, b/y] \equiv a$$

as required. We therefore define

$$Fst \equiv_{df} \lambda p . Cases_{x,y} \ p \ x$$

The term Snd is more problematic, as the type of its result depends upon the value of the first component of its argument. It can be shown that Snd is not derivable from $(\exists E')$, as a consequence of the characterization of the various existential elimination rules by Swaen, examined in Section 8.1.3.

Obviously, if Fst is derivable from $(\exists E')$ then it is derivable from the stronger $(\exists E)$. We now show that Snd is also derivable from $(\exists E)$. To do this we need to be able to cast the judgement

$$y : B$$

in the form $c : C[(x, y)/z]$. c can be y, but we need to cast B as a formula dependent on the pair (x, y) and not simply on the variable x. The way out is provided by Fst, and we write B in the form

$$B[(Fst \ (x, y))/x]$$

so that to meet the rule, we have $C \equiv_{df} B[(Fst \ z)/x]$, giving

$$C[(x, y)/z] \equiv B[(Fst \ z)/x][(x, y)/z] \equiv B[(Fst \ (x, y))/x]$$

We then have

$$Cases_{x,y} \ p \ y \ : \ C[p/z] \equiv B[(Fst \ p)/z]$$

and

$$Cases_{x,y} \ (a,b) \ y \ \rightarrow \ y[a/x, b/y] \equiv b$$

which justifies the definition

$$Snd \equiv_{df} \lambda p . Cases_{x,y} \ p \ y$$

In the opposite direction, we now show that every instance of the rule $(\exists E)$ can be derived from $(\exists E_1')$, introducing Fst and $(\exists E_2')$, introducing Snd.

Suppose that we have a derivation

$$[x:A; y:B]$$
$$\vdots$$
$$c:C[(x,y)/z]$$

and $p:(\exists x:A).B$. By the rules $(\exists E_1')$ and $(\exists E_2')$ we have

$$Fst\ p:A \qquad Snd\ p:B[Fst\ p/x]$$

and so by the rule of substitution (S_6), applied twice, we have

$$c[Fst\ p/x][Snd\ p/y]\ :\ C[p/z]$$

If we substitute (a,b) for p, the judgement becomes

$$c[a/x, b/y]\ :\ C[p/z]$$

as we require.

We shall use whichever of the rules is most convenient in what follows.

Definition 5.3

We call the system of Chapter 4 together with the rules $(\vee E'')$ or $(\vee E^\dagger)$ for disjunction elimination the system TT_0.

Exercise

5.10 Using the rule $(\exists E)$ amongst others, give a proof of the axiom of choice:

$$(\forall x:A).(\exists y:B).C(x,y) \Rightarrow (\exists f:(A \Rightarrow B)).(\forall x:A).C(x,(f\ x))$$

Can you use $(\exists E')$ instead of $(\exists E)$?

5.4   Derivability

In this section we take a general look at derivability in variants of the system TT_0. These results will be proved by induction over derivations. Before looking at particular results, it is worth noting a particular property of the system of type theory we have adopted.

In the system TT_0 any particular judgement, such as

$$fst\ (a,b):A$$

can be derived in two different ways. First we might use the rule which introduces that particular piece of syntax, in this case ($\wedge E_1$). Alternatively, we might use one of the substitution rules, such as (S_2), to derive the same result:

$$\frac{a \leftrightarrow b \quad \mathit{fst}\,(a,a):A}{\mathit{fst}\,(a,b):A}\,(S_2)$$

The main results we prove are that in an appropriately modified system *A is a type* is derivable from $a:A$ and that types are unique.

Definition 5.4

We say that a rule

$$\frac{J_1 \ldots J_k}{J}\,(R)$$

is **derivable** if whenever we have derivations $d_1, \ldots, d_k$ of the judgements $J_1, \ldots, J_k$ then we can construct a derivation d of the judgement J. In the case that application of the rule R discharges any assumptions, then the appropriate assumptions should be discharged in the derivation d constructed.

5.4.1   *A is a type* **is derivable from** $a:A$

One property we might expect of the system is that the rule

$$\frac{a\ :\ A}{A\ is\ a\ type}$$

should be derivable; we should not be able to derive elements of non-types or proofs of non-formulas. For this to be the case we have to modify the rules slightly. If we think about how to prove this property by induction over the derivation tree for $a : A$ then we see how the rules need to be changed. The proof will be constructive in that we define a derivation of *A is a type* in each case.

The base case for the induction is the derivation

$$\frac{A\ is\ a\ type}{x:A}\,(AS)$$

introducing the variable x, which can only be introduced if *A is a type* is derivable.

For a derivation ending with $(\wedge I)$, for instance, we proceed by induction:

$$\frac{a:A \quad b:B}{(a,b):(A \wedge B)}(\wedge I)$$

If we assume the result for the hypotheses, then we can derive A *is a type* and B *is a type*, so using $(\wedge F)$ we derive $(A \wedge B)$ *is a type*.

There are cases for which the rules as they stand are inadequate; we have to add to them additional hypotheses of the form '... *is a type*'. We look at these in turn now.

The first candidate is the rule of $\vee$ introduction:

$$\frac{q \,:\, A}{inl\ q \,:\, (A \vee B)}(\vee I_1) \qquad \frac{r \,:\, B}{inr\ r \,:\, (A \vee B)}(\vee I_2)$$

In each of these rules we have a new type expression (B or A) appearing below the line – we should only introduce such an expression if it is a type. We therefore revise the rules to

$$\frac{q:A \quad B\ is\ a\ type}{inl\ q \,:\, (A \vee B)}(\vee I_1') \qquad \frac{r:B \quad A\ is\ a\ type}{inr\ r \,:\, (A \vee B)}(\vee I_2')$$

We can see now that the judgement $(A \vee B)$ *is a type* can be constructed from a derivation of $\dots \,:\, (A \vee B)$ if the last line of a derivation is a $\vee$ introduction.

In most cases we shall in fact omit the second premiss, as it will be clear from the context that it is derivable.

The next rule we look at is existential introduction

$$\frac{a \,:\, A \quad p \,:\, P[a/x]}{(a,p) \,:\, (\exists x:A).P}(\exists I)$$

In order to see that $(\exists x:A).P$ *is a type* we need to know that the family P is a type, assuming that $x:A$. We make this a third premiss of the rule.

$$[x:A]$$
$$\vdots$$
$$\frac{a \,:\, A \quad p:P[a/x] \quad P\ is\ a\ type}{(a,p) \,:\, (\exists x:A).P}(\exists I')$$

Again, we shall in practice suppress this third premiss.

Other rules which require additional premisses are the variant rules for disjunction $(\vee E'')$ and existential elimination $(\exists E)$, in which we substitute into a type family C. The revised rules are

$$\frac{p:(A \vee B) \quad \overset{[x:A]}{\underset{\vdots}{u:C[inl\ x/z]}} \quad \overset{[y:B]}{\underset{\vdots}{v:C[inr\ y/z]}} \quad \overset{[z:(A \vee B)]}{\underset{\vdots}{C\ is\ a\ type}}}{vcases''_{x,y}\ p\ u\ v\ :\ C[p/z]}(\vee E'')$$

$$\frac{p:(\exists x:A).B \quad \overset{[x:A;y:B]}{\underset{\vdots}{c:C[(x,y)/z]}} \quad \overset{[z:(\exists x:A).B]}{\underset{\vdots}{C\ is\ a\ type}}}{Cases_{x,y}\ p\ c\ :\ C[p/z]}(\exists E)$$

where the additional hypotheses are that C is a type family of the appropriate kind. In practice we shall suppress these extra hypotheses.

The final case we should consider is one in which the last rule applied is a substitution. Consider first the case of (S_2):

$$\frac{c \leftrightarrow a \quad p(c):B(c)}{p(a):B(a)}(S_2)$$

By induction we have a derivation of $B(c)$ *is a type*. Applying the instance of (S_1) which follows, the result is clear.

$$\frac{c \leftrightarrow a \quad B(c)\ is\ a\ type}{B(a)\ is\ a\ type}(S_1)$$

An instance of (S_4) is similarly replaced by an instance of (S_3).

Theorem 5.5

Using the modified system of rules outlined above, given a derivation of $a : A$ we can construct a derivation of A *is a type*.

Proof: The proof proceeds by induction over the derivation of $a : A$ and follows the outline sketched above.   □

We managed to prove the property above by adding sufficient type hypotheses to the rules so that each element derivation contains embedded derivations of the typehood of its various type expressions. In a practical system based on type theory, we would expect to separate these concerns as much as possible; once a type had been derived, we could construct elements of that type without an explicit re-derivation of the type.

Exercise

5.11 Complete the proof of Theorem 5.5.

5.4.2   Unique types

In a language such as Pascal, or indeed Miranda, the types of expressions are unique. Can we expect this to be the case for our system TT_0? In fact as the system is constructed at the moment, there are a number of reasons why this fails. We show why this is so, and how to build a system in which the property holds. The reasons the result fails for TT_0 are as follows.

- The duplication of the function space and product types, since these types can be seen as special cases of the universal and existential types. In future we take $A \Rightarrow B$ and $A \wedge B$ as shorthand for the quantifier forms.

- The injection operators inl and inr do not have unique ranges. Indeed,

$$inl\ 0$$

is a member of $(N \vee A)$ for *any* type A. We remedy this by labelling the injection operators with their range type, so that

$$inl_{(N \vee A)}\ 0\ :\ (N \vee A)$$

We can now see the unlabelled operators as shorthand for these operators.

Theorem 5.6

In the theory TT_0, if from a consistent collection of assumptions we can derive the judgements $a:A$ and $a:B$ then $A \leftrightarrow B$.

Proof: The proof is performed by induction over the derivation of $a:A$.

Consider first the case of a variable $x:A$. Judgements of this sort will be derived in one of two ways. First we may use the rule of assumptions, in which case there is only one choice of type A by the consistency of the assumption set. Alternatively, we can use the substitution rule (S_4) or (S_2). In the former case, we have a derivation ending in

$$\frac{C \leftrightarrow A \quad x:C}{x:A}(S_4)$$

Appealing to induction, the type of x is unique up to convertibility, and the final step simply gives an equivalent typing to x. The case of (S_2) is similar. For each syntactic form we have the possibility of using a substitution rule: it is handled in the same way each time.

At the induction step we perform a case analysis over the rule forming the final deduction of the derivation. We take as an example the rules for disjunction. If the expression has the form $inl_{(A \vee B)}\ q$ then this has type

$(A \lor B)$ if *and only if* q : A, and B *is a type*. If the expression has two types then the second type will be of the form $(A' \lor B)$, in contradiction to the unique type of q, which we assume by induction. In a similar way, for the elimination rule, the (*cases p f g*) expression can only have two types if both f and g have two, a contradiction.   □

Exercises

5.12 Complete the proof of the previous result.

5.13 Show that the rules (S_3) and (S_4) are derivable in the system which results from TT_0 by deleting them. Can the rules (S_1) and (S_2) be derived in a system entirely without substitution rules?

5.5   Computation

Up to now we have devoted the major part of our exposition to the static properties of the system, in looking at how the various judgements are derived. Whilst doing this we have introduced computation rules which are of fundamental importance from the point of view of programming, since it is these rules which define the dynamic behaviour of the system; how the programs are executed, in other words. This section looks at the rules from a general perspective.

The reduction rules are also used to generate a relation of conversion, which is an equivalence relation; convertible objects are seen as being the same, and this allows the substitution of one for the other in any context.

The issues of interest for reduction will be those we discussed first in Sections 2.3, 2.4 and 2.11. Does evaluation terminate (along all paths)? – is the system (strongly) normalizing? Can any two evaluation sequences be extended to yield a common expression – the Church–Rosser property?

This will be the case for the system TT_0; in this section we present two variants for which there are the results we require in the literature. The first, TT_0^*, is one in which reduction, '$\rightarrow$', is limited. This system possesses normalization properties, but has the drawback that it is not Church–Rosser.

The second system, called TT_0^c, is based on a quite different way of introducing functions, and types, though it is equivalent to TT_0. Instead of introducing binding operators such as λ, or type forming operators such as $\forall$ and so on, functions are introduced as constants, each constant having a corresponding reduction rule. Types are introduced in a similar way. This bears a striking resemblance not only to the top-level form of languages such as Miranda, but also in its details to the methods of λ-lifting [Johnsson, 1985] and supercombinators [Hughes, 1983] used in functional language implementations.

5.5.1   Reduction

When we evaluate an expression written in a functional programming language, we expect the final result to be presented in some printable form. We are familiar with Arabic notation for numbers, and lists, trees and so on can be represented in syntactic form. How is a function from (for example) N to N to be printed? Two options present themselves.

- A function is described **extensionally** if we say what is its value on every argument – an infinite amount of information needs to be printed, which is infeasible.

- The alternative is to print some representation of a *program* for the function. Different results will not necessarily denote different functions, yet since (extensional) equality between functions cannot be implemented, we cannot give a standard representation to each function. The difficulty with implementing extensional equality is that, in order to conclude that two functions are equal, an infinite amount of data has to be surveyed, and this operation is simply not computable.

In a sense, this is not a problem, because the results we will be interested in will be finite. (This approach does not ignore the 'infinitary' lists of languages such as Miranda – these are a sequence of finite results, produced one by one, rather than a single infinite result.) We say that a type is *ground* if it involves no (embedded) function or universally quantified types, and we identify the printable values to be those of ground type. The evaluation of an object of functional type is declined politely, at least by the Miranda system.

In the untyped λ-calculus, everything interesting has to be represented by a function, and the unrestricted rule of β-reduction is invaluable. In the untyped context we have to extract meaningful information precisely from representations of functions. ([Abramsky, 1990] gives a penetrating analysis of the untyped λ-calculus from the point of view of making it consistent with evaluation in untyped functional languages.) For this reason, the rule that if $e \rightarrow f$ then $\lambda x . e \rightarrow \lambda x . f$, even with x free in e and f, is of central importance. (We call a redex within an expression such as $\lambda x . e$ a **redex within a lambda**.)

Evaluation of printable values in the typed situation is quite different. Functions are ultimately applied to their arguments, and so any reduction within the body of a λ-abstraction can be deferred until the argument has replaced the bound variable. In a simple case we can see this in action:

$$(\lambda x . (II)x)\, 2 \;\rightarrow\; (\lambda x . Ix)\, 2 \;\rightarrow\; (\lambda x . x)\, 2 \;\rightarrow\; 2$$

can alternatively be reduced thus:

$$(\lambda x . (II)x)\, 2 \;\rightarrow\; (II)2 \;\rightarrow\; I\, 2 \;\rightarrow\; 2$$

Indeed, it is not hard to see that there will be no reductions within a lambda on the leftmost-outermost reduction sequence (cf. Section 2.3). This is because if the leftmost-outermost redex ever lies within a lambda then the lambda will never be reduced, since altering the internal redex will change nothing outside the lambda. (This is illustrated by the example above, where the second sequence is the leftmost outermost.)

The argument we have given is to motivate the definition of reduction for the system TT_0^* which we introduce next.

Exercise

5.14 In the untyped λ-calculus, the natural number n is represented by the function 'apply n times', that is

$$\lambda f . \lambda x . \underbrace{f\,(f\,\ldots\,f\,(f\,x)\ldots)}_{n}$$

and addition is represented by the function

$$add \equiv_{df} \lambda f . \lambda g . \lambda h . \lambda x . f\,h(g\,h\,x)$$

Show that add 2 3 reduces to 5, but observe that the unrestricted β-reduction rule must be used to achieve the result.

5.5.2   The system TT_0^*

The system TT_0^* contains the same rules of formation, introduction, elimination and computation. We only change the definition of the relation '$\rightarrow$', with the consequent effect on '$\twoheadrightarrow$' and '$\leftrightarrow\mkern-10mu\rightarrow$', as follows:

Definition 5.7

We say that one expression e **reduces** to another f in a single step if the following conditions hold. First, e can be represented thus: $e \equiv g[e'/z]$, with the additional property that this z occurs within none of the binding constructs of the language which appear in the expression. We also require that e' reduces to f' according to one of the computation rules, and finally that f is the result of substituting this reduced form into g, that is $f \equiv g[f'/z]$.

This weaker notion of reduction is related to the idea of weak head normal form which we discussed earlier. We have reached a similar notion by changing the definition of reduction itself, rather than the definition of normal form, which we leave alone.

The important result about this system follows.

Theorem 5.8 (Troelstra)

The system TT_0^* is strongly normalizing.

Proof: The proof, given in [Troelstra, 1987], is by means of a translation into another system entirely, for which the strong normalization theorem is a simple generalization of our proof in Section 2.7.

The system in question is that of intuitionistic finite-type arithmetic, which is known as $N - HA^\omega$ in the encyclopaedic [Troelstra, 1973]. The system contains the type structure of products and function spaces built over the type N. The normalization result for the system *without* products is in [Troelstra, 1973], 2.2.30, and it is shown in [Troelstra, 1986] how products may be eliminated from the system.

The translations of the type A and the term a are written A^* and a^*. The crucial property of the translation is that although some of the power of TT_0^* is lost in the translation, reduction is preserved, so that if $a \rightarrow b$ in TT_0^* then $a^* \rightarrow b^*$ in $N - HA^\omega$. A non-terminating sequence in the original system will give rise to one in the target system, contradicting its strong normalization property.

The translation goes as follows (note that '0' is used for the type N in [Troelstra, 1973] – we shall use N):

$$N^* \equiv_{df} N$$

which is the obvious translation. The identity types, which have one element, are represented thus also:

$$(I(A, a, b))^* \equiv_{df} N$$

with its single element being represented by 0. In a similar way we can also represent the booleans, and indeed all the finite types.

In choosing to represent the I types by a constant type N we have removed any dependency of the types on values, so that we say

$$((\forall x : A) . B)^* \equiv_{df} A^* \Rightarrow B^* \qquad ((\exists x : A) . B)^* \equiv_{df} A^* \times B^*$$

representing the quantified types by their non-variable special cases. The elements of these types have images given by

$$(\lambda x . e)^* \equiv_{df} \lambda x . (e^*)$$

$$(a, b)^* \equiv_{df} (a^*, b^*)$$

The only slight trick is in coding the sum type, which is mapped into a product

$$(A \vee B)^* \equiv_{df} N \times A^* \times B^*$$

We represent $(inl\ a)$ by $(0, a, 0_{B*})$ and $(inr\ b)$ by $(1, 0_{A*}, b)$. The values $0_{A*}, 0_{B*}$ are fixed 'dummy' values which are constant zero functions or products of same, depending on the form of the types A, B and so on. The operation of primitive recursion over N is sufficient to implement the *cases* operator over the disjoint sum.

To complete the proof we simply need to check that if $a \rightarrow b$ then $a^* \rightarrow b^*$, which we leave as an exercise for the reader. $\square$

We should remark that the system $N - HA^\omega$ is simpler than TT_0 as it does not contain dependent types. As can be seen from the proof, the reduction properties of the system are preserved by a translation which loses these dependencies, reducing the universal and existential types to function space and product respectively.

There is a problem with the system TT_0^*. The Church–Rosser property fails for it, as can be seen from the following, functional term.

$$\begin{aligned}
(\lambda x . (\lambda y . x)) (II) &\rightarrow (\lambda x . (\lambda y . x)) I \\
&\rightarrow \lambda y . I
\end{aligned}$$

On the other hand if we reduce the outer redex first,

$$(\lambda x . (\lambda y . x)) (II) \rightarrow \lambda y . (II)$$

The final terms of these sequences are normal forms, since no reduction is permitted inside a λ, and distinct, so there is no term to complete the diamond between the two.

This failure is for a term with a functional type, so we might ask whether we can claim a limited result for ground types. It looks as though there should be such a result, but quite how it would be established is an open question. The failure at the functional type is, in fact, still distressing for reasons which will become clearer as we proceed. Without the Church–Rosser property we cannot establish the uniqueness of normal forms, which has in turn the consequence that the relation '$\leftrightarrow$' is decidable: we reduce two terms to their normal forms, and then see whether the two are identical. The system which follows will have these desirable properties.

Exercises

5.15 Show that in the proof of Theorem 5.8 the translation respects reduction, so that if $a \rightarrow b$ then $a^* \rightarrow b^*$.

5.16 Argue that objects in normal form in the system TT_0^* are in weak head normal form in a system with unrestricted β-reduction.

5.5.3   Combinators and the system TT_0^c

In the last section we modified the definition of '$\rightarrow$', disallowing reduction under the λ; here we modify the system giving an entirely different account of functional abstraction and type formation.

All the systems we have looked at so far have shared one aspect: each has used λ-abstraction as a means of forming terms of functional type. Given a term e generally involving the variable x amongst others, we can form the term $\lambda x . e$ with the property that

$$(\lambda x . e)\, a \;\rightarrow\; e[a/x]$$

Instances of this might be the term $\lambda x . (x + y)$, and the term $\lambda x . (II)$, in which the redex (II) is still visible.

An alternative is to make a function or **combinator** definition for the term, saying

$$f\, x \;\rightarrow\; e$$

but there is a problem with doing simply this, exemplified by the addition example we saw above. Our definition would state

$$f\, x \;\rightarrow\; (x + y)$$

which contains an unbound variable on the right-hand side. To make a proper definition of a function we need to include the variable y amongst the arguments, and say

$$f\, y\, x \;\rightarrow\; (x + y)$$

The term $\lambda x . (x + y)$ will now be replaced by the term $(f\, y)$, as it is this application which represents the abstraction over x. In general, a function constant formed in this way needs to have as arguments not only the abstracted variable, but also *all the other variables free in the expression*. These variables can be called the **parameters** of the definition. In order to form the abstraction of interest, these parameters must then be passed to the constant to form the required abstraction. In the case of the addition function above, the abstraction over x is given by the term $(f\, y)$ and not the 'bare' constant f.

For our second example above, $\lambda x . (II)$, the definition is simpler; we just have to write

$$c\, x \;\rightarrow\; (II)$$

and form the term c. Note that in the constant there is no redex. This method of constant definitions *hides* from view the redexes within the bodies of functions, only making them visible when the function is applied to sufficiently many arguments.

Definition 5.9 (combinator abstraction)

Suppose that the derivation of the judgement

$$e : B$$

depends upon the assumptions

$$x_1 : A_1 , \ldots , x_k : A_k , x : A$$

Then we can form a new function constant f which will take arguments of the types $A_1, \ldots, A_k$ (as 'parameters') and A, giving a result of type B. In other words, we can introduce the term

$$f x_1 \ldots x_k$$

of type $(\forall x : A) . B$. The computation rule for the term f is given by

$$f x_1 \ldots x_k x \rightarrow e$$

We can give the type of the new constant f directly:

$$(\forall x_1 : A_1) . \ldots . (\forall x_k : A_k) . (\forall x : A) . B$$

which, when none of the dependencies is exhibited by B, reduces to

$$A_1 \Rightarrow \ldots \Rightarrow A_k \Rightarrow A \Rightarrow B$$

The introduction rule can be written in a familiar form, thus:

$$\frac{\begin{array}{c} [x : A] \\ \vdots \\ e : B \end{array}}{f \ x_1 \ \ldots \ x_k \ : \ (\forall x : A) . B} (\forall I^c)$$

where the undischarged assumptions of the derivation of the hypothesis are $x_1 : A_1, \ldots, x_k : A_k$, and the new constant to be introduced is called f. The computation rule is stated above and the formation and elimination rules for the type $(\forall x : A) . B$ (and therefore for the implication $A \Rightarrow B$) are as before.

Let us consider a simple example. Assuming we have derived that A and B are types then on the basis of the assumptions

$$x : A , y : B$$

we can derive

$$x : A$$

Suppose we wish to form the (informal) expression $\lambda x . \lambda y . x$; we first have to abstract over y. In doing this we produce a *binary* function constant, f, which will take the free variable x as an argument as well as the variable y which is the variable bound by the definition

$$f \, x \, y \; \to \; x$$

and we form the term

$$f \, x \; : \; (B \Rightarrow A)$$

which is based on the assumption of $x : A$. Now we can abstract over x, giving the constant g, with the property

$$g \, x \; \to \; f \, x$$

and the type

$$g \; : \; A \Rightarrow (B \Rightarrow A)$$

(In fact in this case f and g have the same properties, but in general the second and subsequent abstractions are non-trivial.) We can consider the example of the term, which gives a counter-example to the Church–Rosser property for the system TT_0^*,

$$(\lambda x . (\lambda y . x)) \, (II)$$

This is now represented by the term $(g \, (II))$, which reduces thus:

$$g \, (II) \; \to \; f \, (II) \; \to \; f \, I$$

The whole term $f \, (II)$ does not itself form a redex since the function constant f has two formal arguments in its reduction rule, and in this situation it is presented with only one – the Church–Rosser theorem is not violated in this particular case. It is in fact never violated, as we shall see in the next section.

It appears from what we have said so far that no reduction can take place inside an abstraction. In the example of $\lambda x . (II)$ we saw that it was rendered by the constant c with the reduction rule

$$c \, x \; \to \; (II)$$

so that no reduction of the functional term itself, given by c, is possible. The crucial observation to be made here is that the same λ-expression may be represented in *different* ways by constant abstraction. The clue to this is to see the expression II as an *instance of a parameter*, in which case we see the whole expression as an instance of the expression

$$\lambda x \,.\, y$$

with y of the appropriate type. Abstraction here leads to the constant

$$c' \, y \, x \;\longrightarrow\; y$$

with the particular expression represented by

$$c' \, (II)$$

In this representation of $\lambda x \,.\, (II)$ the redex (II) is visible, and so may be reduced, yielding $c' \, I$, which represents $\lambda x \,.\, I$.

Definition 5.10

A proper sub-expression f of a lambda expression e is a **free sub-expression** of e with respect to x if the variable x does not appear free in f. Such an expression is a **maximal free expression** (or *mfe*) with respect to x if it is free with respect to x and moreover is maximal such: it is not a proper sub-expression of an mfe with respect to x.

Definition 5.11 (supercombinator abstraction)

To form the supercombinator abstraction of e over x we first identify the mfes $f_1, \ldots, f_l$ of e with respect to x. We now introduce a new constant g with the reduction rule

$$g \, k_1 \ldots k_l \, x \;\longrightarrow\; e[k_1/f_1, \ldots, k_l/f_l]$$

The abstraction of e over x is given by

$$g \, f_1 \ldots f_l$$

The formal parameters $k_1 \ldots k_l$ replace the maximal free expressions, to which the function constant is then applied.

Now we look at a particular example, the supercombinator abstraction

$$\lambda x \,.\, \lambda y \,.\, ((II)x)$$

First we form the supercombinator abstraction

$$\lambda y \,.\, ((II)x)$$

There is a single mfe in the body, $((II)x)$, so we form the constant c whose reduction rule is

$$c\, k_1\, y \;\rightarrow\; k_1$$

with the expression

$$c\,((II)x)$$

forming the supercombinator abstraction over y. Now we abstract over x. There is a single mfe in the expression above, (II), and we form the constant d with reduction rule

$$d\, k_1\, x \;\rightarrow\; c\,(k_1\, x)$$

the final abstraction being

$$d\,(II)$$

It is important to observe that the redex (II) is visible in this supercombinator abstraction. This is the case in general.

Definition 5.12

The system TT_0^c is defined from TT_0 as follows. All the type forming rules are modified so that types are introduced as constants. The parameters may be chosen to make certain redexes visible and others invisible. The rules of function and universal quantifier introduction are modified as above, as is the rule $(\vee E'')$ which uses the binding operator $vcases_{.,.}$.

Lemma 5.13

If we use the supercombinator abstraction algorithm to give functional abstraction in TT_0^c, then all the redexes which could be reduced in the system TT_0, that is all redexes which are free, can be reduced in TT_0^c.

There is therefore an embedding of the system TT_0 within TT_0^c which preserves the reduction and computation properties of the former. We shall investigate these properties for TT_0^c in the following section, and claim the obvious corollaries for TT_0 there too.

Note that for readability we shall retain the old notation of type forming operations, but we should always recall that it is a shorthand for a notation which is more expressive in allowing a particular expression to be described in different ways, making redexes visible or invisible.

Exercises

5.17 Give the combinator and supercombinator abstractions for the term

$$h \equiv_{df} \lambda a \,.\, \lambda b \,.\, \lambda c \,.\, (abc)$$

5.18 Follow the evaluation behaviour of the expression $h\,(II)\,(II)\,3$ using the two versions of the code compiled in the previous exercise.

5.19 Give a proof of Lemma 5.13.

5.6 TT_0^c: normalization and its corollaries

In this section we shall prove that every term of the type theory TT_0^c has a normal form, a result which can be strengthened to a strong normalization result. The proof is a Tait-style proof, as first seen in Section 2.7, and it is based on Martin-Löf's proof of normalization for his 1975 system, in [Martin-Löf, 1975b]. Its exposition is simpler in omitting the proof information which Martin-Löf's proof carries – this was done originally to make the proof locally formalizable in the (type) theory itself ([Martin-Löf, 1975a], Section 2.1.4) – the approach here is not so formal. The result is proved in such a way that it has a number of important corollaries for the system, including the facts that normal forms are unique, and the Church–Rosser property for reduction holds. Martin-Löf observes that the Church–Rosser property does not have a direct combinatorial proof to his knowledge, this route providing the only means of proof.

As we have seen a number of times up to now, the fact that in type theory the types and the objects are defined by a simultaneous induction means that we have to prove things in a different manner than in the typed λ-calculus. In Section 2.7 we were able first to define stability by induction over the types, and then to show all elements are stable. Here we work by induction over the derivations of closed judgements

$$a \,:\, A \qquad A \text{ is a type}$$

(a closed judgement is one which depends upon no assumptions, and so in particular one for which a and A are closed). The induction defines the following.

- A', a closed normal form of A.
- a', a closed normal form of a so that $a \twoheadrightarrow a'$. a' is also a member of the set $\|A\|$.
- $\|A\|$, the set of **stable** terms of type A, which are members of the type A'. Our proof will show that each closed term is reducible to a stable term, and these terms are clearly seen to be closed and normal.

Because assumptions in open derivations can be discharged, we need also to look at open judgements and derivations. For the open judgement $a : A$, made in the context

$$x_1 : A_1, \ldots, x_n : A_n$$

we also define functions a' and A', depending upon (meta-)variables

$$x_1', \ldots, x_n'$$

which range (respectively) over closed normal terms of type

$$A_1', \ldots, A_n'(x_1', \ldots x_{n-1}')$$

It is important to note that these functions are not defined by terms of the system, in general: they are the operations which assign closed normal forms depending upon the closed normal forms which are their parameters. To choose a concrete example, if $a : N$ depends upon $x : N$, then a' will be a function from numerals to numerals, since numerals are the closed normal forms of natural number type.

We require two conditions of the functions a' and A'.

- First we require that for all closed normal forms

  $$a_1' : A_1', \ldots, a_n' : A_n'$$

  we have the property

  $$a[a_1'/x_1' \ldots, a_n'/x_n'] \twoheadrightarrow a'[a_1'/x_1' \ldots, a_n'/x_n']$$

  (There is a similar definition for A'.)
- We also require that the definitions commute with substitution. Given derivations of

  $$a_1 : A_1 , \ldots , a_n : A_n[a_1/x_1, \ldots, a_{n-1}/x_{n-1}]$$

  we require that

  $$(a(a_1, \ldots, a_n))' \equiv a'(a_1', \ldots, a_n')$$

  with a similar definition for A'. (Recall that we use $\equiv$ to mean 'identical up to change of bound variable'.) In the proof we say that a' is **parametric** if it has this pair of properties.

Theorem 5.14 (normalization for TT_0^c)

Every closed term b of type theory has a normal form b', and moreover if $b \leftrightsquigarrow c$ then $b' \equiv c'$.

Proof: As outlined above we use induction over the length of derivations of judgements. We must go through the constructs of the theory in turn. We must also verify at each step that the normal forms assigned to the two sides of a computability rule such as

$$fst\ (a, b)\ \longrightarrow\ a$$

are equal – this is used in proving that the normal forms given to convertible terms are identical. We shall not cover the cases of function spaces or conjunctions as they are simply special cases of universally and existentially quantified types.

Before we look at the cases in turn, it is worth examining the exact mechanism for type formation in TT_0^c. Suppose we want to form a type such as

$$(\forall x : N)\,.\,I(N, f\ x, 0 + 0)$$

then there are a number of ways of so doing. In the first we simply form a new type constant on this basis, but we may also form a type operator which is parametrized over y, yielding

$$(\forall x : N)\,.\,I(N, f\ x, y)$$

In our particular case we apply this to the (free) expression $0 + 0$, allowing this to be reduced. If an expression is so parametrized, then in the normal form parameters will themselves be reduced to normal form. In the following we assume that types are not parametrized, but this is simply for notational clarity.

Case x a variable: We define x' to be the (informal) variable x'. Obviously this is parametric.

Case $\forall$: The formation rule introduces a new constant, for which we use the shorthand $((\forall x : A)\,.\,B)$. As we said above, we shall assume that the type is not parametrized, and so we define

$$((\forall x : A)\,.\,B)' \equiv_{df} (\forall x : A)\,.\,B$$

We make similar definitions for the other type forming operations, apart from the I types. The set of stable terms of this type, $\|((\forall x : A)\,.\,B)\|$, contains all those closed normal terms c' of type $(\forall x : A)\,.\,B$ with the property that for all closed normal forms (cnfs) a' in A', $(c'\ a')$ reduces to a closed normal form in $B'[a'/x]$.

∀ introduction gives a λ-abstraction, $\lambda x . e$. If we use supercombinator abstraction, we have a new constant f

$$f \, k_1 \ldots k_l \, x \; \rightarrow \; e[k_1/f_1, \ldots, k_l/f_l]$$

where $f_1 \ldots f_l$ are the maximal free expressions of e with respect to x. The abstraction itself is defined to be

$$f \, f_1 \ldots f_l$$

Now, the normal form of f is

$$f' \equiv_{df} f$$

and the normal form for the expression $(f \, f_1 \ldots f_l)$ is given by the clause for ∀ elimination below.

If we restrict ourselves to the simple case of no parameters k_i, then f' is stable since for any cnf a',

$$f' \, a' \; \rightarrow \; e[a'/x] \; \twoheadrightarrow \; e'[a'/x] \equiv (e[a/x])'$$

the equivalence holding by the parametricity property for e, which we assume by induction. For the general case we argue in a similar way, also invoking the case for ∀ elimination below.

∀ elimination gives an application. We define $(f \, a)'$ to be the closed normal form to which $(f' \, a')$ reduces, which exists by induction and the definition of convertibility for the universal type. The computation rule for ∀ states that

$$f \, a \; \rightarrow \; e[a/x]$$

Now observe that

$$(f \, a)' \equiv e'[a'/x] \equiv (e[a/x])'$$

The first equivalence holds by the definition of convertibility for the λ-abstraction and the second by parametricity for e'.

It is not hard to see that the definitions for ∀ introduction and elimination are parametric.

Case ∃ : As for the universal type, we define

$$((\exists x : A) . B)' \equiv_{df} (\exists x : A) . B$$

The stable terms of this type are pairs of stable terms, (a', b'), with $a : A'$

and $b' : B'[a'/x]$. The introduction rules introduce a pair; we say that

$$(a, b)' \equiv_{df} (a', b')$$

The elimination rules $(\exists E_1')$ and $(\exists E_2')$ introduce the projection operators. If we have terms

$$Fst \; p \quad Snd \; p$$

then p', the cnf of p, will be a pair (q', r'). We therefore set

$$(Fst \; p)' \equiv_{df} q' \quad (Snd \; p)' \equiv_{df} r'$$

A pair of parametric terms will be parametric, as will be the components of a parametric pair, so the two constructs preserve parametricity. This will apply similarly in all other cases of non-variable-binding constructs.

Finally we should check that the normal forms of the two sides of the computation rules are identical. The rules state that

$$Fst \; (q, r) \; \rightarrow \; q \quad Snd \; (q, r) \; \rightarrow \; r$$

By the definitions above

$$(Fst \; (q, r))' \equiv (Fst \; (q', r')) \equiv q'$$

as we require. A similar proof shows the result for Snd.

Case $\vee$: We define

$$(A \vee B)' \equiv_{df} (A' \vee B')$$

and take the set of stable elements, $\|(A \vee B)\|$, to be $(\|A\| \vee \|B\|)$.

In introducing an element of a disjunction we inject the object into either the left-hand or the right-hand side. We define

$$(inl \; a)' \equiv_{df} inl \; a' \quad (inr \; b)' \equiv_{df} inr \; b'$$

In eliminating an element by means of $(\vee E')$ we use the *vcases'* construct, $vcases'_{x,y} \; p \; u \; v$. p' will take the form of $(inl \; q')$ or $(inr \; r')$. In the first case, let

$$(cases \; p \; u \; v)' \equiv_{df} u'[q'/x]$$

and in the second

$$(cases \; p \; u \; v)' \equiv_{df} v'[r'/y]$$

The forms defined are stable by the parametricity property, which is also preserved by the definition. It is also easy to check that the definitions respect the computation rules for *vcases*.

Case ⊥ : The cnf of ⊥, ⊥′, is ⊥ itself, and the set of stable terms is the empty set. There are no introduction rules for terms of type ⊥, but there is the elimination rule. We write

$$(abort_A \, p)' \equiv_{df} abort_{A'} \, p'$$

This clearly satisfies parametricity. As there is no introduction rule, there is no computation rule, and therefore no condition to check. In fact this case is a special case of the finite types, which follow.

Case N_n : The cnf of N_n is N_n, and the stable terms are

$$1_n, \ldots, n_n$$

so that it is easy to see that for the introduction rules we have

$$1_n' \equiv_{df} 1_n, \ldots, n_n' \equiv_{df} n_n$$

For the elimination rule we have the n-way case statement

$$cases_n \, e \, c_1 \, \ldots \, c_n$$

The cnf of e will be m_n for some $1 \leq m \leq n$. We define

$$(cases_n \, m_n \, c_1 \, \ldots \, c_n)' \equiv_{df} c_m'$$

Again, parametricity is plain. The computation rule selects the appropriate case according to the value of the object of type N_n – this is respected by the definition.

Note that this also covers the special cases of ⊤, *bool*, and indeed ⊥.

Case N : N' is defined to be N, and the collection of stable terms is defined by (meta-theoretical) induction thus:

- 0 is a stable term;
- $(succ \, n)$ is a stable term if n is.

It should be clear how we define the cnfs for the introduction rules:

$$0' \equiv_{df} 0 \qquad (succ \, n)' \equiv_{df} (succ \, n')$$

In the case of elimination, we have terms of the form

$$prim \, m \, c \, f$$

The cnf m' will be either 0 or $(succ\ n)$ for some n. By an induction over the cnf we say that

$$(prim\ 0\ c\ f)' \equiv_{df} c'$$

$$(prim\ (succ\ n)\ c\ f)' \equiv_{df} y$$

where y is the cnf of the term given by the application

$$f'\ n\ (prim\ n\ c\ f)'$$

which exists by the definition of the cnfs f' of functional type together with the fact that n and $(prim\ n\ c\ f)'$ are themselves cnfs. Parametricity and respecting the computation rule follow.

We treat the type *tree* in an analogous way.

Case I : We say that

$$I(A, a, b)' \equiv_{df} I(A', a', b')$$

and that the set of stable terms consists of $r(a')$. The introduction rule introduces r, and we say

$$(r(a))' \equiv_{df} r(a')$$

In an elimination we form $J(c, d)\ :\ C(a, b, c)$. The only normal form c can have is $r(a')$, and we say

$$(J(r(a'), d))' \equiv_{df} d'$$

Since in the computation rule, we reduce $J(r(a), d)$ to d, we see that this rule is respected by the definition of the cnf. Again, parametricity is preserved.

This exhausts all the cases, and so we have shown all closed normal terms have a closed normal form. We have also verified that for each reduction rule $b \rightarrow c$, the cnfs are equal: $b' \equiv c'$. An induction over the relation '$\leftrightarrow\!\!\!\rightarrow$' is enough to show that if $b \leftrightarrow\!\!\!\rightarrow c$ then $b' \equiv c'$.

This completes the proof of the normalization theorem. $\square$

The normalization result is important in itself, showing that all expressions have a value, and in particular that all expressions of ground type have a printable value, but also the proof itself can yield other results.

Corollary 5.15

There is a model of the system TT_0^c.

Proof: Using the proof of the theorem, types may be modelled by the sets $\|A\|$, and closed terms a by their (closed) normal forms a', which are members of the sets $\|A\|$.   □

Corollary 5.16

If a and b are closed normal terms which are interconvertible then they are identical.

Proof: Martin-Löf attributes this result to Peter Hancock. a and b reduce to a' and b' respectively, but as a and b are normal, $a \equiv a'$ and $b \equiv b'$. Also, we know from the proof that if $a \leftrightarrow b$ then $a' \equiv b'$, which gives the result by the transitivity of '$\equiv$'.   □

Corollary 5.17

Normal forms are unique.

Proof: If a has two normal forms b and c, they are interconvertible, and so by Corollary 5.16 they are identical.   □

Theorem 5.18 (Church–Rosser)

If a and b are closed terms, then $a \leftrightarrow b$ if and only if a and b have a common reduct.

Proof: The 'if' part is obvious. If $a \leftrightarrow b$ then the normal forms a' and b' will be interconvertible, and so identical. This normal form is a common reduct.   □

Theorem 5.19

The normal forms in TT_0^c take the following forms:

Type	Normal form
$A \wedge B$, $(\exists x : A) . B$	(a', b')
$A \Rightarrow B$, $(\forall x : A) . B$	f'
$A \vee B$	$(inl\ a')$, $(inr\ b')$
$I(A, a, b)$	$r(a')$
N_n	m_n
N	0 , $(succ\ n')$
$tree$	$Null$, $Bnode\ n'\ u'\ v'$

where $a', b', \dots$ are themselves closed normal forms.

Proof: The normal forms a' given in the normalization theorem have the forms above. By Corollary 5.17 any normal form will be identical with one of the forms produced in Theorem 5.14.   □

Theorem 5.20

The convertibility relation is decidable – there is a mechanical procedure which decides for arbitrary a, b whether $a \leftrightarrow b$.

Proof: To decide, reduce a and b to their normal forms, as in Theorem 5.14. a and b are convertible if and only if a' and b' are identical.   □

This is a desirable result. We ordained earlier that we would treat interconvertible expressions as denoting the same object, and that we would be able to substitute convertible elements for each other. With this result we are able to decide when two derivations are identical, in that we can check when the terms and types appearing in them can be taken to denote the same object.

Martin-Löf also argues that we can decide whether a given judgement $a : A$ can be derived or not.

Theorem 5.21

Derivability is decidable for TT_0^c.

Proof: Given A and a, we first reduce the type symbol A to normal form, and then we can decide whether it is indeed a normal form of a type. If it is we then reduce the expression a in a similar way, and ask whether a' is a normal form of the type A'.   □

The way that the system is presented, derivability is plainly semi-decidable: a judgement is derivable if and only if there is a derivation of it. It is a surprise that the relation is in fact decidable, but it should not be so. Recall that we derive judgements of the form

a is a proof of the proposition A

or

a is an object of type A

and in many cases these relations are decidable. It is for these properties that we chose to discuss Martin-Löf's earlier *intensional* system [Martin-Löf, 1975b] rather than the more recent extensional [Martin-Löf, 1985]. In the following section we look in more detail at the various equalities of the system, and explain our approach to extensionality in more detail.

Exercises

5.20 Complete the proof sketch for the normalization theorem above.

5.21 What are the terms a' and b' defined in the normalization proof for the terms

$$a \quad \equiv_{df} \quad \lambda y \,.\, x$$
$$b \quad \equiv_{df} \quad \lambda x \,.\, \lambda y \,.\, x$$

5.6.1 Polymorphism and monomorphism

In this short section we comment on another aspect of the system TT_0^c: in the terminology of [Salvesen, 1989b] it is **monomorphic**. Each occurrence of a function such as $\lambda x \,.\, x$ will be a notational shorthand for a function constant of type $A \Rightarrow A$ for a particular type A, with these functions being different for different types A. In formalizing our theory TT_0 we should therefore label all sub-expressions of expressions with their type, so that no typical ambiguity can arise. We shall suppress this information systematically as we continue, but note that it should always be thought of as being present.

An obvious question, raised for example in [Troelstra, 1987], is whether we can re-generate the type information if it is suppressed: in other words whether we can think of the polymorphic system, in which functions such as $\lambda x \,.\, x$ can be given different types at different occurrences, as simply a shorthand for the monomorphic. Salvesen gives a negative answer to this question, showing by a number of counter-examples the differences between the polymorphic and monomorphic theories. For instance, in [Salvesen, 1989b] it is shown that the derivations

$$\cfrac{\cfrac{0:N}{\lambda y_{N \Rightarrow N} \,.\, 0 \,:\, (N \Rightarrow N) \Rightarrow N}(\Rightarrow I) \quad \cfrac{[x:N]}{\lambda x_N \,.\, x \,:\, N \Rightarrow N}(\Rightarrow I)}{(\lambda y_{N \Rightarrow N} \,.\, 0)(\lambda x_N \,.\, x) \,:\, N}(\Rightarrow E)$$

$$\cfrac{\cfrac{0:N}{\lambda y_{B \Rightarrow B} \,.\, 0 \,:\, (B \Rightarrow B) \Rightarrow N}(\Rightarrow I) \quad \cfrac{[x:B]}{\lambda x_B \,.\, x \,:\, B \Rightarrow B}(\Rightarrow I)}{(\lambda y_{B \Rightarrow B} \,.\, 0)\,(\lambda x_B \,.\, x) \,:\, N}(\Rightarrow E)$$

both give rise to derivations of identical conclusions

$$(\lambda y \,.\, 0)\,(\lambda x \,.\, x) \,:\, N$$

and it is simply impossible to derive a single monomorphic type for the variables x and y in this derivation. Building on top of this simple example, there is a derivation in the polymorphic theory which, it is argued, cannot arise from a monomorphic derivation by suppressing type information. More complicated examples show how a Milner-style ([Milner, 1978]) system of *principal* types is not possible.

Finally, we should note that the polymorphism mentioned here is *implicit* polymorphism; we can give definitions which are *explicitly* polymorphic, even in the monomorphic system, by introducing (type) variables which range over the universes U_n.

5.7   Equalities and identities

In the discussion thus far can be found four different notions of equality or identity. We survey their differing roles in this section and, after a discussion of the purpose of these various notions, propose the definition of an extensional equality relation.

5.7.1   Definitional equality

Our first relation is in the meta-language, that is the language in which we discuss the various systems. We say that two terms e and f are identical

$$e \equiv f$$

if they are identical *up to change of bound variable* after all the defined terms, introduced by means of the definitional equality '$\equiv_{df}$', have been expanded out. We simply treat identical expressions as identical – there are no contexts in which we wish to distinguish between two identical expressions.

As an aside, it is worth noting that although it is obvious what this relation is, we have to do some work in a computer implementation to ensure that we can decide exactly when two expressions are identical.

5.7.2   Convertibility

Two expressions are convertible if the computation steps embodied in the computation rules for the system are sufficient to bring them together. Formally we build the relation '$\leftrightarrow$' by taking the reflexive, symmetric transitive and substitutive closure of the relation '$\rightarrow$'. In other words, we ask that, for all expressions $a, b, c, \ldots$ and variables x,

Computation If $a \rightarrow b$ then $a \leftrightarrow b$.

Reflexivity $a \leftrightarrow a$.

Symmetry If $a \leftrightarrow b$ then $b \leftrightarrow a$.

Transitivity If $a \leftrightarrow b$ and $b \leftrightarrow c$ then $a \leftrightarrow c$.

Substitutivity If $a \leftrightarrow b$ and $c \leftrightarrow d$ then $a[c/x] \leftrightarrow b[d/x]$.

We saw in the last section that two terms were convertible if and only if they have the same normal form; this means that the relation of convertibility is decidable.

The definition of convertibility is external to the system – $a \leftrightarrow b$ is intended to embody the fact that the two expressions a and b denote the same object. In the light of the characterization above, we can identify this object as the normal form of the expression, if we wish.

In Section 4.11 we introduced the rules of substitution which allow interconvertible expressions to be substituted for each other in derivations of judgements. This emphasizes the fact that judgements are intended to be about the objects denoted by the expressions, rather than the expressions themselves. We shall come back to this important distinction below.

Because '$a \leftrightarrow b$' is not a proposition of the system, we are unable to build more complex assertions on the basis of it. To do this we turn to our third relation, the identity predicate.

5.7.3   Identity; the I type

As a primitive proposition (or type) forming operator we have the I operation, forming a type thus:

$$\frac{A \; is \; a \; type \quad a:A \quad b:A}{I(A,a,b) \; is \; a \; type}(IF)$$

The type is also written $a =_A b$ or even $a = b$ when no confusion can result. $I(A,a,b)$ is provable, by the object $r(a)$, when $a \leftrightarrow b$, so we can see the type as an internalization of convertibility. On top of the I type we can build more complex assertions, such as

$$(\forall x, y:A) . ((x =_A y) \Rightarrow ((f \; x) =_B (g \; y)))$$

where f and g are functions of type $A \Rightarrow B$. Proof that I is the internalization of '$\leftrightarrow$' is given by the result

Theorem 5.22

For closed a and b, the judgement $I(A,a,b)$ is derivable if and only if $a \leftrightarrow b$.

Proof: Clearly the 'if' part is valid. Suppose that $p:I(A,a,b)$ is derivable; taking normal forms *à la* Theorem 5.14 we have

$$p':I(A',a',b')$$

but for this to be derivable, it must be the case that $a' \equiv b'$, which means that $a \leftrightarrow b$.   □

The expression $x =_A y$ denotes a proposition or type of the system. In order to test for identity in a computation we require a function or operation which returns not a type but rather a value $True$ or $False$ of boolean type.

5.7.4 Equality functions

An equality function is a boolean valued function which can be used in a computation to test for the equality of two objects.

Definition 5.23

An **equality function** (or **equality operation**) over the type A is a term $equal_A$ of type $A \Rightarrow A \Rightarrow bool$ such that the following propositions are valid

$$(\forall a, b : A) . (a =_A b \Rightarrow equal_A\ a\ b =_{bool} True)$$

$$(\forall a, b : A) . (a \neq_A b \Rightarrow equal_A\ a\ b =_{bool} False)$$

Note that one consequence of the definition is that for closed a, b if $a \leftrightarrow b$ then

$$equal_A\ a\ b \leftrightarrow True$$

but on the other hand the non-derivability of $a \leftrightarrow b$ does *not* imply that

$$equal_A\ a\ b \leftrightarrow False$$

Over which types do we have an equality operation? We start our discussion with two definitions.

Definition 5.24

A predicate $P(x_1, \ldots, x_k)$ is **formally decidable** if and only if the following proposition is derivable:

$$(\forall x_1 : A_1) . \ldots . (\forall x_k : A_k) . (P(x_1, \ldots, x_k) \vee \neg P(x_1, \ldots, x_k)) \tag{5.1}$$

Definition 5.25

A predicate $P(x_1, \ldots, x_k)$ is **representable** if and only if for some term r the following propositions are derivable:

$$\begin{aligned} (\forall x_1 : A_1) . \ldots . (\forall x_k : A_k) . \\ (r\ x_1 \ldots x_k =_{bool} True \Rightarrow P(x_1, \ldots, x_k)) \end{aligned} \tag{5.2}$$

$$(\forall x_1 : A_1) . \dots . (\forall x_k : A_k) .$$
$$(r\, x_1 \dots x_k =_{bool} False \Rightarrow \neg P(x_1, \dots, x_k)) \tag{5.3}$$

Theorem 5.26

A predicate is representable if and only if it is formally decidable.

Proof: To prove that a representable predicate is decidable, note first that using the axiom of *bool* elimination we can derive

$$(\forall b : bool) . (b =_{bool} True \lor b =_{bool} False)$$

(a proof of this appears in Section 4.10.1). By means of the propositions 5.2, 5.3, we can derive the formula 5.1, as required.

To prove the converse, we need to take the derivation given by the formula 5.1,

$$d\ :\ (\forall x_1 : A_1) . (\forall x_k : A_k) . (P(x_1, \dots, x_k) \lor \neg P(x_1, \dots, x_k))$$

The term d is a function, which we compose with the function defined over a disjunction which returns *True* over the first disjunct and *False* over the second. This function is given by the term

$$\lambda x . (cases\ x\ (\lambda x . True)\ (\lambda x . False))$$

The resulting function will form a representation of the predicate. □

Corollary 5.27

A type A carries an equality function if and only if the equality over that type is formally decidable.

Proof: The equality function is a representation of equality over the type. The theorem therefore applies the result immediately. □

Theorem 5.28

A ground type A carries an equality function.

Proof: By the previous corollary it is sufficient to show that equality over the type is formally decidable. We can prove by induction over the construction of ground types that equality is decidable for them. Indeed, we have given direct definitions of equality functions in the exercises in the previous chapter. □

Will equality over any other types be decidable? It seems highly unlikely that this is so. Two closed terms of type $N \Rightarrow N$ can be proved equal if and only if they have the same normal form, but there is no way, *internally to type theory*, to compare normal forms. An extensional equality, to which we turn in the following section, has other drawbacks. From an extensional decidability predicate over a functional type we are able to prove a result such as

$$((\forall x:N) . f\ x =_N 0) \vee \neg((\forall x:N) . f\ x =_N 0)$$

which is not in general acceptable to the constructivist, breaking as it does the constraint that properties be finitary.

5.7.5 Characterizing equality

The elimination rules for the various type constructors allow us to derive characterizations of equality for types in terms of their component parts. In Section 4.10.1 we saw that

$$(\forall b:bool) . (b =_{bool} True \vee b =_{bool} False)$$

and we argued that other similar results could also be proved. In particular, we gave as an exercise the proof of

$$(\forall x:N) . (x =_N 0 \vee (\exists y:N) . (x =_N succ\ y))$$

We would also mention the other characterizations

$$(\forall x:A \wedge B) . (\exists y:A) . (\exists z:B) . (x = (y, z))$$

and

$$(\forall x:A \vee B) . ((\exists y:A) . (x = (inl\ y)) \vee (\exists z:B) . (x = (inr\ z)))$$

and for the finite types

$$(\forall x:N_n) . (x = 1_n \vee \ldots \vee x = n_n)$$

with the special case that

$$(\forall x:\top) . x = Triv$$

These results are all proved in similar ways, using the axiom of elimination for the type in question.

Exercises

5.22 Complete the proof of Theorem 5.26 by exhibiting the term r explicitly.

5.23 Give a definition of the equality function over the *tree* type.

5.24 Prove the characterizations of equality for conjunction (product) and disjunction (sum) types given above.

5.8   Different equalities

As we saw in the last section, there are a number of differing notions of equality for a system such as type theory. Here we take a longer view and both ask what the exact purpose of an equality relation is, and propose modified definitions based on the results of these ruminations.

5.8.1   A functional programming perspective

When we first learn arithmetic at school, we write down calculations such as

$$\begin{aligned} (2+3)+(4+5) \;&=\; 5+(4+5) \\ &=\; 5+9 \\ &-\; 14 \end{aligned}$$

which can be thought of as *proofs* that particular equations are true. In a similar way, when we reason about the behaviour of functional programs, we might write chains such as

```
map id (a:x) = id a : map id x
             = a : map id x
             = a : x
```

where `map` is the function which applies its first argument, a function, to every element of its second, a list, and `id` is the identity function.

For the functional programmer (or the primary school child) the interest of such a proof is that two expressions which are not *prima facie* equivalent in fact have the same meaning.

These proofs have in common the fact that they would be considered trivial in the context of type theory; they simply involve showing that two expressions are convertible, and this is formalized *outside* the theory in the convertibility relation.

In order to extend the theory to embrace this kind of equality reasoning, we have radically to modify the theory. The proof objects of the equality (I) types will no longer have the trivial form $r(a)$, but will need to reflect the chains of equalities as above. Also the proposition

$$(2+3)+(4+5) = 14$$

must be distinguished from the proposition

$$14 = 14$$

since the latter is trivial, whilst the former reflects three non-trivial computation steps; proof objects of the two types will be completely different.

The departure here is to consider proofs to be about linguistic expressions (such as $(2 + 2)$) rather than about mathematical objects (such
as the number 4). It would be interesting to see a complete development
of a theory analogous to type theory along the lines proposed here.

5.8.2   Extensional equality

As we said above, type theory addresses itself to objects and their relations, so that we identify expressions which are convertible, allowing their
inter-substitution in any context. This is because we take convertible expressions to have the same meaning, and this is surely correct. What is
more, as a corollary of the normalization theorem we saw that the relation
of convertibility was decidable, so that separately from the system itself
questions of equivalence could be decided.

There remains the question whether convertibility captures *fully* what
it is for two expressions to mean the same thing. For objects of ground type
there is no question that this is so, but for functions the question is more
complex. We saw in Section 4.11.2 that two different ways of adding one to
an arbitrary natural number gave the same value on every argument, and
an **extensional** equality would deem them to be equal. Can we augment
the system to make equality extensional? We shall review a number of
proposals now.

A first attempt might be made to augment the convertibility rules,
with a rule such as η-conversion, which we saw first in Section 2.3:

$$\lambda x . (f\, x) \;\rightarrow\; f$$

if the variable x is not free in the expression f. Given the definition of
convertibility in Chapter 2 which allows conversion under the λ, we can
say that if

$$f\, x \;\leftrightarrow\; g\, x \qquad\qquad\qquad (5.4)$$

then by two η-conversions we have

$$f \;\leftrightarrow\; \lambda x . (f\, x) \;\leftrightarrow\; \lambda x . (g\, x) \;\leftrightarrow\; g$$

so it appears that we have an extensional convertibility.

This is not the case, however, as the equivalence 5.4 is a weak one, based as it is on convertibility between two expressions involving an arbitrary value represented by the variable x. In our proof of the equivalence of the two functions adding one, we inferred

$$(\forall x : N) . f\, x = g\, x$$

by induction, a *proof-theoretic* technique based on a case analysis over the variable x, rather than simply a rewriting *à la* property 5.4. It appears then that we cannot capture a fully extensional equality as a conversion relation. Martin-Löf proposes a rule in his 1979 system [Martin-Löf, 1985] which contains a fully extensional conversion, by means of the rule

$$\frac{c : I(A, a, b)}{a \leftrightarrow b} (IE_{ext})$$

This addition has unfortunate consequences for the general properties of the system: convertibility is undecidable, the system fails to be strongly normalizing and so on, and it is for these reasons that we have chosen to adopt Martin-Löf's earlier system as the basis of ours here. It is no surprise that these are the consequences of the rule (IE_{ext}), since it makes the relation of conversion have a proof-theoretic link which it fails to have in the earlier system.

Before we leave the topic of convertibility, it is worth referring back to our commments of Section 2.11 on the superfluity of the (so-called) conversion rules like η-reduction. In particular the remark that these rules are not needed to reduce closed terms of ground type to normal form still applies in the context of TT_0.

Is there an alternative to Martin-Löf's method of including an extensional equality in the system?

Turner has proposed in the unpublished [Turner, 1989] that an extensional I type can be defined. He argues that the type

$$I(N \Rightarrow N, f, g)$$

can be inhabited by terms other than r – a proof of the equality of all the values of the function, in other words an object p of type

$$(\forall n : N) . (f\, n = g\, n)$$

can be injected into the type also, giving

$$ext\, p \; : \; I(N \Rightarrow N, f, g)$$

If we add new canonical elements to a type we require new rules of elimination and computation if the classes of canonical objects of other types are not to be enlarged with spurious members. Some rules to accomplish this are to be found in [Turner, 1989], and it appears that a system in which no spurious canonical forms are introduced could be built on the basis of the system there. The complete presentation might involve a theory of structured equality objects, so that proofs of equality of pairs would be pairs of equality proofs, equalities between functions would be functions proving the equality of all results, and so on.

A variant of this approach suggests itself, and that is to introduce an element of the equality thus

$$\frac{p:(\forall x:A)\,.\,(f\,x =_B g\,x)}{r\,:\,I(A \Rightarrow B, f, g)}(II')$$

but this means that the proof-theoretic information contained in the object p is lost. This happens in the standard introduction rule, yet in that case the information lost is convertibility information, which can be recovered by the decision procedure for conversion. If we are to adhere to the principle of complete presentation, then we should reject this course; if not, this presents a way to proceed.

5.8.3   Defining extensional equality in TT_0

The option we explore here is to define explicitly the relation of extensional equality within the theory TT_0 whose equality is intensional. We retain the decidability of '$\leftrightarrow$', as well as adhering to the principle of complete presentation.

Definition 5.29

By induction over the construction of the type A we can define the operator $\simeq_A$ embodying **extensional equality** over A. Formally, we have the derived rule

$$\frac{A\ is\ a\ type \quad a:A \quad b:A}{(a \simeq_A b)\ is\ a\ type}(EEF)$$

For base types N, N_n, $bool$, $I(T, n, m)$ and so on we define

$$a \simeq_A b \equiv_{df} I(A, a, b)$$

Omitting the type subscripts from now on, for function types we say

$$f \simeq g \equiv_{df} (\forall x, y:A)\,.\,((x \simeq y) \Rightarrow (f\,x \simeq g\,y))$$

For product types,

$$u \simeq v \equiv_{df} (fst\,u \simeq fst\,v) \wedge (snd\,u \simeq snd\,v)$$

and similarly for disjunctions.

For f and g of the universally quantified type

$$(\forall x : A) . B$$

the proposition

$$(\forall x, y : A) . ((x \simeq y) \Rightarrow (f\,x \simeq g\,y))$$

is only well formed if the type family B is itself extensional, that is if $x \simeq x'$ then $B \leftrightarrow B[x'/x]$.

The relation '$\simeq$' is a **partial equivalence relation**, in that

Lemma 5.30

The relation '$\simeq_A$' has the following properties

Symmetry If $f \simeq g$ is derivable, then so is $g \simeq f$.

Transitivity If $f \simeq g$ and $g \simeq h$ are derivable, then so is $f \simeq h$.

Semi-reflexivity If $f \simeq g$ is derivable, then so is $f \simeq f$.

Proof: The proof is by induction over construction of the type A. The interesting case is that of the function type $B \Rightarrow C$. We look at the various properties in turn. First suppose that we have $f \simeq g$, that is

$$(\forall x, y : B) . ((x \simeq y) \Rightarrow (f\,x \simeq g\,y))$$

by the symmetry of '$\simeq$' for the type C we have

$$(\forall x, y : B) . ((x \simeq y) \Rightarrow (g\,y \simeq f\,x))$$

as required. Now suppose that we have $f \simeq g$ and $g \simeq h$, and suppose that $x \simeq_B y$. By the first proposition, we have

$$f\,x \simeq g\,y$$

Since $x \simeq y$, we have by symmetry and semi-reflexivity for B that $y \simeq y$, so by $g \simeq h$ we can derive

$$g\,y \simeq h\,y$$

and finally by transitivity for $\simeq$ over C we have

$$f\,x \simeq h\,y$$

which establishes transitivity. Semi-reflexivity is a consequence of symmetry and transitivity.   □

Definition 5.31

If a is an open term with free variables $x_1, \ldots, x_k$ then its **closure** is the term $\lambda x_1, \ldots, x_k . a$.

Definition 5.32

We call a closed term a of type A **extensional** if $a \simeq_A a$. If a is open, we call it extensional if its closure is.

Not all terms are extensional. Take the function

$$h \equiv_{df} \lambda x . (x, r(x)) \; : \; (A \Rightarrow (\exists x : A) . I(A, x, x))$$

Suppose that we take the type A to be $N \Rightarrow N$, and choose two functions f and g of this type so that $f \simeq g$ yet $f \not\twoheadrightarrow g$. The two addition functions of Section 4.11.2 will do for f and g. Now,

$$h f \twoheadrightarrow (f, r(f))$$

$$h g \twoheadrightarrow (g, r(g))$$

These two values are not extensionally equal, as the objects $r(f)$ and $r(g)$ are of different types, since the family $I(A, x, x)$ is not extensional.

We could leave the development here, with a definition of what it is for two terms to be extensionally equal. Unfortunately, what we have developed thus far is not very useful – we have no way of using the defined relation directly, and instead we must expand out its definition to use it. The equality relation $I(A, a, b)$ is characterized by its elimination rule, stating that a and b may be substituted for each other in any context. '$\simeq$' is a weaker relation than identity, and so we cannot expect to substitute extensionally equal terms for each other in *all* contexts. Instead, we prove that substitution can be performed safely in a large class of contexts.

Definition 5.33

We call a proposition P **extensional** if it satisfies the following. Any sub-term of P of the form $I(A, a, b)$ must satisfy

- A is a ground type, and
- the terms a and b are extensional.

Theorem 5.34

If P is extensional, $f \simeq g$ and we can derive $p : P[f/x]$ then we can find p' so that $p' : P[g/x]$ is derivable.

Proof: We prove this result by induction over the derivation p.   □

We would also **conjecture** that any closed term of an extensional type is itself extensional. This would include in particular all terms of types which do not involve the identity types $I(A, a, b)$, which would include all the types of a traditional functional programming language such as Miranda. We can prove the more limited theorem which follows.

Theorem 5.35

The class of extensional terms is closed under the operations of pairing, projection, injection (into sum types), case analysis, primitive recursion over natural numbers and *trees*, abstraction, application, function composition and so on.

Proof: The proof is simply a matter of checking the definitions in each case.   □

To summarize this section, we have shown that within an intensional system of type theory (with pleasant meta-mathematical properties) we can build an identity relation which is extensional. Moreover, we can prove that we can substitute extensionally equal terms for each other in a wide variety of contexts. This approach seems to combine the advantages of both the extensional and intensional theories, without anything being sacrificed.

Exercise

5.25 Complete the proofs of Theorems 5.34 and 5.35.

5.9 Universes

The system TT_0 makes a rigid distinction between types, such as N, $A \wedge B$ and $I(A, a, b)$, and the objects which inhabit them, 0, (a, b), $r(a)$ and so on. There are situations in which this distinction can usefully be blurred.

- We may wish to make an object depend upon a type parameter – this is often called type polymorphism.

- We might want to assert the existence of a type with certain properties – this is the content of an *abstract type* definition.

- Some functions are most naturally defined over the collection of all objects of all types.

For these and other reasons, we can see the merit of introducing a type T of all types, and this was indeed what Martin-Löf did in an early version [Martin-Löf, 1971] of his type theory. It was later shown by Girard [Girard, 1972] that this addition made the logic of type theory inconsistent, in the sense that every proposition became provable. Girard's proof is based on the set-theoretic Burali-Forti paradox, which proves the inconsistency of the set of all well-founded sets, which is a member of itself, and therefore not well founded.

A common thread to paradoxes such as this and Russell's is the *impredicativity* of the objects defined: in describing what the members of T are, we have to mention T itself. This is one point at which the logical and programming interpretations of type theory diverge; the logical inconsistency of the system means in programming terms that every type has a member. This inhabitation is something we are used to in languages such as Miranda, since every type contains an undefined element, identified by the semantics with the bottom element of a domain. Of course, also, the self-reference in the definition of T is simply that of general recursion, and inconsistency becomes partiality. For detailed analysis of the computational behaviour of the paradox, see [Meyer and Reinhold, 1986] and Howe's analysis in [Howe, 1988, Chapter 4] of the paradox in the related system Nuprl.

If it is our aim to maintain a coherent logical interpretation of the system, T must be avoided. Instead of introducing a single universe, we introduce a hierarchy of universes, U_n for $n = 0, 1, 2, \ldots$. The types given by the formation rules of TT_0 are in U_0; hence the subscript of TT_0. If we then add U_0 as a type, using the same formation rules we form types in U_1, and so on, through the hierarchy.

Formally, we obtain the system TT by modifying the formation rules as follows. Occurrences of the judgements *A is a type* are replaced by

$$A : U_n$$

and the rule

$$\frac{A_1 \text{ is a type} \ \cdots \ A_k \text{ is a type}}{T(A_1, \ldots, A_k) \text{ is a type}}(TF)$$

is replaced by

$$\frac{A_1 : U_{n_1} \ \cdots \ A_k : U_{n_k}}{T(A_1, \ldots, A_k) \ : \ U_{max(n_1, \ldots, n_k)}}(TF)$$

In other rules which have premises of the form *A is a type*, those premises are replaced by $A : U_n$. We also add the following formation rule:

Formation rule for U

$$\frac{}{U_n \ : \ U_{n+1}}(UF)$$

The system of universes is not cumulative; each type is a member of exactly one universe, U_k say, rather than being a member of all the universes

$U_k, U_{k+1}, \ldots$.

We end this introduction by remarking that the results of Section 5.6 carry over to TT with no modification, so that

Theorem 5.36

TT is strongly normalizing, has the Church–Rosser property, and both convertibility and the derivability of judgements of the form $a : A$ are decidable.

Proof: Exactly as Section 5.6. □

5.9.1   Type families

Because the universes are types just like any other, we can form new objects of these types. For example, we have

$$\frac{x : bool \quad \bot : U_0 \quad \top : U_0}{if\ x\ then\ \bot\ else\ \top\ :\ U_0}(bool\ E)$$

The term $B \equiv_{df} (\ if\ x\ then\ \bot\ else\ \top\ )$ is a type family over the variable $x : bool$, with the property that

$$B(True) \quad \rightarrow \quad \bot$$
$$B(False) \quad \rightarrow \quad \top$$

This gives a more direct definition of type family than that described in Section 4.10.3.

Now we prove a theorem using the universe U_0 to give a result we cannot prove in TT_0.

Theorem 5.37

In TT we can derive $\neg(True =_{bool} False)$.

Proof: Suppose that we have $p : True =_{bool} False$. Applying the function

$$\lambda x\ .\ (\ if\ x\ then\ \bot\ else\ \top\ )$$

to the two sides, and reducing, we find

$$p' : \bot =_{U_0} \top$$

If we then perform the substitution of $\bot$ for $\top$ in

$$Triv\ :\ \top$$

we have the result

$$Triv \; : \; \bot$$

Discharging the original assumption, we have an element of

$$\neg(True =_{bool} False)$$

which we assumed as an axiom in TT_0. $\qquad\qquad\qquad\qquad\qquad\qquad$ □

Smith gives a formal proof that the result cannot be derived in (an extension of) TT_0 in his paper [Smith, 1987].

5.9.2 Quantifying over universes

Many functions can be derived for arbitrary types; among the examples are all the functions of Section 4.5. We can rewrite the derivation of the identity function thus

$$\cfrac{\cfrac{\cfrac{\cfrac{\overline{U_0 \; : \; U_1}(UF)}{[A \; : \; U_0]^2}(AS)}{[x:A]^1}(AS)}{\lambda x_A . x \; : \; (A \Rightarrow A)}(\Rightarrow I)_1}{\lambda A_{U_0} . \lambda x_A . x \; : \; (\forall A{:}U_0).(A \Rightarrow A)}(\forall I)_2$$

The informal assumption that A *is a type* had been derived is replaced here by the formal assumption $A \; : \; U_0$, which is subsequently discharged. The function defined will give the identity function over any type A in U_0 when applied to that type. For example,

$$(\lambda A_{U_0} . \lambda x_A . x) \, N \;\; \rightarrow \;\; \lambda x_N . x \; : \; (N \Rightarrow N)$$

This gives a form of polymorphism; the identity function is thus defined for all 'small' types (as we call the members of U_0) uniformly.

If we are given an abstract type, this usually means that we are given a type which we can access only through certain operations over that type, rather than all the operations available over the type.

Consider a type such as

$$(\exists A{:}U_0).P(A)$$

What do objects of this type look like? They are pairs (A, p) of objects,

$$A{:}U_0 \quad \text{and} \quad p{:}P(A)$$

A is a (small) type, and p is a proof that it has the property $P(A)$. Suppose we have defined $P(A)$ to be

$$(A \Rightarrow A) \wedge (A \Rightarrow A)$$

then an object of the existential type will be a type A together with

$$p : (A \Rightarrow A) \wedge (A \Rightarrow A)$$

that is a pair of functions from A to itself. An object of this type is equivalent to an implementation of an abstract type, with signature (written in Miranda notation)

```
abstype A
    with f1 :: A -> A
         f2 :: A -> A
```

where f1 and f2 are the first and second projections of p, of course.

We shall have more to say about quantified types in the following chapter, where we look at a series of examples.

5.9.3 Closure axioms

The usual way that we characterize the members of a type is by a pair of rules: the introduction rule explains what objects are permitted to be elements of the type, and the elimination rule (together with the computation rule) characterizes these elements as the *only* elements of the type. We could call the latter rules the **closure** axioms for the type. It is the closure axioms for a type A which allow us to prove properties for all elements of A, and to define functions by recursion over A.

The rules we have given for universes correspond to introduction rules; if we wish to define functions by recursion over the universe we need a closure axiom to that effect. In Martin-Löf's treatment of the system, these axioms have been omitted deliberately; for philosophical reasons he has chosen to make the universes open ended, so that other type forming operations can be added to the system without violating the closure axioms.

The closure axioms permit us to define polymorphic functions which fail to be parametric [Strachey, 1967]. We could, for instance, define a function which was the identity function on all types but N, and which was the successor function $\lambda n . (succ\ n)$ on N. This would have the type

$$(\forall A : U_0) . (A \Rightarrow A)$$

just as did the polymorphic identity function, which had a parametric definition – we did not perform any analysis on the type variable A in the definition of the identity function, it was simply a *parameter*.

5.9.4   Extensions

Why do we stop with a chain of universes $U_0, U_1, \ldots$, when there are natural functions which cannot be defined in the system? The obvious one which springs to mind is

$$(\lambda n : N) . U_n$$

which clearly inhabits none of the U_n. To give this a type we need to add the first **transfinite** universe U_ω, which is itself a member of $U_{\omega+1}$, and so we can iterate through the constructive ordinals. Whether this extension is interesting, either proof theoretically or from the point of view of programming, is open to question, but the interested reader may wish to consult [Andrews, 1965] for a similar transfinite theory.

Another possible direction is to distinguish between the types which are sets, such as N and *tree*, and the propositions, and to try to extend the type theory with a type of propositions. This has itself been shown to be inconsistent in [Jacobs, 1989].

If one is prepared to limit the type forming operations, then systems with a type of types can be built consistently. The work of Girard on system F [Girard, 1980] and of Huet and Coquand [Coquand and Huet, 1985] testifies to this. More details of these systems are given in Section 9.1.5.

5.10   Well-founded types

When we first introduced algebraic types in the previous chapter, Section 4.9, we described what we meant by an algebraic type, and then introduced the rules for a particular type, *tree*, of binary trees. It is not difficult to see how we might form the rules for a type of lists along similar lines; we do that in a moment.

There is a general framework into which we can fit the types defined in this way. By an analysis of the *tree* type we find the rules for a general well-founded type, and this we do in the section which follows.

5.10.1   Lists

A list is either empty, [ ], or can be thought of as having a first element, or **head**, a and a remainder, or **tail**, x. The list with head a and tail x is written

$$(a :: x)$$

The double colon '::' is often pronounced 'cons'. Definitions by recursion take the form

$$sum\,[\,] \quad \equiv_{df} \quad 0$$
$$sum\,(a :: x) \quad \equiv_{df} \quad a + (sum\,x)$$

where in this case we look at a function defined over a numerical list. (Note that we have used the *reverse* convention to Miranda, in which a single colon denotes the 'cons' operator, and the double colon is used for 'has the type' – the convention is that of the SML language, in fact.) Elements of lists can have any type, as long as we keep the lists **homogeneous** – all the elements of any particular list should be of the same type, otherwise many definitions, such as those of the standard functions *map*, *filter* and *foldr* simply cannot be stated. Lists form one of the standard data types in functional programming; definitions of these standard functions and many other examples can be found in the textbooks [Bird and Wadler, 1988] and [Reade, 1989].

With this introduction, we should now be able to understand the rules, in which we write $[A]$ for the type of lists with elements of type A.

Formation rule for *list*

$$\frac{A \text{ is a type}}{[A] \text{ is a type}}(list\ F)$$

Introduction rules for *list*

$$\frac{}{[\,] \,:\, [A]}(list\ I_1) \qquad \frac{a:A \quad l:[A]}{(a :: l) \,:\, [A]}(list\ I_2)$$

Elimination rule for *list*

$$\frac{\begin{array}{l} l:[A] \\ s:C[\,[\,]\,/x] \\ f:(\forall a:A)\,.\,(\forall l:[A])\,.\,(C[l/x] \Rightarrow C[(a :: l)/x]) \end{array}}{lrec\ l\ s\ f \,:\, C[l/x]}(list\ E)$$

Computation rules for *list*

$$lrec\,[\,]\,s\,f \quad \rightarrow \quad s$$
$$lrec\,(a :: l)\,s\,f \quad \rightarrow \quad f\,a\,l\,(lrec\,l\,s\,f)$$

'::' is taken to be right associative, and the shorthand $[a_1, \ldots a_n]$ will be used for the list $(a_1 :: \ldots :: a_n :: [\,])$. We call functions defined using the elimination rule *primitive recursive*.

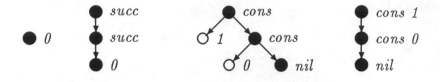

Figure 5.1   Natural numbers and lists.

Exercises

5.26 Using *lrec* define the function *map* which takes as arguments a function f and a list $[a_1, \ldots a_n]$, and returns the list $[f\ a_1, \ldots f\ a_n]$.

5.27 Define the function *segs* of type $[A] \Rightarrow [[A]]$ with the property that

$$segs\ [n_1, \ldots, n_m] \equiv_{df} [[\ ]\ ,\ [n_1]\ ,\ [n_1, n_2]\ ,\ \ldots\ ,\ [n_1, \ldots, n_m]]$$

5.28 Using *segs* or otherwise, define the function *sums* of type $[N] \Rightarrow [N]$ with the property that

$$sums\ [n_1, \ldots, n_m] \equiv_{df} [0\ ,\ n_1\ ,\ n_1 + n_2\ ,\ \ldots\ ,\ n_1 + \cdots + n_m]$$

What is a suitable value for the empty list $[\ ]$?

5.29 Formulate what it means for one list to be a sublist of another, and define the function

$$sublists\ :\ [A] \Rightarrow [[A]]$$

which returns the list of all sublists of a list. How would you remove duplicate entries from the list if necessary?

5.30 How is the equality operation on the list type $[A]$ defined from the equality operation on A?

5.10.2   The general case – the W type

In general, we can think of the elements of *any* algebraic type as trees. In Figure 5.1 we see trees representing the natural numbers 0 and 2, that is *succ* (*succ* 0), and the list $[1, 0]$, shown in two slightly different forms. In the first, we show the numerical components as pointed to by a node; in the second we show them as components of the *cons* node itself. Figure 5.2 shows an example from our type *tree* of binary numeric trees.

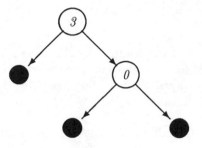

Figure 5.2   A binary tree of type *tree*.

The general form of these types is that each **node** is built from a certain collection of **predecessors** of the same type. Considering our type *tree*, a *Null* node, illustrated by a black disc, has no predecessors, whereas a node of sort *Bnode* 0, *Bnode* 1,..., shown in white, has two predecessors. (The terminology *immediate* predecessor is sometimes used for our 'predecessor'.)

For a general algebraic type we will have a *type A* of **sorts** of node. In the case of trees this type is best thought of as a *sum* type,

$$A \equiv_{df} (\top \vee N)$$

where $\top$ is the one-element type, for the *Null* node, and the other summand, N, is for the *Bnode* nodes, which carry numbers. To make the subsequent account more readable, we rename the injection functions *nu* and *bnode*, and use *null* for the application (*nu Triv*). This means that we can think of the elements of A as *null* together with (*bnode n*) for natural numbers n.

Different kinds of nodes have different numbers of predecessors. For a particular kind of node $a:A$ we specify what form the predecessors of the node take by supplying a type $B(a)$, which we can think of as the type of **names of predecessor places**.

For a particular node of that sort we specify the collection of predecessors of the node by a function from $B(a)$ to the type in question.

Considering the particular case of the type *tree*, since the *Null* node has no predecessors, we say

$$B(null) \equiv_{df} \bot$$

and for the binary nodes ($Bnode\, n$), we have two predecessors, so we define

$$B(bnode\, n) \equiv_{df} N_2$$

We could make N_2 more readable by replacing $1_2, 2_2$ by *Left* and *Right*, as we would expect for the names of the two predecessor places of the *Bnode*. To define the family $B(x)$ in this way requires the use of the universe U_0; without using a universe we can say

$$B(x) \equiv_{df} ((isnull\, x = True) \wedge \perp) \vee ((isnull\, x = False) \wedge N_2)$$

where the function *isnull* of type $A \Rightarrow bool$ is defined thus:

$$isnull\, x \equiv_{df} (cases\, x\, \lambda y . True\, \lambda z . False)$$

The type we build is determined by the class of sorts of node, A, and the family determining the nature of the set of predecessors of each sort of node, $B(x)$. The type thus constructed is called $(W\, x : A) . B(x)$, the W being used as a reminder that the type is well founded.

Formation rule for W

$$[x\ :\ A]$$
$$\vdots$$
$$\frac{A\ is\ a\ type \quad B(x)\ is\ a\ type}{(W\, x : A) . B(x)\ is\ a\ type}(WF)$$

As far as our type *tree* is concerned, it is clear that we have satisfied the hypotheses of the rule with our definitions of A and $B(x)$.

A general node of type $(W\, x : A) . B(x)$ can be built from a node sort, $a : A$, and a collection of predecessors

$$f\ :\ B(a) \Rightarrow (W\, x : A) . B(x)$$

The node given by f and a is called

$$node\, a\, f\ :\ (W\, x : A) . B(x)$$

This is formalized in the introduction rule.

Introduction rule for W

$$\frac{a\ :\ A \quad f\ :\ (B(a) \Rightarrow (W\, x : A) . B(x))}{node\, a\, f\ :\ (W\, x : A) . B(x)}(WI)$$

Going back to our example *tree* type, how do we form nodes? Choose first the element *null* of A. The set of predecessor names is $B(null)$, which is the empty type, $\perp$. For any type T there is a function from the type $\perp$ to T, given by the abort construct,

$$efun \equiv_{df} \lambda x \,.\, abort_T \; x$$

Taking T to be $(W \, x : A) \,.\, B(x)$ itself, we produce one element of the W type:

$$node \; null \; efun$$

This is the representative of the node $Null$, which has no predecessors, and the argument above constitutes an informal derivation of the rule $(tree I_1)$. How can we derive the other tree introduction rule from (WI)? The hypotheses of $(tree I_2)$ are that $n : N$, $u : tree$ and $v : tree$. The term

$$f_{u,v} \equiv_{df} \lambda x \,.\, (cases_2 \; x \; u \; v)$$

is of type $(N_2 \Rightarrow tree)$, and $N_2 \equiv B(bnode \; n)$, which means that this is a predecessor function for a $(bnode \; n)$ node. Formally, (WI) allows the formation of

$$node \; (bnode \; n) \; f_{u,v}$$

which represents the node $(Bnode \; n \; u \; v)$. Using the notation $Null$ for the term $(node \; null \; efun)$, the node

$$node \; (bnode \; 3) \; f_{Null,g}$$

where $g \equiv (node \; (bnode \; 0) \; f_{Null,Null})$, represents the tree

$$Bnode \; 3 \; Null \; (Bnode \; 0 \; Null \; Null)$$

as illustrated in Figure 5.2.

We eliminate a node by the operator which performs recursion or induction, which we shall call Rec. The idea of an induction is to prove

$$C(node \; a \; f)$$

on the basis of proofs of

$$C(p)$$

for all the predecessors p of the node. Remember that the predecessors are given by the values of the function f over the type $B(a)$, so that this collection of proofs will have the form

$$pr \; : \; (\forall y : B(a)) \,.\, C(f \; y)$$

The object which performs the proof transformation, that is the induction step of the proof, for a particular node $(node\ a\ f)$ is therefore an object $tr_{a,f}$ of type

$$tr_{a,f}\ :\ ((\forall y : B(a)).C(f\ y)) \Rightarrow C(node\ a\ f)$$

Finally, this should be parametrized over f and a, giving our general *proof transformer* or *induction step* as an object of type

$$(\forall a : A)(\forall f : (B(a) \Rightarrow (W\ x : A)\,.\,B(x)))$$
$$((\forall y : B(a))C(f\ y) \Rightarrow C(node\ a\ f))$$

which we shall abbreviate $Ind(A, B, C)$. Now we can state our rule.

Elimination rule for W

$$\frac{w : (W\ x : A)\,.\,B(x) \quad R : Ind(A, B, C)}{(Rec\ w\ R)\ :\ C(w)}(WE)$$

Note that on the basis of this, if we discharge the first assumption, we have

$$\lambda w.(Rec\ w\ R)\ :\ (\forall w : ((W\ x : A)\,.\,B(x)))\,.\,C(w)$$

showing that the rule (WE) defines a function over the well-founded type $(W\ x : A)\,.\,B(x)$ by induction. What is the computation rule for these objects? The value at a node $(node\ a\ f)$ is computed from the values at the predecessors, and those predecessors themselves, using the R operator.

Computation rule for W

$$Rec\,(node\ a\ f)\,R\ \rightarrow\ R\ a\ f\,(\lambda x\,.\,Rec\,(f\ x)\,R)$$

Observe that as x ranges over $B(a)$, $(f\ x)$ ranges over the predecessors of $node\ a\ f$, so that

$$\lambda x\,.\,Rec\,(f\ x)\,R$$

ranges over the values of the recursive function on the predecessors of the node $node\ a\ f$. Also the parameter f specifies the predecessors themselves.

Consider the type *tree* again. How do the elimination and computation rules for the W type generalize those for *tree*? In the case of *tree*, recall that

$$
\begin{aligned}
A &\equiv_{df} (\top \vee N) \\
B(null) &\equiv_{df} \bot \\
B(bnode\ n) &\equiv_{df} N_2
\end{aligned}
$$

How can we define an operator R

$$R : (\forall a : A)(\forall f : (B(a) \Rightarrow (W\ x : A)\,.\,B(x)))$$
$$((\forall y : B(a))C(f\ y) \Rightarrow C(node\ a\ f))$$

for these types? We need to define $R(a)$ for each a in A. Starting with *null*, we have to define an object of type

$$(\forall f : (\bot \Rightarrow (W\ x : A)\,.\,B(x)))((\forall y : \bot)C(f\ y) \Rightarrow C(node\ a\ f))$$

What are the functions f of type $(\bot \Rightarrow (W\ x : A)\,.\,B(x))$? If we adopt an *extensional* approach there is but one, the function *efun*, since the domain of the function is the empty type. In that case we have to define an object of type

$$((\forall y : \bot)C(f\ y) \Rightarrow C(Null))$$

(where we replace $(node\ null\ efun)$ with $Null$). What is the domain type here? Again it is easy to argue that there is a single function in the dependent type $(\forall y : \bot)C(f\ y)$, so that the function type above collapses to

$$C(Null)$$

In other words, our starting value for the induction is a single value c of type $C(Null)$, just as it is in the rule $(treeE)$. A similar argument, with fewer simplifications, allows us to see that the case of the nodes

$$(Bnode\ n\ u\ v)$$

is also covered by R applied to the elements $(bnode\ n)$ – we leave this as an exercise for the reader.

Finally, we look at the computation rule in the case of the $Null$ node. We assume that R is determined for *tree* as outlined above, and note that the general rule is

$$Rec\,(node\ a\ f)\,R \;\to\; R\ a\ f\ (\lambda x\,.\,Rec\,(f\ x)\ R)$$

In the case of $(node\ null\ efun)$, it becomes

$$Rec\,Null\,R \;\to\; R\ null\ efun\ (\lambda x\,.\,Rec\,(efun\ x)\ R)$$

but recalling the definition above, the right-hand side is simply the value $c : C(null)$. A similar argument applies in the $Bnode$ case.

It is worth observing that we needed to move to an extensional equality between functions to prove the uniqueness of the function from an empty domain. If it is wished to remain in an intensional system, the alternative seems to be to introduce the rules explicitly, type by type. Another alternative is to introduce a type of *finite* functions, which can be treated extensionally in an intensional system; this would only work for a limited class of W types, in which A is finite and $B(a)$ is finite for each $a:A$.

Making the argument above more formal, we can say that we have established that certain types are extensionally isomorphic, where this is defined thus.

Definition 5.38

Two types A and B are **extensionally isomorphic** if there are two functions

$$f:A \Rightarrow B \qquad g:B \Rightarrow A$$

so that the following proposition is derivable.

$$(\forall x:A).(g(f\ x) \simeq_A x) \wedge (\forall y:B).(f(g\ y) \simeq_B y)$$

The two functions f, g form an isomorphism pair, up to extensional equality.

We can simplify some of the notation above when we are looking at the recursive definitions of functions of non-dependent type – in these cases C will not be parametrized. Note that in proofs, though, it is crucial that C *is* parametrized, as otherwise we are proving the same proposition repeatedly, which is safe but not very useful.

As we remarked earlier, these recursions and inductions are made much more readable by the introduction of *names*. This is clearly a feature which has to be added to the W types as 'syntactic sugar' if they are to be used in a real programming environment.

Definition 5.39

We call the system of TT with the full rules for W TT^+, retaining the name TT for the system containing just *tree* or equivalently all W types for which all the predecessor types $B(a)$ are finite.

Theorem 5.40

TT^+ is strongly normalizing, has the Church–Rosser property, and both convertibility and the derivability of judgements of the form $a:A$ are decidable.

Proof: Exactly as Section 5.6.   □

5.10.3   Algebraic types in Miranda

Our method here has been adopted for two reasons. It provides a simple way of writing down objects such as trees without our having to introduce *names* for constructors, which is what we do in (for example) Miranda. We also see that it provides a non-trivial generalization of finite 'algebraic' types. There was no stipulation that the sets of predecessor places, $B(a)$, need be finite, and so we can have *infinitely branching* trees as objects of our language. This allows us to define, for example, the countable ordinal numbers. In fact, we can do a similar thing in Miranda, thus:

```
ordinal ::= Zero |
            Succ ordinal |
            Limit (nat -> ordinal)
```

In fact, in Miranda we can define more general types still.

- We can define a number of types by definitions which are mutually recursive. These, if they are well founded, can be modelled in TT by a definition of a sum type, from which we project the types of interest.

- The Miranda mechanism allows definitions in which the type under construction can appear in the domain position of a function space, such as

```
model ::= Atom nat |
          Function (model -> model)
```

Such a type can be seen as a model of the untyped λ-calculus – it is not a well-founded type, however, and it cannot be fitted into the W-type framework. If we wish to include only well-founded types in the Miranda algebraic type mechanism, we would have to disallow the type under definition from appearing in the domain type of a function space which is the argument to a constructor. (In fact we could be more liberal than this, only disallowing the type being defined from negative occurrences: the polarity of an occurrence is reversed, recursively, for an occurrence in the domain position of a function space constructor.)

   Reasoning about general non-well-founded types and objects is performed by so-called fixed point induction [Stoy, 1977].

   In fact mutually recursive types can be given a type-theoretic treatment similar to that of trees and lists above. For more details see [Backhouse *et al.*, 1989, Section 6], or the paper [Petersson and Synek, 1987].

Exercises

5.31 Argue that in the case of $a \equiv (bnode\ n)$, for which $B(a) \equiv N_2$, the type

$$(\forall f : (N_2 \Rightarrow tree))((\forall y : N_2)C(f\ y) \Rightarrow C(node\ a\ f))$$

is extensionally isomorphic to the type

$$(\forall u : tree) . (\forall v : tree) . (C[u/x] \Rightarrow C[v/x] \Rightarrow C[(Bnode\ n\ u\ v)/x])$$

It might be useful to think of the f as one of the $f_{u,v}$ defined above. You should then argue that the types

$$(\forall y : N_2)C(f_{u,v}\ y) \Rightarrow C(node\ a\ f)$$

and

$$(C[u/x] \Rightarrow C[v/x] \Rightarrow C[(Bnode\ n\ u\ v)/x])$$

are extensionally isomorphic.

5.32 Show that the computation rule for R specializes to that for $trec$ for the nodes $(Bnode\ n\ u\ v)$.

5.33 Show that the natural numbers can be represented as a W type.

5.11   Expressibility

This section gives a characterization of the functions which can be written in the system TT_0.

Definition 5.41

A term e of TT_0 (or TT, TT^+) **represents** the function f over the natural numbers if and only if for all natural numbers $n_1, \ldots, n_k$,

$$e\ \underline{n_1}\ \ldots\ \underline{n_k} \twoheadrightarrow \underline{f\ n_1\ \ldots\ n_k}$$

where $\underline{n}$ is the representation of the natural number n, given by

$$\underbrace{succ\ (succ\ \ldots\ (succ\ 0))}_{n}$$

How can we characterize the functions f which are representable? First we know by the normalization theorem that they are *recursive*, since for each term e, to find the value of

$$e \, \underline{n_1} \, \ldots \, \underline{n_k}$$

we simply have to reduce the expression to normal form, and the application of the rules is certainly a mechanical process. It is equally clear that we cannot represent *all* recursive functions in this way, since if we could a *diagonalization* argument would lead to a contradiction. (For an exposition of the elementary details of computability theory see, for example, [Cutland, 1981; Rogers, 1967].)

We thus have that the class of functions is properly contained between the classes of primitive recursive functions and total recursive functions. A clue to the precise characterization lies in the normalization result, and the formalization of its proof *term by term*.

Theorem 5.42

For each term e of TT_0, the proof of normalization of e can be formalized in the theory of first-order intuitionistic arithmetic, HA, or its classical counterpart PA.

Proof: The proof uses a coding (or Gödel numbering) of the system TT_0 within the theory of arithmetic. It involves checking that the steps of the proof outlined in Section 5.6 can be encoded thus.   □

Note that the result does *not* claim that the complete normalization proof can be coded as a whole – the coding is uniform, but the individual results cannot be combined into a single proof, as the logical complexity of the individual proofs grows unboundedly with the complexity of the expression e.

Just as we explained what it was for a function f to be representable in one of our type theories, we can define how a function is representable in PA.

Definition 5.43

The term g of PA **represents** a k-ary function f if and only if for all $n_1, \ldots, n_k$,

$$PA \vdash g \, \underline{n_1} \, \ldots \, \underline{n_k} = f \, n_1 \, \ldots \, n_k$$

where $\underline{n}$ is the representation of the natural number n in PA.

Definition 5.44

A representable k-ary function f is **provably total** in PA (HA) if and only if we can prove in PA (HA) that its representative is total, that is

$$PA \vdash (\forall x_1, \ldots, x_k)(\exists y)(g \, x_1 \, \ldots \, x_k = y)$$

Theorem 5.42 can be seen now in a slightly different light, showing that every function representable in TT_0 is provably total in PA. We can also prove a converse to this, which shows that all functions provably total in PA can be represented in TT_0. The origins of this result lie with Gödel's *Dialectica* interpretation of PA in a theory of functions which itself can be viewed as a subtheory of TT_0 [Gödel, 1958]. More details of this and many other topics relating to the meta-mathematics of intuitionism can be found in [Troelstra, 1973].

Theorem 5.45

A function f over the natural numbers is representable in TT_0 if and only if it is provably total in PA (or HA).

The author is unaware of precise characterizations of the functions representable in the stronger theories TT and TT^+, although [Beeson, 1985] gives some partial results, including one for a system with a single universe. Whatever the case, the class of functions representable in the type theories is very large, and indeed it can be argued that this more than encompasses all the functions we might ever wish to program. In terms of sheer computation *time* all the functions we program are primitive recursive, in the sense that by suitable transformation any more complex calculations can be *bounded* by primitive recursive bounds. This is not the most natural way to proceed; in the next chapter we look at the ways in which functions are most naturally implemented in the language.

Exercise

5.34 One function which cannot be written in TT is an interpreter for the expressions of TT itself. Discuss how a *bounded* interpreter for the language can be written.

5.12   The Curry–Howard isomorphism?

The identification of propositions and types, proofs and objects has been fundamental to our investigation so far. In this section we look at two aspects of the system which seem not to fit with this identification.

5.12.1 Assumptions

Suppose we have a proof p of the proposition B depending upon the assumption A. The rule of $\Rightarrow$ introduction allows us to derive $A \Rightarrow B$ without the assumption of A. There may be a number of occurrences of A in p; without loss of generality *all* these are discharged by the implication introduction. This intuitive account is *not* an accurate account of the rule $(\Rightarrow I)$; only the assumptions of A named x are discharged in the application

$$\frac{\begin{array}{c} [x:A] \\ \vdots \\ e:B \end{array}}{\lambda x.e \ : \ A \Rightarrow B}(\Rightarrow I)$$

and if e also contains $y:A$, the proof of $A \Rightarrow B$ still depends upon A. The alternative rule, which we call $(\Rightarrow I)_{alt}$ would discharge *all* assumptions of A. It might be argued that the rule $(\Rightarrow I)$ allows the user of the system more freedom in proof construction. This is the case, but nonetheless it allows no more theorems to be proved, for we can simply replace all occurrences of $(\Rightarrow I)$ by $(\Rightarrow I)_{alt}$, some of the applications of the latter resulting in vacuous discharges of the hypothesis of the implication.

On the other hand, named *variables* are crucial, as can be seen by the derivation

$$\frac{\dfrac{[x:N]^2 \quad [y:N]^1}{(x+y) \ : \ N}}{\dfrac{\lambda y.(x+y) \ : \ N \Rightarrow N}{\lambda x.\lambda y.(x+y) \ : \ N \Rightarrow N \Rightarrow N}(\Rightarrow I)_1}(\Rightarrow I)_2$$

For the object $\lambda x.\lambda y.(x+y)$ to have the proper computational behaviour, it is crucial that the two assumptions $x:N$ and $y:N$ are distinct, and that $x:N$ is not identified with $y:N$. As far as the *inhabitation* of the proposition $N \Rightarrow N \Rightarrow N$ is concerned, it is irrelevant, naturally.

The mismatch here can be traced to the divergence of interests between the users of a logical system, who are primarily interested in proving theorems, that is in showing that particular types are *inhabited*, and the users of a programming language who are interested in the behaviour of many different objects of a given type. On the other hand, the proof theorist who studies the general behaviour of logical systems *is* interested in such behaviour. We look at this next.

5.12.2 Normal forms of proofs

When we discussed computation and reduction in Section 5.5 the emphasis was from the programming point of view: we argued that the expressions we were interested in studying were closed expressions of ground type: these are the printable values of a functional language. If we think of the expressions as denoting *proofs* of formulas, then neither assumption is tenable. We are interested in proofs of expressions such as

$$(A \Rightarrow B) \Rightarrow (A \Rightarrow C)$$

which are not of ground type, and which may depend upon assumptions (in this case, on $A \Rightarrow (B \Rightarrow C)$ say).

Proof theorists, such as Prawitz in his pioneering study of natural deduction, [Prawitz, 1965], are interested in showing that

> [The] rules allow the deduction to proceed in a certain direct fashion, affording an interesting normal form for deductions.

[Prawitz, 1965] shows the normal form theorem for proofs in a number of different systems of deduction, including first- and second-order classical and intuitionistic logic. The crucial reduction to ensure 'directness of proof' is that embodied in our computation rules: the elimination of a formula just introduced can be avoided. For example, the rule of β-reduction is interpreted as saying that the natural deduction proof

$$
\cfrac{A \qquad \cfrac{\begin{array}{c}[A]\\\vdots\\B\end{array}}{A \Rightarrow B}(\Rightarrow I)}{B}(\Rightarrow E)
$$

can be transformed to

$$
\begin{array}{c}\vdots\\A\\\vdots\\B\end{array}
$$

in which the proof of A replaces the assumption(s) of A in the proof of B.

The computation rules are not the only simplifications possible. For the reasons above, the arguments of Section 2.11 do not apply, and so we have another mismatch. The extra rules come in two different forms. Instead of replacing 'introduction then elimination' we can also replace 'elimination then introduction'. These are examples of the equivalence rules we discussed earlier. For example, we might encounter the following steps in a proof.

$$\frac{\dfrac{[A] \quad A \Rightarrow B}{B}(\Rightarrow E)}{A \Rightarrow B}(\Rightarrow I) \qquad \frac{\dfrac{A \wedge B}{A}(\wedge E_1) \quad \dfrac{A \wedge B}{B}(\wedge E_2)}{A \wedge B}(\wedge I)$$

both of which are completely irrelevant to the result of the proof. The corresponding reduction rules in type theory are

$$\lambda x \,.\, (f\, x) \quad \rightarrow \quad f \quad \text{if } x \text{ not free in } f$$
$$(fst\, p, snd\, p) \quad \rightarrow \quad p$$

and for each type we can devise a similar rule. The reading we have given to the rules above shows that as far as proofs are concerned, they do perform a simplification.

The other class of **commutation** rules are included in the system studied by Prawitz for more technical reasons, which are discussed by him and also in [Girard *et al.*, 1989, Section 10]. The simplest is the equivalence between

$$\frac{\dfrac{\dfrac{\mathcal{P}_1}{\exists x.B} \quad \dfrac{\mathcal{P}_2}{F}}{F}(E\exists) \quad \mathcal{P}_3}{D}(R) \qquad \frac{\dfrac{\mathcal{P}_1}{\exists x.B} \quad \dfrac{\dfrac{\mathcal{P}_2}{F} \quad \mathcal{P}_3}{D}(R)}{D}(E\exists)$$

in which we can see that the proof of D from F and the proof $\mathcal{P}_3$ can be performed before or after the existential elimination. Any orientation of this equivalence into a reduction rule will be arbitrary. Prawitz chooses to reduce the left-hand to the right-hand side.

These considerations seem to be motivated by proof-theoretic considerations, but a final twist is added by their link with the discussion of the computational efficiency (or otherwise) of certain rules, and in particular the considerations which lead us to the strong elimination rules of Section 7.7.

Chapter 6
Applying Type Theory

This chapter investigates the different ways in which the system of type theory can be used.

- We are already familiar with type theory as a constructive logic, and have seen a number of examples of proofs being built in, for example, Sections 4.5 and 4.6.1.

- We have also seen that TT can be seen as a functional programming language, with a number of novel features, such as the following.

  - Every expression has a defined value; every program terminates.
  - The system of types is more expressive than those in common use, allowing as it does dependent product and function spaces.
  - The functional language is integrated with a logic in which to reason about the programs.

- Another view of program development is provided by the insight that in TT we can think of programs as being *extracted* from constructive proofs. This combines the two interpretations in an elegant and powerful way.

- Not only can we use the logical system to reason about the properties of programs, we can also use the system to support program transformation.

- Finally, we show how we can develop imperative programs within a type-theoretic framework.

We begin our discussion by looking at TT as a functional language. We assume that the reader is familiar with the elements of functional programming as covered in [Bird and Wadler, 1988] and [Reade, 1989], so that in choosing examples we look for *distinctive features* of programming in TT, rather than running through the traditional repertoire of functional programming techniques. In Section 6.1 we show how primitive recursion is used to define functions *and types (or propositions)*. Because the language is terminating, a number of familiar functions, such as the function taking the head of a list, need to be defined in novel ways. Using the more expressive type system we are able to give the head function its 'proper' type, as a function acting over the type of *non-empty* lists. TT contains only primitive recursion over each primitive type; we show how more complex forms of recursion, such as course-of-values recursion, can be programmed in TT.

In Section 6.2 we investigate a larger example, that of the quicksort function over lists. Here we develop the program first and then prove that it meets its specification, showing that we have a system in which programming and verification are integrated. We follow this with a more detailed survey of the uses of dependent types, especially in the presence of universes. These give dependent function and sum types, which can be seen to support polymorphic functions, abstract data types, type classes (*à la* Haskell [Hudak and Wadler, 1990]) and modules. In Section 6.4 we apply these ideas in developing a type of vectors.

We look at how programs can be extracted from a number of simple derivations in Section 6.5, before discussing a general strategy for program derivation in Section 6.6. We also use this opportunity to give a novel view of specifications in type theory, and examine the ideas in the context of the well-known problem of the Dutch (or Polish) national flag.

Our view of programming has been exclusively functional up to this point. In Section 6.8 we argue that imperative programs can be seen as functional programs of a particularly restricted sort, the *tail-recursive* functions. We can thus view TT as extending an imperative programming language and we give a general result about the transformation of primitive recursive programs into tail-recursive form, after looking at various concrete examples.

We conclude the chapter with a survey of other examples discussed in the literature of type theory.

6.1   Recursion

One of the properties of the systems of type theory TT_0, TT and TT^+ is strong normalization: every computation sequence terminates. This means that the system does not permit full general recursion to be used, as in an unrestricted form this can lead to non-termination. A simple example is given by

$$f\,0 \quad \equiv_{df} \quad 0$$
$$f\,(n+1) \quad \equiv_{df} \quad f\,(n+2)+1$$

and other, less obvious, examples can be constructed.

As a counterbalance to the weaker recursion operation, we have a more powerful type system than is common in programming languages. We are able thus to express more precisely the true types of functions, using for instance the existential quantifier to build a subset type, over which the function is total.

In some cases, the definition of the function itself depends upon an inductive proof that it terminates; the effect of this is to give functions whose definitions manipulate information *witnessing* certain facts, as well as the computational data. This intermingling of verification and computation is characteristic of type theory.

We concentrate on examples over the natural numbers and lists in this section, with some introduction of quantified types as we go along. We look in more depth at these types in Section 6.3.

Before examining particular examples of definitions, it is worth mentioning that two general methods present themselves.

- Theorem 5.45 shows that anything provably total in PA can be programmed in TT_0, and indeed the proof will provide a term. This does beg the question of *how* the function is proved total; we would argue that the system TT_0 provides exactly the right environment in which to give such proofs, as it allows a *constructive* derivation of the function which assures its totality.

- Proof theorists have characterized classes of provably total functions by means of the *well-orderings* which can be used in defining these functions by recursion [Schütte, 1977]. We could use this characterization to give functions in TT_0, but again would argue for the natural nature of the system itself. There have been a number of proposals for incorporating principles of well-founded or *general* recursion; we look at these in Section 7.9.

6.1.1 Numerical functions

We look at some examples embodying common patterns of recursion, and show how they are coded in TT_0. First, consider the naïve addition algorithm,

$$add\,a\,0 \quad \equiv_{df} \quad a$$

$$add\, a\, (n+1) \quad \equiv_{df} \quad add\, (a+1)\, n$$

This appears to be primitive recursive, except for the fact that the argument a is *increased* on the recursive call. To make a properly primitive recursive definition, we observe that we can define the values $add\, a\, n$ simultaneously for all a, by induction on n. In other words, we define the functions

$$\lambda a\, . \, (add\, a\, n)$$

by induction over n. That this is possible is due to the fact that in the definition of $add\, a\, (n+1)$ we appeal to a value of add with second argument n. Formally, if we let $C \equiv_{df} (N \Rightarrow N)$, then at the base case we define

$$c \equiv_{df} \lambda a\, . \, a \; : \; C$$

To give the recursion step, we say

$$f\, n\, h\, a \equiv_{df} h\, (a+1)$$

where $n, a : N$ and $h : C$. This gives

$$f \; : \; (N \Rightarrow C \Rightarrow C)$$

and so by a simplified form of (NE) in which C is constant,

$$\frac{n \; : \; N \quad c \; : \; C \quad f \; : \; (N \Rightarrow C \Rightarrow C)}{prim\, n\, c\, f \; : \; C}(NE)$$

with the reduction properties

$$\begin{aligned}
prim\, 0\, c\, f\, a \quad &\to \quad c\, a \\
&\equiv \quad (\lambda a\, . \, a)\, a \\
&\to \quad a \\
prim\, (n+1)\, c\, f\, a \quad &\to \quad f\, n\, (prim\, n\, c\, f)\, a \\
&\to \quad (prim\, n\, c\, f)\, (a+1)
\end{aligned}$$

We therefore have the definition

$$add \equiv_{df} \lambda a\, . \, \lambda n\, . \, (prim\, n\, c\, f\, a)$$

There is an analogy between the generalization we had to make here, from defining one function to defining a class of functions simultaneously, and the generalizations of induction hypotheses we often have to make when we prove a result by induction. If $+$ is the usual addition operator and we wish to prove that

$$add\ a\ n = (a + n)$$

by induction, then the hypothesis we shall have to take is that

$$(\forall a: N).(add\ a\ n = (a + n))$$

rather than the 'bare' equation with a as a parameter.

Primitive recursion defines a value at $(n + 1)$ from the value at the immediate predecessor n – sometimes it is natural to use a value at a number m smaller than n. A case in point is the *power* function

$$power\ k\ 0 \quad \equiv_{df} \quad 1$$
$$power\ k\ n \quad \equiv_{df} \quad (power\ k\ (n\ div\ 2))^2 * k^{(n\ mod\ 2)}$$

where the value at positive n is derived from that at $(n\ div\ 2)$. (Note that we are not using the power function in the second multiplicand: this is either 1 or k depending upon whether n is even or odd. Observe also that in contrast to the first argument of *add* that here k is simply a *parameter* of the definition – its value is unchanged on the recursive call.)

This definition provides an example of a general phenomenon, called **course-of-values** recursion. To give a sketch of the method, we replace a definition of the form

$$f\ 0 \quad \equiv_{df} \quad a$$
$$f\ (n + 1) \quad \equiv_{df} \quad \ldots f\ 0 \ldots f\ 1 \ldots f\ n \ldots$$

by a definition of the function

$$g\ n \equiv_{df} [f\ 0, \ldots, f\ n]$$

which has as its value at n the *list* of values of f on numbers up to n. The definition of $g\ (n + 1)$ is made by defining $f\ (n + 1)$ from the list $g\ n$ and appending the value to the list. We obtain the value $f\ n$ by taking the last value in the list $g\ n$. We shall show how to realize this form of definition in type theory after looking at lists in more detail.

Exercises

6.1 Show how to define the 'natural subtraction' operation over the natural numbers

$$natsub\ m\ n \equiv_{df} max\ 0\ (m - n)$$

where $(m - n)$ is intended to denote integer subtraction.

6.2   In Section 5.3 we gave a definition of the type of integers: how would you define the arithmetic operations of addition, subtraction and multiplication over the integers defined in that way?

6.1.2   Defining propositions and types by recursion

Using the universes $U_0, U_1, \ldots$ we can make definitions of parametric types or propositions by recursion. Consider the predicate '*non-zero*' over the natural numbers. One way to define it is to use the equality relation over N and say

$$nonzero\, n \equiv_{df} \neg(n =_N 0)$$

If n is zero then an element of this type will be a function

$$(0 =_N 0) \Rightarrow \bot$$

which when applied to the equality witness will yield $\bot$, so this type is inhabited if and only if every type is. On the other hand it can be shown that for every other element of N, the type will be inhabited, a consequence of the axiom which asserts that the two boolean values are distinct:

$$ax\; :\; \neg(True =_{bool} False)$$

which was introduced in Chapter 4.

Rather than defining the predicate in terms of other predicates, we can simply give a direct definition of it, as a function with result in U_0. We say that

$$
\begin{aligned}
nz\, 0 &\equiv_{df} \bot \\
nz\, (n+1) &\equiv_{df} \top
\end{aligned}
$$

The proof objects in this case are either non-existent, in the case of 0, or $Triv$, the trivial proof, in the case of $(n+1)$. Recalling the type of lists introduced earlier, we can give a similar definition of the predicate for non-empty lists:

$$
\begin{aligned}
nonempty &: [A] \Rightarrow U_0 \\
nonempty\, [\,] &\equiv_{df} \bot \\
nonempty\, (a :: x) &\equiv_{df} \top
\end{aligned}
$$

Given this predicate we can define the type of non-empty lists thus:

$$nelist\, A \equiv_{df} (\exists l : [A]) \,.\, (nonempty\, l)$$

elements of which will be pairs

$$(l, p)$$

with $p : (nonempty \, l)$. In the case that l is empty, this p will be a proof of $\perp$ and in any other case it will be $Triv$.

In the cases above we have simply used the case analysis aspect of primitive recursion in making the definitions. Now we look at an example which uses the full power of recursion in defining the 'less than' relation over the natural numbers.

Informally, nothing is smaller than zero, zero is smaller than $n + 1$, and $m + 1$ is smaller than $n + 1$ if and only if m is smaller than n. Two possibilities suggest themselves for the representation of the relation. We can define the *bool*ean function

$$
\begin{aligned}
lt_1 \quad &: \quad N \Rightarrow N \Rightarrow bool \\
lt_1 \, m \, 0 \quad &\equiv_{df} \quad False \\
lt_1 \, 0 \, (n + 1) \quad &\equiv_{df} \quad True \\
lt_1 \, (m + 1) \, (n + 1) \quad &\equiv_{df} \quad lt_1 \, m \, n
\end{aligned}
$$

The proposition that m is smaller than n is given by the equality

$$I(bool, \, lt_1 \, m \, n \, , True)$$

The alternative is direct.

$$
\begin{aligned}
lt_2 \quad &: \quad N \Rightarrow N \Rightarrow U_0 \\
lt_2 \, m \, 0 \quad &\equiv_{df} \quad \perp \\
lt_2 \, 0 \, (n + 1) \quad &\equiv_{df} \quad \top \\
lt_2 \, (m + 1) \, (n + 1) \quad &\equiv_{df} \quad lt_2 \, m \, n
\end{aligned}
$$

so that for m and n in N

$$lt_2 \, m \, n$$

is itself a proposition. (Note that in both these cases, we have to make the definitions simultaneously on all the values of the first argument.) In what follows we shall use the second of these definitions, so that $lt \equiv_{df} lt_2$ and we shall write $lt \, m \, n$ thus: $m < n$.

Exercises

6.3 Show that, given the axiom asserting that the boolean values are distinct, the proposition

$$(\forall x : N) . ((x =_N 0) \lor \neg (x =_N 0))$$

is inhabited.

6.4 Show that for all natural numbers n and m the propositions $lt_1\, m\, n$ and $lt_2\, m\, n$ are equivalent.

6.5 How would you formulate the relation 'less than or equal to' by analogy with the formulations above?

6.6 Give a recursive definition of the iterated cartesian product operator, which maps a type A and a natural number n to the product

$$\underbrace{A \land (A \land \ldots (A \land A) \ldots)}_{n}$$

where the product of zero copies of A is defined to be $\top$. How would you define the projection operations on these types?

6.1.3   Recursion over lists – 1

Lists were introduced in Section 5.10 as an example of a well-founded type, which carries a recursion/induction operator, *lrec*. In this section some of the more common list-manipulating functions are discussed. A number of these come from the standard environment of Miranda which is a library of function definitions made available to the Miranda user. As we mentioned above, a non-empty list, $(a :: x)$, has a head, a, and a tail, x. Can we define functions returning these values? There is a problem here – what are we to do with the *empty* list, $[\,]$, which has neither head nor tail? The solutions we present here can be applied to many examples of ostensibly *partial* functions.

- We can supply an extra parameter to the function, which is to be returned in the case that the list argument is the empty list. For example

$$
\begin{aligned}
head_1 \quad &: \quad A \Rightarrow [A] \Rightarrow A \\
head_1\, h\, [\,] \quad &\equiv_{df} \quad h \\
head_1\, h\, (a :: x) \quad &\equiv_{df} \quad a
\end{aligned}
$$

In some situations, there is a 'natural' choice for this element, as the case of the tail function:

$$tail_1 \quad : \quad [A] \Rightarrow [A]$$
$$tail_1\,[\,] \quad \equiv_{df} \quad [\,]$$
$$tail_1\,(a :: x) \quad \equiv_{df} \quad x$$

- We can make the result type of the function a *sum* type. Recalling our naming conventions from Section 5.2.1, we can write

$$error\ A \equiv_{df} ok\ A + err\ \top$$

where we abbreviate ($err\ Triv$) by $error$. Now we can define

$$head_2 \quad : \quad [A] \Rightarrow error\ A$$
$$head_2\,[\,] \quad \equiv_{df} \quad error$$
$$head_2\,(a :: x) \quad \equiv_{df} \quad ok\ a$$

and similarly,

$$tail_2 \quad : \quad [A] \Rightarrow error\ [A]$$
$$tail_2\,[\,] \quad \equiv_{df} \quad error$$
$$tail_2\,(a :: x) \quad \equiv_{df} \quad ok\ x$$

- Instead of enlarging the range of the function, we can restrict the domain, which is perhaps the most natural thing to do. We want to apply the functions to non-empty lists, so we define

$$nelist\ A \equiv_{df} (\exists l : [A]) \,.\, (nonempty\ l)$$

as we did in Section 6.1.2. The head function can be given the type

$$head_3 \,:\, nelist\ A \,\Rightarrow\, A$$

so we aim to derive the head of the list l on the basis of the pair (l, r). Working by cases, if l is $(a :: x)$ then the head is a, and we are done. If, on the other hand, l is $[\,]$, we have

$$nonempty\ l \equiv_{df} \bot$$

so that $r : \bot$. We then have

$$abort_A\ r \,:\, A$$

which gives us the element of A which was required. A similar derivation gives us

$$tail_3 \; : \; nelist \; A \; \Rightarrow [A]$$

- We can define functions $head_4$ and $tail_4$ of type

$$(\forall l : [A]) . (nonempty \; l \Rightarrow A) \quad \text{and} \quad (\forall l : [A]) . (nonempty \; l \Rightarrow [A])$$

with the appropriate properties since these types are extensionally isomorphic with the types of $head_3$ and $tail_3$ respectively, a property we proved in Section 4.6.1.

Whichever choice of definition we make there will be a proof-theoretic obligation to show that the argument is non-empty, as if it is not then

- if we are using $head_1$ we may get the default value as a result;
- if we are using $head_2$ we may get the value *error* as the result rather than an '*ok*' value; and finally,
- if we are using $head_3$ we need a proof that the list is non-empty in order to apply the function itself.

In what follows we shall use the third definition, so that $hd \equiv_{df} head_3$ and $tl \equiv_{df} tail_3$. We leave the definition of the function which returns the *last* element of a non-empty list,

$$last : nelist \; A \; \Rightarrow A$$

as an exercise

Two standard functions which we can define without difficulty are the function returning the length of a list, usually written $\#$, and the function which joins two lists together, $\mathbin{+\!\!+}$. Equationally they are given by

$$
\begin{aligned}
\# \, [\,] \;\; &\equiv_{df} \;\; 0 \\
\# \, (a :: x) \;\; &\equiv_{df} \;\; \# x + 1
\end{aligned}
$$

$$
\begin{aligned}
[\,] \mathbin{+\!\!+} y \;\; &\equiv_{df} \;\; y \\
(a :: x) \mathbin{+\!\!+} y \;\; &\equiv_{df} \;\; a :: (x \mathbin{+\!\!+} y)
\end{aligned}
$$

The reader should have no problem putting them in *lrec* form.

With the example of course-of-values recursion in mind, we need to define a function which will extract one of the values from a list. Informally,

$$[a_0, \ldots, a_{n-1}] \, ! \, m \equiv_{df} a_m$$

What do we do when m is out of the range $0, \ldots, n - 1$? One option is to return a default value, or the *last* value in the case of a non-empty list, but we can define the function so that its type is sufficiently restricted not to allow indexing which is 'out of range'. Given a list l the permissible indices are those less than the length $\# l$. The next subsection explores various options for this.

Exercises

6.7 Give a definition of the function *last* mentioned in the section above.

6.8 Give an explicit definition of the function

$$head_4 \; : \; (\forall l : [A]) . (nonempty \, l \Rightarrow A)$$

discussed above.

6.9 A type of non-empty lists can be defined as an algebraic type in a similar way to $[A]$. Formulate the rules of formation, introduction, elimination and computation for this type, and define the *head*, *last* and *tail* functions for this type.

6.10 Formulate a version of the indexing function '!' for the type of non-empty lists which will return the last element in the list as a default if the index is 'out of range'.

6.1.4   Recursion over lists – 2

In this section we look at the list-indexing function and return to the issue of course-of-values recursion over the natural numbers.

Recall the definition of $<$ in Section 6.1.2. We define the function *index* to have the type

$$(\forall l : [A]) . (\forall n : N) . ((n < \# l) \Rightarrow A)$$

Given a list l, a natural number n, *and* a proof that n is smaller than the length of l we return the nth element of l. How is index defined?

$$
\begin{aligned}
index \, [\,] \, n \, p \; &\equiv_{df} \; abort_A \, p \\
index \, (a :: x) \, 0 \, p \; &\equiv_{df} \; a \\
index \, (a :: x) \, (n + 1) \, p \; &\equiv_{df} \; index \, x \, n \, p
\end{aligned}
$$

The second and third clauses are clear. What is happening in the first? p is a proof that $(n < \#[\,])$ that is $(n < 0)$, which is $\perp$ – we can define an element of A from p using $abort_A$.

It is interesting to see that the definition of *index* can be made either by induction over N with a subsidiary induction over $[A]$, or vice versa – the two arguments are independent of each other.

Now we can return to the example of course-of-values recursion, as we have defined all the auxiliary functions that are needed. Taking a special case of the *power* function, we have

$$pow\ 0 \quad \equiv_{df} \quad 1$$
$$pow\ n \quad \equiv_{df} \quad (pow\ (n\ div\ 2))^2 * 2^{(n\ mod\ 2)}$$

which can be rewritten thus, where h is a primitive recursive function,

$$pow\ 0 \quad \equiv_{df} \quad 1$$
$$pow\ (n+1) \quad \equiv_{df} \quad h\ (pow\ (n+1\ div\ 2))\ n$$

Transforming this into a list definition, we have

$$g\ 0 \quad \equiv_{df} \quad [1]$$
$$g\ (n+1) \quad \equiv_{df} \quad (g\ n) \mathbin{++} [h\ ((g\ n)\ !\ (n+1\ div\ 2))\ n]$$

The sub-expression $g\ !\ (n+1\ div\ 2)$ is informal; *index* takes a third argument which is a proof object, legitimizing the application. The application will be legitimate if we can show that

$$(n+1\ div\ 2) < \#(g\ n)$$

This will follow from proofs of

$$(0 < m) \Rightarrow (m\ div\ 2 < m)$$

which is standard, and

$$\#(g\ n) = (n+1) \tag{6.1}$$

which we have to establish by induction, simultaneously with the definition itself. Transforming again, we define a function which returns a *pair*

$$(\,g\ n\ ,\ p_n\,)$$

where p_n proves the assertion 6.1. To extract the result $(f\ n)$ from the value $(g\ n)$ we apply the head function. Remember that to do this we need a proof that the list is non-empty. We can use the assertion 6.1 again here to show this, as it states that all the values $(g\ n)$ have positive length, and so none of them can be empty.

We can see from the derivation of the function above that the system is quite different from a traditional functional programming system, in that the definition of a function cannot be separated from a proof that it terminates. In fact, this is not quite accurate – if we had adopted the approach which gives default or error values to *head* and *index* we could perform the derivation without the inferences we needed above, but once derived we would have to prove that the values returned by the function are 'ok' and not error or default values.

Exercises

6.11 Using induction over $m : N$ prove that $(m \ div \ 2) < m$ for all $m > 0$.

6.12 Formalize the derivation of the functions g and pow above.

6.13 Give a proof that for all lists l and m,

$$\#l + \#m = \#(l + \!\!+ m)$$

6.14 Consider the example of 'Russian multiplication' given by the definition

$$mul \ a \ 0 \quad \equiv_{df} \quad 0$$
$$mul \ a \ b \quad \equiv_{df} \quad (mul \ (2 * a) \ (b \ div \ 2)) + a * (b \ mod \ 2)$$

How would you argue that this is definable in type theory?

6.15 Show how the following functions, defined informally, can be given definitions in type theory

$$
\begin{aligned}
merge \quad &: \quad [N] \Rightarrow [N] \Rightarrow [N] \\
merge \ [\,] \ y \quad &\equiv_{df} \quad y \\
merge \ (a :: x) \ [\,] \quad &\equiv_{df} \quad (a :: x) \\
merge \ (a :: x) \ (b :: y) \quad &\equiv_{df} \quad a :: (merge \ x \ (b :: y)) \quad \textbf{if } less \ a \ b \\
&\equiv_{df} \quad b :: (merge \ (a :: x) \ y) \quad \textbf{if not}
\end{aligned}
$$

$$
\begin{aligned}
foldl \quad &: \quad (A \Rightarrow B \Rightarrow A) \Rightarrow A \Rightarrow [B] \Rightarrow A \\
foldl \ f \ a \ [\,] \quad &\equiv_{df} \quad a \\
foldl \ f \ a \ (b :: y) \quad &\equiv_{df} \quad foldl \ f \ (f \ a \ b) \ y
\end{aligned}
$$

6.2 A case study – quicksort

This section surveys the general area of sorting numerical lists and gives a complete development and verification of the quicksort function over these lists. In the course of the development we will have occasion to define other useful functions and discuss proofs of general theorems.

6.2.1 Defining the function

The function quicksort over numerical lists can be defined in a functional language language such as Miranda thus:

$$qsort \quad : \quad [N] \Rightarrow [N]$$
$$qsort\,[\,] \quad \equiv_{df} \quad [\,]$$
$$qsort\,(a :: x) \quad \equiv_{df} \quad qsort\,(filter\,(lesseq\,a)\,x)$$
$$+\!\!+\,[a]\,+\!\!+$$
$$qsort\,(filter\,(greater\,a)\,x)$$

where the function $filter$, which selects the elements of a list which have the property $p:(A \Rightarrow bool)$, has the type-theoretic definition

$$filter \quad : \quad (A \Rightarrow bool) \Rightarrow [A] \Rightarrow [A]$$
$$filter\,p\,[\,] \quad \equiv_{df} \quad [\,]$$
$$filter\,p\,(a :: x) \quad \equiv_{df} \quad a :: (filter\,p\,x) \qquad \textbf{if } (p\,a)$$
$$filter\,p\,(a :: x) \quad \equiv_{df} \quad filter\,p\,x \qquad \textbf{if not}$$

which is by an induction over the list argument.

The function $lesseq$, of type $(N \Rightarrow N \Rightarrow bool)$, is defined thus

$$lesseq\,0\,x \quad \equiv_{df} \quad True$$
$$lesseq\,(n+1)\,0 \quad \equiv_{df} \quad False$$
$$lesseq\,(n+1)\,(m+1) \quad \equiv_{df} \quad lesseq\,n\,m$$

which is formalized as a primitive recursive definition of the functions

$$\lambda m\,.\,(lesseq\,n\,m)$$

over the variable $n:N$. The function $greater$ is defined in the analogous way.

We shall also use a proposition $(m \le n)$ asserting 'less than or equal to'. It is defined by the analogous recursion thus:

$$0 \le x \quad \equiv_{df} \quad \top$$
$$(n+1) \le 0 \quad \equiv_{df} \quad \bot$$
$$(n+1) \le (m+1) \quad \equiv_{df} \quad n \le m$$

How can we give a type theoretic version of the definition of $qsort$? The crucial observation is that the *length* of the lists on which the recursive call is made is *smaller* than the length of $(a :: x)$, so the recursion is justified by course-of-values recursion over N.

The modified definition of quicksort is by means of a function with three arguments. This first is a number n, the second a list l to be sorted and the third a proof that $(\#l \leq n)$. The functions

$$\lambda l \,.\, \lambda p \,.\, qsort' \, n \, l \, p$$

are defined by recursion over n:

$$
\begin{aligned}
qsort' \quad &: \quad (\forall n : N) \,.\, (\forall l : [N]) \,.\, ((\#l \leq n) \Rightarrow [N]) \\
qsort' \, n \, [\,] \, p \quad &\equiv_{df} \quad [\,] \\
qsort' \, 0 \, (a :: x) \, p \quad &\equiv_{df} \quad abort_{[N]} p' \\
qsort' \, (n+1) \, (a :: x) \, p \quad &\equiv_{df} \quad qsort' \, n \, (filter \, (lesseq \, a) \, x) \, p_1 \\
&\qquad +\!\!+ \, [a] +\!\!+ \\
&\qquad qsort' \, n \, (filter \, (greater \, a) \, x) \, p_2
\end{aligned}
$$

What are the proof objects p', p_1, p_2?

By assumption $p : (\#(a :: x) \leq 0)$; we can also prove $(0 < \#(a :: x))$. These two proof objects are combined to give an element p' of $0 < 0$, which is the type $\bot$.

Suppose that $p : (\#(a :: x) \leq (n+1))$. Since

$$\#(a :: x) \;\leftrightarrow\; \#x + 1$$

we have

$$(\#(a :: x) \leq (n+1)) \;\leftrightarrow\; \#x \leq n$$

so by the substitution rules,

$$p : (\#x \leq n)$$

Now we note a general result.

Lemma 6.1

For all lists x and properties p,

$$\#(filter \, p \, x) \leq \#x$$

Proof: Straightforward induction over the list x. $\square$

Now, by the transitivity of the relation $\leq$, whose proof we also leave to the reader, we can define proofs of

$$\#(filter \, (lesseq \, a) \, x) \leq n \qquad \#(filter \, (greater \, a) \, x) \leq n$$

These are the objects p_1 and p_2. We leave it as an exercise to define these values formally, to be the results of functions h_i, where the type of h_1 is, for instance,

$$(\forall a \colon N) . (\forall n \colon N) .$$
$$(\forall x \colon [N]) . (\forall p \colon (\#(a :: x) \leq (n+1))) .$$
$$(\#(filter\ (lesseq\ a)\ x) \leq n)$$

We must define these values p_i in order for the recursive application of $qsort'$ to be properly typed.

The function $qsort$ itself is defined by

$$qsort\ l \equiv_{df} qsort'\ (\#l)\ l\ Triv$$

since $Triv$ constitutes the canonical proof that $(\#l \leq \#l)$.

6.2.2   Verifying the function

We have implemented the quicksort algorithm before having specified its purpose: we expect it to sort a list, so that it should

- return a result which is sorted, and,

- return a result which is a permutation of its argument.

A list is sorted if and only if, for each pair of elements chosen from the list, the element which lies to the left is smaller than or equal to the other. Formally,

$$(\forall m \colon N) . (\forall n \colon N) .$$
$$(\forall p \colon (m < n)) . (\forall q \colon (n < \#l)) .$$
$$(index\ l\ m\ p' \leq index\ l\ n\ q)$$

where p' is the proof of $(m < \#l)$ derived from p and q by transitivity of the ordering relation. List indexing was defined above; the reader might recall that in order for an application of the function to be legitimate, there needs to be evidence that the index is less than the length of the list argument.

The proof can be developed for this characterization, but we choose instead to define sorting in an inductive way, over the structure of the list.

$$
\begin{array}{rcl}
sorted & : & [N] \Rightarrow U_0 \\
sorted\,[\,] & \equiv_{df} & \top \\
sorted\,[a] & \equiv_{df} & \top \\
sorted\,(a :: b :: x) & \equiv_{df} & (a \leq b) \wedge (sorted\,(b :: x))
\end{array}
$$

We say that one list is a permutation of another if the number of occurrences of any possible element is the same in both the lists.

$$perm \; l \; l' \equiv_{df} (\forall a : N) . (occs \; a \; l =_N occs \; a \; l')$$

The function counting the occurrences is given by

$$
\begin{aligned}
occs \; a \; [\,] & \equiv_{df} & 0 & \\
occs \; a \; (b :: x) & \equiv_{df} & 1 + occs \; a \; x & \quad \textbf{if } eq_N \; a \; b \\
occs \; a \; (b :: x) & \equiv_{df} & occs \; a \; x & \quad \textbf{if not}
\end{aligned}
$$

In stating a number of auxiliary results we will need one further definition:

$$
\begin{aligned}
mem & \quad :: & A \Rightarrow [A] \Rightarrow U_0 \\
mem \; a \; [\,] & \equiv_{df} & \bot \\
mem \; a \; (b :: x) & \equiv_{df} & (a = b) \vee (mem \; a \; x)
\end{aligned}
$$

The lemma which follows enumerates a number of basic properties of the ordering relation, the functions *occs*, *mem* and the relation *perm*.

Lemma 6.2

The following types are inhabited.

(1) $(\forall x, y : N) . (lesseq \; x \; y = True \Rightarrow x \leq y)$

(2) $(\forall x, y : N) . (lesseq \; x \; y = True \vee greater \; x \; y = True)$

(3) $(\forall x, y : N) . \neg (lesseq \; x \; y = True \wedge greater \; x \; y = True)$

(4) $(\forall p : N \Rightarrow bool) . (\forall l : [N]) . (\forall x : N) . (mem \; x \; (filter \; p \; l) \Rightarrow p \; x = True)$

(5) $(\forall l : [N]) . (\forall a, x : N) . (mem \; x \; (filter \; (lesseq \; a) \; l) \Rightarrow x \leq a)$

(6) $(\forall x : N) . (\forall l : [N]) . (mem \; x \; l \Leftrightarrow occs \; x \; l > 0)$

(7) $(\forall l, l' : [N]) . (perm \; l \; l' \Rightarrow (\forall x : N) . (mem \; x \; l \Leftrightarrow mem \; x \; l'))$

(8) $(\forall a : N) . (\forall l, m : [N]) . (occs \; a \; (l \mathbin{+\!\!+} m) = occs \; a \; l + occs \; a \; m)$

(9) $(\forall l, m, x : [N]) . (\forall a : N) . (perm(l \mathbin{+\!\!+} m) x \Rightarrow perm(l \mathbin{+\!\!+} [a] \mathbin{+\!\!+} m)(a :: x))$

(10) $(\forall l, l', m, m' : [N]) . perm \; l \; l' \wedge perm \; m \; m' \Rightarrow perm \; (l \mathbin{+\!\!+} m) \; (l' \mathbin{+\!\!+} m')$

(11) $(\forall l : [N]) . (\forall a : N) . perm \; l \; (filter \; (lesseq \; a) \; l \mathbin{+\!\!+} filter \; (greater \; a) l)$

(12) *perm* is an equivalence relation

Proof: Results 1–3 are proved by induction over N; 4, 6 by induction over the list l. 5 is a corollary of 1 and 4. 7 is a corollary of 6; 8–10 are again proved by induction over the list l. 11 is a consequence of 2, 3 and 8. 12 is a simple consequence of the definition of permutation.   □

The crucial lemma concerning sorting is

Lemma 6.3

The following proposition is inhabited.

$$(\forall l, m : [N]) . (sorted\, l \,\wedge\, sorted\, m \,\wedge\, (\forall b : N) . (mem\, b\, l \Rightarrow b \leq a) \,\wedge$$
$$(\forall b : N) . (mem\, b\, m \Rightarrow a \leq b) \Rightarrow sorted\, (l +\!+[a] +\!+m))$$

Proof: The result is established by an induction over the list l, with an auxiliary case analysis over the list m in the case that l is $[\,]$.   □

We can now assert the theorem on the correctness of quicksort.

Theorem 6.4

The following proposition is provable.

$$(\forall m : N) . (\forall l : [N]) . (\forall p : (\#l \leq m)) .$$
$$sorted\, (\, qsort'\, m\, l\, p\,) \,\wedge\, perm\, l\, (\, qsort'\, m\, l\, p\,)$$

Proof: The proof is by induction over the variable m, just as the function was defined by recursion over this variable. In each part of the proof we use a case analysis over lists: such a form of proof is a special case of induction in which the induction hypothesis is not used.

Case $m \equiv 0$: There are two sub-cases according to whether the list is empty or not. In the former, the result is $[\,]$ and this is both sorted and a permutation of itself, giving the result. Suppose we have a non-empty list; just as when we were defining the function, from the proof p we can extract a proof of $\bot$ and thence a proof of anything, including the correctness conditions. This completes the proof in the base case.

Case $m \equiv (n+1)$: Again there are two sub-cases. In the case of an empty list we proceed exactly as above, so suppose that we have a non-empty list $l \equiv (a :: x)$. Now

$$qsort'\, (n + 1)\, (a :: x)\, p \equiv l_1 +\!+[a] +\!+l_2$$

where

$$l_1 \equiv_{df} qsort'\, n\, (filter\, (lesseq\, a)\, x)\, p_1$$
$$l_2 \equiv_{df} qsort'\, n\, (filter\, (greater\, a)\, x)\, p_2$$

By induction we know that

$$sorted\, l_1 \,\wedge\, sorted\, l_2 \tag{6.2}$$

$$perm\, (filter\, (lesseq\, a)\, x)\, l_1 \,\wedge\, perm\, (filter\, (greater\, a)\, x)\, l_2 \tag{6.3}$$

We aim to use Lemma 6.3 to show that $l_1 +\!+[a] +\!+l_2$ is sorted. The sortedness hypotheses are given by assertion 6.2, so we need to show that every element of l_1 is less than or equal to a, and to show that every element of l_2 is greater than or equal to a. By proposition 6.3 and Lemma 6.2 (parts 5 and 7) we can deduce

$$(\forall x:N).(mem\ x\ l_1 \Rightarrow x \leq a)$$

and a similar proof establishes

$$(\forall x:N).(mem\ x\ l_2 \Rightarrow a \leq x)$$

Now, by Lemma 6.3 we can deduce that the result is sorted.
    To prove that

$$perm\ (a :: x)\ (\ l_1 + \!\!+[a] + \!\!+l_2\ )$$

we use a series of lemmas. By Lemma 6.2(11) the list x is a permutation of the two halves of the partition, which have permutations l_1 and l_2 by relation 6.3. Using Lemma 6.2, parts 9, 10 and 12, we have the desired result. This completes the induction step and the proof itself.   □

Corollary 6.5
For all lists l,

$$sorted\ (qsort\ l)\ \wedge\ perm\ l\ (qsort\ l)$$

Proof: Simply take the appropriate case of the theorem.   □

    A number of remarks are in order.

- In most cases of program verification, the induction used in verifying the result is of the same form as that used in the definition of the function; the proof we have given is no exception. *qsort* is defined to be a special case of *qsort'*, and we verified a generalization of the result using the same induction as we used to derive *qsort'*.

- The function *qsort'* appears to be less efficient than the Miranda algorithm, as the former contains the proof-theoretic information, transmitted through the recursive calls. This is the case if we use applicative order evaluation, which forces the evaluation of function arguments prior to evaluation of the body. On the other hand, if we use lazy evaluation, it can be seen that the terms p_1, p_2 in the recursive calls will never be evaluated. We come back to this point in Chapter 7.

- The presentation of sorting we have given here presents the algorithm first and the verification second. It is possible to reverse this, deriving the result that

$$(\forall l:[N]).(\exists l':[N]).(\ sorted\ l'\ \wedge\ perm\ l\ l'\ ) \tag{6.4}$$

and extracting the quicksort function from the proof. This seems highly artificial in this case where the function is well known, but the reader may wish to reconstruct the result in this way.

The definition of quicksort is an example of a general phenomenon, in which a general recursive definition of a function g over a type A

$$g\,x \equiv_{df} \dots g\,(h\,x)\dots$$

is justified by appeal to induction over another type B, where there is a function

$$f\,:\,A \Rightarrow B$$

so that

$$f\,(h\,x)$$

is a predecessor of $(f\,x)$ in B. The recursion g is justified by the **inverse image** of recursion over B using the function f. In the case of quicksort, we use the inverse image of induction over N under the length function. In related areas this function is often called a **norm**. This method justifies many important definitions, some of which are included in the exercises which follow.

Exercises

6.16 There are many other sorting algorithms over lists, amongst which are insertion sort and tree sort. Show first how these are expressed in type theory and then show how they meet the specification of a sorting algorithm. Alternatively prove the result 6.4 in such a way as to make the function extracted from the proof the algorithm you wish to express.

6.17 How would you show that the greatest common divisor function defined by

$$
\begin{aligned}
gcd\,n\,m &\equiv_{df} & n & \qquad \textbf{if } n = m \\
gcd\,n\,m &\equiv_{df} & gcd\,m\,n & \qquad \textbf{if } n < m \\
gcd\,n\,m &\equiv_{df} & gcd\,(n-m)\,m & \qquad \textbf{if } n > m > 0 \\
gcd\,n\,0 &\equiv_{df} & 0 & \qquad \textbf{if not}
\end{aligned}
$$

can be defined in type theory?

6.18 Show how the algorithm for the permutations of a list, which uses the Miranda list comprehension notation, can be coded in type theory.

$$
\begin{aligned}
perms\,[\,] &\equiv_{df} & [\,[\,]\,] \\
perms\,x &\equiv_{df} & [\,(a :: p)\,|\,a \leftarrow x\,;\,p \leftarrow perms\,(x - - a)\,]
\end{aligned}
$$

6.3 Dependent types and quantifiers

One of the features of TT which distinguishes it from traditional programming languages is its ability to express *dependent* types. These are types, or more correctly type expressions, which depend upon the value of one or more variables which they contain. The operations $\forall$, $\exists$ and W form types from these families of types, namely the dependent product type, the dependent sum or subset type and a well-founded type. This section concentrates on the two quantifiers, $\forall$ and $\exists$, after a discussion of how dependent types, or type families, can be defined.

6.3.1 Dependent types

By a dependent type we mean any type (expression) which contains one or more free variables. Under the logical interpretation such types are simply predicates, of course. Dependency is introduced in two ways.

The rule of I formation introduces values into the types. Recall the rule

$$\frac{A \ is \ a \ type \quad a:A \quad b:A}{I(A,a,b) \ is \ a \ type}(IF)$$

which forms the atomic *equality* proposition which is also written $a =_A b$. Clearly the expressions a and b can contain free variables, and thus are variables introduced into the types; depending on the complexity of a and b we build more or less complex propositions. Other dependent types are then formed using the propositional connectives and quantifiers, but these introduce no *additional* dependency. We have already seen examples of this, in Sections 4.10 and 6.1.2; another atomic example is the type

$$(\#l =_N n)$$

where l and n are variables of type $[A]$ and N, and from this we can form the dependent type

$$(\exists l:[A]) . (\#l =_N n)$$

which contains the variable n free. For a fixed value of n, this is the type of lists of that length, or more strictly, *pairs*

$$(l,r)$$

where r is a witness to (or proof of) the proposition $(\#l =_N n)$.

One general class of propositions we can define in this way are those which are representable by a boolean-valued function, such as the 'less than' relation which is represented by

$$lt_1 \ : \ (N \Rightarrow N \Rightarrow bool)$$

This is turned into a proposition by forming

$$I(bool \ , \ lt_1 \ m \ n \ , \ True)$$

with n,m free. Propositions representable by boolean-valued functions are decidable, and so this class of propositions is not closed under quantification over infinite domains. Once we have turned such a representation into a proposition as above its universal and existential closure as a proposition can be formed. This method of forming propositions is indirect: we define a boolean-valued function, by recursion say, and then make a proposition by equating its application to $True$ or $False$.

Using the universes $U_0, \ldots$ we can define dependent propositions directly. The 'small' types are members of the type U_0, and so we can use the *expression forming* operators, such as *cases* and recursion, to form type expressions. This approach is not restricted to the members of U_0; we can make the same constructions at each level U_n, and from an informal point of view these constructions are often uniform in n. We have already seen a number of examples of these definitions in Section 6.1.2.

It has been proposed that a facility be added to TT_0 which allows the definition of types (or propositions) inductively without using the universe U_0 – we return to this topic in Section 7.10.

6.3.2 The existential quantifier

The type $(\exists x : A) . B$ consists of pairs (a, b) with $a : A$ and $b : B[a/x]$. If $B[a/x]$ is thought of as a type, then the construct looks like a *sum* of the types $B(x)$ as x ranges over A. On the other hand if B is a predicate, then the construct can be seen as a *subset* of A, consisting of those a in A with the property $B[a/x]$. Consistent with the principle of complete presentation, the objects a are paired with the proofs b of the property $B[a/x]$. We saw an application of the subset type in the definition of the type of non-empty lists earlier.

An interesting class of subsets of $[A]$ is given by the family

$$[A]_n \equiv_{df} (\exists l : [A]) . (\#l = n)$$

of lists of length n, where $n : N$. Taking the sum over N, we have

$$(\exists n : N) . (\exists l : [A]) . (\#l = n)$$

which is isomorphic to $[A]$, by the functions

$$f \quad : \quad [A] \Rightarrow (\exists n : N) \,.\, (\exists l : [A]) \,.\, (\#l = n)$$
$$f\, l \quad \equiv_{df} \quad (\#l, (l, r(\#l)))$$

where $r(\#l)$ is the canonical member of $(\#l = \#l)$, and

$$g \quad : \quad (\exists n : N) \,.\, (\exists l : [A]) \,.\, (\#l = n) \Rightarrow [A]$$
$$g\,(n, (l, s)) \quad \equiv_{df} \quad l$$

This division of the type seems arbitrary, and indeed we could have divided the type according to any function

$$h \; : \; [A] \Rightarrow \ldots$$

but in this case it is interesting that many standard functions on lists can be made to commute with this **stratification**, since they preserve the lengths of the lists to which they are applied. One example is the *map* function, mentioned on page 184, and we have a family of functions

$$map_n \; : \; (A \Rightarrow B) \Rightarrow [A]_n \Rightarrow [B]_n$$

so that

$$map_n \; f \; (l, r) \equiv_{df} (map \; f \; l \, , \; r)$$

which is legitimate since $\#(map \; f \; l) = \#l$ is provable for all l, by induction. These map_n functions behave like *map*, except that they carry along the proof-theoretic information about the length of the list, which can be used by functions that use the result.

　　We usually read a judgement $a : A$ as asserting either that the object a has type A, or that a is a proof of A. There is a particular case in which *both* interpretations are used. This is the assertion that

$$(a, p) \; : \; (\exists x : A) \,.\, P$$

which we can read as saying that object a, of type A, meets the specification $P(x)$, witnessed by the proof $p : P[a/x]$ – we shall come back to this topic later.

6.3.3 The universal quantifier

The universal quantifier $\forall$ defines a dependent function space, so that if $f : (\forall x : A) . B$ then

$$f\, a \;:\; B[a/x]$$

We have already seen this used to good effect in the quicksort function above, amongst others. We shall see it used again in the coming example of vectors, in which the operations over vectors are parametrized over the size of the vector.

Both quantifiers have interesting properties when quantification is over a universe; before we look at that we examine a slightly larger-scale application, the implementation of a logic.

6.3.4 Implementing a logic

We take as an example the propositional logic of 'and' and 'implies'. Using our earlier notation, we have a well-founded type which describes the syntax of the formulas, thus:

$$fmla \quad \equiv_{df} \quad Vbl\, var + T + F +$$
$$And\, fmla\, fmla + Imp\, fmla\, fmla$$

where T and F represent the propositions 'true' and 'false', and var is a type representing the propositional variables, perhaps by character strings. A definition by primitive recursion over $fmla$ will give outright definitions for variables and the two constant propositions, and at $And\, f_1 f_2$, $Imp\, f_1 f_2$ will make recursive calls to the values at f_1 and f_2.

There are two approaches to defining the **proofs** of the logic. The first is to make an embedding into the logic of TT itself, by means of a function from formulas to types.

$$
\begin{aligned}
proof \quad &: \quad fmla \Rightarrow U_0 \\
proof\,(Vbl\, v) \quad &\equiv_{df} \quad \{Assum\, v\} \\
proof\, T \quad &\equiv_{df} \quad \top \\
proof\, F \quad &\equiv_{df} \quad \bot \\
proof\,(And\, f_1 f_2) \quad &\equiv_{df} \quad (proof\, f_1) \wedge (proof\, f_2) \\
proof\,(Imp\, f_1 f_2) \quad &\equiv_{df} \quad (proof\, f_1) \Rightarrow (proof\, f_2)
\end{aligned}
$$

$\{Assum\, v\}$ is intended to denote the type with the single element $Assum\, v$.

Proofs are to be constructed in this system using the mechanisms of TT itself; unfortunately, the method is flawed. Consider the proof

(*Assum v*) of the propositional variable (*Var v*). In order to construct a proof of the tautology

$$Imp\,(Var\,v)\,(Var\,v)$$

we need to be able to build a function from the one-element type to itself: this is trivial, but so is finding a function of type

$$Imp\,(Var\,v)\,(Var\,v')$$

for *any* variable v' in the system! This is not a sound representation. The difficulty is that the proofs of assumptions are not really variables of the system TT, which they would have to be for the embedding to be sound. Nonetheless, the embedding is sound if we leave out the variables, giving a system with constants and connectives.

In order to achieve a sound implementation in general, we look at the traditional 'LCF' approach to the problem [Paulson, 1987]. Under this approach we build an abstract type of proofs, with each deduction rule represented by a function over the type. The TT mechanism for abstract types is discussed in the section to come, here we look at the implementation of the proof type. We define

$$proof \quad \equiv_{df} \quad Tr \; + \; ConjI\,proof\,proof \; + \\ ConjE_1\,proof \; + \; ConjE_2\,proof \; + \\ ImpI\,proof\,fmla \; + \; ImpE\,proof\,proof$$

The type can be interpreted case by case.

Tr is the trivial proof of T.

ConjI $p_1\,p_2$ is a proof of (*And* $f_1\,f_2$) if the p_i are proofs of f_i.

ConjE$_1$ p is a proof of f_1 if p is a proof of the pair (f_1, f_2). If p does not have this form, the object does not represent a proof. A similar analysis applies to *ConjE*$_2$.

ImpI $p\,g$ is a proof of the formula (*Imp* $g\,f$), if p is a proof of f.

ImpE $p_1\,p_2$ is a proof of f if p_1 proves g and p_2 proves (*Imp* $g\,f$). If not, the object does not represent a proof.

The cases of *ConjE* and *ImpE* are difficult. Some applications of the constructors do not produce proofs. In the LCF approach, this gives rise to an error, or an exception if the SML language is used. We can use the dependent type mechanism to make proof construction secure without raising errors or exceptions.

First we define a function

$$proves \; : \; proof \Rightarrow (fmla + dummy)$$

which returns the object proved by an element of the type *proof*, giving the *dummy* value when one of the exceptional cases above arises. Then we define the subtypes

$$prf\ f \equiv_{df} (\exists p:proof).(proves\ p = f)$$

Using these we can give types to the functions which eliminate conjunctions

$$conjE_1\ :\ (\forall f:fmla).(\forall g:fmla).(prf(And\ f\ g) \Rightarrow prf\ f)$$

and implications.

$$impE\ :\ (\forall f:fmla).(\forall g:fmla).(prfg \Rightarrow prf(Imp\ g\ f) \Rightarrow prf\ f)$$

The essential effect of the functions *conjE* and *impE* is to apply the corresponding constructor. We know that their application is only permitted when it will take legitimate proofs into a legitimate proof, and thus the possibility of raising errors is excluded.

We can define functions *tr*, *conjI* and *impI* corresponding to the action of the constructors *Tr*, *ConjI* and *ImpI*, and then build on top of the type *proof* an abstract type of secure proofs, *secproof*, whose signature consists of these functions only. The type *secproof* will only contain legitimate proofs.

Exercises

6.19 Give definitions of the functions *proves*, *conjE*$_1$ and *impE* introduced above.

6.20 Give types for and then define the functions *tr*, *conjI* and *impI*.

6.21 Prove that the type *secproof* contains only legitimate proofs, and that all such proofs are contained therein.

6.3.5   Quantification and universes – $\forall$

Quantification over the universes $U_0, \ldots, U_n, \ldots$ allows us to assert the existence of types with certain properties, and to make definitions which are parametrized by a type parameter. To take the latter example first, we saw in Section 5.9.2 that a form of polymorphism was given by definitions such as

$$\lambda A_{U_0}.\lambda x_A.x\ :\ (\forall A:U_0).(A \Rightarrow A)$$

in which the first parameter ranges over the universe U_0. Such definitions are not restricted to the first universe, and we can derive uniformly in n

the judgements

$$(\lambda A\!:\!U_n)\,.\,(\lambda x\!:\!A)\,.\,x \;:\; (\forall A\!:\!U_n)\,.\,(A \Rightarrow A)$$

since the role played by the A is purely that of a parameter.

We have already seen how the quicksort function *qsort* can be defined over lists of numbers. In fact, it can be defined over any type A which carries a function

$$lesseq \;:\; A \Rightarrow A \Rightarrow bool$$

so the definition may be construed thus:

$$qsort \;:\; (\forall A\!:\!U_0)\,.\,((A \Rightarrow A \Rightarrow bool) \Rightarrow ([A] \Rightarrow [A]))$$

This parametrization is possible in a language such as Miranda, but with the more expressive type system of TT we can go further and demand that the function supplied is an ordering. This we define thus:

$$\begin{aligned}
Ordering(A) \quad \equiv_{df} \quad &(\exists\, lesseq\!:\!(A \Rightarrow A \Rightarrow bool))\,.\,(\forall a\!:\!A)\,. \\
&(\;lesseq\ u\ u = True\ \land \\
&(\forall a,b\!:\!A)\,.\,lesseq\ a\ b = lesseq\ b\ a\ \land \\
&(\forall a,b,c\!:\!A)\,.\,lesseq\ a\ b = lesseq\ b\ c = True \Rightarrow \\
&lesseq\ a\ c = True\;)
\end{aligned}$$

The subtype of sorted elements of $[A]$ is given by

$$Slist(A) \equiv_{df} (\exists l\!:\![A])\,.\,(sorted\ l)$$

where the predicate *sorted* was defined above, and we can then show that there is a verified version of quicksort

$$vsort \;:\; (\forall A\!:\!U_0)\,.\,(Ordering(A) \Rightarrow ([A] \Rightarrow Slist(A)))$$

The examples we have seen so far resemble the parametric polymorphic functions permitted by the Hindley–Milner type system [Milner, 1978] which is used in the languages Miranda and SML. Milner polymorphic types contain free type variables which resemble the $A\!:\!U_0$ of the examples above; there is no operation under which these variables are bound – a free type variable is equivalent to a variable bound *at the top level*. A polymorphic typing under the Hindley–Milner system can be seen as a shorthand for a class of monomorphic typings: those which arise as substitution instances of the polymorphic type.

In the system TT we can express different types. One of the simplest examples is the type

$$(\forall A : U_0).(A \Rightarrow A) \Rightarrow (\forall A : U_0).(A \Rightarrow A)$$

this type cannot be seen as a shorthand for a collection of monotypes: it is the type of functions from a polymorphic type to itself. A function of this type is given by

$$\lambda f.(\,if\ f\ bool\ (eq_N\ (f\ N\ 0)\ (f\ N\ 1))\ then\ f\ else\ id\,)$$

In the condition $f\ bool\ (eq_N\ (f\ N\ 0)\ (f\ N\ 1))$ the function f is used on *both* the booleans and the natural numbers. The function must therefore be of the polymorphic type $(\forall A : U_0).(A \Rightarrow A)$. The result returned is either the function f itself or the identity function

$$id \equiv_{df} \lambda A_{U_0}.\lambda x_A.x$$

Quantifiers over a universe can be used to define weak versions of various familiar type constructors. For example, the type

$$Prod\ A\ B \equiv_{df} (\forall C : U_0).((A \Rightarrow B \Rightarrow C) \Rightarrow C)$$

resembles the product of the types A and B (which we assume inhabit the universe U_0). Given elements $a : A$ and $b : B$ we can define

$$
\begin{aligned}
F_{a,b} \quad &: \quad Prod\ A\ B \\
F_{a,b} \quad &\equiv_{df} \quad (\lambda C : U_0).(\lambda f : A \Rightarrow B \Rightarrow C).(f\ a\ b)
\end{aligned}
$$

and we can also define two 'projections' thus:

$$
\begin{aligned}
p \quad &: \quad Prod\ A\ B \Rightarrow A \\
p\ F \quad &\equiv_{df} \quad F\ A\ (\lambda x_A.\lambda y_B.x)
\end{aligned}
$$

$$
\begin{aligned}
q \quad &: \quad Prod\ A\ B \Rightarrow B \\
q\ F \quad &\equiv_{df} \quad F\ B\ (\lambda x_A.\lambda y_B.y)
\end{aligned}
$$

Observe that

$$
\begin{aligned}
p\ F_{a,b} \quad &\equiv_{df} \quad F_{a,b}\ A\ (\lambda x_A.\lambda y_B.x) \\
&\equiv_{df} \quad (\lambda C : U_0).(\lambda f : A \Rightarrow B \Rightarrow C).(f\ a\ b)\ A\ (\lambda x_A.\lambda y_B.x) \\
&\rightarrow \quad (\lambda f : A \Rightarrow B \Rightarrow A).(f\ a\ b)\ (\lambda x_A.\lambda y_B.x) \\
&\rightarrow \quad (\lambda x_A.\lambda y_B.x)\ a\ b \\
&\rightarrow \quad \lambda y_B.a\ b \\
&\rightarrow \quad a
\end{aligned}
$$

In a similar way, $q\ F_{a,b} \twoheadrightarrow b$. This shows that the function $F_{a,b}$ can be thought of as representing the pair formed from a and b. *Prod A B* is a *weak* representative of the product as it is not possible to prove from the rules of TT that every member of the type is such a pair: we fail to have a general enough elimination or closure condition.

Other representations of types such as the disjunction (or sum type) and algebraic types can be found in Chapter 11 of [Girard *et al.*, 1989].

Exercises

6.22 Give a derivation of the verified quicksort function above.

6.23 Show that the type

$$(\forall C:U_0).((A \Rightarrow C) \Rightarrow (B \Rightarrow C) \Rightarrow C)$$

can be thought of as a weak sum type, and that the type

$$(\forall C:U_0).(C \Rightarrow (C \Rightarrow C) \Rightarrow C)$$

can be seen as a representation of the type of natural numbers.

6.24 Compare the weak representations of types given in the section and exercise above with the elimination rules for the types represented – can you see a general pattern emerging?

6.3.6   Quantification and universes – $\exists$

Existential quantification over a universe offers a rich collection of examples. In Section 5.9.2 it was explained that objects of type $(\exists A : U_0).P$ were pairs (A,p) with A a (small) type and p a member of the type P, which depends upon A. In the simplest case, of $P \equiv A$, we have a *sum* of the types in U_0.

An important case is when $P(A)$ is a conjunction of types

$$P_1 \wedge \ldots \wedge P_n$$

Objects of the existential type consist of a type A, together with elements $p_i : P_i$. We can think of $P_1 \wedge \ldots \wedge P_n$ as a **signature** and the tuple $(p_1, \ldots, p_n)$ as an implementation of the signature. A traditional example in such cases is

$$A \wedge (N \Rightarrow A \Rightarrow A) \wedge (A \Rightarrow A) \wedge (A \Rightarrow N)$$

which gives elements which can usefully be named thus:

$$
\begin{aligned}
empty &: \quad A \\
push &: \quad (N \Rightarrow A \Rightarrow A) \\
pop &: \quad (A \Rightarrow A) \\
top &: \quad (A \Rightarrow N)
\end{aligned}
$$

The type $(\exists A : U_0) . P$ can therefore be thought of as an abstract type, or more precisely the collection of implementations of an abstract type, in this case the type of *stacks*.

We observed earlier, in Section 5.3.3, that the rule $(\exists E')$ was weaker than the rule $(\exists E)$ or the equivalent pair $(\exists E_1')$ and $(\exists E_2')$. We discuss their formal differences in Section 8.1.3, but we ought to look here at how their difference affects the abstract data type or module construct.

The weak rule has been characterized by MacQueen in [MacQueen, 1986] as giving only a **hypothetical** witness to the existential statement. It is this interpretation which underlies the Miranda **abstype**, [Turner, 1985], and constructs in a number of other languages. This interpretation has the disadvantage that the encapsulation cannot be re-opened once formed, making it difficult to extend the functionality of the abstype once formed, a basic tenet of object-oriented design. Specific examples can be found in MacQueen's paper and in the survey [Cardelli and Wegner, 1985]. Mac-Queen therefore argues in [MacQueen, 1986] and [MacQueen, 1990], which discusses the module mechanism in Standard ML, that the appropriate notion is the *strong* one, which makes the witnesses **transparent**, allowing both the underlying type and the implementation functions to be extracted, and thus permitting such extensions of types. Naturally, there are advantages to each approach, and perhaps both could usefully be included in a programming language, each serving its own purpose.

We can interpret existential quantification over a universe in a different way. The Haskell programming language uses Wadler and Blott's idea of **type classes**, first introduced in [Wadler and Blott, 1989]. The motivation behind type classes is to give a cleaner treatment of the quasi-polymorphism of the equality operation in languages such as Miranda and SML. In the former, an equality is defined over every type, despite the fact that it is the undefined function on all but ground types. In SML a special kind of type variable is introduced to range over only those types bearing an equality. Type classes are defined to be collections of types each member of which must have functions over it implementing the signature which defines the type. For instance, every type t in the Eq class must carry a function **eq** of type

```
eq : t -> t -> bool
```

In type theory, a type class will be given by

$$(\exists t : U_0) . S$$

where S is the signature defining the class, in the case of **Eq** this being $t \Rightarrow t \Rightarrow bool$. An example using **Eq** is the function which removes every occurrence of an element from a list

$$
\begin{array}{lll}
remove \; [\,] \; b & \equiv_{df} & [\,] \\
remove \; (a :: x) \; b & \equiv_{df} & remove \; x \; b & \textbf{if } eq \; a \; b \\
remove \; (a :: x) \; b & \equiv_{df} & a :: (remove \; x \; b) & \textbf{if not}
\end{array}
$$

which has the special Haskell type

```
remove : (Eq t) => [t] -> t -> [t]
```

which is intended to mean that `remove` is only defined over elements of the class **Eq**. If we write

$$Eqt \equiv_{df} (\exists A : U_0) . (A \Rightarrow A \Rightarrow bool)$$

then we can model the function *remove* in TT thus:

$$remove : (\forall (A, eq) : Eqt) . ([A] \Rightarrow A \Rightarrow [A])$$

where we use the pattern (A, eq) to range over elements of the existential type purely for readability. The restricted polymorphism is expressed explicitly, since the type variable A ranges only over those A which possess a function of type $(A \Rightarrow A \Rightarrow bool)$.

Instead of the predicate part P of the type $(\exists A : U_0) . P$ being simply a type, it can contain proof information as well. For instance we might want to stipulate that any implementation of the stack signature satisfies

$$(\forall n : N) . (\forall a : A) . (pop \, (push \, n \, a) = a)$$

$$(\forall n : N) . (\forall a : A) . (top \, (push \, n \, a) = n)$$

We do this by forming a subtype of

$$A \wedge (N \Rightarrow A \Rightarrow A) \wedge (A \Rightarrow A) \wedge (A \Rightarrow N)$$

thus:

$$
\begin{aligned}
& (\exists \, (empty, push, pop, top) : A \wedge (N \Rightarrow A \Rightarrow A) \wedge (A \Rightarrow A) \wedge (A \Rightarrow N)) . \\
& ((\forall n : N) . (\forall a : A) . (pop \, (push \, n \, a) = a) \wedge \\
& (\forall n : N) . (\forall a : A) . (top \, (push \, n \, a) = n))
\end{aligned}
$$

In exactly the same way we can form **logical type classes** for which we specify not only the existence of objects of a certain type, but also demand that they have certain properties. In the case of Eq, we might ask for the relation to be an equivalence relation, rather than an arbitrary binary boolean-valued function. The extra information supplied in one of these type classes would allow us to infer properties of the functions defined over the class.

It is interesting to observe that abstract data types and type classes are modelled by exactly the same construction in type theory. In Haskell the difference between the two lies in their *use*. In a Miranda abstype declaration, we see a signature defined and bound immediately to a particular implementation. Any code which uses the abstype must be capable of using *any* implementation of the signature, and so can be thought of as a function over the appropriate type class. The novel feature of type classes is that these functions over classes can be declared *explicitly* and can be applied to more than one implementation of the specification within a given scope.

Type classes can be thought of as adding one aspect of object-oriented programming to a functional language. A member of a type class might be thought of as an *object*. From this perspective, it is interesting to see that there is support for (multiple) inheritance. A subclass of the class

$$C_1 \equiv_{df} (\exists t : U_0) . S_1$$

is defined by extending the signature part by adding more operations (or in the case of a logical type class more operations or properties) to give the signature S_2 and the corresponding class C_2. Because S_2 extends S_1 there will be a projection function

$$\pi_{2,1} : S_2 \Rightarrow S_1$$

which can be extended to

$$
\begin{aligned}
forget_{2,1} \quad &: \quad C_2 \Rightarrow C_1 \\
forget_{2,1} \quad &\equiv_{df} \quad \lambda p . (Fst\ p, \pi\ (Snd\ p))
\end{aligned}
$$

Any function $F : C_1 \Rightarrow R$ defined over the class C_1 can be applied to members of C_2 by composing with the function $forget_{2,1}$:

$$F \circ forget_{2,1} : C_2 \Rightarrow R$$

Multiple inheritance is supported by different extensions to signatures: the *forget* functions will be defined uniquely by the signatures involved.

6.4   A case study – vectors

Vectors are fixed-length sequences of values from a given type. One way to model them is using the subtypes $[A]_n$ of the list type $[A]$; this section explores a different treatment, representing vectors as functions over finite types. First we define the finite types, then the vectors and finally we show how functions can be defined *uniformly* over the different sizes of vector.

6.4.1   Finite types revisited

TT contains the finite types N_n, which are an obvious candidate for the domains of the vectors – why are they unsuitable? The difficulty is that they are not defined in a uniform way; in other words the mapping

$$n \mapsto N_n$$

cannot be defined in type theory. We now show how the finite types can be defined as subtypes of N in a uniform way. Recall the definition of the 'less than' relation in Section 6.1.2

$$
\begin{aligned}
m < 0 \quad &\equiv_{df} \quad \bot \\
0 < (n+1) \quad &\equiv_{df} \quad \top \\
(m+1) < (n+1) \quad &\equiv_{df} \quad m < n
\end{aligned}
$$

We first establish that the relation is a total ordering on the natural numbers.

Theorem 6.6

The relation '$<$' is a total ordering over the natural numbers, as each of the following propositions is inhabited.

(1) Reflexivity: $x \not< x$

(2) Symmetry: $\neg(x < y \wedge y < x)$

(3) Transitivity: $(x < y) \Rightarrow (y < z) \Rightarrow (x < z)$

(4) Totality: $(x < y) \vee (x = y) \vee (x > y)$

(5) Successor: $x < (x + 1)$

Proof: Each of the parts is proved by induction. We look at the first and the penultimate. For reflexivity, we work by induction over x. The base case $0 \not< 0$ is given by the clause $m < 0 \equiv_{df} \bot$ of the definition. Now suppose that $(n + 1) < (n + 1)$. By the third clause of the definition we have $n < n$, which gives $\bot$ by induction, so $(n + 1) \not< (n + 1)$.

To prove totality, we work by induction on x with a subsidiary induction over y. Take x to be 0 – if y is zero then $x = y$, otherwise by the second clause of the definition $x < y$. The induction step is analogous. □

Definition 6.7

The **finite types** C_n are defined thus

$$C_n \equiv_{df} (\exists m : N) . (m < n)$$

This definition *is* uniform in the variable n.

We can view the transitivity of '$<$' as asserting the existence of canonical embeddings

$$f_{p,q} \; : \; C_p \Rightarrow C_q$$

when $p \leq q$. If $p = q$ the function is simply the identity, whilst if $p < q$, for any $(m, r) : C_p$, $m < p$ and $p < q$ gives $m < q$ and thus $(m, s) \; : \; C_q$ for some proof s of the inequality.

We can also establish a characterization like that of the types N_n.

Theorem 6.8

For each C_n we can show that the following proposition is provable.

$$(\forall x : C_n) . (\; x = \overline{0} \lor x = \overline{1} \lor \ldots \lor x = \overline{n-1} \;)$$

where by $\overline{n}$ we mean the pair

$$(\; \underbrace{succ\,(succ \ldots (succ\; 0) \ldots)}_{n} , \; Triv\;)$$

Proof: The proof is by a *meta-theoretic* induction over n. We cannot formalize in a uniform way the sequence of formulas asserted, and so we cannot formalize the argument. □

Do the C_n have exactly the properties of the N_n? Given the last propositions, the rules for introducing elements of the two types are equivalent. The $cases_n$ construct can be represented by a function with domain C_n, where we can take account of the different types of the various values by mapping into a sum type. Specifically, to model

$$(\lambda m : N_n) . (cases_n \; m \; a_1 \ldots a_n)$$

with $a_i : A_i$ we define the function

$$(\lambda x : C_n) . (\; if \; (eq_n \; x \; \overline{0}) \; then \; (in_1 \; a_1) \; else$$
$$if \; (eq_n \; x \; \overline{1}) \; then \; (in_2 \; a_2) \ldots else \; (in_n \; a_n) \;)$$

of type

$$C_n \Rightarrow (A_1 \vee \ldots \vee A_n)$$

where we use in_k for the injection of the component type A_k into the n-ary sum $(A_1 \vee \ldots \vee A_n)$, and eq_n for the equality function over C_n.

The construct $(cases_n \ m \ a_1 \ldots a_n)$ is characterized by the values m and $a_1, \ldots, a_n$. For a function modelling this to be thus characterized, we need to adopt an extensional approach, as outlined in Section 5.8.

Exercise

6.25 Show that given definitions of addition and multiplication the following propositions are inhabited:

$$(a < b) \wedge (c < d) \Rightarrow (a + c < b + d)$$
$$(a < b) \wedge (0 < c) \Rightarrow (a * c < b * c)$$

6.4.2   Vectors

Using the finite types of the previous section we are in a position to define the vector types.

Definition 6.9

The type of **vectors** of length n over type A, $Vec \ A \ n$, is defined thus

$$Vec \ A \ n \equiv_{df} (C_n \Rightarrow A)$$

The definition of $Vec \ A \ n$ is uniform in A and n, and so definitions of vector operations can be made parametric in either A, n or both. We now give a number of definitions of vector operations.

A constant vector is formed by

$$const \quad : \quad (\forall A : U_0) . (\forall n : N) . (A \Rightarrow Vec \ A \ n)$$
$$const \ A \ n \ a \quad \equiv_{df} \quad \lambda x . a$$

A vector v is updated in position m with b by

$$update \ A \ n \quad : \quad Vec \ A \ n \Rightarrow C_n \Rightarrow A \Rightarrow Vec \ A \ n$$
$$update \ A \ n \ v \ m \ b \quad \equiv_{df} \quad \lambda x . (\ if \ (eq_n \ m \ x) \ then \ b \ else \ (v \ x) \ )$$

A permutation of the indices C_n is represented by a function $p : (C_n \Rightarrow C_n)$, and the elements of the vector v are permuted by composing the permutation p with v.

Given a binary operator on the type A, θ, we **reduce** the vector

$$< a_1, \ldots, a_n >$$

using θ to form

$$(\ldots (a_1 \, \theta \, a_2) \, \theta \, \ldots \, \theta \, a_n)$$

The type of *reduce* is given by

$$(\forall A : U_0) . (\forall n : Pos) . ((A \Rightarrow A \Rightarrow A) \Rightarrow Vec \, A \, n \Rightarrow A)$$

where Pos is the set of positive natural numbers $(\exists n : N) . (0 < n)$. The definition is by induction over the positive natural numbers. For vectors of length one, we return the single value, and for the vector v

$$< a_1, \ldots, a_n, a_{n+1} >$$

we reduce $v' \equiv_{df} < a_1, \ldots, a_n >$ giving r, say, which is then used to form $r \, \theta \, a_{n+1}$. To make the definition above precise we need to explain how an element of a vector is accessed. If $m : C_n$ and $w \,:\, Vec \, A \, n$ then the mth element is given by the application $(w \, m)$. How is the vector $v' : C_n$ formed from $v : C_{n+1}$? We simply define the composition

$$v \circ f_{n,n+1} \,:\, (C_n \Rightarrow A) \equiv Vec \, A \, n$$

where $f_{n,n+1}$ is the canonical embedding given above.

Exercises

6.26 Give a type and definition for the function giving the inner product of a numerical vector.

6.27 How would you define a general sorting function for vectors?

6.28 Explain how the model above can be extended to treat rectangular arrays of any dimension.

6.29 Using the types defined in the previous question, define the array product and inversion operations. In the latter case you can use a subtype to restrict the domain to those arrays which possess inverses.

6.5   Proof extraction; top-down proof

Up to now in these examples, we have treated the system as a functional programming language, reasoning about objects, their types and their computational behaviour. It is possible to give a different presentation of the rules in which some of the information about the proof objects is suppressed. The information can be used to *extract* a proof object from the derivation given. This approach underlies the Nuprl system [Constable and others, 1986]. The first two examples are discussed in [Constable and others, 1986, Sections 4.3 and 4.4] – the reader can compare the two treatments.

6.5.1   Propositional logic

If we look at the rules for propositional logic, taking $(\vee E')$ as the rule of disjunction elimination, they have an interesting characteristic: there is no link between the right-hand and left-hand sides of the judgements

$$proof \ : \ proposition$$

which they involve. Taking the rule $(\vee E')$ as an example, we can strip the proof information from the rule, leaving

$$
\begin{array}{ccc}
 & [A] & [B] \\
 & \vdots & \vdots \\
(A \vee B) & C & C \\
\hline
 & C &
\end{array}
\ (\vee E')
$$

Of course, we still know that given the appropriate proofs of the hypotheses we can form the proof object $vcases'_{x,y} \ p \ u \ v$ which proves the conclusion, C.

Without the proof information, the rule admits of a second reading:

> In order to derive C (from hypotheses Γ) it is sufficient to derive $(A \vee B)$ (from Γ) and to derive C in the two cases that A and B are assumed (together with Γ).

We call this the backwards or **top-down** interpretation. Other rules admit a similar reading. $(\Rightarrow I)$ can be construed as saying

> In order to derive $(A \Rightarrow B)$ it is sufficient to derive B from the (additional) assumption A.

We now use these ideas to give a 'proof-free' derivation of the formula

$$(P \vee \neg P) \Rightarrow (\neg P \Rightarrow \neg Q) \Rightarrow (Q \Rightarrow P)$$

Using $(\Rightarrow I)$ top-down three times, it is sufficient to derive the formula P from the assumptions

$$(P \vee \neg P) \, , \, (\neg P \Rightarrow \neg Q) \, , \, Q$$

The backwards reading of $(\vee E')$ above suggests how to use a disjunctive assumption. To derive P from $(P \vee \neg P), (\neg P \Rightarrow \neg Q), Q$ it is enough to derive P from the two sets of assumptions

$$P \, , \, (\neg P \Rightarrow \neg Q) \, , \, Q \quad \text{and} \quad \neg P \, , \, (\neg P \Rightarrow \neg Q) \, , \, Q$$

The derivation from the first set is trivial, as P is a member. In the second case, we apply *modus ponens* to the first two formulas, giving $\neg Q$, and from this and Q, *modus ponens* gives $\bot$, which by *ex falso quodlibet* gives us any formula, and in particular P. It is interesting to note that, as is often the case, a top-down construction reaches a point beyond which it yields to a bottom-up approach. Making the description above into a formal derivation, we have

$$
\cfrac{P \vee \neg P \;\; [P]^1 \qquad \cfrac{Q \quad \cfrac{\cfrac{[\neg P]^1 \quad \neg P \Rightarrow \neg Q}{\neg Q}(\Rightarrow E)}{\cfrac{\bot}{P}(\bot I)}(\Rightarrow E)}{P}}{P}(\vee E')_1
$$

From this we can discharge the assumptions thus

$$[Q]^2, [\neg P]^1, [\neg P \Rightarrow \neg Q]^3$$
$$\vdots$$

$$
\cfrac{\cfrac{\cfrac{\cfrac{[P \vee \neg P]^4 \;\; [P]^1 \qquad P}{P}(\vee E')_1}{Q \Rightarrow P}(\Rightarrow I)_2}{(\neg P \Rightarrow \neg Q) \Rightarrow (Q \Rightarrow P)}(\Rightarrow I)_3}{(P \vee \neg P) \Rightarrow (\neg P \Rightarrow \neg Q) \Rightarrow (Q \Rightarrow P)}(\Rightarrow I)_4
$$

We can now extract the proof information, naming the assumptions and forming terms as described by the full proof rules.

$$
\cfrac{x:(P \vee \neg P) \;\; [u:P]^1 \qquad \cfrac{z:Q \quad \cfrac{\cfrac{[v:\neg P]^1 \quad y:(\neg P \Rightarrow \neg Q)}{(y\,v):\neg Q}(\Rightarrow E)}{\cfrac{((y\,v)\,z):\bot}{abort_P\,((y\,v)\,z):P}(\bot I)}(\Rightarrow E)}{}}{cases'_{u,v}\,x\,u\,(abort_P\,((y\,v)\,z)) \; : \; P}(\vee E')_1
$$

If we write e for $cases'_{u,v} \; x \; u \, (abort_P \, ((y \, v) \, z))$, we obtain finally

$$[z:Q]^2, [v:\neg P]^1, [y:(\neg P \Rightarrow \neg Q)]^3$$
$$\vdots$$

$$\cfrac{\cfrac{[x:(P \vee \neg P)]^4 \quad [u:P]^1 \qquad\qquad P}{\cfrac{\cfrac{\cfrac{e \; : \; P}{\lambda z . e \; : \; (Q \Rightarrow P)}(\Rightarrow I)_2}{\lambda y . \lambda z . e \; : \; (\neg P \Rightarrow \neg Q) \Rightarrow (Q \Rightarrow P)}(\Rightarrow I)_3}}(\vee E')_1}{\lambda x . \lambda y . \lambda z . e \; : \; (P \vee \neg P) \Rightarrow (\neg P \Rightarrow \neg Q) \Rightarrow (Q \Rightarrow P)}(\Rightarrow I)_4$$

which gives the proof object

$$\lambda x . \lambda y . \lambda z . (\; cases'_{u,v} \; x \; u \, (abort_P \, ((y \, v) \, z)) \,)$$

as a witness of the proof of the formula.

6.5.2   Predicate logic

The proof extraction technique can be extended to some of the rules of predicate logic. For the universal quantifier we obtain

$$[x : A]$$
$$\vdots$$

$$\cfrac{P}{(\forall x:A) . P}(\forall I) \quad \text{and} \quad \cfrac{a \; : \; A \quad (\forall x:A) . P}{P[a/x]}(\forall E)$$

whilst for the existential quantifier we have

$$[x:A; B]$$
$$\vdots$$

$$\cfrac{a \; : \; A \quad P[a/x]}{(\exists x:A) . P}(\exists I) \quad \text{and} \quad \cfrac{(\exists x:A) . B \qquad C}{C}(\exists E')$$

Some proof information seems to remain here, in the judgement $a \; : \; A$ of $(\exists I)$ for instance. Since the logic is typed, this minimum of type information must be retained to ensure the well-formedness of propositions. An example of a 'proofless' derivation of $(\forall x \; : \; A) . (\exists y \; : \; B) . P$ from

$(\exists y : B) . (\forall x : A) . P$ follows.

$$\dfrac{[y:B]^2 \quad \dfrac{\dfrac{[x:A]^1 \quad [(\forall x:A).P]^2}{P}(\forall E)}{\dfrac{(\exists y:B).P}{(\forall x:A).(\exists y:B).P}(\exists I)}(\forall I)_1}{(\forall x:A).(\exists y:B).P}(\exists E')_2$$

with $(\exists y : B) . (\forall x : A) . P$ on the left of the final line.

The derivation can now have the proof object extracted from it, if we name p and q the proofs of $(\exists y : B) . (\forall x : A) . P$ and $(\forall x : A) . P$ which are assumed to exist. The q will be discharged, as we shall see.

$$\dfrac{[y:B]^2 \quad \dfrac{\dfrac{[x:A]^1 \quad [q:(\forall x:A).P]^2}{(q\,x):P}(\forall E)}{\dfrac{(y,q\,x)\ :\ (\exists y:B).P}{\lambda x.(y,q\,x)\ :\ (\forall x:A).(\exists y:B).P}(\exists I)}(\forall I)_1}{Cases_{y,q}\,p\ (\lambda x.(y,q\,x))\ :\ (\forall x:A).(\exists y:B).P}(\exists E')_2$$

with $p\ :\ (\exists y:B).(\forall x:A).P$ on the left of the final line.

The only free variable in the proof object is p which represents the undischarged assumption $(\exists y : B) . (\forall x : A) . P$.

We have only considered the *weak* existential elimination rule in this way as the stronger rule, in either the forms $(\exists E'_2)$ or $(\exists E)$, introduces a proposition as a conclusion which depends upon the proof object of the proposition above the line. To use these rules, which we need to do to prove the axiom of choice,

$$(\forall x : A) . (\exists y : B) . P \Rightarrow (\exists f : A \Rightarrow B) . (\forall x : A) . P[(f\,x)/y]$$

for instance, we need to reason about the proof terms explicitly. Similar remarks apply to the choice of disjunction elimination rule.

6.5.3   Natural numbers

We can extend this proofless derivation to results involving data types such as the natural numbers. Obviously the introduction rules still need to mention the elements of N, and so are unchanged, but we can re-state the (NE) rule thus:

$$\dfrac{n:N \quad C[0/x] \quad (\forall n:N).(C[n/x] \Rightarrow C[succ\,n/x])}{C[n/x]}(NE)$$

An example we might prove thus is $(\forall n : N) . (0 < fac\,n)$ where the proposition $(m < n)$ was first defined in Section 6.1.2, and fac has the definition

$$fac\,0 \quad \equiv_{df} \quad 1$$

$$fac\,(n+1) \quad \equiv_{df} \quad (n+1) * (fac\,n)$$

We first have to derive $(0 < 1)$ which is a special case of $(0 < n+1)$, which is itself trivially derivable. In the second case we have to derive

$$(\forall n : N)\,.\,((0 < fac\,n) \Rightarrow (0 < fac\,(n+1)))$$

for which, using the rules $(\forall I)$ and $(\Rightarrow I)$ top-down, it is sufficient to derive $(0 < fac\,(n+1))$ on the assumption that $n\ :\ N$ and $(0 < fac\,n)$. Since $fac\,(n+1)$ is the product

$$(n+1) * (fac\,n)$$

and as it is a standard result (and exercise!) that a product of positive numbers is positive, the result is derived.

Exercises

6.30 Give 'proofless' derivations of the formulas $(B \vee C) \Rightarrow \neg(\neg B \wedge \neg C)$, $A \Rightarrow \neg\neg A$ and $(\neg A \vee \neg B) \Rightarrow \neg(A \wedge B)$, and from your derivations extract the corresponding proof objects.

6.31 Find a 'proofless' derivation of the formula

$$(\forall x : X)\,.\,(A \Rightarrow B) \Rightarrow ((\exists x : X)\,.\,A \Rightarrow (\exists x : X)\,.\,B)$$

and extract a proof object from the derivation.

6.32 Formalize the 'proofless' derivation of the fact that all values of fac are positive, assuming the lemma on multiplication, and give the proof object that it generates.

6.33 Making a suitable definition of the multiplication operation '$*$' over N, give a 'proofless' derivation of the lemma that a product of positive numbers is positive.

6.6   Program development – Polish national flag

This section addresses the problem of the Polish national flag, which is an inessential simplification of the problem of the Dutch national flag. This was first addressed in [Dijkstra, 1976]. In the context of type theory it was first investigated in [Petersson and Smith, 1985] and later in Section 22.2 of [Nordström *et al.*, 1990]. The problem, baldly stated, is this: given a sequence of items which are either red or white, return a permuted sequence in which all the red items precede the white.

Our approach differs from that in [Nordström *et al.*, 1990] in two ways. First, we express the specification in a different way, so as to separate the computational from the proof theoretic; secondly, we eschew the use of the subset type. We shall discuss this type in some detail in Chapter 7. We also use an 'equational' notation which is closer to that in use in the majority of functional programming languages.

Our development depends upon some of the functions and predicates which were introduced earlier; in particular we shall use $+\!\!+$, the list concatenation operator, the predicate $perm\ l\ m$, which expresses the fact that the list l is a permutation of the list m, together with the auxiliary $occs\ a\ l$, which counts the number of occurrences of a in the list l. We assume that the colours are represented by the boolean type, $bool$ (which we shall abbreviate C, for colour), with the value $True$ representing the colour red. We therefore say $isRed\ a \equiv_{df} a = True$ and similarly for $isWhite$. Also, we define

$$
\begin{array}{lcl}
allRed & : & [bool] \Rightarrow U_0 \\
allRed\ [\,] & \equiv_{df} & \top \\
allRed\ (a :: x) & \equiv_{df} & isRed\ a \wedge allRed\ x
\end{array}
$$

with the corresponding definition for $allWhite$. One way to express the specification of the problem is then to say

$$
\begin{array}{l}
(\forall l : [C]) \cdot (\exists (l', l'') : [C] \wedge [C]) \cdot \\
\quad (allRed\ l' \wedge allWhite\ l'' \wedge perm\ l\ (l' +\!\!+ l''))
\end{array} \tag{6.5}
$$

What we seek is, in fact, a function which returns the pair of lists (l', l'') corresponding to each l, so we modify the specification to read

$$
\begin{array}{l}
(\exists f : [C] \Rightarrow [C] \wedge [C]) \cdot (\forall l : [C]) \cdot \\
\quad allRed\ (fst\ (f\ l)) \wedge allWhite\ (snd\ (f\ l)) \wedge \\
\quad perm\ l\ ((fst\ (f\ l)) +\!\!+ (snd\ (f\ l)))
\end{array} \tag{6.6}
$$

What will a proof of this formula consist of? It will be a pair (f, p) with

$$
f : [C] \Rightarrow [C] \wedge [C]
$$

and p a proof that for all lists l

$$
\begin{array}{l}
allRed\ (fst\ (f\ l)) \wedge allWhite\ (snd\ (f\ l)) \wedge \\
perm\ l\ ((fst\ (f\ l)) +\!\!+ (snd\ (f\ l)))
\end{array} \tag{6.7}
$$

This pair consists precisely of the *function* required together with a *proof* that is has the property required of it. This is the general form that an implementation of a *specification* in type theory should take – we return to this topic in Chapter 7. Note that the transformation of the first specification into the second is by no means *ad hoc* – we have applied the axiom of choice to the first to obtain the second; indeed given this axiom the two specifications are logically equivalent. The axiom of choice is the statement

$$(\forall x:A).(\exists y:B).P(x,y) \Rightarrow (\exists f:A \Rightarrow B).(\forall x:A).P(x,f\,x)$$

It is not hard to show that this type is inhabited; it is left as an exercise for the reader, who will be able to find a proof in [Martin-Löf, 1985].

There are two distinct ways of proving a statement such as 6.6.

- We can prove the statement by giving a term f and proving the formula 6.7. This method corresponds to traditional program development in a functional programming language: we first define the function we think has the desired property and separately we prove that it does have the property, an exercise in program verification. This was the method we used in developing quicksort in Section 6.2.

- Alternatively, we can develop the proof from the top down, reducing the existential statement 6.6 to 6.5. We then try to prove this formula directly and from the proof we extract a function by applying the axiom of choice. This *program extraction* technique is the one which we follow here: note that both methods can lead to the same definition of the required function.

Using the first method we would define the function

$$
\begin{array}{llll}
split & : & [C] \Rightarrow [C] \wedge [C] & \\
split\,[\,] & \equiv_{df} & ([\,],[\,]) & \\
split\,(a :: m) & \equiv_{df} & (a :: l', l'') & \textbf{if } a \\
& \equiv_{df} & (l', a :: l'') & \textbf{if not} \\
& & \textbf{where} & \\
& & (l', l'') \equiv split\ m &
\end{array}
$$

and then attempt to verify, by induction, that *split* has the property 6.7. Alternatively we try to prove the result 6.5 directly; this we do now.

Theorem 6.10

For all lists $l : [C]$,

$$(\exists(l',l''):[C] \wedge [C]).$$
$$(allRed\ l' \wedge allWhite\ l'' \wedge perm\ l\ (l' +\!+l'')) \qquad (6.8)$$

Proof: We prove the result by induction over the list l. We shall call the statement 6.8 $P(l)$.

Case: $l \equiv [\,]$. It is immediate that the types $allRed\,[\,]$ and $allWhite\,[\,]$ are inhabited. Also $[\,] +\!+ [\,] \equiv [\,]$ and as *perm* is reflexive (see Lemma 6.2, part 12) we have

$$perm \ l \ (l' +\!\!+ l'')$$

is inhabited. Putting the proof objects together we have some p_0,

$$p_0 \ : \ P([\,])$$

as required in an inductive proof.

Case: $l \equiv (a :: m)$. Suppose that $p_m \ : \ P(m)$. Now,

$$p_m \equiv ((l', l''), q)$$

where $q \equiv (q_1, q_2, q_3)$ and

$$(q_1, q_2, q_3) \ : \ (allRed \ l' \wedge allWhite \ l'' \wedge perm \ m \ (l' +\!\!+ l''))$$

Now, since there are only two booleans, a will be either red or white. The proof proceeds now by a case analysis. Suppose that

$$cs_w \ : \ isWhite \ a$$

It is not hard to see that

$$q_2' \equiv_{df} (cs_w, q_2) \ : \ allWhite \ (a :: l'')$$

and certainly

$$q_1 \ : \ allred \ l'$$

Now, by an earlier result on the simple properties of $perm$, Lemma 6.2, parts 9 and 11, we can find

$$q_3' \ : \ perm \ (a :: m) \ (l' +\!\!+ (a :: l''))$$

where q_3' depends upon the proof object q_3. Pulling this together, we have

$$q_w \equiv_{df} (q_1, q_2', q_3') \ : \\ (allRed \ l' \wedge allWhite \ (a :: l'') \wedge perm \ m \ (l' +\!\!+ (a :: l'')))$$

and so

$$p_w \equiv_{df} ((l', (a :: l'')), \ q_w \ ) \ : \ P(a :: m)$$

In a similar way if we assume

$$cs_r \ : \ isRed \ a$$

then we can find

$$p_r \equiv_{df} (\,(\,(a :: l'),l''\,)\,,\,q_r\,) \;:\; P(a :: m)$$

Since every element a is either red or white, we have

$$p' \equiv_{df} \textit{if a then } p_r \textit{ else } p_w \;:\; P(a :: m)$$

This gives us an inductive construction of an element of $P(a :: m)$ from objects $a : C$, $m : [C]$ and a proof $q : P(m)$, and so amounts to the proof of the induction step.

Formalizing the derivation, we have

$$\lambda l \,.\,(lrec\; l\; p_0\; (\lambda a \,.\, \lambda m \,.\, \lambda q \,.\, p')) \;:\; (\forall l : [C]) \,.\, P(l)$$

which completes the derivation of an object of the type required.   □

We can see that the function extracted from the proof by the method which was outlined above will be exactly the function *split* defined earlier.

6.7   Program transformation

We have so far seen a number of approaches to program construction in type theory. In this section we consider the *transformational* approach to program development. We show how a program may be transformed *within the system TT* into another program which has the same behaviour yet which has other desirable properties such as time or space efficiency or parallelizability.

How might the starting point of a sequence of transformations arise? Two ways suggest themselves:

- A program may be written directly to reflect the specification, an *executable specification* in the popular jargon.

- A program may be extracted from a proof: often a proof will use 'brute force' rather than subtlety to achieve its result.

The example we look at in this section can be thought of as arising in either way, in fact. Our example has been examined in a number of places including [Thompson, 1989a] and the excellent [Bentley, 1986], Column 7. It is the problem of finding the maximum sum of a contiguous segment of a finite sequence of integers. For the sequence

$$-2 \;\; \underbrace{3\;\; 4\;\; -3\;\; 5}_{9} \;\; -2\;\; 1$$

the segment indicated has the maximum value.

The essence of program transformation is to take a program into another with the *same applicative behaviour*, yet improved in some aspect such as time efficiency or space usage. Two functions have the same behaviour when they return the same results for all arguments, when they are *extensionally equal*, in other words. In TT program transformation will therefore involve the replacement of an object by an extensionally equivalent one, through a series of simple steps of the same kind.

In the discussion of the problem here, a *list* of integers is used to implement the sequence. One implementation of the integers was given on page 138.

We begin our discussion by introducing the operators *map* and *fold*, and examining some of their properties, including how they are modified to operate over non-empty lists. Readers who are familiar with these functions may prefer to move straight on to the transformation, returning to the next subsection when and if necessary.

6.7.1   *map* and *fold*

Two of the most useful operations over lists are *map* and *fold*. *map* applies a function to every element of a list, and has the primitive recursive definition

$$
\begin{array}{rcl}
map & : & (A \Rightarrow B) \Rightarrow [A] \Rightarrow [B] \\
map\, f\, [\,] & \equiv_{df} & [\,] \\
map\, f\, (a :: x) & \equiv_{df} & (f\, a) :: (map\, f\, x)
\end{array}
$$

which can be written formally

$$\lambda f . \lambda l . (lrec\, l\, [\,]\, h_f)$$

where

$$h_f\, a\, l\, p \equiv_{df} (f\, a) :: p$$

By the rule of I introduction and the computation rules for $lrec$, we can see that for all f, the types

$$
\begin{array}{rcll}
map\, f\, [\,] & = & [\,] & \text{(6.9)} \\
map\, f\, (a :: x) & = & (f\, a) :: (map\, f\, x) & \text{(6.10)}
\end{array}
$$

are inhabited. The composition operator $\circ$, which is written in an infix form for readability, has the definition

$$(g \circ f) \equiv_{df} \lambda x . (g\, (f\, x)) \tag{6.11}$$

Recall also that the ++ operator joins two lists together.

The transformations we give later are based on the application of a small number of general 'laws' embodying properties of the standard functions. The first law relates *map* and the append operation.

Theorem 6.11

$map\ f\ (l + \!\!+ m) = (map\ f\ l) + \!\!+ (map\ f\ m)$ for all lists l and m.

Proof: The proof is by induction over l.   □

The second law relates *map* and composition.

Theorem 6.12

$map\ g \circ map\ f \simeq map\ (g \circ f)$ for all functions f and g.

Proof: We show that for all x

$$(map\ g \circ map\ f)\ x = map\ (g \circ f)\ x$$

which we do by induction over the list argument x. In the base case we have to prove that

$$(map\ g \circ map\ f)\ [\ ] = map\ (g \circ f)\ [\ ]$$

By the definition 6.11

$$(map\ g \circ map\ f)\ [\ ] = map\ g\ (map\ f\ [\ ])$$

which by the Equation 6.9

$$= map\ g\ [\ ]$$

which by Equation 6.9 again is $[\ ]$. A single application of the same equation shows that the right-hand side also equals $[\ ]$.

At the induction step, we aim to show

$$(map\ g \circ map\ f)\ (a :: x) = map\ (g \circ f)\ (a :: x) \tag{6.12}$$

using

$$(map\ g \circ map\ f)\ x = map\ (g \circ f)\ x \tag{6.13}$$

Expanding the left-hand side of the Equation 6.12 first by the definition 6.11 and then by Equation 6.10 twice, we have

$$\begin{aligned}
&= map\ g\ (map\ f\ (a :: x)) \\
&= map\ g\ ((f\ a) :: (map\ f\ x)) \\
&= (g\ (f\ a)) :: (map\ g\ (map\ f\ x))
\end{aligned}$$

By the definition 6.11, twice, this is

$$= (g\,(f\,a))\; ::\; ((map\,g \circ map\,f)\,x)$$
$$= ((g \circ f)\,a)\; ::\; ((map\,g \circ map\,f)\,x)$$

and by the induction hypothesis 6.13

$$= ((g \circ f)\,a)\; ::\; (map\,(g \circ f)\,x)$$

By Equation 6.10 for $(g \circ f)$, this is

$$= map\,(g \circ f)\,(a :: x)$$

which is the right-hand side of the Equation 6.12. This completes the induction step and therefore the proof itself.   □

The elements of a *non-empty* list can be combined together using the operator *fold*. For instance, we get the product of the elements of a list by folding in the multiplication operator.

$$fold \quad : \quad (A \Rightarrow A \Rightarrow A) \Rightarrow (nel\,A) \Rightarrow A$$
$$fold\,f\,(\,[\,],p\,) \quad \equiv_{df} \quad abort_A\,p$$
$$fold\,f\,(\,(a :: [\,]),p\,) \quad \equiv_{df} \quad a$$
$$fold\,f\,(\,(a :: (b :: x)),p\,) \quad \equiv_{df} \quad f\,a\,(fold\,f\,(\,(b :: x),Triv\,))$$

where the type of non-empty lists, $(nel\,A)$, is defined by

$$(nel\,A) \equiv_{df} (\exists l : [A])\,.\,(nempty\,l)$$

where

$$nempty\,[\,] \quad \equiv_{df} \quad \bot$$
$$nempty\,(a :: x) \quad \equiv_{df} \quad \top$$

We would like to use the standard functions *map* and ++ over non-empty lists as well as over the usual list type. We cannot use the functions directly, but we can define analogues of them, *map′* and ++′, operating over the type $(nel\,A)$ because of the following lemma.

Lemma 6.13

If l and m are non-empty, then so are $map\,f\,l$ and $l ++ m$.

Proof: The proofs are by induction.   □

Formally, the last lemma gives functions map_p, app_p of type

$$map_p \quad : \quad (\forall l:[A]) . (\, (nempty \; l) \Rightarrow (nempty \; (map \; f \; l)) \,)$$
$$app_p \quad : \quad (\forall l:[A]) . (\forall l:[A]) . (\, (nempty \; l) \Rightarrow$$
$$(nempty \; m) \Rightarrow (nempty \; (l +\!\!+ m)) \,)$$

The functions map' and $+\!\!+'$ are now defined

$$map' \quad : \quad (A \Rightarrow A) \Rightarrow (nel \; A) \Rightarrow (nel \; A)$$
$$map' \; f \; (l, p) \quad \equiv_{df} \quad (map \; f \; l \, , \; map_p \; l \; p)$$

$$+\!\!+' \quad : \quad (nel \; A) \Rightarrow (nel \; A) \Rightarrow (nel \; A)$$
$$(l, p) +\!\!+' (m, q) \quad \equiv_{df} \quad (l +\!\!+ m \, , \; app_p \; l \; m \; p \; q)$$

These functions combine computation with proof, as they transmit the information witnessing the non-emptiness of the argument(s) to the same information about the result.

We also have analogues of Theorems 6.11 and 6.12.

Theorem 6.14

For all functions f, and non-empty lists l', m'

$$map' \; f \; (l' +\!\!+' m') = (map' \; f \; l') +\!\!+' (map' \; f \; m')$$

Theorem 6.15

For all functions f, g,

$$map' \; g \circ map' \; f \simeq map' \; (g \circ f)$$

Proofs: As the theorems above. □

Theorem 6.16

If f is an associative function, that is for all a, b and c,

$$f \; a(f \; b \; c) = f \; (f \; a \; b) \; c$$

then for non-empty l' and m'

$$fold \; f \; (l' +\!\!+' m') = f \; (fold \; f \; l') \; (fold \; f \; m')$$

Proof: The proof is by induction over the non-empty list l'. □

The final law we give relates the action of $fold$ and map', and shows a case in which a map before a fold is transformed into a single function application following a fold.

Theorem 6.17

If f and g satisfy $f\,(g\,a)\,(g\,b) = g\,(f\,a\,b)$ then

$$(fold\,f) \circ (map'\,g) \simeq g \circ (fold\,f)$$

The analogue of $fold$ over $[A]$ is called $foldr$. It takes an extra parameter, which is the value returned on the empty list; a starting value, in other words. It is defined by

$$
\begin{aligned}
foldr \quad &: \quad (A \Rightarrow B \Rightarrow B) \Rightarrow B \Rightarrow [A] \Rightarrow B \\
foldr\,f\,st\,[\,] \quad &\equiv_{df} \quad st \\
foldr\,f\,st\,(a :: x) \quad &\equiv_{df} \quad f\,a\,(foldr\,f\,st\,x)
\end{aligned}
$$

This is in fact a specialization of the recursion operator $lrec$, which omits to use the tail of the list, x, in the recursive call at $(a :: x)$. Using $foldr$ we can define many operations over lists, including

$$sum \equiv_{df} foldr\,(+)\,0$$

where (θ) denotes the prefix form of the infix operator θ.

Theorem 6.18

For all f and st,

$$(foldr\,f\,st) \circ ((::)\,a) \simeq (f\,a) \circ (foldr\,f\,st)$$

Proof: This is proved without induction, simply by expanding both sides when applied to an argument x. □

6.7.2   The algorithm

The problem we aim to solve is finding the maximum sum of a segment of a finite list of integers. There is a naïve solution, which forms the starting point of the transformation. In this we

- take all the (contiguous) sublists of the list,
- find the sum of each, and
- take the maximum of these sums.

We can write this as the composition

$$maxsub \equiv_{df} (fold\,bimax) \circ (map'\,sum) \circ sublists'$$

where *bimax* is the binary maximum function over the integers and *sublists'* is the function of type $[A] \Rightarrow (nel\,[A])$, returning the *non-empty* list of sublists of a list. The result is non-empty since even an empty list has itself as a sublist. We then apply *map' sum* to the result, transmitting the proof information, and so permitting the application of *fold* which demands a non-empty argument.

How is the function *sublists'* to be defined? We define a function *sublists* which returns a list of the sublists, and then combine its result with a proof that it is non-empty. This proof is an inductive one, which it is not hard to construct given the definitions which follow. To explain them, observe that a sublist of $(a :: x)$ is either a sublist of x, or includes a, in which case a must be followed by a sublist of x which starts at the front of x; these lists are returned by *frontlists x*.

$$
\begin{aligned}
sublists &: & &[A] \Rightarrow [\,[A]\,] \\
sublists\,[\,] &\equiv_{df} & &[\,[\,]\,] \\
sublists\,(a :: x) &\equiv_{df} & &map\,((::)\,a)\,(frontlists\,x) \\
& & &+\!\!\!+\ sublists\,x
\end{aligned}
$$

where

$$
\begin{aligned}
frontlists &: & &[A] \Rightarrow [\,[A]\,] \\
frontlists\,[\,] &\equiv_{df} & &[\,[\,]\,] \\
frontlists\,(a :: x) &\equiv_{df} & &map\,((::)\,a)\,(frontlists\,x) \\
& & &+\!\!\!+\ [\,[\,]\,]
\end{aligned}
$$

We have presented this solution as a direct implementation of the specification. Such a program might also be extracted from a proof of the existence of a maximum segment sum: maxima of finite collections exist simply by exhaustion arguments, and such a strategy would give rise to an algorithm as we have just defined.

So, derived in whatever way, we have our naïve solution, which is unsatisfactory for two reasons. The first is an efficiency consideration: to compute the result, we use time (and space) *quadratic* in the length of the list, as we examine all the (contiguous) sublists of the list, and the number of these grows as the square of the length of the list. Secondly, we carry proof-theoretic information through the computation, which seems to be unnecessary. The transformation remedies both these difficulties.

6.7.3   The transformation

We transform the program for $maxsub$ beginning with a case analysis. Take the argument $[\,]$

$$
\begin{aligned}
maxsub\,[\,] & \\
= &\ ((fold\,bimax) \circ (map'\,sum) \circ sublists')\,[\,] \\
= &\ (fold\,bimax)\,((map'\,sum)\,(sublists'\,[\,])) \\
= &\ (fold\,bimax)\,((map'\,sum)\,([\,[\,]\,],\,Triv)) \\
= &\ (fold\,bimax)\,(0\,,\,Triv) \\
= &\ 0
\end{aligned}
$$

where each of the steps above is justified by the definition of the appropriate function. Now we examine the case of $(a :: x)$.

$$
\begin{aligned}
& ((fold\,bimax) \circ (map'\,sum) \circ sublists')\,(a :: x) \\
= &\ (fold\,bimax)\,((map'\,sum)\,(sublists'\,(a :: x))) \\
= &\ (fold\,bimax)\,((map'\,sum)\,(l_1 +\!\!+'l_2))
\end{aligned}
$$

where

$$
\begin{aligned}
l_1 & \equiv_{df} \quad map'\,((::)\,a)\,(frontlists'\,x) \\
l_2 & \equiv_{df} \quad sublists'\,x
\end{aligned}
$$

both of which are non-empty. By Theorem 6.14, the expression equals

$$(fold\,bimax)\,((map'\,sum\,l_1) +\!\!+'(map'\,sum\,l_2))$$

which by Theorem 6.16 is

$$
\begin{aligned}
bimax \quad & (fold\,bimax\,(map'\,sum\,l_1)) \\
& (fold\,bimax\,(map'\,sum\,l_2))
\end{aligned}
$$

Recalling that $l_2 \equiv_{df} sublists'\,x$, and the definition of $maxsub$, this is

$$
\begin{aligned}
bimax \quad & (fold\,bimax\,(map'\,sum\,l_1)) \\
& (maxsub\,x)
\end{aligned} \tag{6.14}
$$

We now concentrate on the first argument in the expression, which when expanded is

$$(fold\,bimax)\,\underbrace{(map'\,sum\,(map'\,((::)\,a)\,(frontlists'\,x)))} \tag{6.15}$$

The sub-expression indicated is a composition of two map's, so we replace it with

$$map'\,(sum \circ ((::)\,a))\,(frontlists'\,x)$$

Now, by Theorem 6.18, since $sum = foldr\,(+)\,0$ we have

$$sum \circ ((::)\,a) \simeq ((+)\,a) \circ sum$$

so this gives

$$map'\,(((+)\,a) \circ sum)\,(frontlists'\,x)$$

which by Theorem 6.15 is

$$(\,(map'\,((+)\,a)) \circ (map'\,sum)\,)\,(frontlists'\,x)$$

This means that the argument 6.15 becomes, using the associativity of 'o',

$$(\,(fold\,bimax) \circ (map'\,((+)\,a)) \circ (map'\,sum)\,)\,(frontlists'\,x)$$

Here we have an interaction between $fold$ and map', and as the conditions of Theorem 6.17 apply, we have

$$a + (\,(((fold\,bimax) \circ (map'\,sum) \circ frontlists')\,x)$$

If we now write

$$maxfront \equiv_{df} (fold\,bimax) \circ (map'\,sum) \circ frontlists'$$

we have the original expression 6.14 equal to

$$bimax\,(a + maxfront\,x)\,(maxsub\,x)$$

A similar transformation of $maxfront$ yields

$$
\begin{aligned}
maxfront\,[\,] &= 0 \\
maxfront\,(a :: x) &= bimax\,0\,(a + maxfront\,x)
\end{aligned}
$$

and for the original function we have the final form

$$
\begin{aligned}
maxsub\,[\,] &= 0 \\
maxsub\,(a :: x) &= bimax\,(maxsub\,x)\,(a + maxfront\,x)
\end{aligned}
$$

We can make these equations a definition of the $maxsub$ function, and it can be seen that its complexity depends on the length of the list. Also, the functions are free of any of the proof information which appeared in the original algorithm, because it used non-empty lists.

Exercises

6.34 What is the principle of induction for the type of integers *int* introduced above? [Hint: it can be derived from the principles of induction on the component parts of the type *int*.]

6.35 In the proof of Theorem 6.11 why is the induction over the list l and not the list m?

6.36 Complete the proofs which were only sketched in the text.

6.37 State and prove the theorem corresponding to Theorem 6.16 for the operator *foldr* rather than *fold*.

6.38 Give a formal derivation of the function

$$sublists' \; : \; [A] \Rightarrow (nel \; A)$$

6.39 Explain why the original definition of *maxsub* has quadratic complexity and why the final one is linear.

6.8   Imperative programming

Our programming focus has been functional in the development so far. Can similar techniques be brought to bear on imperative programs? The full answer to this is a topic of current research, but a partially positive answer can be given, via an identification of a particular class of functional programs, the *tail-recursive functions*, with imperative programs.

Definition 6.19

A function is **tail recursive** if its definition takes the form

$$
\begin{array}{llll}
f \, a_1 \, \dots \, a_n & \equiv_{df} & f \, (g_{1,1} \, \vec{a}) \, \dots \, (g_{1,n} \, \vec{a}) & \textbf{if } c_1 \, \vec{a} \\
& \equiv_{df} & \dots & \textbf{if } \dots \\
& \equiv_{df} & f \, (g_{k,1} \, \vec{a}) \, \dots \, (g_{k,n} \, \vec{a}) & \textbf{if } c_k \, \vec{a} \\
& \equiv_{df} & h \, \vec{a} & \textbf{if not}
\end{array}
$$

where $\vec{a}$ denotes the sequence $a_1 \dots a_n$, and each of the functions $c_1, \dots, c_k$, $g_1, \dots, g_k$ and h does not mention f.

First note that these functions are called tail recursive since the only recursive calls the right-hand sides make to f are in the *tail* of the code, after evaluating all the function arguments (assuming applicative order evaluation of the code, of course). Why should these functions be identified with imperative programs? Take the simple case of

$$
\begin{aligned}
f \, a_1 \, \ldots \, a_n \quad &\equiv_{df} \quad f \, (g_1 \, \vec{a}) \, \ldots \, (g_n \, \vec{a}) \quad \textbf{if } c \, \vec{a} \\
&\equiv_{df} \quad h \, \vec{a} \qquad\qquad\qquad\quad \textbf{if not}
\end{aligned}
$$

If the condition $c \, \vec{a}$ is true, we make a recursive call which transforms the argument a_i to $g_i \, \vec{a}$, if not we return the result $h \, \vec{a}$. Rephrasing this slightly, **while** the condition $c \, \vec{a}$ is true, we perform the **parallel assignment**

$$
a_1 , \, \ldots , \, a_n := (g_1 \, \vec{a}) , \, \ldots , \, (g_n \, \vec{a})
$$

and so in an imperative pseudo-code we have

> **while** $c \, \vec{a}$ **do**
> $\quad a_1 , \, \ldots , \, a_n := (g_1 \, \vec{a}) , \, \ldots , \, (g_n \, \vec{a})$;
> **return** $h \, \vec{a}$;

To illustrate the point, there follows a tail-recursive version of the factorial function:

$$
\begin{aligned}
fac \, n \quad &\equiv_{df} \quad tfac \, n \, 1 \\
tfac \, 0 \, p \quad &\equiv_{df} \quad p \\
tfac \, (n + 1) \, p \quad &\equiv_{df} \quad tfac \, n \, ((n + 1){*}p)
\end{aligned}
$$

This is not an isolated phenomenon; every primitive recursive function can be given a tail-recursive definition using the function $tprim$

$$
tprim \; : \; N \Rightarrow C \Rightarrow (N \Rightarrow C \Rightarrow C) \Rightarrow N \Rightarrow C \Rightarrow C
$$

$$
\begin{aligned}
tprim \, n \, c \, f \, 0 \, v \quad &\equiv_{df} \quad v \\
tprim \, n \, c \, f \, (m + 1) \, v \quad &\equiv_{df} \quad tprim \, n \, c \, f \, m \, (f \, (n - m - 1) \, v) \\
&\qquad\qquad\qquad\qquad\quad \textbf{if } (m < n) \\
&\equiv_{df} \quad v \qquad\qquad\qquad\quad \textbf{if not}
\end{aligned}
$$

where we assert that for all n, c and f,

$$
prim \, n \, c \, f = tprim \, n \, c \, f \, n \, c
$$

The idea of the transformation is that the last argument starts off at c, which is $prim \, 0 \, c \, f$, and is transformed by the successive application of $f \, 0$, $f \, 1$, ... into $prim \, 1 \, c \, f$, $prim \, 2 \, c \, f$, ... The result is a corollary of the following theorem.

Theorem 6.20

For all n, c, f and $m \leq n$,

$$tprim \; n \; c \; f \; (n - m) \; (prim \; m \; c \; f) = prim \; n \; c \; f$$

Proof: The proof is by induction over the difference $n - m$ which is non-negative by hypothesis. The base case is that of $n - m = 0$. In that case

$$
\begin{aligned}
& tprim \; n \; c \; f \; (n - m) \; (prim \; m \; c \; f) \\
= \; & tprim \; n \; c \; f \; 0 \; (prim \; n \; c \; f) \\
= \; & (prim \; n \; c \; f)
\end{aligned}
$$

the second equality being an immediate consequence of the definition of $tprim$. At the induction step, suppose that $n - m = p + 1$ and that the result holds for a difference of p.

$$
\begin{aligned}
& tprim \; n \; c \; f \; (n - m) \; (prim \; m \; c \; f) \\
= \; & tprim \; n \; c \; f \; (p + 1) \; (prim \; m \; c \; f) \\
= \; & tprim \; n \; c \; f \; p \; (f \; m \; (prim \; m \; c \; f)) \\
= \; & tprim \; n \; c \; f \; p \; (prim \; (m + 1) \; c \; f)
\end{aligned}
$$

By the induction hypothesis, since $n - (m + 1) = p$,

$$= \; prim \; n \; c \; f$$

which completes the induction step and the proof itself.   □

Corollary 6.21

For all n, c and f,

$$tprim \; n \; c \; f \; n \; c = prim \; n \; c \; f$$

Proof: Take $m = 0$ in the theorem.   □

Note that in the action of $tprim$ the first three arguments are not modified in the recursive calls – they act as parameters or constants of the program, and no storage locations need to be allocated to them; the other two parameters *do* of course need to be allotted space.

The corollary justifies the transformation of any primitive recursive function into a tail-recursive one, and thus into an imperative form. We can prove similar theorems for the other recursion operators in the system, so a functional program can form an intermediate step in the development of an imperative program, as long as the imperative target language can support all the higher-order data types of TT. In the case that it cannot, other coding techniques can be found, but the correspondence is less direct.

If we take any imperative program there will be a functional form for it, in which the only recursion is tail recursion. However, that tail recursion may not be formalizable in TT, since it may lead to non-termination. If we can supply a proof of termination for the imperative program, and the proof can be formalized in first-order arithmetic (see Section 5.11), then there will be an equivalent of the program in TT.

Exercises

6.40 Give tail-recursive forms of the recursion operators over lists and trees.

6.41 Comment on the space efficiency of the tail-recursive form of the factorial function. Does your observation depend upon the form of evaluation chosen for terms of TT?

6.9   Examples in the literature

This section provides a survey of examples in the published literature of proof and program development in theories similar to TT. Many of the examples use the subset type; we shall discuss this and its relevance to program development in the chapter to come, which contains examples of new concepts as they are introduced.

6.9.1   Martin-Löf

In Martin-Löf's work there are few examples. The extensional version of the theory, [Martin-Löf, 1985], contains a proof of the axiom of choice,

$$(\forall x : A) . (\exists y : B) . C \Rightarrow (\exists f : (\forall x : A) . B) . (\forall x : A) . C[(f\ x)/y]$$

which involves the strong existential elimination rule, $(\exists E)$, in an essential way. As well as a proof of the axiom of choice, the Padova notes [Martin-Löf, 1984], contain small examples but nothing large scale. Martin-Löf's notes on constructive mathematics, [Martin-Löf, 1970], contain examples of mathematical proofs developed from a constructive standpoint, but it is fair to say that they bear little formal relation to proofs in TT.

6.9.2   Goteborg

A source of many examples is the Programming Methodology Group at the University of Goteborg and Chalmers University of Technology, in Sweden.

In [Dybjer, 1987] type theory is examined as one of a number of systems applied to the example of the derivation of an algorithm to normalize the syntactic form of propositional expressions.

Generalizing the idea of a multilevel array, as used in VDL and VDM, is the type of multilevel functions, which also encompasses the types of vectors, natural numbers, lists and others. A formal presentation of this type as an addition to TT is given in [Nordström, 1985]. The types could also be developed using the W types of TT^+ but the authors argue that it is more natural to add the new rules to embody the type directly.

In [Nordström and Petersson, 1985] there is a discussion of how the quantifiers and dependent types of TT can be used to provide specifications of modules.

6.9.3   Backhouse *et al.*

Roland Backhouse and his co-workers at the Universities of Groningen and Eindhoven have written widely on the topic of type theory. We shall look at their work later when we look at extensions of the theory, but there are a number of sources we should mention now. The tutorial notes [Backhouse, 1987a] contain a number of shorter examples, chosen to illustrate the system construct by construct. The paper [Backhouse *et al.*, 1989], which introduces a number of additions, also contains useful examples, such as the Boyer-Moore majority vote algorithm and a collection of game playing operations, similar to those in [Hughes, 1990].

A substantial derivation of a parsing algorithm is given in [Chisholm, 1987]. The parser is specified by the assertion

$$(\forall w : Word) . Parse\ w \vee \neg Parse\ w$$

where the proposition $Parse\ w$ is an assertion of the fact that the string w is a sentence of the language. Proofs of this proposition consist of showing that there is a valid parse tree for the word, as expressed by

$$w = spell\ pt$$

spell being the function to 'spell out' the word coded by a parse tree pt. The implementation is compared with the result of an earlier effort to derive a program using the LCF system [Cohn and Milner, 1982].

6.9.4   Nuprl

Constable's group at Cornell University have concentrated on their Nuprl system, which we shall discuss in more detail in Section 9.1.1 on 'Implementing Mathematics', which is indeed the title of their exposition of Nuprl

[Constable and others, 1986]. The system is sufficiently close to type theory for the majority of their examples to be comprehensible if not translatable. [Constable and others, 1986] contains short expository examples, of course, but also develops a number of libraries of mathematical objects in Chapter 11.

Howe's thesis, [Howe, 1988], gives a detailed analysis of Girard's paradox in Chapter 4. Sections 3.10 and 3.11 contain a number-theoretic example, and a saddleback search, and Chapter 5 addresses the issue of reflection, which is taken up by [Knoblock and Constable, 1986]. The addition of partial objects to type theory is discussed in [Constable and Smith, 1987].

A more concrete application to hardware specification and verification is presented in [Basin and del Vecchio, 1989]. The specific component investigated is the front end of a floating point adder/subtractor.

6.9.5 Calculus of constructions

One other system which bears a rather less close relation to TT is Huet and Coquand's calculus of constructions [Coquand and Huet, 1985]. An example of algorithm development is to be found in [Paulin-Mohring, 1987] and the extraction of programs from proofs in the calculus is examined in [Paulin-Mohring, 1989]. An analysis of Girard's paradox is given in [Coquand, 1986].

Chapter 7
Augmenting Type Theory

Using type theory as a program development system has led a number of people to propose that new constructs be added to the theory. Although we have seen that in theory the system is highly expressive, there are questions of whether it expresses what is required in either a natural or an efficient way. This chapter contains an account of the proposals concerning ways in which the system may be augmented.

An important point which should be made before we embark is that each of the additions, whilst arguably adding to the power of the system in some way, also makes it more complicated, either from a user's point of view, or for foundational reasons, such as the loss of strong normalization. We shall discuss the pros and cons of each proposal section by section, and shall in the conclusion to the book have something more to say on the topic.

Central to the proposals is the notion of a subset type, distinct from the existential type, whose members are simply those elements of the base type with the required property, rather than such objects *paired* with a *witness* to that property. To set the discussion in its proper context, we begin in Section 7.1 by looking at the exact nature of specifications, a topic we first examined when we looked at the case study of the Polish national flag. What precisely are specifications in type theory has been the subject of some confusion in the literature; we hope to clarify the issue here.

Another general topic connected with the introduction of the subset type is that of computational relevance: some parts of expressions seem to have a purely logical role, rather than contributing to the result of a computational process. We discuss two approaches to capturing this intuition, and also look at how it is linked with lazy evaluation. Naturally, any argument about computational relevance or efficiency can only be conducted relative to some evaluation scheme, and we argue that many of the reasons advanced for a more complicated type system in view of computational efficiency are irrelevant in the case that the system is implemented using lazy evaluation.

After this background discussion, in Section 7.2 we introduce the naïve definition of the subset type, and examine some of its theoretical drawbacks. As we said above, much of the motivation for subsets is to achieve a separation between logical and computational aspects of type theory; in Section 7.3 we look at how subsets can properly be expressed only in a system in which propositions and types are no longer identified.

We give a review of the proposals in Section 7.4 where we argue that all the examples of subsets in the literature can be handled quite smoothly within TT, without recourse to the new type. This is achieved by a lazy implementation together with a judicious choice of types in specifications: we choose to specify a function by asserting its existence rather than by a $\forall\exists$ formula, for instance. We provide a number of general and concrete examples by way of illustration.

The primitive type forming operation, W, constructs *free* data types, whilst there are examples in which an abstract object can best be represented by a collection of concrete items: a set represented as a list is one case. To reason and program most simply with such a type it is argued that a *quotient* type, consisting of equivalence classes, be formed. We examine two variants of this idea in Section 7.5.

An important application area for constructive mathematics is real analysis. Section 7.6 gives the beginnings of a treatment of the topic, and also serves as a case study in which to examine the utility of the subset and quotient type.

Various infelicities have been shown in the rules for elimination – the following section examines proposals to overcome these by means of the *strong* elimination rules. A generalization of these, the *polymorphic* types of Backhouse *et al.*, is also introduced. It is interesting to observe that an addition of this sort can lead to a term which has no normal form and indeed no weak head normal form: a genuine non-termination is thus present in the augmented system. This will maybe underline the fact the 'reasonable' additions to a system made in an *ad hoc* way can lead to unforeseen circumstances, and that we should make quite certain that any addition we make does not destroy something more important than it adds.

As we saw in the last chapter, recursions can be coded in type theory only in terms of the primitives provided. The most general form of terminating recursion is called *well-founded* recursion. We first look at what this is in a set-theoretic context in Section 7.8, and then in the following section we look at two different ways that well-founded recursion can be added to type theory. The general mechanism provided derives once and for all the principles of which particular cases, such as quicksort, were derived in the course of the proof developments of the last chapter.

A different approach again is to provide new methods of defining types, together with definition mechanisms. Equivalent to well-founded recursion we can add types defined by a general principle of induction, which we do in Section 7.10. We discuss the relation between these types and the W types of TT, and argue that the latter can be used to provide a representation of the former.

A novel idea, at least from the programming point of view, is to define the *co-inductive* types, which are the *largest* solutions of certain type equations. If we solve the equation characterizing lists, then the smallest solution contains simply the finite elements, whilst the largest contains *infinite* elements also. The presence of infinite lists is not a surprise to the lazy functional programmer, but remarkable is the *absence* of partial lists. We show how a general scheme of co-induction is introduced, and then examine in more detail the type of infinite lists or *streams*. In this context it is interesting to note that if we use infinite lists as models for communications between communicating processes (*à la* Kahn and MacQueen) then in type theory we can be sure that if a recursion is possible it gives a completely defined list, ruling out the possibility of *deadlock*.

Consistency of TT as a logical system will be lost if partial objects are permitted to inhabit every type, since then the undefined element will be a member of each type, which from a logical point of view means that every theorem is provable. There are other ways for partial objects to be added, however – a proposal for the incorporation of a representation of such objects is given in Section 7.12. This is done without sacrificing the Curry–Howard isomorphism or the consistency of the logical system.

The proposals thus far are general, but another kind of extension is possible. Martin-Löf has always stressed the *open-endedness* of the system, and in the final section we look at how a particular kind of object, the semi-group, can be modelled by adding a set of new rules governing its behaviour. We contrast this approach with that of forming an explicit model of the type within the theory. Naturally, this approach is not limited to semi-groups but can be used in any particular application area.

7.1   Background

This section explores some of the background to the introduction of the subset type into TT, before we go on to discuss exactly how this might be done, and indeed whether it is necessary.

7.1.1   What is a specification?

We first examined this question in Section 6.6 in the particular context of the Polish national flag problem. Here we reconsider it from a more general point of view.

The judgement $a : A$ can be thought of as expressing 'a proves the proposition A' and 'a is an object of type A', but it has also been proposed, in [Martin-Löf, 1985; Petersson and Smith, 1985] for example, that it be read as saying

a is a program which meets the specification A $\qquad$ (†)

This interpretation does *not* apply in general to every judgement $a : A$. Take for instance the case of a function f which sorts lists; this has type $[A] \Rightarrow [A]$, and so,

$$f \ : \ [A] \Rightarrow [A]$$

Should we therefore say that it meets the specification $[A] \Rightarrow [A]$? It does, but then so do the identity and the reverse functions! The type of a function is but one aspect of its specification, which should describe the relation between its input and output. This characterization takes the form

the result $(f\, l)$ is ordered and a permutation of the list l

for which we will write $S(f)$. To assert that the specification can be met by some implementation, we write

$$(\exists x : [A] \Rightarrow [A]) . S(x)$$

What form do objects of this type take? They are pairs (f, p) with $f : [A] \Rightarrow [A]$ and p a proof that f has the property $S(f)$. The confusion in (†) is thus that the object a consists not only of the program meeting the specification, but also of the *proof* that it meets that specification.

In the light of the discussion above, it seems sensible to suggest that we conceive of specifications as statements $(\exists o : T) . P$, and that the formal assertion

$$(o, p) \ : \ (\exists o : T) . P$$

be interpreted as saying

the object o, of type T, is shown to meet the specification P by the proof object p

an interpretation which combines the logical and programming interpretations of the language in an elegant way. This would be obvious to a constructivist, who would argue that we can only assert (†) if we have the appropriate evidence, namely the proof object.

In developing a proof of the formula $(\exists o : T) . P$ we construct a pair consisting of an object of type T and a proof that the object has the property P. Such a pair keeps separate the computational and logical aspects of the development, so that we can extract directly the computational part simply by choosing the first element of the pair.

There is a variation on this theme, mentioned in [Nordström *et al.*, 1990] and examined in Section 6.6, which suggests that a specification of a function should be of the form

$$(\forall x : A) . (\exists y : B) . P(x, y) \tag{7.1}$$

Elements of this type are functions F so that for all $x : A$,

$$F\, x\ :\ (\exists y : B) . P(x, y)$$

and *each* of these values will be a pair (y_x, p_x) with

$$y_x : B \quad \text{and} \quad p_x : P(x, y)$$

The pair consists of value and proof information, showing that under this approach the program and its verification are inextricably mixed. It has been argued that the only way to achieve this separation is to replace the inner existential type with a subset type, which removes the proof information p_x. This can be done, but the intermingling can be avoided without augmenting the system. We simply have to give the intended function a *name*. That such a naming can be achieved in general is a simple consequence of the axiom of choice, which states that

$$(\forall x : A) . (\exists y : B) . P(x, y) \Rightarrow (\exists f : A \Rightarrow B) . (\forall x : A) . P(x, f\, x)$$

and applying *modus ponens* to this and the specification 7.1 we deduce an 'existential' specification as above. Note that the converse implication to that of the axiom of choice is easily derivable, making the two forms of the specification logically equivalent.

The equivalent specifications can be thought of as suggesting different program development methods: using the $\exists\forall$ form, we develop the function and its proof as separate entities, either separately or together, whilst in the $\forall\exists$ form we extract a function from a proof, *post hoc*.

This analysis of specifications makes it clear that when we seek a program to meet a specification, we look for the *first* component of a member of an existential type; the second proves that the program meets the constraint part of the specification. As long as we realize this, it seems irrelevant whether or not our system includes a type of first components, which is what the subset type consists of. There are other arguments for the introduction of a subset type, which we review now.

Exercises

7.1 How would you specify the operations $+$ and $*$ over the natural numbers N? In general, how would you specify functions whose natural specifications are their primitive recursive definitions?

7.2 How would you specify the head and tail functions, $+\!\!+$, and the length and sorting functions over lists?

7.3 When we discussed quicksort, we specified permutation by means of the predicate *perm*, which used the equality function eq_N over the type N. Give a definition of permutation which does not depend upon the existence of an equality function and which can therefore be used over any type of lists.

7.4 Discuss ways in which specifications can be made modular, using the universal and existential quantifiers.

7.1.2 Computational irrelevance; lazy evaluation

Recall our discussion in Section 6.1 of the 'head' function over lists. It is defined only over those lists which have a head, the non-empty lists, where we say

$$(nelist\ A) \equiv_{df} (\exists l\!:\![A]) . (nonempty\ l)$$

where the predicate *nonempty* has the inductive definition

$$
\begin{aligned}
nonempty\ [\,] \quad &\equiv_{df} \quad \bot \\
nonempty\ (a :: x) \quad &\equiv_{df} \quad \top
\end{aligned}
$$

and the head function, *hd*, itself is given by

$$
\begin{aligned}
hd \quad &: \quad (nelist\ A) \Rightarrow A \\
hd\ ([\,],p) \quad &\equiv_{df} \quad abort_A\ p \\
hd\ ((a :: x),p) \quad &\equiv_{df} \quad a
\end{aligned}
$$

(This is formalized in TT by a list induction over the first component of a variable of the existential type.) Given an application

$$hd\ ((2 :: \ldots), \ldots)$$

computation to 2 can proceed with no information about the elided portions. In particular, the *proof* information is not necessary for the process of computation to proceed in such a case. Nonetheless, the proof information is crucial in showing that the application is properly typed; we cannot apply the function to a bare list, as that list might be empty. There is thus a tension between what are usually thought of as the *dynamic* and *static* parts of the language. In particular it is thought that if no separation is achieved, then the efficiency of programs will be impaired by the welter of irrelevant information which they carry around – see Section 3.4 of [Backhouse *et al.*, 1989] and Section 10.3 (page 213) of [Constable and others, 1986].

Any conclusion about the efficiency of an object or program is predicated on the evaluation mechanism for the system under consideration, and we now argue that a *lazy* or outermost-first strategy has the advantage of not evaluating the computationally irrelevant, a topic we first discussed at the end of Section 6.2.

Recalling the results of Section 5.6, since the system is strongly normalizing, *any* sequence of reductions will lead us to a result. Since we also have the Church-Rosser property, every reduction sequence leads to the *same* result. We can therefore choose how expressions are to be evaluated. There are two obvious choices. **Strict** evaluation is the norm for imperative languages and many functional languages (Standard ML [Harper, 1986] is an example). Under this discipline, in an application such as

$$f \; a_1 \; \ldots \; a_n$$

the arguments a_i are evaluated fully before the whole expression is evaluated. In such a situation, if an argument a_k is computationally irrelevant, then its evaluation will degrade the efficiency of the program. The alternative, of **normal order** evaluation is to begin evaluation of the whole expression, prior to argument evaluation: if the value of an argument is unnecessary, then it is not evaluated.

Definition 7.1

Evaluation in which we always choose the leftmost-outermost redex (cf. Definition 2.13) is called **normal order** evaluation. If in addition we ensure that no redex is evaluated more than once we call the evaluation **lazy**.

In a language with structured data such as pairs and lists, there is a further clause to the definition: when an argument is evaluated it need not be evaluated to normal form; it is only evaluated to the extent that is necessary for computation to proceed. This will usually imply that it is evaluated to weak head normal form. This means that, for example, an argument of type $A \wedge B$ will be reduced to a pair (a, b), with the subexpressions a and b as yet unevaluated. These may or may not be evaluated in subsequent computation.

Recent research has shown that efficient lazy implementations of functional languages such as Miranda are feasible, and there is every reason that the same techniques could be used for an implementation of TT. It would take us away from our theme to go into this any further; the interested reader can consult the book [Peyton Jones, 1987] which is an excellent introduction to the topic.

Under lazy evaluation computationally irrelevant objects or components of structured objects will simply be ignored, and so no additional computational overhead is imposed. Indeed, it can be argued that the proper definition of computational relevance would be that which chose just that portion of an expression which is used in calculating a result under a lazy evaluation discipline.

There is another possible approach to computational relevance, and that involves an examination of the different forms that types (that is propositions) can take.

Since there are no closed normal forms in $\bot$ and there is only the trivial $Triv$ in $\top$, computation of objects of these types will never be important. What *is* of importance is whether the type is inhabited or not in any particular case. This is exactly the role played by these types in the definition of the head function hd, where we should recall that

$$nelist\ A \equiv_{df} (\exists l:[A]) . (nonempty\ l)$$

with

$$
\begin{aligned}
nonempty \quad & : \quad [A] \Rightarrow U_0 \\
nonempty\ [\,] \quad & \equiv_{df} \quad \bot \\
nonempty\ (a :: x) \quad & \equiv_{df} \quad \top
\end{aligned}
$$

An application of hd to a list l is only possible if we can pair l with a proof p that l is non-empty; the proof will contribute nothing to further evaluation, rather it ensures (through the type system of the language) that the application is to a non-empty list.

It can be argued that this sort of computational irrelevance is preserved when combinations are taken using the connectives $\wedge$, $\Rightarrow$ and $\forall$. A different perspective on the topic in the context of the extensional theory of [Martin-Löf, 1985] is given in Section 3.4 of [Backhouse *et al.*, 1989].

Exercises

7.5 Compute the result of the expression $hd\ ((2 :: a), b)$ using the lazy evaluation strategy discussed above.

7.6 Discuss why combination of formulas by the connectives $\wedge$, $\Rightarrow$ and $\forall$ should preserve computational irrelevance.

7.7 Examine the examples of the previous chapter to find cases of computational irrelevance.

7.2   The subset type

How should we represent the collection of objects of type A with the property B? According to the principle of complete presentation, we would form the type

$$(\exists x : A) . B$$

consisting of pairs of objects and the proofs that they have the property P. This is how we have dealt with the type so far in this exposition. An alternative approach is to build the 'subset' type

$$\{ x : A \mid B \}$$

whose members consist of those a in A which have the property $B[a/x]$, that is those for which the type $B[a/x]$ is inhabited. This has the consequence that we lose the uniqueness of types in the system TT; an object a will be a member of the type $\{ x : A \mid B \}$ for every B which is a property of a.

What are the formal rules for the subset type? The rules we give now are those first proposed in [Nordström and Petersson, 1983], and used in [Constable and others, 1986], page 167, and [Backhouse et al., 1989], Section 3.4.2. Formation is completely standard:

Formation rule for *Set*

$$\frac{A \text{ is a type} \quad B \text{ is a type}}{\{ x : A \mid B \} \text{ is a type}} (SetF)$$

$$[x : A]$$
$$\vdots$$

and objects are introduced as we described above,

Introduction rule for *Set*

$$\frac{a : A \quad p : B[a/x]}{a \ : \ \{ x : A \mid B \}} (SetI)$$

How should a set be eliminated? If we know that $a : \{ x : A \mid B \}$ then we certainly know that $a : A$, but also that $B[a/x]$. What we do not have is a specific proof that $B[a/x]$, so how could we encapsulate this? We can modify the existential elimination rule ($\exists E$) so that the hypothetical judgement $c \ : \ C$ is derived assuming some $y : B[a/x]$, but that c and C cannot depend upon this y. We use the fact that $B[a/x]$ is provable, but we cannot depend on the proof y itself:

Elimination rule for *Set*

$$[x:A; y:B]$$
$$\vdots$$
$$\frac{a:\{\,x:A \mid B\,\} \qquad c(x):C(x)}{c(a)\ :\ C(a)}(SetE)$$

Since no new operator is added by the elimination rule, there is no computation rule for the subset type. We should note that this makes these rules different from the others in type theory. This is also evident from the fact that they fail to satisfy the *inversion principle* of Section 8.4.

We shall write TT_0^S for the system TT_0 with the above rules for subsets added. How are TT_0 and TT_0^S related? The following theorems are proved in [Chisholm, 1988a].

Theorem 7.2

From a derivation d in TT_0^S of the judgement $p\ :\ (\exists x:A).B$ a derivation of

$$fst\ p\ :\ \{\,x:A \mid B\,\}$$

from the same set of assumptions can be constructed.

Proof: Use the rule $(SetI)$. □

Theorem 7.3

If in TT_0^S we can derive $p:\{\,x:A \mid B\,\}$ from the assumptions Γ, then from this derivation we can, for some $q:B$, construct a derivation in TT_0 of

$$(p,q)\ :\ (\exists x:A).B$$

from the assumptions Γ'. The assumptions Γ' result from Γ by replacing assumptions of the form $y\ :\ \{\,y:C \mid D\,\}$ by $y:C; y':D$ where y' is chosen to be a new variable.

Proof: The proof is by induction over the size of the derivation of the judgement $p:\{\,x:A \mid B\,\}$; details can be found in [Chisholm, 1988a].   □

Neither of these results should be a surprise. The first simply uses subset introduction, whilst the second shows that if we are able to derive membership of a subset type then *implicit* in that derivation is a proof that the element has the property required of it. Examining the derivation allows us to extract that proof object. On the other hand, Smith and Salvesen show by an elaboration of Martin-Löf's normalization proof (in Section 5.6 and [Martin-Löf, 1975b]) that

Theorem 7.4

If the judgement

$$t \ : \ (\forall x : \{ z : A \mid P(z) \}) . P(x) \qquad\qquad (7.2)$$

is derivable in TT_0^S, and A and P do not contain the subset type, then for some term t',

$$t' : (\forall x : A) . P(x) \qquad\qquad (7.3)$$

can be derived.

Proof: See [Salvesen and Smith, 1989].   □

This shows that the rules for subsets are very weak. In the judgement 7.2 the term t witnesses the property P of the objects in the subset type. The result says that we can only extract this information when the judgement 7.3 is derivable, in other words when *all* the elements of the type A have the property P! Wherein lies the weakness of the rules for subset? Examining the rule $(SetE)$, we should look at the hypothesis

$$x : A; y : B$$
$$\vdots$$
$$c(x) : C(x)$$

We are allowed to use the assumption $y : B$, *but* y cannot occur free in c or C. Examining the rules for TT_0, if any of the rules contains a variable free in an undischarged hypothesis, then this variable will appear free in the conclusion. In other words, if we use the assumption, and it is not discharged, then it will appear free in the conclusion.

The theorem shows that many functions are not derivable in TT_0^S. Looking first at lists, suppose that we can derive functions

$$head' \ : \ \{ l : [A] \mid nonempty\, l \} \Rightarrow A$$
$$tail' \ : \ \{ l : [A] \mid nonempty\, l \} \Rightarrow [A]$$

with the property that for a non-empty list l

$$l = (head'\, l \ :: \ tail'l)$$

From this we can construct a proof of $(nonempty\, l)$. This is the hypothesis 7.2 and so we can infer

$$(\forall l : [A]) . (nonempty\, l)$$

resulting in a contradiction.

7.2.1 The extensional theory

The case of the extensional theory, [Martin-Löf, 1985], is different, since the proof rule (IE_{ext}) (introduced on page 173) together with the rule (II) allow the derivation of $r(a):I(A,a,b)$ from $e:I(A,a,b)$ for any expression e. Since $r(a)$ is a constant, this results in a proof object of type $I(A,a,b)$ containing no free variables. This in turn makes it possible to give a derivation of a proof object which contains a number of variables in its hypotheses, yet with these variables not appearing free in the proof object: this condition is exactly what is required for the application of the rule $(SetE)$. In [Salvesen, 1989a] there is a derivation of

$$(\forall x:[N]).(\forall n:\{\,z:N\mid(\,z\;in\;x\,)\,\}).(\,n\;in\;x\,)$$

where $(\,n\;in\;x\,)$ is the inductively defined proposition expressing that n is a member of the list x. This derivation is by no means straightforward, using the type U_0 and the type substitution rule in an essential way, but this is not an isolated phenomenon.

Definition 7.5

A formula P over A is **stable** if

$$(\forall x:A).(\neg\neg P\Rightarrow P)$$

Salvesen and Smith show that for all stable formulas,

$$(\forall x:\{\,z:A\mid P(z)\,\}).P(x)$$

is derivable in the extensional version of type theory.

A syntactic characterization of (some of) the stable formulas was first given by Harrop in [Harrop, 1960], and similar characterizations of computationally irrelevant formulas can be found in [Backhouse *et al.*, 1989]. (Note that as is remarked in [Salvesen, 1989a] it is more difficult to recognize the stable formulas when universes are present, as non-normal type expressions can be introduced with the aid of a universe.) The result on stable formulas is in some sense the best possible, as it is also shown in [Salvesen and Smith, 1989] that $(\forall x:\{\,z:A\mid P(z)\,\}).P(x)$ cannot be proved for all formulas. Their proof is based on an idea of Troelstra's for the refutation of Church's thesis in an extensional context.

This limitation has led to a re-evaluation of the subset type by the Goteborg group, with a different approach being adopted. We look at this in Section 7.3.

Exercises

7.8 Complete the proof of Theorem 7.3.

7.9 Formalize the argument above that the existence of the *head'* and *tail'* functions leads to an inconsistency.

7.10 Can the functions *head'* and *tail'* be defined in the extensional version of type theory discussed above?

7.11 Show that the propositions N, N_n, are stable, and that if equality over A is formally decidable then $x =_A y$ is stable. Show that if A and B are stable, then so are $A \wedge B$, $A \Rightarrow B$ and $(\forall x : A) . B$.

7.12 Give examples of formulas which are not stable using disjunction and existential quantification.

7.3   Propositions *not* types

Immediately after introducing the rules for subsets in Section 7.2 we saw in Theorem 7.4 that they were unsatisfactory. The question remains of how to improve the representation of subsets in type theories. The proposed resolutions all involve a representation of propositions as distinct from types. There is intuitive sense in this; *prima facie* the user of a logic is interested in establishing judgements of the form

> *A is true*

rather than in showing that a particular proof object makes the proposition true.

7.3.1   'Squash' types

The first approach to representing the proposition is to consider the 'squash' type, defined in [Constable and others, 1986] to be

$$\|A\| \equiv_{df} \{ t : \top \mid A \}$$

which will be inhabited by the object $Triv$ if and only if there is some proof object $a : A$. It is called the squash type, as all the information about the proof is 'squashed' out of it. We should ask whether the judgement

> $Triv \ : \ \|A\|$

gives a reasonable representation of the judgement '*A is true*'. What would this entail? We would expect that all the rules of constructive logic, as presented in TT_0 say, would remain true when judgements of the form $b : B$ are replaced by others stating B *is true*. For example, we should have

$$\frac{A \ is \ true \quad B \ is \ true}{A \wedge B \ is \ true} \tag{7.4}$$

This we can prove. Suppose that we assume, in accordance with $(SetE)$,

$$x:\top \, , \; p:A$$

and

$$y:\top \, , \; q:B$$

From these we can infer $(p,q) \; : \; (A \wedge B)$, and so by the law $(SetI)$,

$$Triv \; : \; \{ \, t:\top \mid A \wedge B \, \}$$

a judgement in which neither p nor q is free. This means that by subset elimination twice, we have the same result on the assumption

$$Triv \; : \; \{ \, t:\top \mid A \, \} \; , \;\; Triv \; : \; \{ \, t:\top \mid B \, \}$$

which is precisely rule 7.4.

This programme comes to grief when we try to prove that

$$
\begin{array}{c}
[x:A] \\
\vdots \\
\underline{B(x) \; is \; true} \\
(\forall x:A) . \, B(x) \; is \; true
\end{array}
\qquad\qquad (7.5)
$$

as it is not difficult to show that a derivation of this will contradict the counter example to Theorem 7.4; see [Salvesen, 1989a, Section 3]. Intuitively we might argue that knowing that B is true at each instance is not sufficient to establish in a uniform way that it is true universally. This is the only rule for which the criterion fails, but it shows that a different approach must be adopted if we are to find a proper representation of the judgement A *is true* in type theory.

7.3.2   The subset theory

If the representation of the judgement is to be an improvement on TT, as far as subsets are concerned, it is desirable that the system validates the rule

$$
\begin{array}{c}
[x:A \, , \; P \; is \; true] \\
\vdots \\
\underline{a \; : \; \{ \, x:A \mid P \, \} \qquad Q(x) \; is \; true} \\
Q(a) \; is \; true
\end{array}
(SetE')
$$

which has the consequence, setting P and Q the same, that

$$\frac{a \ : \ \{\,x\!:\!A \mid P\,\}}{P(a) \ is \ true}$$

For this to be valid, we need to move to a system in which propositions and types are distinct, for we cannot have this rule if P is a type, as seen by Theorem 7.4.

In [Nordström *et al.*, 1990] the Goteborg group, 'following ideas of Martin-Löf', have introduced a system called the **subset theory** in which the new judgements

$$P \ prop \quad and \quad P \ is \ true$$

are added to the system, together with a set of *logical* connectives, distinct from the type forming operations introduced in their extensional version of TT. Their system uses the names $\times, +, \Pi, \ldots$ for the type forming operations, reserving $\wedge, \vee, \forall, \ldots$ for the operations on propositions. They introduce the rules which, looking at the example of the *logical* $\forall$, state

$$\frac{\begin{array}{c}[x\!:\!A]\\ \vdots\\ A \ prop \quad P(x) \ prop\end{array}}{(\forall x\!:\!A).P(x) \ prop} \qquad \frac{\begin{array}{c}[x\!:\!A]\\ \vdots\\ P(x) \ is \ true\end{array}}{(\forall x\!:\!A).P(x) \ is \ true}$$

$$\frac{(\forall x\!:\!A).P(x) \ is \ true \quad a\!:\!A}{P(a) \ is \ true}$$

As well as this, they give the following rules for subsets,

$$\frac{\begin{array}{c}[x\!:\!A]\\ \vdots\\ A \ is \ a \ type \quad P(x) \ prop\end{array}}{\{\,x\!:\!A \mid P(x)\,\} \ prop} \qquad \frac{a\!:\!A \quad P(a) \ is \ true}{a \ : \ \{\,x\!:\!A \mid P(x)\,\}}$$

$$\frac{a \ : \ \{\,x\!:\!A \mid P(x)\,\} \qquad \begin{array}{c}[x\!:\!A \ , \ P(x) \ is \ true]\\ \vdots\\ c(x)\!:\!C(x)\end{array}}{c(a)\!:\!C(a)}$$

$$\frac{a \ : \ \{\,x\!:\!A \mid P(x)\,\} \qquad \begin{array}{c}[x\!:\!A \ , \ P(x) \ is \ true]\\ \vdots\\ Q(x) \ is \ true\end{array}}{Q(a) \ is \ true}$$

There are two elimination rules for subsets: the first for types, as previously, and the second for propositions, which is $(SetE')$, the rule we wanted to be valid. These rules can be seen to satisfy the inversion principle of Section 8.4.

An elegant aspect of the subset theory is its justification. It can be given an interpretation in the 'basic' type theory, an extensional version of TT along the lines of [Martin-Löf, 1985], thus:

Types are pairs A, A' in the basic theory, where A is a type in the theory, and A' a predicate over A.

Propositions in the new theory are propositions, that is types in the old theory, which may of course contain quantifications over the new types, and so not all propositions of the old theory are propositions of the new. The interpretation is defined construct by construct.

Under this interpretation, all the rules for the propositions are derivable in the basic system, so that the consistency of the basic system lifts to the subset theory.

7.3.3   Gödel interpretation

A second representation of propositions as distinct from types is given by [Salvesen, 1989a, Section 4]. Motivated by the results on Harrop formulas in [Salvesen and Smith, 1989], propositions are interpreted as a certain subclass of types, arising by means of the Gödel double negation interpretation of classical logic in intuitionistic logic; see [Dummett, 1977] for details. Informally, the interpretation is given by prefacing each existential quantification, disjunction and equality type by $\neg\neg$, weakening its constructive content. We can derive rules similar to those above including $(SetE')$, as well as the classical

$$\frac{A \; prop}{A \vee \neg A \; is \; true}$$

which requires a derivation of $\neg\neg(A \vee \neg A)$ in TT.

Exercises

7.13 Give the proofless version of (NE), and show that if we use the judgement $Triv : \|A\|$ to represent A is true, this version of the rule is valid.

7.14 Show how the validity of the derivation 7.5 contradicts the counter example to Theorem 7.4.

7.15 Derive the result $\neg\neg(A \vee \neg A)$ in TT_0.

7.4 Are subsets necessary?

Is the introduction of a subset type necessary for a usable proof and program development system? We began this discussion in Section 7.1, where we saw that the major argument for its introduction was to provide some means of separating (to some degree) the computational and logical aspects of the system from each other. This is ironic, as one of the most appealing aspects of type theory is its identification of propositions and types, proofs and programs, but it was argued that it was necessary for two major reasons.

- Specifications and functions are made more complicated by the presence of proof theoretic information. It is argued in [Nordström *et al.*, 1990], page 125, that the inhabitants of a type such as

$$(\forall x \colon A) . (\exists y \colon B) . P(x, y)$$

should be functions which solve the problem of finding, for each a in A, an element b of B with the property $P(a, b)$. This is not the case, since for each a we will have a *pair* (b, p_b) consisting of such a b together with a proof that it indeed has the required property. Using the subset type,

$$(\forall x \colon A) . \{ y \colon B \mid P(x, y) \}$$

we obtain a function giving only the b without the witnessing information.

- In general, the development of many well-known functions, such as quicksort in Section 6.2, involves the introduction of proof information into the functions, and this will have a deleterious effect on the evaluation efficiency of the function, compared with a 'purely computational' version.

Any discussion of efficiency, like the latter point above, rests on the implementation envisaged, and we would argue, as we did in Section 7.1.2, that a *lazy* implementation of type theory will result in only the computationally relevant information being evaluated. Now we examine the first argument in more detail.

The idea is that we should be able to separate from a complex derivation exactly the part which is computationally relevant, and that this is to be done by replacing some occurrences of existential types by subset types, from which the witnessing information is absent. We would propose an alternative which we believe is superior for two reasons:

- it is a solution which requires no addition to the system of type theory, and

- it allows for more delicate distinctions between proof and computation.

The solution is simply to *name* the appropriate operations and objects sought, which in the case cited above involves us in invoking the axiom of choice to change the specification to

$$(\exists f : A \Rightarrow B) . (\forall x : A) . P(x, (f\,x))$$

Now, inhabitants of this type are pairs, (f, p), which are the function sought together with a proof that it has the required property. Giving this function an explicit name, which is known as **skolemizing** the quantifiers in a logical context, has resulted in a specification which expresses more naturally what is required. This method applies to more complex specifications as well.

Take as an example a simplification of the specification of the Polish/Dutch national flag problem as given in [Nordström *et al.*, 1990]. We now show how it may be written without the subset type. The original specification has the form

$$(\forall x : A) . \{\, y : \{\, y' : B \mid C(y') \,\} \mid P(x, y) \,\}$$

with the intention that for each a we find b in the subset $\{\, y' : B \mid C(y') \,\}$ of B with the property $P(a, b)$. If we replace the subsets by existential types, we have

$$(\forall x : A) . (\exists y : (\exists y' : B) . C(y')) . P(x, y)$$

This is logically equivalent to

$$(\forall x : A) . (\exists y : B) . (\, C(y) \wedge P(x, y) \,) \tag{7.6}$$

and by the axiom of choice to

$$(\exists f : A \Rightarrow B) . (\forall x : A) . (\, C(f\,x) \wedge P(x, (f\,x)) \,)$$

which is inhabited by functions *together with proofs of their correctness*. It can be argued that this expresses in a clear way what was rather more implicit in the specification based on sets – the formation of an existential type bundles together data and proof, the transformation to the specification 7.6 makes explicit the unbundling process.

As a final example, consider a problem in which we are asked to produce for each a in A with the property $D(a)$ some b with the property $P(a, b)$. There is an important question of whether the b depends just upon the a, or upon both the a and the proof that it has the property $D(a)$. In the latter case we could write the specification thus:

$$(\forall x : (\exists x' : A) . D(x')) . (\exists y : B) . P(x, y)$$

and skolemize to give

$$(\exists f:((\exists x':A).D(x') \Rightarrow B)).(\forall x:(\exists x':A).D(x')).P(x,(f\ x))$$

If we use the Curry equivalence, first proved in Section 4.6.1, page 93, which replaces existential quantifiers in the domain position of a function type, we have

$$(\exists f:((\forall z:A).(D(z) \Rightarrow B))).(\forall x':A).(\forall p:D(x')).P((x',p),(f\ x'\ p))$$

which makes manifest the functional dependence required. Observe that we could indeed have written this formal specification directly on the basis of the informal version from which we started.

If we do *not* wish the object sought to depend upon the proof of the property D, we can write the following specification:

$$(\exists f:A \Rightarrow B).(\forall x':A).(\forall p:D(x')).P((x',p),(f\ x')) \tag{7.7}$$

in which it is plain that the object $(f\ x')$ in B is not dependent on the proof object $p:D(x')$. Observe that there *is* still dependence of the property P on the proof p; if we were to use a subset type to express the specification, thus, we would have something of the form

$$(\forall x':\{\ x':A \mid D(x')\ \}).(\exists y:B).P'(x',y)$$

where the property $P'(x,y)$ relates $x':A$ and $y:B$. This is equivalent to the specification

$$(\exists f:A \Rightarrow B).(\forall x':A).(\forall p:D(x')).P'(x',(f\ x'))$$

in which the property P' must not mention the proof object p, so that with our more explicit approach we have been able to express the specification 7.7 which cannot be expressed under the naïve subset discipline.

It is instructive to examine examples from the literature in which the subset type has been used. We have already discussed the Polish flag problem; a second example is the parsing algorithm of [Chisholm, 1987]. In fact we find that in Chisholm's derivation of the parsing algorithm, the subset type is not used in an essential way: the solution is presented as a member of the type

$$(\forall w:Word).(Parse\ w) \vee \neg(Parse\ w)$$

where

$$Parse\ w \equiv_{df} \{\ pt:PT \mid w = spell\ pt\ \}$$

the function *spell* giving the word spelt out by the parse tree *pt* which is a member of the algebraic type *PT* of parse trees. The subset type is used nowhere else in the derivation, and it is used here only because the proof object for $w = spell\ pt$ can be ignored 'because it has no computational content'. It makes no difference to the derivation to replace the set by

$$(\exists pt:PT)\ .\ (w = spell\ pt)$$

which carries the proof objects explicitly. Our remarks in Section 7.1.2 would apply as far as the efficiency of the final algorithm is concerned.

As a final example, consider the problem of finding a root of a function. It is argued, in [Constable and others, 1986], Section 2.4, for example, that the natural specification for such a function is

$$(\forall f:\{\ f:N \Rightarrow N\ |\ (\exists n:N)\ .\ (f\ n) = 0\ \})\ .\ (\ (\exists n:N)\ .\ (f\ n) = 0\ )$$

which might be read 'given a function for which a root exists, we can find a root'. It is a simple consequence of Theorem 7.4 that the existence of an object of this type leads to a contradiction.

In any case, this specification seems to miss the point about root finding. The sorts of algorithms we find used in practice are those embodied by theorems of the form

$$(\forall f:N \Rightarrow N)\ .\ (\ C(f) \Rightarrow (\exists n:N)\ .\ (f\ n) = 0\ )$$

which we would read 'if f satisfies the condition $C(f)$ then we can find a root'. Many of the most important and difficult theorems of number theory and numerical analysis are precisely theorems of this kind, from which algorithms are derived. In contrast, the specification above begs the question of where the proof of existence of the root comes from.

To summarize, there are two responses to the computationally irrelevant. We can first ignore it, exploiting lazy evaluation. The second expedient is to transform the specification so that the computation and verification are separated. We did this above by a simple series of transformations; in general, simply *naming* the function we aim to compute and writing the specification and derivation in terms of that function can achieve the desired effect. This approach seems to achieve the separation between the logical and the computational to the appropriate degree, without introducing the subset type. We have found no example in the literature which is not amenable to this kind of treatment.

Using the subset type to represent a subset brings problems; as we saw in the previous section, it is not possible in general to recover the witnessing information from a subset type, especially in an intensional system such as *TT*, and so, in these cases, the existential type should be used, retaining the witnessing information.

7.5   Quotient or congruence types

An important tool for the programmer and the mathematician is the capability to define an equality relation over a class of objects. For instance in this account we stipulated that we would consider as the same two expressions which differ only in their bound variables. In a program we might choose to represent finite sets by finite lists, by taking as equal those lists which have the same elements, irrespective of their multiplicity or ordering. In both cases we can be seen to define a new type by taking the **quotient** of a type by an equivalence relation (a relation which is reflexive, symmetric and transitive).

These types are a part of the Nuprl system [Constable and others, 1986] and a variant of them, *congruence* types, appears in the type theory of [Backhouse *et al.*, 1989]. We start with an exposition of the quotient type adapted to the context of TT, and then compare it with the congruence type. Because of the number of hypotheses in the following rule, we write them in a vertical list.

Formation rule for $A//E_{x,y}$

$$
\frac{
\begin{array}{l}
A \text{ is a type} \\
x:A \ , \ y:A \vdash E \text{ is a type} \\
x:A \vdash r \ : \ E[x/x, x/y] \\
x:A \ , \ y:A \ , \ r:E \vdash s:E[y/x, x/y] \\
x:A \ , \ y:A \ , \ z:A \ , \\
\quad r:E \ , \ s:E[y/x, z/y] \vdash t:E[x/x, z/y]
\end{array}
}{A//E_{x,y} \text{ is a type}}(QF)
$$

In this rule we have written hypothetical judgements such as

$$
[x:A \ , \ y:A]
$$
$$
\vdots
$$
$$
E \text{ is a type}
$$

in the horizontal form

$$
x:A \ , \ y:A \vdash E \text{ is a type}
$$

In each case the hypotheses to the left of the '$\vdash$' are discharged by the application of the rule.

In forming the type, we have to verify that the predicate is an equivalence relation – that is the purpose of the final three premises of the rule. We use the subscript of x, y to indicate that it is these two variables, free in E, which are bound by the type construct. When no confusion can result, they will be omitted.

The introduction rule breaks unicity of typing. An alternative would be to 'tag' variables in some way to indicate to which type they belong.

Introduction rule for $A//E_{x,y}$

$$\frac{a:A}{a:A//E_{x,y}}(QI)$$

If we define a function over a quotient type, then the value on equivalent elements has to be equal, otherwise the function is not well defined, giving different values when different representatives of the same equivalence class are chosen. The elimination rule for the quotient type, which is the rule introducing functions over the type, must reflect this.

In eliminating an element of a quotient type, we behave in the same way as for an element of type A, producing some object $c(x):C(x)$, except that for the elimination to be well defined, c should give the same values for equivalent elements. This gives an extra hypothesis in the rule.

Elimination rule for $A//E_{x,y}$

$$\frac{a:A//E_{x,y} \quad \overset{[x:A]}{\underset{\vdots}{c(x):C(x)}} \quad \overset{[x:A\,,\ y:A\,,\ p:E]}{\underset{\vdots}{t:I(C(x),c(x),c(y))}}}{c(a)\ :\ C(a)}(QE)$$

There is no separate computation rule for the quotient type, but there is a rule indicating that equivalent elements are deemed to be equal, so making the equivalence relation the equality over the type.

Equality rule for $A//E_{x,y}$

$$\frac{a:A \quad b:A \quad p:E[a/x,b/y]}{r(a)\ :\ I(A//E_{x,y},a,b)}(Q{=})$$

This has the effect of allowing equivalent elements to be substituted for equivalents in any context involving elements of the type $A//E_{x,y}$, and so it is by this rule that the new equality is defined on the type. Given the judgement $r(a):I(A//E_{x,y},a,b)$ we can substitute b for a in any context where a is considered to be of type $A//E_{x,y}$ – such contexts are of course restricted to those where these substitutions can be performed safely. Note that it is *not* asserted that the type $I(A,a,b)$ is inhabited, so that we cannot substitute b for a in *every* context.

If it is thought confusing that a has both the type A and the type $A//E_{x,y}$ we could introduce a label to suggest when a is being considered as an element of the quotient type. There is no inverse to this operation, in general, unless each equivalence contains a 'canonical' member, such as the representatives

$$0,1,\ldots,k-1$$

of the equivalence classes for the relation $|x - y| \, mod \, k = 0$.

A typical example of a quotient type is that of the rationals, which can be represented by pairs (n, m) with n an integer and m a positive integer. (We suggested a representation of the integers in Section 6.7.) Two pairs are equivalent

$$(n, m) \sim (n', m')$$

if $n * m' = n' * m$. The sum of two rationals n/m and p/q is defined to be

$$\frac{n * q + p * m}{m * q}$$

It is an exercise for the reader to verify that this respects the relation $\sim$. Similarly, if we define the 'less than' relation over the integers by analogy with the definition of lt_2 over N in Section 6.1.2, then defining

$$(n, m) \prec (n', m') \equiv_{df} (n * m' < n' * m)$$

then the predicate is well defined. (In the Nuprl development, [Constable and others, 1986, page 210] this is not true, because a stronger version of type equality is adopted than that here.) A definition which fails is the function

$$denom \, (n, m) \equiv_{df} m$$

but we can give a definition,

$$denom \, (n, m) \equiv_{df} m \, div \, (gcd \, n \, m)$$

based on the canonical representative $(n \, div \, g \, , \, m \, div \, g)$ of the rational (n, m), where $g = gcd \, n \, m$.

A second example is given by the extensional equality of Section 5.8. In that section we described '$\simeq$' as a partial equivalence relation, since it is not in general reflexive. It will be reflexive on the domain consisting of those functions which are themselves extensional. The substitution check in the elimination rule for the type means that we only perform substitutions in what we called extensional propositions. An advantage of our approach there is that we have a syntactic criterion for extensionality of propositions which obviates the necessity of checking the conditions time after time. We shall look at a further example in the following section on congruence types.

What is the advantage of the quotient type, over a simple definition of an equivalence relation with which we work explicitly? The major one is to carry over the rules for substitution and so on to the equivalence relation, when the formula in which the substitution is being made is insensitive to the representative of the equivalence class chosen. We examine the real numbers as a further case study in Section 7.6.

7.5.1   Congruence types

A similar construction is given in the paper [Backhouse *et al.*, 1989], where it is called the **congruence type** construction. When introducing a (free) algebraic type, such as that of finite lists, we introduce the constructors [ ] and :: and the objects built from these are distinct unless they are identical. If we want to represent finite bags, we might choose finite lists as a representation, but we shall identify two lists which contain the same elements, in different orders. This identification is an equivalence relation, and so we could just write down the equivalence relation, and form the quotient type as above. The approach of congruence types is slightly different, as we can simply state that the equation

$$a \bullet b \bullet x = b \bullet a \bullet x \tag{7.8}$$

should hold for all a, b and x, where $\bullet$ is the (infix) list constructor for this type. The requirement 7.8 is considerably simpler to express than the explicit form for the equivalence relation generated by that equation, and the property of respecting such an equation, as is required in the elimination rule, is also easier to express. Apart from this the rules for such algebraic types are exactly as for the quotient type.

Can we express a general quotient $A//E_{x,y}$ by these means? We can indeed, by means of the trivial constructor, $\star$ say. We have the formation rule

$$\overline{\quad Star_E\ A\ is\ a\ type \quad}$$

and the introduction rule

$$\frac{a:A}{\star a\ :\ Star_E\ A}$$

In eliminating the type, we have

$$\frac{s:Star_E\ A \quad c(a)\ :\ C(\star a) \quad t:I(C(\star x),c(x),c(y))}{\star - elim_x(c,s)\ :\ C(s)}$$

$$[a:A] \qquad\qquad [x:A\ ,\ y:A\ ,\ p:E]$$
$$\vdots \qquad\qquad\qquad \vdots$$

with the computation rule

$$\star - elim_x(c, \star a) \; \rightarrow \; c(a)$$

We have simply replaced the equation with a general requirement that the formula introduced by the elimination respects the relation E. One advantage of the approach here is that the elements are 'tagged' with the constructor '$\star$' so that we can distinguish between an object $a : A$ and its equivalence class $\star a$ in the congruence type.

The example of the type of binary numerals implemented as a congruence type appears in [Backhouse *et al.*, 1989, Section 5].

This method is similar to the idea of *laws* in early versions of the Miranda language; on introducing an algebraic type by means of its constructors, the user was allowed to write down rewrite rules which would be applied to any expression of the type. To implement the type of ordered lists, one was allowed to write

```
Ocons a (Ocons b x) => Ocons b (Ocons a x)        , if a>b
```

which would swap any pairs which were out of order. This is more limited than the general type-theoretic construct both because the language in which the equivalences could be written was much simpler, and also because each of the rules had to be oriented, so that rewriting would only take place in one direction. Further details of the types and the techniques available to reason about them can be found in [Thompson, 1986; Thompson, 1900].

As a coda to this discussion, we should mention [Chisholm, 1988b], in which it is shown that the subset type can be used to advantage with the congruence type, reducing the proof burden which arises in checking the conditions for the elimination rule. The author shows the difference between the derivations of the cardinality function over types of finite sets implemented with and without using the subset construct. The example chosen is one in which the equivalence classes under the equivalence relation fail to have canonical members, and it is in this sort of example that the advantage is most marked.

Exercises

7.16 Complete the arguments that $+$ and $\prec$ are well defined over the rationals.

7.17 How would you define the division function over the rationals?

7.18 Give an explicit definition of the equivalence relation generated by Equation 7.8.

7.6   Case study – the real numbers

Nowhere is the difference between classical and constructive mathematics more evident than in the treatment of the real numbers and real analysis. The classical mathematician is happy to treat the reals as equivalence classes of convergent (or *Cauchy*) sequences of rationals, choosing arbitrary representatives of equivalence classes when necessary. He or she is also accustomed to using non-constructive principles such as that which states that every increasing sequence of rationals has a least upper bound, which as we saw in Chapter 3 numbers the law of the excluded middle amongst its consequences. Attention is paid to computation only in numerical analysis, which can only use the results of classical analysis in a most indirect manner.

In a constructive setting we can define the reals to be convergent sequences of rational numbers (written Q). We define $Real_C$ to be the type

$$(\exists s:N \Rightarrow Q).(\exists m:Q \Rightarrow N).$$
$$(\forall q:Q).(\forall n:N).(q \succ 0 \wedge n > (m\,q) \Rightarrow |s_n - s_{(m\,q)}| \prec q)$$

where we have used the subscript s_n instead of a function application for readability. What are elements of this type? They have the form

$$(s,(m,p))$$

where s is a sequence, m is a modulus of continuity for s and p is a proof of this fact, which is an element of

$$(\forall q:Q).(\forall n:N).(q \succ 0 \wedge n > (m\,q) \Rightarrow |s_n - s_{(m\,q)}| \prec q)$$

In computing with reals, this latter proof information will be computationally irrelevant, but nonetheless has to be dealt with – as we define new reals, that is a new sequence and its modulus of continuity, we are obliged to show that the latter is indeed a modulus function.

There is a slightly more streamlined approach which has been adopted in [Bishop and Bridges, 1985] amongst other places. We can take the sequences which have a fixed modulus of continuity, the **regular** sequences, and write

$$Real \equiv_{df} (\exists s:Seq).Reg(s)$$

where $Seq \equiv_{df} (N \Rightarrow Q)$ and

$$Reg(s) \equiv_{df} (\forall m,n:N).\left(|s_n - s_m| \prec \frac{1}{m+1} + \frac{1}{n+1}\right)$$

Elements of this type will be pairs

$$(s, p)$$

with s a sequence and p a proof that s is regular. As we said earlier, the information p is computationally irrelevant.

How can addition be defined? Given two reals (s, p) and (t, q) we can define a sum sequence thus:

$$x_n \equiv_{df} s_{2*n+1} + t_{2*n+1}$$

but we also need proof that this sequence is regular. Note that

$$|x_n - x_m|$$
$$\equiv |s_{2*n+1} + t_{2*n+1} - s_{2*m+1} - t_{2*m+1}|$$
$$\preceq |s_{2*n+1} - s_{2*m+1}| + |t_{2*n+1} - t_{2*m+1}|$$

and using the proofs p and q we have that this is

$$\prec \frac{1}{2*m+1+1} + \frac{1}{2*n+1+1} + \frac{1}{2*m+1+1} + \frac{1}{2*n+1+1}$$

$$\equiv \frac{1}{m \mid 1} + \frac{1}{n \mid 1}$$

From this we can build an object v which proves that x is regular, giving a real (x, v). This has been an informal development, but it is not hard to see that we can on the basis of this write a function add' of type

$$Real \Rightarrow Real \Rightarrow Real$$

This definition mixes the computationally relevant with the irrelevant, and we can in fact write, following Bishop, a version add of type

$$(\exists f : (Seq \Rightarrow Seq \Rightarrow Seq)) .$$
$$(\forall s, t : Seq) . (Reg(s) \land Reg(t) \Rightarrow Reg(f\ s\ t))$$

whose members consist of a (sequence) function of type $Seq \Rightarrow Seq \Rightarrow Seq$ together with a verification that it preserves regularity. We shall write add_S for the sequence function defined above. We can develop other arithmetic operations in a similar way. We have used our earlier strategy of naming functions appropriately rather than using a subset type. Other approaches, such as that in Section 11.5 of [Constable and others, 1986], define the reals thus:

$$Real_{Set} \equiv_{df} \{ s : Seq \mid Reg(s) \}$$

In this context it seems more appropriate to use our approach, which makes explicit the proofs, yet which separates them from the computation operations over sequences.

Each number on the real line has an infinite number of representatives in the type *Real*. Consider zero for instance: it is represented by the constant zero sequence, as well as by the sequence

$$z_n \equiv_{df} \frac{1}{k + 2 * n + 3}$$

for each natural number k. We say that two reals (s, p) and (t, q) are **equal** if the following type is inhabited

$$Eq(s, t) \equiv_{df} (\forall n : N) . \left(|s_n - t_n| \prec \frac{1}{2 * n + 1} \right)$$

Note that this definition depends only upon s and t and not on the proof information p and q.

We leave it as an exercise for the reader to prove that this equality is an *equivalence relation* over the type *Real*. It is not difficult to see that each of the representatives of zero above is equal, and to see that the definition of addition above respects equality, so that the following type is inhabited.

$$Eq(s, s') \land Eq(t, t') \Rightarrow Eq(add_S \, s \, t \, , \, add_S \, s' \, t')$$

As Eq is an equivalence relation over *Real*, it seems sensible to investigate the quotient $Real_q \equiv_{df} Real // Eq_{s,t}$. We have already seen that addition respects the relation Eq, so we can define a version of addition

$$add_q \, : \, Real_q \Rightarrow Real_q \Rightarrow Real_q$$

In many applications we need to select a particular representative sequence for a real. A classic example is to select, given a real r and a positive rational x, a rational within a distance x of r. This is trivial given a particular representative sequence, but the rational chosen will depend upon the particular sequence, different sequences giving different approximations. This means that for a general treatment of the reals we need to use the type *Real*; as is remarked in [Constable and others, 1986], the type $Real_q$ can provide a useful framework for substitution if nothing else.

It is no surprise that our constructive approach to the reals is quite different from a classical one, focusing as it does on convergent sequences of rationals. When we compute with 'real numbers' we do precisely this – it is only in the idealized framework of classical mathematics that we are able to deal with infinitary objects such as equivalence classes of infinite sequences.

For further material we would refer the reader to [Constable and others, 1986], on which we have relied here, which develops the theory a little further, and of course to [Bishop and Bridges, 1985] which gives a re-development of much of classical analysis, in a rigorous but informal way.

Exercises

7.19 Show that equality as defined above is an equivalence relation, and give definitions of subtraction, absolute value and multiplication which respect this relation.

7.20 How would you define equality and the arithmetic operations over the type of Cauchy reals, $Real_C$? How would you separate the computational from the proof theoretic in making these definitions?

7.21 Give definitions of convergence of sequences of reals, and so of continuity of functions, and using this give a proof of Theorem 3.2, the constructive intermediate value theorem.

7.7 Strengthened rules; polymorphism

Experienced users of type-theoretic systems, such as Roy Dyckhoff, the Cornell group and Backhouse and his co-workers, have noticed that a number of proofs seem to contain steps which though necessary seem less than 'intuitive'. After examining an example of this, we look at Dyckhoff's strong elimination rules and Backhouse's 'hypothetical hypotheses', a topic to which we return in Section 8.4. We conclude with a discussion of the polymorphic type $A \mapsto B$ defined in [Malcolm and Chisholm, 1988], which can be seen to generalize the other rules introduced in this section.

7.7.1 An example

In [Dyckhoff, 1987] the example of the proof of

$$(\exists z : A \vee B) . P(z) \Rightarrow ((\exists x : A) . P(inl\ x) \vee (\exists y : B) . P(inr\ y))\ \ (\textbf{7.9})$$

is cited as the motivation for a re-examination of the rules of type theory. How does the proof proceed? Working top-down we assume

$$p : (\exists z : A \vee B) . P(z)$$

and aim to show that the consequent of the implication above is inhabited. We have an existential assumption, which is used by means of the rule $(\exists E)$. We should therefore try to prove

$$((\exists x : A) . P(inl\ x) \vee (\exists y : B) . P(inr\ y))$$

on the basis of the assumptions

$$z : A \vee B \ , \ r : P(z) \tag{7.10}$$

To use the disjunctive assumption $z : A \vee B$, we would like to reason in the two cases that z is in the left- and right-hand sides of the sum; we cannot do this as the variable z is free in the second assumption. In order to be able to perform the case analysis, we have to make this extra assumption a part of the goal: we make it the hypothesis of an implication, so we aim to prove

$$Q(z) \equiv_{df} P(z) \Rightarrow (\ (\exists x : A) . P(inl \ x) \ \vee \ (\exists y : B) . P(inr \ y) \ )$$

from the single assumption that $z : A \vee B$. This proceeds thus

$$\cfrac{\cfrac{\cfrac{x : A \quad [q : P(inl \ x)]^1}{(x, q) \ : \ (\exists x : A) . P(inl \ x)}(\exists I)}{inl \ (x, q) \ : \ (\ (\exists x : A) . P(inl \ x) \ \vee \ (\exists y : B) . P(inr \ y) \ )}(\vee I_1)}{\lambda q . inl \ (x, q) \ : \ Q(inl \ x)}(\Rightarrow I)_1$$

By a similar argument we show that $\lambda s . inr \ (y, s)$ is a member of $Q(inr \ y)$ and so by $(\vee E'')$,

$$vc \equiv_{df} vcases''_{x,y} \ z \ \lambda q . inl \ (x, q) \ \lambda s . inr \ (y, s)$$

is a member of

$$P(z) \Rightarrow (\ (\exists x : A) . P(inl \ x) \ \vee \ (\exists y : B) . P(inr \ y) \ )$$

assuming that $z : A \vee B$. Also assuming $r : P(z)$, we have

$$vc \ r \ : \ (\ (\exists x : A) . P(inl \ x) \ \vee \ (\exists y : B) . P(inr \ y) \ )$$

and by a final application of $(\exists E)$,

$$Cases_{x,y} \ p \ (vc \ r) \ : \ (\ (\exists x : A) . P(inl \ x) \ \vee \ (\exists y : B) . P(inr \ y) \ )$$

Commentators have argued that the abstractions $\lambda q . \ldots, \lambda s . \ldots$ in the term vc and the application of this term to the proof r are *spurious* as they arise by our need to transfer the assumption $p : P(z)$ into the goal so that the case analysis on the z can take effect.

It would be preferable when we perform a case analysis on the z in the assumptions 7.10 for that case analysis to percolate through to the other assumptions which depend upon it, to give the two sets of assumptions

$$x : A \ , \ p : P(inl \ x) \quad \text{and} \quad y : B \ , \ p : P(inr \ y)$$

It is essentially this which is achieved by the strong rule of [Dyckhoff, 1987], which we present now.

7.7.2 Strong and hypothetical rules

The stronger version of the elimination rule for disjunction is

$$\frac{p:(A \vee B) \qquad u:C[inl\ x/z] \qquad v:C[inr\ y/z]}{decide_{x,y}\ p\ u\ v\ :\ C[p/z]}(\vee SE)$$

$$\begin{array}{cc} [x:A & [y:B \\ r:(p = inl\ x)] & r:(p = inr\ y)] \\ \vdots & \vdots \end{array}$$

with the computation rules

$$\begin{aligned} decide_{x,y}\ (inl\ a)\ u\ v &\ \rightarrow\ u[a/x] \\ decide_{x,y}\ (inr\ b)\ u\ v &\ \rightarrow\ v[b/y] \end{aligned}$$

The terminology *'decide'* is used for the operator, as this is the Nuprl terminology [Constable and others, 1986], and the Nuprl rules for the union and the existential type indeed are strong versions of the rules of TT.

With the extra hypotheses, it is easy to build a proof of the implication 7.9 without the spurious abstractions and application. We start as before, from the assumptions 7.10, but now we can perform a case analysis, giving the two sets of assumptions

$$x:A\ ,\ p:P(z)\ ,\ r:(z = inl\ x) \quad \text{and} \quad y:B\ ,\ p:P(z)\ ,\ r:(z = inr\ y)$$

From the first set, we have by substitution

$$p\ :\ P(inl\ x)$$

giving in a direct fashion first

$$(x,p)\ :\ (\exists x:A)\,.\,P(inl\ x)$$

and then

$$inl\ (x,p)\ :\ (\,(\exists x:A)\,.\,P(inl\ x) \vee (\exists y:B)\,.\,P(inr\ y)\,)$$

We derive in a similar way from the second

$$inr\ (y,p)\ :\ (\,(\exists x:A)\,.\,P(inl\ x) \vee (\exists y:B)\,.\,P(inr\ y)\,)$$

and by an application of $(\vee E'')$ we have the required result, with no spurious abstractions.

An alternative way of expressing these stronger rules is by rules which contain 'hypothetical hypotheses'. Up to now, the hypotheses of a rule have been judgements, such as $p:A \vee B$ or $u:C[inl\ x/z]$, from the derivations of which certain assumptions may be discharged on the application of the rule.

A hypothetical hypothesis should be thought of as the hypothesis that a particular judgement can be derived on the basis of certain assumptions, rather than being derivable outright. In an adaptation of Backhouse's notation, as presented in [Backhouse, 1987b], where we write the hypotheses in a vertical list and we use the notation

$$\{\ J_1, \ldots, J_k\ \triangleright\ J\ \}$$

for the hypothetical hypothesis that J is derivable from the assumptions J_1 to J_k, the stronger rule for disjunction elimination is

$$\frac{\begin{array}{l} p:(A \vee B) \\ \{\ v:(A \vee B), w:C\ \triangleright\ E\ is\ a\ type\ \} \\ \{\ x:A, w:C[inl\ x/w]\ \triangleright\ b:E[inl\ x/w]\ \} \\ \{\ y:B, w:C[inr\ y/w]\ \triangleright\ c:E[inr\ y/w]\ \} \end{array}}{\{\ w:C[a/w]\ \triangleright\ when_{x,y}\ a\ b\ c\ :\ E[a/w]\ \}}(\vee EH)$$

The rules of computation for *when* are exactly the same as those for *vcases* and *decide*. More details on this material can be found in [Malcolm and Chisholm, 1988], and we shall have more to say in general about derivations containing hypothetical hypotheses in Section 8.4.

The elimination rules for all constructs can be given a hypothetical form; some details of this are to be found in [Saaman and Malcolm, 1987], where it is argued that their use leads to more compact proof objects, for reasons similar to those which improved the proof above. One slightly unsatisfactory point about the rules is the case of inductively defined types, such as lists, where the rules are less general than might be hoped (if consistency is to be preserved!). In the next section we look at an alternative approach.

7.7.3 Polymorphic types

Another case in which spurious abstractions and applications appear is that of the head function over lists. Even if we work in a theory such as the subset theory of Section 7.3, although the type of the function can be specified to be

$$\{\ l:[A]\ |\ l \neq [\ ]\ \} \Rightarrow A \qquad\qquad (7.11)$$

the best that can be done is to derive a function of type

$$(\forall l : [A]) . (l \neq [\,]) \Rightarrow A$$

which is equivalent to the type using the existential representation of the set of non-empty lists. Again, as in the earlier example, the problem is how to incorporate information about an argument without making that information (in this case the proof that the list is non-empty) an extra argument of the function.

A new class of *polymorphic* types, which can be used to overcome this problem, is defined in Section 3.4.3 of [Backhouse *et al.*, 1989].

The non-dependent **polymorphic** type $A \mapsto B$ is characterized by the rules

$$\frac{\begin{array}{c} [x:A] \\ \vdots \\ b:B \end{array}}{b \; : \; A \mapsto B}(\mapsto I) \qquad \frac{b:A \mapsto B \quad a:A}{b \; : \; B}(\mapsto E)$$

where in the introduction rule neither b nor B contains the variable x. b is thought of as a polymorphic constant, as although it depends upon the assumption $x:A$, the *value* of b is independent of the value of x.

In an extensional system, such as that of [Martin-Löf, 1985], it is possible to derive that

$$head \, l \; : \; (l \neq [\,]) \mapsto A \tag{7.12}$$

and then by the elimination rule,

$$head \, l \; : \; A$$

This technique can be used to derive the stronger rules of elimination of [Dyckhoff, 1987], as well.

7.7.4 Non-termination

There are consequences of introducing the polymorphic type $A \mapsto B$ in an extensional system. It is well known that not every term of [Martin-Löf, 1985] has a normal form, as we can derive

$$(\lambda p : \bot) . ((\lambda x . xx)(\lambda x . xx)) \; : \; \bot \Rightarrow A \tag{7.13}$$

for any type A. This is because assuming that $p : \bot$, we can deduce that

$$r \; : \; I(U_n, A, A \Rightarrow A)$$

and then

$$A \leftrightarrow (A \Rightarrow A)$$

Using substitution of types, from $x:A$ we can deduce that $x:(A \Rightarrow A)$ and so that

$$(xx) \ : \ A$$

Further deductions give the judgement 7.13. On the other hand, we *can* show that every closed expression has a canonical value, or weak head normal form (cf. Section 2.3), so that with this weaker notion, the system is terminating. If we include the polymorphic type, then there are terms without canonical form, so the system is not terminating. Take the derivation that

$$((\lambda x \,.\, xx)(\lambda x \,.\, xx)) \ : \ A$$

depending upon the assumption $p:\bot$. By $(\mapsto I)$, we have

$$((\lambda x \,.\, xx)(\lambda x \,.\, xx)) \ : \ \bot \mapsto A$$

depending upon *no* assumptions. This term has no canonical form, since

$$((\lambda x \,.\, xx)(\lambda x \,.\, xx)) \ \rightarrow \ e$$

if and only if $e \equiv ((\lambda x \,.\, xx)(\lambda x \,.\, xx))$.

In an intensional theory such as TT, there is no difficulty of this kind in adding the polymorphic type, but note that the polymorphic types will contain fewer objects since as was argued in [Salvesen and Smith, 1989] none of the rules of TT loses mention of objects mentioned in their hypotheses.

Exercises

7.22 Give a strengthened elimination rule for the existential quantifier, and an example in which its use simplifies a proof object.

7.23 Show how the strong elimination rule for $\vee$ is a consequence of the hypothetical rule $(\vee EH)$.

7.24 Give 'hypothetical' versions of the strengthened rules for $\exists$ and N elimination.

7.25 Give a derivation of the judgement 7.12 and use this to show that *head* can be given the type 7.11.

7.26 Complete the derivation of the judgement 7.13.

7.8   Well-founded recursion

Rather than giving completely explicit definitions of functions, or proofs of universal propositions, we often have to use *recursion*, which allows functions to be defined in terms of their values at 'simpler' arguments, or properties to be proved assuming that they already hold of 'simpler' objects.

The recursions in the system TT are **structural**, that is they are linked to the inductive generation of a data type such as N, *lists*, *trees* and the W types. For these types we say that the component parts of an object, such as the subtrees u and v of the tree

$Bnode\ n\ u\ v$

are simpler than the tree itself. The elimination rule for these types legitimizes definition by recursion and proof by induction over the types. Such recursions are limited, in that we limit our notion of what is simpler to a structural one: component parts are simpler than the whole. The question we address in this section is whether there is a more general notion of 'simpler than' over which we can make recursive definitions and inductive proofs. We shall see that indeed there is, and that some of the examples of recursion we have seen in Chapter 6 can be cast in a more natural form in this way.

We shall go on to look at other ways in which the recursive capabilities of the system may be increased. In particular we shall also examine how a wider class of 'inductive' type definitions can be added to the system, and also how a treatment of partial functions can be included, without breaking the important property of strong normalization. First, however, we examine well-founded types and recursion.

As this section is intended to be an introduction to the idea of well-founded recursion, we shall use ideas and notation of naïve set theory, as discussed in [Enderton, 1977] for instance, going on in the next section to examine how these ideas can best be incorporated into type theory.

Definition 7.6

A binary relation $\prec$ is a **partial order** if for all x, y, z,

$$x \nprec x$$
$$x \prec y \wedge y \prec z \Rightarrow x \prec z$$

We can think of $x \prec y$ as expressing 'x is simpler than y', as we are certain by the first clause that we have no loops $x \prec x$, and in combination with the second that we have nothing of the form

$$x_o \prec x_1 \prec \ldots \prec x_n \prec x_0$$

However, being a partial order is insufficient to guarantee that we can perform recursion over the ordering, and the classic example is the relation

$$n \prec m \equiv_{df} m < n$$

so that

$$\ldots n+1 \prec n \prec \ldots \prec 1 \prec 0$$

How would a recursion over this type work? We would have to define the value at 0 in terms of the value at $1, 2, \ldots$. In turn, the value at 1 is determined by values at $2, 3, \ldots$: never at any point do we make a start with the definition. Consider the concrete case of the definition $f : (N \Rightarrow N)$ by 'recursion' over $\prec$:

$$f\, n \equiv_{df} f\,(n+1) - 1 \qquad\qquad (7.14)$$

The problem with this is that it does not define a *unique* function, for the functions f_k with

$$f_k\, n \equiv_{df} n + k$$

are *all* solutions of the recursion equation 7.14. Not only is this example classic, but it characterizes those orderings over which recursion fails.

Definition 7.7

A partial ordering $\prec$ over A is **well founded** if and only if there are no sequences $<x_n>_n$ in A so that

$$\ldots x_{n+1} \prec x_n \prec \ldots \prec x_1 \prec x_0$$

Such a sequence is called an **infinite descending chain**.

In any ordering with an infinite descending chain, we can reproduce the example above, showing that 'recursive' definitions do not lead to unique solutions. On the other hand, we can show that recursive definitions *are* well defined over well-founded orderings.

This characterization of well-foundedness has classical equivalents which are more suited to a constructive context, as they are more explicit. The one we shall use is

Theorem 7.8

A partial ordering is well founded if and only if it satisfies

$$\forall x(\forall y(y \prec x \Rightarrow y \in z) \Rightarrow x \in z) \Rightarrow \forall x(x \in z) \qquad\qquad (7.15)$$

for all sets z.

Proof: Standard set theory; see [Enderton, 1977] for example.   □

This characterization legitimizes proof by induction over the ordering. To prove that $P(x)$ holds for all x, we take $z \equiv_{df} \{y \in A | P(y)\}$ so that the relation 7.15 reads, in rule form

$$\frac{\forall x (\forall y (y \prec x \Rightarrow P(y)) \Rightarrow P(x))}{\forall x P(x)}$$

Every partial ordering has a well-founded, or accessible, part.

Definition 7.9

The well-founded or **accessible** part $Acc(A, \prec)$ of the ordering $\prec$ over A is defined to be

$$\{x \in A \mid \neg \exists <x_n>_n \text{ such that } x \succ x_0 \succ \ldots x_n \succ x_{n+1} \ldots\}$$

Theorem 7.10

The accessible part of a partial ordering $\prec$ over A is the smallest subset z of A with the property that

$$(\forall y (y \prec x \Rightarrow y \in z)) \Rightarrow x \in z$$

Proof: As for Theorem 7.8.   □

Corollary 7.11

The principle of induction over $\prec$ given above holds for $Acc(A, \prec)$.

Theorem 7.10 shows that we can think of defining functions either by recursion over a well-founded ordering, or by recursion over the well-founded part of an arbitrary partial ordering. In the latter case the definition will often be linked to a characterization of $Acc(A, \prec)$, so as to show that particular arguments of interest lie within the accessible part.

How are functions defined by recursion over a well-founded ordering? We define the value at an argument a using the values at simpler arguments $x \prec a$.

Definition 7.12

The function f is defined by **well-founded recursion** over the relation $\prec$ if it has the form

$$f\, a \equiv_{df} \ldots f\, a_1 \ldots f\, a_n \ldots \tag{7.16}$$

where each $a_i \prec a$

As an example, it is easy to see that the definition of *pow* from Section 6.1.4

$$pow\ 0 \quad \equiv_{df} \quad 1$$
$$pow\ n \quad \equiv_{df} \quad (pow\ (n\ div\ 2))^2 * 2^{(n\ mod\ 2)}$$

is justified by induction over the well-founded ordering $<$ on N.

The formal treatment of well-founded recursion is slightly more general. If we write $f{\downarrow}a$ for the function f restricted to the domain

$$\{y \in x | y \prec a\}$$

then the recursion is defined by a function F, taking the values so far and a itself to the value at a

$$F\ (f{\downarrow}a)\ a = fa \qquad\qquad (7.17)$$

This generalizes *course-of-values* recursion – we define the value at a using the values at all the points preceding a in the ordering, just as we did in Section 6.1.1 for the natural numbers. We now argue that recursion is well defined over well-founded orderings.

Theorem 7.13

For every function F as above, there is a unique solution to the Equation 7.17.

Proof: The proof is by induction over the relation $\prec$. $\qquad\qquad$ □

Just to show how the formal treatment works, we look again at the *pow* function. The function F defining the recursion is given by

$$F\ h\ 0 \quad \equiv_{df} \quad 1$$
$$F\ h\ n \quad \equiv_{df} \quad (h\ (n\ div\ 2))^2 * 2^{(n\ mod\ 2)}$$

where the function h gives the values of the recursion on arguments smaller than the second argument. h is only applied to smaller arguments here: in the first case it is not used, and in the second it is only applied to $(n\ div\ 2) < n$ when $n > 0$. The F notation is slightly cumbersome, so we shall tend to present function definitions in the form of 7.16.

What examples of well-founded orderings are there? For each of the types A in TT with a recursion operator we can define a well-founded ordering $\prec_A$ which embodies that recursion. We can read off the relation from the introduction rules, the elements of the type which appear above the line being the immediate predecessors of those appearing below it.

For instance, for the type of trees there are two cases as there are two introduction rules. The node *Null* has no predecessors, and for a *Bnode*, we have

$$u \prec_1 (Bnode\ n\ u\ v) \qquad v \prec_1 (Bnode\ n\ u\ v)$$

and for $n + 1 > 1$,

$$t \prec_{n+1} t' \equiv_{df} \exists u(t \prec_1 u \wedge u \prec_n t')$$

Finally, we say that

$$t \prec t' \equiv_{df} \exists n(t \prec_n t')$$

The definition of $\prec$ specifies the formation of the **transitive closure** of the **immediate predecessor** relation $\prec_1$.

Using the original definition of well-foundedness, it is easy to see that there is a wealth of well-founded orderings. We summarize them now, leaving proofs to the reader.

- The orderings induced by the introduction rules for the types N, $[A]$, *tree* and the W types in general are well founded.
- If $\prec'$ is a well-founded ordering on B and $f : (A \Rightarrow B)$ then the ordering $\prec$ on A defined by

$$a \prec a' \equiv_{df} (fa) \prec' (fa')$$

is well founded. We call the ordering $\prec$ the **inverse image** $\prec'$ under f. An example of this is the ordering on lists given by the length function, #,

$$l \prec m \equiv_{df} \#l < \#m$$

- A sub-ordering $\prec\!\!\prec$ of a well-founded ordering will be well founded. By a sub-ordering we mean that for all a, b,

$$a \prec\!\!\prec b \Rightarrow a \prec b$$

- Given orderings $\prec$ on A and $\prec'$ on B, we can define a number of well-founded orderings.
  - The product ordering on $A \times B$: $(a, b) \prec\!\!\prec (a', b')$ if and only if $a \prec a'$ and $b \prec' b'$.
  - The lexicographic product ordering on $A \times B$: $(a, b) \prec\!\!\prec (a', b')$ if and only if either $a \prec a'$ or $a = a'$ and $b \prec' b'$. This is called the lexicographic ordering, as it is the way that words are ordered in a dictionary, and indeed it can be extended to n-ary products and lists in general.

— The sum ordering on $A \vee B$: for which we define

$$(inl\ a) \twoheadleftarrow\!\!\prec (inl\ a') \equiv_{df} a \prec a'$$
$$(inr\ b) \twoheadleftarrow\!\!\prec (inr\ b') \equiv_{df} b \prec' b'$$

with items from different sides of the sum incomparable.

Having introduced the general subject in a free-wheeling way, we must now show how we can introduce well-founded recursion into type theory in a suitable manner. There are a number of proposals to look at, and we do this in the section to come.

Exercises

7.27 Show that the set $Acc(A, \prec)$ is downwards closed; that is, if $y \prec x$ and $x \in Acc(A, \prec)$ then $y \in Acc(A, \prec)$.

7.28 Give explicit definitions of the well-founded orderings induced on lists and on a general W type by their structure.

7.29 Argue that sub-orderings, and the product, lexicographic product and sum orderings are well founded if their component orderings are.

7.30 Try to discover the orderings over which definitions in Chapter 6 are most naturally expressed. Look in particular at the examples of quicksort and the Ackermann function.

7.9   Well-founded recursion in type theory

Having introduced the idea of well-founded recursion, here we look at how best to add it to our system TT. The most straightforward idea, first investigated in [Paulson, 1986], is to take the characterization of well-foundedness given by Theorem 7.8, to translate it into type theory and then to ask which orderings meet the definition. It transpires that all the well-founded orderings mentioned in the last section can be shown to be well founded under the type-theoretic characterization.

A second approach, introduced in [Nordström, 1988] and developed in [Saaman and Malcolm, 1987], is to permit recursion along the accessible parts of any partial ordering $\prec$. The collection of elements $Acc(A, \prec)$ has then to be defined in some way, and this is done by giving type-theoretic rules, just as for other types. The characterization is unusual, in that we have to reason about the membership relation

$$b\ :\ B$$

to characterize properly the class $Acc(A, \prec)$, and so some proposition representing this judgement has to be introduced, analogous to the internal representation of equality by '$=$'.

7.9.1   Constructing recursion operators

In our earlier discussion, we characterized the well-foundedness of the ordering $\prec$ by

$$\forall x (\forall y (y \prec x \Rightarrow y \in z) \Rightarrow x \in z) \Rightarrow \forall x (x \in z) \qquad (7.18)$$

for all sets z. How can we express the quantification 'for all sets z' in type theory? We can think of it as expressing 'for all properties P', where by a property we mean a predicate over A. A predicate $P(z)$ over A gives a proposition $P(a)$ for every $a : A$, so we can think of a predicate as a member of

$$A \Rightarrow U_0$$

(In fact, of course, there are also predicates in the larger universes U_n, but we restrict ourselves to the 'small' predicates in U_0.) As the ordering $\prec$ is a binary relation, we can think of it as a function in $A \Rightarrow A \Rightarrow U_0$. We shall continue to write it in infix form.

Definition 7.14

A partial ordering $\prec$ is **well founded** in TT if and only if the type

$$\begin{aligned} (\forall P : A & \Rightarrow U_0) . \\ & (\ (\forall x : A) . ((\forall y : A) . (y \prec x \Rightarrow P \, y) \Rightarrow P \, x) \\ & \Rightarrow (\forall x : A) . (P \, x) \ ) \end{aligned} \qquad (7.19)$$

is inhabited by an object Ξ satisfying

$$\Xi \, P \, F \, x = F \, (\lambda y . \lambda r . (\Xi \, P \, F \, y)) \qquad (7.20)$$

It is worth examining the premiss of the implication 7.19.

$$(\forall x : A) . ((\forall y : A) . (y \prec x \Rightarrow P \, y) \Rightarrow P \, x)$$

An object of this type is like the F of the relation 7.20, taking the values on the predecessors y of x to the value on x, in $P \, x$. Given such a function, we return a function of type $(\forall x : A) . (P \, x)$ that is defined on the whole of A. Asking purely that we have an object of type 7.19 guarantees that we have proof by induction over the type; we add the rider 7.20 to guarantee that we can also define functions by recursion. The equation states that the value at x, $\Xi \, P \, F \, x$, is got by applying F to the values at the predecessors

$$\lambda y . \lambda r . (\Xi \, P \, F \, y)$$

Note that the second argument to the function is the proof that $y \prec x$.

Given the operator Ξ we can define functions using the syntactic form

$$f\,a \equiv_{df} \ldots f\,a_1 \ldots f\,a_n \ldots$$

where each $a_i \prec a$ and we shall do this in what follows.

To show that the orderings over well-founded types such as *lists*, *trees* and N are well founded, we have to show that the course-of-values recursion operator is defined, where the previous values are presented in the form of a function of type

$$(\forall y : A).(y \prec x \Rightarrow P\,y)$$

rather than as a list as we did for the natural numbers in Section 6.1.4. This is not difficult to achieve, and we leave it as an exercise for the reader.

As an example derivation, we show that

Theorem 7.15

If $\prec'$ is a well-founded ordering on B, and $f : A \Rightarrow B$, then the ordering $\prec$ defined on A by

$$y \prec x \equiv_{df} f\,y \prec' f\,x \tag{7.21}$$

is well founded.

Proof: We need to construct an operator Ξ of type 7.19 given an operator Ξ' of type

$$
\begin{aligned}
&(\forall P' : B \Rightarrow U_0).\\
&\quad (\,(\forall x' : A).((\forall y' : B).(y' \prec' x' \Rightarrow P'\,y') \Rightarrow P'\,x')\\
&\quad \Rightarrow (\forall x' : B).(P'\,x')\,)
\end{aligned}
\tag{7.22}
$$

To construct an operator of function type such as the type 7.19 we assume that we have objects of the argument type and aim to derive an object of the range type. We therefore assume we have

$$
\begin{aligned}
P &: \quad A \Rightarrow U_0\\
F &: \quad (\forall x : A).((\forall y : A).(y \prec x \Rightarrow P\,y) \Rightarrow P\,x)
\end{aligned}
$$

and try to deduce an object of type $(\forall x : A).P\,x$. We shall try to use the operator Ξ' in this enterprise, and we use this by applying it to P' and F' of the appropriate type. How should we define P'? Given f we say

$$P'\,x' \equiv_{df} (\forall x : A).(\,f\,x = x' \Rightarrow P\,x\,) \tag{7.23}$$

saying that $P'\, x'$ holds if and only if P holds for all elements of the inverse image of x'. Note that if we can conclude that

$$(\forall x':B)\,.\,P'\, x' \tag{7.24}$$

then we have in particular

$$(\forall x:A)\,.\,P'\,(f\,x)$$

which by the definition 7.23 expands to

$$(\forall x:A)\,.\,(\forall z:A)\,.\,(\,f\,x = f\,z \Rightarrow P\,x\,)$$

implying $(\forall x:A)\,.\,(P\,x)$. Our goal now is therefore to prove the assertion 7.24. We can conclude this if we can define

$$F' \;:\; (\forall x':B)\,.\,((\forall y':B)\,.\,(y' \prec' x' \Rightarrow P'\,y') \Rightarrow P'\,x')$$

To do this we assume that

$$\theta \;:\; (\forall y':B)\,.\,(y' \prec' x' \Rightarrow P'\,y') \tag{7.25}$$

and try to find an object of type $P'\,x'$, that is of type

$$(\forall x:A)\,.\,(\,f\,x = x' \Rightarrow P\,x\,)$$

so we also assume that $x:A$ and $x' = f\,x$ and aim to find an object of type $P\,x$. By substitution into the judgement 7.25 we have

$$\theta \;:\; (\forall y':B)\,.\,(y' \prec' (f\,x) \Rightarrow P'\,y')$$

so that in particular,

$$\theta' \;:\; (\forall y:A)\,.\,((f\,y) \prec' (f\,x) \Rightarrow P'\,(f\,y))$$

but then by the definition of P', and of $\prec$

$$\theta'' \;:\; (\forall y:A)\,.\,(y \prec x \Rightarrow P\,y)$$

We can apply F to this θ'' to give the result we required, that is

$$P\,x$$

We extract from the proof a definition of the function F' and so define Ξ by

$$\Xi\,P\,F \equiv_{df} \Xi'\,P'\,F'$$

as we discussed above.   □

The product and lexicographic product orderings can also be shown to preserve well-foundedness. We leave these as exercises for the reader, who can also find derivations of them in [Paulson, 1986].

Theorem 7.15 is important not only in showing that particular orderings are well founded. It also forms a part of a characterization of the well-founded orderings, proved in Section 14 of [Paulson, 1986]:

Theorem 7.16

An ordering $\prec$ on A is well founded if and only if there is some W type B and a function $norm : A \Rightarrow B$ so that $\prec$ is logically equivalent to the inverse image under $norm$ of the canonical ordering on B.

Exercises

7.31 Check that orderings on the types N, lists, trees and so forth are well founded according to the definition above – this will involve using the recursion operators in an essential way.

7.32 Complete the proof of Theorem 7.15 by giving an explicit definition for the expression Ξ, and checking that it has the property 7.20.

7.33 Show that the well-founded orderings defined in the previous section, including the product and lexicographic product, satisfy Definition 7.14.

7.34 Can you define an ordering on A which is well founded according to predicates $A \Rightarrow U_0$ but *not* with respect to predicates in $A \Rightarrow U_1$?

7.9.2   The accessible elements

The approach taken in [Nordström, 1988] is to axiomatise definition by recursion over the set of accessible elements of the ordering $\prec$. We first give the rules as introduced by Nordström, and then discuss them, and their subsequent elaboration in [Saaman and Malcolm, 1987].

Formation rule for *Acc*

$$[x : A, y : A]$$
$$\vdots$$
$$\frac{A \text{ is a type} \quad (x \prec y) \text{ is a type}}{Acc(A, \prec) \text{ is a type}}(AccF)$$

Introduction rule for *Acc*

$$[y:A, y \prec a]$$
$$\vdots$$

$$\frac{a:A \quad y:Acc(A, \prec)}{a:Acc(A, \prec)} (AccI)$$

Elimination rule for *Acc*

$$\left[\begin{array}{l} x:Acc(A, \prec) \\ z:A, z \prec x \ \triangleright \ (f\,z):C(z) \end{array} \right]$$
$$\vdots$$

$$\frac{p \ : \ Acc(A, \prec) \qquad\qquad (e\,x\,f):C(x)}{rec\,e\,p \ : \ C(p)} (AccE)$$

Computation rule for *Acc*

$$rec\,e\,p \ \rightarrow \ e\,p\,(rec\,e)$$

The formation and computation rules are standard, but the other two rules deserve some comment. In the elimination rule, the second hypothesis in the deduction of $(e\,x\,f):C(x)$ is itself hypothetical; assuming that z is a predecessor of x, f has a value on z. This f gives the values on the predecessors which are used in the expression e to calculate the value at x itself. We shall say more about this form of rule in Section 8.4.

More unfamiliar is the rule $(AccI)$. To fulfil the second hypothesis, we have to infer that

$$y:Acc(A, \prec)$$

on the basis of the assumptions

$$y:A, y \prec a$$

This is an unlikely inference, and misleading, as what we want to infer is the *proposition* that

$$y \in Acc(A, \prec)$$

on the basis of $y \in A$ and $y \prec a$. In order to do this, we have to give an internal form of the membership relation, just as '$=$' gives an internalization of equality. This can be done, and indeed was done in [Saaman and Malcolm, 1987]. The introduction and elimination rules for '$\in$' are

Introduction rule for $\in$

$$\frac{b \;:\; B}{el \;:\; (b \in B)}(\in I)$$

Elimination rule for $\in$

$$\frac{c \;:\; (b \in B)}{b \;:\; B}(\in E)$$

In fact Saaman and Malcolm use a collection of simplified elimination rules, based on the presence of the '$\in$' types, of which an example is the rule for N.

$$\frac{n:N \quad v[0/x]:C[0/x] \quad \overset{\displaystyle [\,i:N, v[i/x]:C[i/x]\,]}{\underset{\displaystyle \vdots}{}} \quad v[succ\,i/x]:C[succ\,i/x]}{v[n/x]:C[n/x]}(SNE)$$

These rules can be thought of as performing the appropriate reductions on the expressions usually introduced by the elimination rules, and using these the '$\in$' type does not need to be discussed explicitly.

A relation on a type A will be well founded if $Acc(A, \prec)$ is the whole set. Saaman and Malcolm derive this result for the examples in [Paulson, 1986]. They also derive an unbounded search program, of type

$$(\forall f : \{\, f \mid (\exists x:N)\,.\,f\,x = 0\,\})\,.\,(\exists x:N)\,.\,(\,f\,x = 0\,)$$

which they build using the observation that the ordering $m \prec n \equiv_{df} m > n$ *is* well founded on the set

$$\{\, n:N \mid (\forall m:N)\,.\,(m < n \Rightarrow fm \neq 0)\,\}$$

Exercises

7.35 Show that the class of elements accessible under the ordering '$<$' on N is N itself.

7.36 Given orderings $\prec$ and $\prec'$ on A and A', how would you characterize the elements accessible in the product, lexicographic product and sum orderings on $A \wedge B$ and $A \vee B$?

7.9.3   Conclusions

Two alternatives have been suggested to augment the 'structural' recursions over types such as N, lists, trees and so on. In the first, in [Paulson, 1986], the theory TT is shown to be sufficiently powerful to *define* many of the recursion operators over well-founded relations. This has the advantage that no changes need to be made to the system, and also the advantage over the derivations given in Chapter 6, in which implicitly at least, the derivation of well-foundedness has to be repeated for each function definition. In this respect Paulson's approach adds a useful *modularity* to the system.

Saaman and Chisholm's proposal is more far-reaching, involving the introduction of a new predicate '∈' of uncertain effect on, for example, the termination properties of the system. On the other hand, they claim that it simplifies considerably the proof objects given by Paulson's approach, as well as allowing the definition of the root-finding program.

7.10   Inductive types

The idea examined in this section is that types can be generated by induction. We begin with an informal introduction, and then turn to a discussion of how the process can be formalized in type theory. [Moschovakis, 1974] gives an elegant treatment of inductive definitions from a set-theoretic standpoint, the type-theoretic treatment appearing in [Mendler, 1987] and [Dybjer, 1988].

7.10.1   Inductive definitions

We look at the idea of inductive generation of types using the running example of finite lists of natural numbers. We have already seen that lists can be introduced by means of the W type mechanism, but an informal specification might say

> [ ] is a list, and if n is a number, and x a list, then $(n :: x)$ is also a list ...

The type of lists L has to contain [ ], and if it contains x it must contain $(n :: x)$ also. Moreover, the intention of the definition is that L is the *smallest* such set, as the informal specification has the implicit conclusion

> ... and lists can only arise in this way.

We can formalize by saying that L is the smallest solution of the equation

$$L \equiv_{df} \{[\,]\} \vee (N \wedge L)$$

if we represent the list $(n :: x)$ by the pair (n, x). We shall in fact continue to use the familiar notation $(n :: x)$ instead of the pair. Not every equation

$$T \equiv \Theta\, T$$

has a solution or a least solution: a sufficient condition for a least solution is that the operator Θ is **monotonic**, so that if $S \subseteq T$ then

$$\Theta\, S \subseteq \Theta\, T$$

The least solution of the equation is called the **least fixed point** of the operator Θ, and we write it $Fix\ \Theta$. To show that the equation has a solution we consider the sequence of sets

$$\Theta^0 \equiv_{df} \emptyset \subseteq \ldots \subseteq \Theta^{\alpha+1} \equiv_{df} \Theta\, \Theta^{\alpha} \subseteq \ldots$$

Assuming that we are working in some universe set, this sequence must have a fixed point, $\Theta^{\beta+1} = \Theta^{\beta}$. In general, the superscript β may be an *infinite* ordinal number, reflecting the complexity of the type thus defined. This fixed point is the least fixed point of Θ, but we can also deduce that a least fixed point exists from the fact that for a monotonic operator, the intersection of all the solutions is itself a solution, and that will be the least such.

We shall use the notation $\mathcal{L}$ for the operator of which L is the least fixed point:

$$\mathcal{L}\, T \equiv_{df} \{[\,]\} \vee (N \wedge T)$$

The equation

$$L \equiv \{[\,]\} \vee (N \wedge L)$$

characterizes that L is *a* fixed point of $\mathcal{L}$. How do we characterize that L is the least solution?

We need to express that elements *only* go in by the action of the operator $\mathcal{L}$. We do this by giving an elimination rule which constructs a function by recursion over L. To make such a definition it is necessary and sufficient to state a value at $[\,]$ and a way of going from a value at x to a value at $(n :: x)$. Looking at this in a slightly different way, we have given a way of going from a value at an object of type T to a value at an object of type $\mathcal{L}\, T$, since a value of type

$$\mathcal{L}\, T \equiv \{[\,]\} \vee (N \wedge T)$$

will be either $[\,]$ or $(n :: x)$ with $x : T$.

Abstracting from this, to define a function

$$fix\ g\ :\ Fix\ \mathcal{L} \Rightarrow R$$

we give a function

$$g\ :\ (T \Rightarrow R) \Rightarrow (\mathcal{L}\,T \Rightarrow R)$$

Consider the example of the *sum* function, which returns the sum of a numerical list. This is characterized by the function g,

$$
\begin{aligned}
g\ f\ [\,] &\equiv_{df} & 0 \\
g\ f\ (n,x) &\equiv_{df} & n + (f\ x)
\end{aligned}
$$

since if we define its fixed point, $fix\ g$, it will satisfy

$$
\begin{aligned}
fix\ g\ [\,] &\equiv & 0 \\
fix\ g\ (n,x) &\equiv & n + (fix\ g\ x)
\end{aligned}
$$

In the general case this is encapsulated by the computation rule

$$(fix\ g)\ \rightarrow\ g\,(fix\ g)$$

Before we give a type-theoretic treatment of inductive definitions, we observe that there is a link between inductively defined sets and well-founded orderings. Every inductive set has an ordering given by comparing the **stages** at which the elements go into the set. We define

$$\|x\| \equiv_{df} \text{ the } \alpha \text{ such that } x \in \Theta^{\alpha+1} - \Theta^{\alpha}$$

Now we say that $x \prec y$ if and only if $\|x\| < \|y\|$; this ordering is well founded as it is the inverse image of the ordering of the ordinal numbers. This characterization also suggests that we can give a representation of inductively defined sets by means of well-founded recursion, and ultimately by means of the W types.

Exercises

7.37 Show that the type of finite and infinite lists of natural numbers is a solution of the equation

$$L \equiv_{df} \{[\,]\} \vee (N \wedge L)$$

How would you argue that it does not meet the inductive characterization of the least fixed point?

7.38 Argue that the operator which sends T to $\{1\}$ if $0 \in T$, and to $\{0\}$ if not, has no fixed point.

7.39 Show that the intersection of a non-empty set of fixed points of a monotonic operator Θ is a fixed point of Θ, and therefore that a *least* fixed point exists.

7.40 Give fixed point definitions of the types of natural numbers and trees.

7.41 How would you define a type of lists whose elements are either natural numbers or lists themselves?

7.42 Give a fixed point definition of a type of finite and countable ordinal numbers.

7.10.2   Inductive definitions in type theory

Formation of inductive types is permitted when we have a monotonic operation

$$\Theta \; : \; Type \Rightarrow Type$$

There are two approaches to verifying the monotonicity of an operator. In the first, which is adopted in [Dybjer, 1988], a meta-theorem guarantees that operations of a restricted syntactic form are monotonic. If the symbol T does not appear embedded in the domain part of any function or universal type in $\mathcal{T}$, then the operation

$$\Theta : T \mapsto \mathcal{T}$$

is called **positive**, and can readily be shown to be monotonic. We can refine this to sanction *negative* appearances of T in the domain part, where such appearances have the dual definition to positive ones.

In [Mendler, 1987], an explicit check for monotonicity is added to the rule, forcing the verification of a statement such as

$$T_1 \subseteq T_2 \; \triangleright \; \mathcal{T}[T_1/T] \subseteq \mathcal{T}[T_2/T]$$

To facilitate this, various straightforward rules for the new judgement form $T_1 \subseteq T_2$ have to be added to the system. The two approaches are complementary, and there is no reason at all why they should not be used together.

The rules for the inductive type take the following forms.

Formation rule for Ind

$$\frac{\Theta \; \text{monotonic}}{Fix\; \Theta \; \textit{is a type}}(IndF)$$

There is no introduction rule for the type, rather we have a rule of type equality.

Type equality rule for *Ind*:

$$Fix\ \Theta \ \rightarrow \ \Theta\,(Fix\ \Theta) \qquad\qquad\qquad (7.26)$$

This rule is sufficient to give the usual introduction rule in the case of the operator $\mathcal{L}$. We have

$$[\,] \ : \ \mathcal{L}\,(Fix\ \mathcal{L})$$

so that by (7.26), $[\,]\ :\ Fix\ \mathcal{L}$. Similarly, if $n : N$ and $x : Fix\ \mathcal{L}$ then

$$(n :: x) \ : \ \mathcal{L}\,(Fix\ \mathcal{L})$$

and thus $(n :: x)$ is in $Fix\ \mathcal{L}$ itself.

The elimination rule can be written in a number of forms. Giving it the full parametricity, we have

Elimination rule for *Ind*

$$[\,T \subseteq Fix\ \Theta\,]$$
$$\vdots$$
$$\frac{g \ : \ (\forall x : T)\,.\,C \Rightarrow (\forall y : \Theta\ T)\,.\,C[y/x]}{fix\ g \ : \ (\forall z : Fix\ \Theta)\,.\,C[z/x]}\,(IndE)$$

and the computation rule is

Computation rule for *Ind*

$$fix\ g \ \rightarrow \ g\,(fix\ g)$$

Examples of types thus definable are lists, trees, and the general W types. Mendler augments the mechanism by allowing the definitions to be *parametric*. This means that types can be defined by simultaneous recursion, and in this context the types can readily be thought of as predicates. For instance, the definition

$$Root\ f\ n \equiv_{df} (f\ n = 0) \vee (Root\ f\ (n+1))$$

defines a family of types by a simultaneous recursion over $n : N$. The predicate defined expresses the property that f has a root greater than or equal to n. Note that here we have a predicate which depends upon a value n but which is defined without using the universes U_i. Using the recursion operator over this type and the subset type to hide information, Mendler is able to give a function implementing unbounded search.

[Dybjer, 1988] argues that, in many cases, the traditional introduction and elimination rules of the types can be read off from the operator Θ, as indeed we saw for the operator $\mathcal{L}$ above. Certainly if it is a sum of products of expressions, it is easy to see that this bears a resemblance to, say, the Miranda algebraic types

```
ty ::= con1 t11 ... t1k |
       con2 t21 ... t2l |
            ...
```

with one constructor per summand, and one selector per constructor argument, or product component. This paper also explores a representation of these inductively defined sets in TT, by means of the W types. This representation is proved to be an isomorphism in case the type theory carries an extensional equality.

One drawback to the addition of these types is that equality between types is made undecidable: we can adopt a tighter notion of equality, such as name equality (see, for example, [Tennent, 1979]) but this seems to be in conflict with the remainder of the system, for which a structural equality of types can be maintained.

Exercises

7.43 What is the rule of induction for lists given by $(IndE)$? Compare it with the rule given earlier in Section 5.10.

7.44 Using the rules for sets given in Section 7.2, derive a root-finding program of type

$$\{ f : N \Rightarrow N \mid (\exists n : N) . (Root\ f\ n) \} \Rightarrow (\exists n : N) . I(N, (f\ n), 0)$$

7.45 Give inductive definitions of the transitive closure of R and of the smallest equivalence relation extending R when R is a binary relation over a type A, say.

7.46 (*For logicians*) Given a formal system $\mathcal{F}$ for first-order arithmetic, give an inductive definition of the set of theorems provable in the system. Explain how to give an interpretation of the system over the type N of type theory, and write down an inductive definition of the formulas of $\mathcal{F}$ which are valid under that interpretation.

7.11 Co-inductions

Readers who are familiar with languages which feature lazy evaluation of all function applications, including those of *constructor* functions such as the (infix) cons, '::' will see the type of *lists* as sadly deficient, containing as it does only the finite lists. The Miranda programmer is accustomed to being able to define infinite lists such as

```
2::3::5::7::11::...
```

The approach in such a language is to evaluate any structured expression only to the extent that is necessary for computation to proceed. In combination with general recursion, this means that lists may be completely undefined, or more subtly, *partially* defined. If we write

```
lis1 = 3 :: undef
```

where `undef=undef` is the definition of the tail of the list, this list has a head of 3; only if we examine the tail do we find that it is undefined. We can see that the combination of unrestricted recursion and lazy evaluation leads naturally to these partial lists, which we obviously cannot accommodate in a hereditarily *total* type theory. Is there any way that we can retain some of the power of programming with lazy lists, which is described so clearly in [Hughes, 1990], Section 4? We shall see that by looking at the class of co-inductive definitions, that is definitions of *greatest* fixed points of operators, we can build types with infinite objects *without* adding partially defined data items. We pursue the example of the type of infinite lists of numbers as a running illustration.

Infinite lists are described in quite a different way to their finite counterparts. Instead of saying what are the component parts, $[\,], 0, 1, \ldots$, and the 'glue', ::, from which they are built, by introduction rules, all we can say is that given an infinite list, we can split it up into a head and a tail, which is again infinite. The equation

$$I \equiv_{df} N \wedge I \tag{7.27}$$

describes this in another way, for it says if $l : I$ then

$$l : N \wedge I$$

so that $l \equiv (n :: l')$, with $n : N$ and $l' : I$. The Equation 7.27 has many solutions, the smallest of which is $\emptyset$! Surely *anything* which decomposes $l \rightarrow (n :: l')$ has a right to be called an infinite list, so we should choose the largest and not the smallest of the solutions of Equation 7.27, that is the largest fixed point of the operator $\mathcal{I}$,

$$\mathcal{I}\,I \equiv_{df} N \wedge I$$

How can we guarantee that we have chosen the largest fixed point? We should ensure that any definition of a list is a member of the type, being careful *not to introduce any partiality*. As a guide to the form of the equations, think of how the infinite list of ones can be defined. We can say

$$ones \equiv_{df} 1 :: ones$$

where on the right-hand side of the equation we have ensured that we have given a clearly defined head to the list. Assuming the same about the recursive call means that we are certain of being able to 'unfold' *ones* any finite number of times. Using such a form of definition we can make the radical step of defining all the constant infinite lists! To make any further progress, such as defining the list $1 :: 2 :: 3 :: \ldots$ we need to be a bit more ingenious, and think of defining a whole collection of lists simultaneously.

$$from_n \equiv_{df} n :: from_{n+1}$$

is a definition of the lists $from_n$ enumerating the natural numbers staring from $n : N$. Again, the right-hand side guarantees that each list has a head, recursion supplying the tail. A final example along these lines is a function making a list from a function $f : (N \Rightarrow N)$

$$makel_f \equiv_{df} (f\ 0) :: makel_{f'}$$

where the function f' is defined by

$$f'\ n \equiv_{df} f\ (n+1)$$

This defines $(N \Rightarrow N)$-many infinite lists simultaneously, each of which is guaranteed to have a head by the form of the definition. How are these recursions structured?

There is a domain D, from which the parameter is taken. How do we form the right-hand sides of the definitions we saw above? We can use the parameter, call it y, and the lists themselves, $z : D \Rightarrow T$, say. From these we have to form a list, but this must be a list with a defined head. Recalling the definition 7.27, the right-hand side must be a member of the type $\mathcal{I}\ T$, rather than simply the type T itself. Given such a term, we can form the fixed point, which will be the object defined as above.

Let us set this down as a rule, using Ψ for the general monotonic operator.

Introduction rule for $Coin$

$$[y : D\ ,\ z : D \Rightarrow T]$$
$$\vdots$$

$$\frac{d\ :\ D \qquad b\ :\ \Psi\ T}{xif_{y,z}\ b\ d\ :\ Xif\ \Psi}(CoinI)$$

where we need also the following rules.

Formation rule for *Coin*

$$\frac{\Psi \text{ monotonic}}{(Xif \ \Psi) \ is \ a \ type}(CoinF)$$

Computation with the *xif* object is straightforward,

Computation rule for *Coin*

$$xif_{y,z} \ b \ d \ \rightarrow \ b[d/y \,, \ \lambda w \,.\, (xif_{y,z} \ b \ w)/z]$$

where we can see that in the unfolded recursion the function z is replaced by the whole family of recursively defined objects $\lambda w \,.\, (xif_{y,z} \ b \ w)$, as we described the recursion above.

In the case of a co-induction, the role of the defining Equation 7.27 is that of an *elimination* rule, for if we know that $l : (Xif \ \mathcal{I})$ then

$$l \ : \ \mathcal{I} \ (Xif \ \mathcal{I}) \tag{7.28}$$

eliminating the (bare) type $(Xif \ \mathcal{I})$.

The nature of recursion over a co-inductive type is quite different from that over an inductive type, where the definition is grounded by the fact that at each appeal we make a call to the value of the function at a simpler object. Here recursion does not directly explain how a function is defined over the type $Xif \ \Psi$, rather it explains how individual objects of the type are defined. How *are* such functions defined? There are two methods. First, by proposition 7.28 we have the *selector functions* head and tail over the type. Given the selectors we can define such functions as

$$sum27 \ [a_0, a_1, \ldots, a_n, \ldots] \equiv_{df} a_0 + a_1 + \cdots + a_{27}$$

We can give fully recursive definitions to standard operators over infinite lists using the selectors in combination with $(CoinI)$. An example is

$$mapi \quad : \quad (N \Rightarrow N) \Rightarrow (Xif \ \mathcal{I}) \Rightarrow (Xif \ \mathcal{I})$$
$$mapi \ f \ (a :: x) \quad \equiv_{df} \quad (f \ a) :: mapi \ f \ x$$

which defines the value of *mapi f l* simultaneously for all infinite lists l.
Functions of the form

$$sumi \ n \ [a_0, a_1, \ldots, a_n, \ldots] \quad \equiv_{df} \quad a_0 + a_1 + \cdots + a_n$$
$$index \ n \ [a_0, a_1, \ldots, a_n, \ldots] \quad \equiv_{df} \quad a_n$$

can either be defined by tail recursion over the parameter $n \ : \ N$, or by a simultaneous recursion over all infinite lists.

Other types which can be defined by co-inductions are the type of finite *and* infinite lists, the largest fixed point of the operator $\mathcal{L}$, infinite trees and the like.

We can define sophisticated functions over the type of infinite lists if we are prepared to incorporate some proof-theoretic information into the domain. One example might be a function which splits a stream of characters into a stream of words, splitting at each white space character. We cannot define this function over all the infinite lists, but only those with white space occurring infinitely often. We can describe exactly this class as an existential or subset type, and therefore define the function.

Equality over these types is interesting also. If it is intensional, then we will only identify (for example) two infinite lists if they are defined in the same way. An alternative is to adopt an extensional approach, saying that

$$l \simeq l' \Leftrightarrow (\forall n : N) . (\, index \; n \; l = index \; n \; l' \,)$$

This approach is adopted in a logic for Miranda [Thompson, 1989b] where it axiomatizes equality of infinite lists. Using the denotational semantics for Miranda, we can of course prove that this is the case.

In conclusion, we would suggest that many of the advantages advanced for lazy lists accrue here also. In particular, the examples of [Hughes, 1990, Section 4] seem to carry over with no difficulty.

Exercises

7.47 Give formal definitions of the functions *mapi*, *sumi* and *index* defined above.

7.48 Define the functions

$$iterate \; f \; st \equiv_{df} [\, st \, , \; f \; st \, , \; f \, (f \; st) \, , \; \ldots]$$

$$infold \; f \; st \; [a_0, a_1, \ldots, a_n, \ldots] \equiv_{df} [st, \; f \; st \; a_0, \; f \, (f \; st \; a_0) \; a_1, \; \ldots]$$

7.49 A natural number greater than one is called a **Hamming number** if its only prime factors are 2, 3 and 5. Show how to define a function which will merge two infinite lists, removing duplicate occurrences which appear in both lists and preserving order in the case that the lists are ordered. Using this function and the *iterate* function above give a definition of the list of Hamming numbers, enumerated in ascending order. (This problem is described in more detail in [Dijkstra, 1976].)

7.50 Give a definition of the list of prime numbers.

7.51 Write a definition of a general *map* function over the finite and infinite lists.

Figure 7.1 Three communicating processes.

7.52 Why cannot an analogue of the *filter* function over finite lists be defined over the infinite lists? Can you define one over the type of finite and infinite lists?

7.53 Give a type and definition of the character stream splitting function discussed above.

7.11.1 Streams

One of the most prominent applications of the infinite lists of Miranda is to streams between interacting processes. We model a system such as that in Figure 7.1 by giving explicit definitions of the communications along the three channels. These communications form lists l_0, l_1, l_2, and we can in the liberal environment of Miranda write definitions of networks of processes which will result in deadlock – just define each of the processes to copy its input to its output. What happens if we look at an example like this in the context of type theory, using the infinite lists of the last section? We will have in the case above to define the three lists l_0, l_1, l_2 by a mutual recursion, and moreover by one which ensures that each of the lists l_i has at least a head. In other words, the condition on infinite lists ensures that we *never have deadlock* in networks of processes that we define – the process of definition itself prevents that.

In a similar way, we can model streams which can close down by taking the streams to be in the greatest fixed point of $\mathcal{L}$ which gives the type of finite and infinite lists – the absence of partial lists again shows that if a system can be defined, then it will not deadlock: it will either continue forever, or will close down.

Exercise

7.54 Give a solution to the dining philosophers problem using the infinite lists of type theory.

7.12   Partial objects and types

The literature contains a number of proposals for adding non-terminating or 'partial' objects to type theory. The naïve proposal would be simply to allow unrestricted recursion and thus non-terminating computations in the systems TT_0 and so forth. As a programming language this results in something much closer to current systems such as Miranda and Haskell, but we also appear to *lose* the logical interpretation of the system. Since the undefined object, $\uparrow$, or bottom (which is confusingly denoted $\perp$ in the literature on denotational semantics) is a member of every type, the logical interpretation is inconsistent, as every formula is provable, by the proof $\uparrow$. Moreover, principles such as induction have to be modified to take account of the additional members of types such as N. (Details of how this is done can be found in [Paulson, 1987; Thompson, 1989b].)

Can a logical interpretation be given to such a system? It would seem that there is at least a chance of so doing, if we can identify precisely those objects which represent 'total' and not 'partial' proofs. The logic for Miranda alluded to earlier shows how the total objects can be identified at simple types, but there is a choice in what should be deemed the total objects at type

$$(N \Rightarrow N) \Rightarrow (N \Rightarrow N)$$

say. It would be an interesting research project to see precisely how such a logical interpretation would work.

A quite different approach is suggested in[Constable and Smith, 1987], which supersedes the earlier version of partial types discussed in [Constable and others, 1986], Section 12.2. This proposes the addition of types $\overline{T}$ which consist of **computations** of elements of T, the partial objects which may or may not result in values in the type T itself. The advantage of this approach over the naïve one is the degree of descriptive power that it affords. For instance, we can distinguish the following types of numerical functions

$$N \Rightarrow N \quad N \Rightarrow \overline{N} \quad \overline{N} \Rightarrow \overline{N} \quad \overline{N \Rightarrow N} \quad \overline{N \Rightarrow \overline{N}} \quad \overline{\overline{N} \Rightarrow \overline{N}}$$

each of which is sensible and embodies a different notion of function from N to N. It is a revealing exercise to discover the relations between the types by finding which embeddings exist between them, and by showing which do not exist by finding the appropriate counter-examples. A basic relationship between types is that members of T are members of $\overline{T}$, and in the converse direction, if an element of $\overline{T}$ is shown to have a canonical form then it is in T. So as to allow explicit reasoning about termination, we will have to introduce the membership predicate, $a \in A$, as in Section 7.9.2.

Elements of partial types are introduced by parametrized general recursion, with an object f of type $A \Rightarrow \overline{B}$ being defined in terms of itself:

$$[q : A \Rightarrow \overline{B}]$$
$$\vdots$$
$$\frac{f : A \Rightarrow \overline{B}}{rec_q\, f\ :\ A \Rightarrow \overline{B}}(recI)$$

with the associated computation rule

$$rec_q\, f\ \rightarrow\ f[(rec_q\, f)/q]$$

There are a number of induction rules which licence proofs about these recursively defined functions. They fall into two classes. First we can reason over the structure of the **computation** which leads to a result, and this rule admits a number of formalizations, which have obvious links with the rules of Section 7.9. Second, we can add the rule of fixed point induction which can only be applied to *admissible* predicates (see [Paulson, 1987]). This is not so easy in type theory where in the presence of universes we can have non-canonical forms for types. Further discussion of these points, the justification for the addition of the types and their links with classical recursion theory can be found in [Constable and Smith, 1987] and [Smith, 1988].

7.13   Modelling

Thus far we have looked at *generic* extensions of the system; for the individual, the problem at hand will normally be to model a small number of specific kinds of object, such as groups, stacks, records and so forth. Two approaches suggest themselves:

- A model of the objects is built within type theory, as a series of abstract data types, for instance.
- The system is itself augmented with new rules describing the objects.

The contrast between these approaches is investigated in [Dyckhoff, 1985], which examines how to model elementary category theory up to the level of natural transformations. We look at a simpler case here, that of *semi-groups*.

Definition 7.17

A **semi-group** is a set A together with an associative operation $\star$ over A. An **identity** element is an element ι so that for all $a \in A$,

$$a \star \iota = a = \iota \star a$$

and an **inverse** a^{-1} of a satisfies

$$a \star a^{-1} = \iota = a^{-1} \star a$$

We can model the class of semi-groups as an abstract data type as follows. First we define the formula $Semi\ A \star$ to be

$$(\forall a, b, c : A).(\ (a \star b) \star c = a \star (b \star c)\ )$$

Elements of this type are functions f with $f\ a\ b\ c$ providing the proof of associativity at the triple a, b, c. We then define the class of semi-groups thus:

$$Semigroup \equiv_{df} (\exists A : U_0).(\exists \star : A \Rightarrow A \Rightarrow A).(\ Semi\ A \star\ )$$

Elements of this type are triples $(A, (\star, f))$, with f as above.

An elementary result about semi-groups is that the identity is unique. We show this formally now. Using the notational conventions of Section 5.2.1, we write *set*, *op* and *assoc* for the three projection functions from the triples above.

Theorem 7.18

Given a particular member $S : Semigroup$ we shall write $A, \star, f$ for the three projections *set* S, *op* S and *assoc* S. If we assume that

$$(\forall a : A).a \star \iota = a \wedge a = \iota \star a \quad (\forall a : A).a \star \iota' = a \wedge a = \iota' \star a$$

are inhabited, then we can show that

$$\iota = \iota'$$

is inhabited. This shows that the identity is *unique* if it exists.

Proof: Take

$$g : (\forall a : A).a \star \iota = a \wedge a = \iota \star a$$

apply it to ι', and take the first projection. We have

$$fst\ (g\ \iota') : \iota' \star \iota = \iota' \tag{7.29}$$

Similarly, if we take

$$h : (\forall a : A).a \star \iota' = a \wedge a = \iota' \star a$$

apply it to ι, and take the second projection, we obtain

$$snd\,(h\,\iota)\ :\ \iota = \iota' \star \iota \tag{7.30}$$

From the judgements 7.29 and 7.30 and the transitivity of equality, we have that

$$\iota = \iota'$$

is inhabited, as required.   □

Theorem 7.19

Using the same convention as above, if for a particular element a of A it is the case that

$$a \star a' = \iota \ \wedge \ \iota = a' \star a$$

$$a \star a'' = \iota \ \wedge \ \iota = a'' \star a$$

are both inhabited, then $a' = a''$ is inhabited, proving that inverses are unique if they exist.

Proof: Exercise: the proof uses the fact that the operation '$\star$' is associative.   □

The results depend upon us repeatedly unpacking the triples $(A, (\star, f))$ and upon the system having the capability of giving temporary names to objects. Dyckhoff found that as this was difficult in the implementation available to him, it would be more appropriate to axiomatize the theory directly. For semi-groups, axioms would take the form.

Formation rule for *Semigroup*

$$\frac{}{Semigroup\ is\ a\ type}(SemiF)$$

Writing the three hypotheses in a vertical list, we have the introduction rule:

Introduction rule for *Semigroup*

$$\frac{\begin{array}{l} A\ is\ a\ type \\ \star\ :\ A \Rightarrow A \Rightarrow A \\ r\ :\ (\forall a, b, c : A) . (\,(a \star b) \star c = a \star (b \star c)\,) \end{array}}{SG\ A\ \star\ r\ :\ Semigroup}(SemiI)$$

Elimination rules for *Semigroup*

$$\frac{S:Semigroup}{set\ S\ is\ a\ type}(SemiE_1)$$

$$\frac{S:Semigroup}{op\ S\ :\ setS \Rightarrow set\ S \Rightarrow set\ S}(SemiE_2)$$

$$\frac{S:Semigroup}{assoc\ S\ :\ (\forall a,b,c:set\ S).\quad (\ (a\,(op\,S)\,b)(op\,S)\,c}{=\ a\,(op\,S)(b\,(op\,S)\,c)\,)}(SemiE_3)$$

The computation rules show that *set*, *op* and *assoc* behave as projections:

Computation rules for *Semi*

$$set\,(SG\ A \star r) \quad \rightarrow \quad A$$
$$op\,(SG\ A \star r) \quad \rightarrow \quad \star$$
$$assoc\,(SG\ A \star r) \quad \rightarrow \quad r$$

Using these rules we can prove results such as Theorems 7.18, 7.19 in a similar way to those above.

In comparing the two approaches, it is clear that they are very close. The positive effect of moving to rules is that we have access to a naming facility, but we have shown that this can be integrated with a representational approach. A disadvantage of adding rules to the system is that we may well disturb the formal properties of the system, such as logical consistency or strong normalization. In this case there is no difficulty, as we could read the rules as being *derived* from the representation, providing a cleaner interface to the particular data abstraction. This possible disruption of the formal properties of the system by the addition of rules is something which might be said of all the additions of this chapter; we shall look into it in more depth in the chapter to come.

[Dyckhoff, 1985], on which this section is based, gives a similar comparison of approaches for the more significant example of categories.

Exercises

7.55 What are the types of the projection functions *set*, *op* and *assoc*?

7.56 Prove Theorem 7.19.

7.57 Prove versions of the Theorems 7.18, 7.19 using the rules for the new type *Semigroup*.

Chapter 8
Foundations

This chapter marks a return to looking at the system as a whole, rather than at particular examples of terms and proofs derivable in it, or at possible extensions. We investigate various questions about the mathematical foundations of the system. From the point of view of traditional proof theory, we can compare its strength with other formal systems for arithmetic – this we do in the first section. The technique used here is that of realizability, which forms one sort of model of the formal system. We discuss the motivation for developing a model theory of TT in the subsequent section, giving other methods of model construction.

The topic of realizability is interesting not just from the proof-theoretic point of view: it provides a general mechanism for extracting the computational content of a derivation, and as such may give a means of deriving more efficient programs from type-theoretic derivations.

We conclude the discussion with an overview of Schroeder-Heister and Dybjer's work on the *inversion* of proof rules. At an intuitive level, if we are given the introduction rules for a type then we seem to know all the forms that elements can take, and this really characterizes the type. The inversion principle gives a formal description of how an introduction rule can be inverted to generate the elimination and computation rules. We also look at a primitive justification of the inversion principle itself.

8.1   Proof theory

In this section we look at the relationship between the systems $TT_0, \ldots$ and more traditional presentations of constructive arithmetic. In particular we examine the system HA of first-order intuitionistic arithmetic and its generalization to the simple types, HA^ω. The 'H' in these titles is in honour of the intuitionist Heyting, who was one of the first constructivists. We follow this with a discussion of the technique of *realizability*, which is used to give interpretations of intuitionistic systems, and which can form the basis of a more flexible algorithm extraction discipline than that of type theory. We conclude with a discussion of the various rules for existential elimination, and what consequences the choice of rules has for our implementation of modules.

8.1.1   Intuitionistic arithmetic

Definition 8.1

A full definition of the system of **first-order Heyting arithmetic**, HA, is given in [Troelstra, 1973], section I.3. The system consists of a first-order theory of the natural numbers, with a function constant for each primitive recursive function. Axioms assert the basic properties of equality; the standard Peano axioms stating that zero is not a successor, that the successor is 1–1 and the axiom scheme of induction

$$\phi(0) \wedge \forall n.(\phi(n) \Rightarrow \phi(n+1)) \Rightarrow \forall n.\phi(n)$$

for every formula ϕ; and finally the defining equations of each of the primitive recursive functions.

The rules of deduction are the standard set for constructive predicate calculus, which can be derived, by omitting the proof objects, from our introduction and elimination rules for $\wedge$, $\vee$, $\Rightarrow$, $\perp$, $\forall$, $\exists$, choosing the *weak* rules for the elimination of disjunction and the existential quantifier, that is $(\vee E)$ and $(\exists E')$.

Definition 8.2

The system of **Heyting arithmetic at finite types**, HA^ω, and called $N - HA^\omega$ in the definition [Troelstra, 1973], Section I.6, is similar to HA, except that objects can be of any of the finite types formed from N by the function space constructor. An operator which embodies definition by primitive recursion is included at each type. Quantifiers range over particular types, rather than the whole domain.

These systems have been studied extensively, and their relation with TT_0 can tell us something about the system itself. Obviously the system HA^ω is an extension of HA in a sense to be made clearer by the next definition. We write $\mathcal{S} \vdash \phi$ for 'ϕ is a theorem of the formal system $\mathcal{S}$'.

Definition 8.3

Given two formal systems $\mathcal{S}_1$ and $\mathcal{S}_2$, a function f from the formulas of $\mathcal{S}_1$ to those of $\mathcal{S}_2$ is an **embedding** of the first system in the second if for all formulas ϕ,

$$\mathcal{S}_1 \vdash \phi \text{ implies } \mathcal{S}_2 \vdash (f\ \phi)$$

If the relationship above is an equivalence, then $\mathcal{S}_2$ is called a **conservative extension** of $\mathcal{S}_1$, and we can call the function f an **interpretation** of $\mathcal{S}_1$ in $\mathcal{S}_2$.

The system $\mathcal{S}_2$ is a conservative extension of $\mathcal{S}_1$ if the two theories prove the same theorems in the language of the smaller, $\mathcal{S}_1$; they give consistent pictures of their common domain.

Obviously there is an embedding of HA in HA^ω. We can also embed the formulas of HA^ω as formulas of TT_0, and prove the result that

Theorem 8.4

For any formula ϕ, if $HA^\omega \vdash \phi$ then for some term t, we can derive in TT_0 the judgement $t : \phi$.

Proof: The term t is a coding of the proof of ϕ in HA^ω. More details are given in [Beeson, 1985], Theorem XI.17.1.   □

Moreover, if we add to HA^ω the axiom of choice over finite types, AC_{FT},

$$\forall x.\exists y.A(x,y) \Rightarrow \exists f.\forall x.A(x, f\ x)$$

this is also validated by TT_0. Showing that the axiom of choice is derivable in type theory is one of Martin-Löf's few concessions to examples in his papers. See [Martin-Löf, 1985; Martin-Löf, 1984], and observe that the derivation does not use extensionality. If we adopt the extensional theory of [Martin-Löf, 1985], then our type theory extends the extensional version $HA^\omega + Ext + AC_{FT}$.

What results can we derive on the basis of this relationship?

Our first result, due to Troelstra, is typical of the gain we can get by looking at these inter-relationships: we are able to transfer a *negative* result from HA^ω to type theory. First we give another definition.

Definition 8.5

A function F from $N \Rightarrow N$ to N is called **continuous** if for all $f : (N \Rightarrow N)$ there is an n, so that if $f\ i = g\ i$ for all $i \leq n$, then $F\ f = F\ g$. The value n is called a **modulus of continuity** of F at f.

Continuity is an assertion of the *finitary* nature of the functions over $N \Rightarrow N$: the value of such a function at f is determined by a finite amount of information about f. We would therefore expect that this would be true of all the functions F definable in TT_0. However, we can show that TT_0 does not prove the formal statement of this,

$$(\forall F:(N \Rightarrow N) \Rightarrow N).Cont(F)$$

This itself follows from the theorem

Theorem 8.6

The theory

$$HA^\omega + AC_{FT} + Ext + (\forall F:(N \Rightarrow N) \Rightarrow N).Cont(F)$$

is inconsistent (that is derives $\perp$)

Proof: See [Beeson, 1985], Theorem XI.19.1. Using the axiom of choice, we can define a function μ returning the modulus of continuity of a function F at the argument f. Extensionality means that this modulus is determined by function *values* rather than representations, and this can be shown to lead to a finite procedure solving the limited principle of omniscience, a contradiction. □

Corollary 8.7

The theory TT_0 does not prove

$$(\forall F:(N \Rightarrow N) \Rightarrow N).Cont(F)$$

Proof: If TT_0 proves this, then the extensional version of type theory proves it also and, as it also derives the axiom of choice, by the theorem is inconsistent. We have a proof of consistency, and so the original assumption is untrue. □

Can we characterize the arithmetical theorems provable in type theory? Again, the answer is yes:

Theorem 8.8

TT_0 is a conservative extension of HA, where we say that TT_0 makes a proposition A valid when we can derive $t:A$ for some expression t.

Proof: This is due to a number of authors, including Beeson and Renardel [Beeson, 1985; Diller and Troelstra, 1984]. The proof uses the technique of realizability, to which we turn in the next section. □

It is worth noting what the theorem says. It asserts that the system of TT_0 – which extends first-order arithmetic by embedding it in a system of types, for which the axiom of choice is assumed to hold (and which might be made extensional as far as this result is concerned) – is no stronger than first-order arithmetic as far as arithmetical statements are concerned.

We have said nothing about the theories TT, TT^+ and TT_0^+. Each of these is stronger than TT_0. We have already shown that TT is stronger than TT_0; other remarks about this can be found in [Beeson, 1985], Section XIII.5. We know of no results for the theories with the full W type.

8.1.2   Realizability

We remarked that the proof of Theorem 8.8 was by the realizability method. We take the opportunity of explaining that method here, as it forms the foundation of an important piece of research which we also describe.

Realizability was introduced by Kleene in 1945 as a way of forming recursive models of intuitionistic theories. Given the informal explanations of the connectives which we first encountered in Chapter 3, we can see that central to any explanation of a constructive system is a notion of transformation, as it is thus that implication and universal quantification are interpreted. Kleene's idea was to use recursive functions as the transforming functions. Of course, recursive functions can be coded by natural numbers, and so we shall define a relation

$$e \Vdash \phi$$

with e a natural number and ϕ a formula. We also write $\{e\}(q) \downarrow$ for 'the recursive function e terminates on argument q'. Now we define realizability as originally given in [Kleene, 1945]:

Definition 8.9

Realizability for arithmetic (**r**-realizability, in fact) is defined by the following clauses.

$$
\begin{array}{lll}
e \Vdash (A \Rightarrow B) & \text{iff} & \forall q.(q \Vdash A \Rightarrow \{e\}(q) \downarrow \wedge \{e\}(q) \Vdash B) \\
e \Vdash \forall x.A & \text{iff} & \forall x.(\{e\}(x) \downarrow \wedge \{e\}(x) \Vdash B) \\
e \Vdash \exists x.A & \text{iff} & first\ e \Vdash A(second\ e) \\
e \Vdash A \wedge B & \text{iff} & first\ e \Vdash A \wedge second\ e \Vdash B \\
e \Vdash A \vee B & \text{iff} & (first\ e = 0 \Rightarrow second\ e \Vdash A) \wedge \\
& & (first\ e \neq 0 \Rightarrow second\ e \Vdash B)
\end{array}
$$

Finally, any number realizes a true atomic formula.

We can think of the interpretation as giving a *model* of the logical system, with the valid formulas those ϕ for which some $e \Vdash \phi$. The important point about realizability is the theorem

Theorem 8.10 (soundness)

If HA proves ϕ then there is some natural number e which realizes ϕ, that is $e \Vdash \phi$.

Proof: Is by induction over the size of the proof of ϕ. A detailed proof is given in [Beeson, 1985], Section VII.1. $\square$

This can be read as saying that for any theorem ϕ, we have a term which gives the formula a computational interpretation, as is seen by examining a formula such as

$$\forall x.\exists y.P(x,y)$$

where P is atomic.

$$e \Vdash \forall x.\exists y.P(x,y)$$
$$\text{iff}\quad \forall x.(\{e\}(x) \downarrow \wedge \{e\}(x) \Vdash \exists y.P(x,y))$$
$$\text{iff}\quad \forall x.(\{e\}(x) \downarrow \wedge first\ \{e\}(x) \Vdash P(x\,,\ second\ \{e\}(x)))$$

which means in particular that there is a recursive function g such that

$$\forall x.P(x, g\ x)$$

There are a number of notable aspects of realizability. First observe that the right-hand sides of the definitions 8.9 are themselves expressions of arithmetic. This is crucial to the earlier result that type theory gives a conservative extension of HA. Because of this identification, we can study the relation between a formula and the formal expression of its realizability: it transpires that for r-realizability the formulas ϕ which are equivalent to the statement of their own realizability $\exists e.(e \Vdash \phi)$ are those which have no existential import: those with no computational significance, in other words.

Secondly we should note how general the definition is: all we need to give a different notion of realizability is a different collection of realizing functions, or a slightly different right-hand clause. Given a soundness theorem, we can extract some computational information from a proof of a formula. This applies equally well to target theories: the definition above is for first-order arithmetic, but in general we might look at other theories, such as higher-order versions of arithmetic.

Given this, our theory TT_0 begins to look like a *particular version of realizability* for a higher-order type system. Might some disadvantages accrue from too intimate a link between the logic and the notion of realizability which can be used to give computational content to the theorems of the system? One area which we looked at in Section 7.1.2 is that of 'computational relevance', where we saw that in certain circumstances our proof objects contained information which was unnecessary from a computational point of view. A decoupling of the logical rules from the function extraction mechanism could well result in more efficient extracted objects, without modification of the logic itself.

The major advantage of such an approach is that the logic in which proofs are written can remain fixed whilst different proof extraction techniques (that is notions of realizability) are applied to the proofs. This contrasts with the complications introduced by the augmented versions of TT in the previous chapter.

This decoupling lies at the heart of investigations into the system TK by Henson and Turner, to which we turn in the following chapter.

8.1.3   Existential elimination

We observed earlier, in Section 5.3.3, that the rule $(\exists E')$ was weaker than the rule $(\exists E)$ or the equivalent pair $(\exists E'_1)$ and $(\exists E'_2)$. These rules are investigated in depth in the thesis [Swaen, 1989], where it is shown that the use of $(\exists E)$ in the proof of the axiom of choice is essential:

Theorem 8.11

The strong rule $(\exists E)$ is equivalent to the weak rule, together with the axiom of choice.

Moreover, conservation results analogous to those above apply to this theory.

Theorem 8.12

TT_0^w, that is TT_0 with the weakened rule of existential elimination, is conservative over HA^ω.

The system TT_0^w is discussed in its own right in [Diller, 1980].

8.2   Model theory

Model theory attempts to give a meaning to formal systems such as TT_0 and TT. In order to avoid circularity and the attendant problems of ambiguity or incoherence, the semantics should explain the system using notions *outside* the system itself.

Why is a semantics important?

- The simplest reason is that a completely uninterpreted system is of no interest to anyone. Every system has an *informal* semantics, investing its symbols with deeper meaning than simply marks on paper.

- A semantics can show that a system is consistent, or more strictly, consistent relative to the theory in which its semantics lies. This is not of idle interest, as it is quite possible to write down intuitively plausible systems, such as Martin-Löf's earliest version of type theory, or the formal theory

$$HA^\omega + AC_{FT} + Ext + (\forall F:(N \Rightarrow N) \Rightarrow N).Cont(F)$$

which subsequently turn out to be inconsistent. A semantics gives the assurance that this does not happen (assuming that a more primitive system is itself consistent). Moreover, a semantics may prove other meta-theoretical results, such as the Church–Rosser property.

- A semantics can delimit the proof-theoretic strength of a system, thus showing that the system will prove some theorems and not others.

- A semantics can not only establish that particular additions to the system maintain consistency but also suggest that certain strengthenings of the system (extending it by certain operations in the semantics, say) are also legitimate.

What forms can the semantics of TT_0 take? We look at the explanations given by Martin-Löf, Smith, Beeson and Allen in turn. First we should mention an important reference [Martin-Löf, 1975a] which examines the general notion of a constructive model for an intuitionistic theory, which fits those models introduced by Martin-Löf himself, Smith and Beeson.

8.2.1   Term models

The most direct explanation is that given in [Martin-Löf, 1975b], which is given a gloss in both [Martin-Löf, 1985] and [Nordström et al., 1990]. The model is one of a class called **term models**. These models depend upon the notions of reduction and normal form, ideas external to the system itself.

The interpretation of a closed expression $a:A$ is as a canonical form a' in A', the canonical form of the type A. For the theories TT_0 and TT we interpret 'canonical form' as 'normal form', and Section 5.6 contains a proof that the collections of closed normal terms form a model of the theory. Whilst making plain the meaning of closed expressions, we should say exactly how an expression $b(x) : B(x)$ is given a meaning. $b(x)$ is a canonical term of type $B(x)$ if for all canonical a, $b(a)$ reduces to a canonical term in $B(a)$.

Term models form the canonical(!) model of type theory: the distinct nature of the normal forms attests to its non-triviality, and an informal explanation of the term model forms the basic intuitive semantics of the system, according to [Martin-Löf, 1985]. By examining the model we were able to show a number of additional properties of the system, including the Church–Rosser theorem and the decidability of judgements.

Because a term model is bound so tightly to the syntactic form of the system, it is difficult to use it to derive results such as conservation results, or to justify extensions to a theory: in this case a new term model formed from a wider class of expressions has to be shown to exist.

8.2.2 Type-free interpretations

It can be argued that one of the complications of the systems TT_0, TT is in their complex type systems, with a simpler theory being provided by a type-free system. This can be said of the simple λ-calculus as against the typed λ-calculus, and for type theory, a type-free theory of logic and computation as given in [Smith, 1984] or by the Frege structures of [Aczel, 1980] is a suitable candidate.

Smith gives such an interpretation in [Smith, 1984], and he characterizes this interpretation on page 730 as

> The interpretation we will give ... is based on the semantical explanation of type theory given in [Martin-Löf, 1985]. Indeed it may be viewed as a metamathematical version of the semantical explanation, formalized in the logical theory.

It also has relationships with realizability, and in particular the model **M** of [Beeson, 1985], Section XI.20; Smith uses type-free λ-terms as realizing functions whilst Beeson uses numbers, and of course Smith's theory is formalized.

As we saw above, one advantage of realizability models is that they can be used in characterizing the proof-theoretic strength of a theory. Beeson used the model **M** in showing that TT_0 is conservative over HA.

The models of Aczel, Beeson and Smith are all general: a number of differing notions of realizability exist, and it can be shown that every model of the type-free λ-calculus can be extended to a Frege structure, which in turn can provide a model of type theory.

8.2.3 An inductive definition

An alternative approach to the semantics of the system is described in [Allen, 1987a; Allen, 1987b] and is summarized in [Constable and Smith, 1987, Section 2.2]. Allen examines the definition of the system [Martin-Löf, 1985], aiming to give an inductive definition of the types as equivalence classes of sets of (untyped) expressions. That two expressions t and t' denote equivalent objects at type T is denoted

$$t = t' \in T$$

and $t \in T$ is shorthand for $t = t \in T$. An important clause is that for membership of the type $(\forall x : A) . B$. t is in this type if $(\forall x : A) . B$ is a type and

$$
\begin{aligned}
\exists u, b. \quad & t \to \lambda u . b \wedge \\
& \forall a, a' (a = a' \in A \Rightarrow b[a/u] = b[a'/u] \in B)
\end{aligned}
\tag{8.1}
$$

A general reference on inductive definitions is [Moschovakis, 1974], where we can discover that not all inductive definitions have least solutions (or indeed solutions at all). There is always a least solution of a monotone inductive definition, and a sufficient condition for monotonicity is for the defining formula 8.1 to be positive in the relation

$$
\dots = \dots \in \dots
$$

This is *not* the case, as the relation appears in the hypothesis of an implication. This failure means that the definition cannot be given simply as an inductive definition in this form.

Instead, Allen defines his system in a more complicated way, specifying a definition of an operator $\mathcal{M}$, which can be thought of as a monotone operator on *type theories*. In turn, a type theory is seen as a two-place relation $\mathcal{T}$ where

$$
\mathcal{T} A \sim_A
$$

holds if and only if A is a type, carrying the equality relation $\sim_A$ in the type theory $\mathcal{T}$. Since the operator $\mathcal{M}$ *is* monotone, a semantics is then given by the least fixed point of the operator.

In both [Allen, 1987a] and [Allen, 1987b] it is argued that this approach is close to that of Beeson, with Allen's more faithful to the lazy evaluation in Martin-Löf's informal semantics of the system.

An advantage of an inductive definition is that it can readily be extended to augmented systems. In [Constable and Smith, 1987] it is shown how to extend the semantics to the partial types of that paper. Allen himself argues that it can be used in justification of some of the 'direct computation rules' of Nuprl, which allow the reduction of terms under fewer hypotheses than would be permitted in TT.

8.3   A general framework for logics

Our introduction to the theories TT_0 and TT has been somewhat informal as far as syntax is concerned, and in this section we review how the presentation can be formalized.

The operations which form types and elements have a definite *meta-theoretical* type. For example, $\Rightarrow$ is of meta-type

$$Type \rightarrow Type \rightarrow Type$$

where we write '$\rightarrow$' for the function space constructor *at the meta-level*, and *Type* is the meta-type of types. Similarly, the injection *inl* can be given the meta-type

$$(\Pi t : Type).(\Pi s : Type).(\ El(s) \rightarrow El(s \vee t)\ )$$

where 'Π' is the dependent function space constructor in the meta-language, and *El* is a constant of meta-type

$$(\Pi t : Type).Elem$$

which associates with a type expression the collection of elements it is intended to denote. These two examples suggest that as a meta-theory we can use a **typed λ-calculus with dependent product types**, with rules of β- and η-conversion.

All the operations of the system TT, including those such as λ which bind variables, can be presented as **constants** in the meta-theory, taking advantage of the binding in the meta-language. The operator λ over the non-dependent types can be described by

$$\lambda\ ::\ (\Pi t : Type).(\Pi s : Type).(\ (El(t) \rightarrow El(s)) \rightarrow El(t \Rightarrow s)\ )$$

where '$e :: \alpha$' means 'e has meta-type α'. The application operator is a constant of type

$$app\ ::\ (\Pi t : Type).(\Pi s : Type).(\ El(t \Rightarrow s) \rightarrow El(t) \rightarrow El(s)\ )$$

The computation rule for the function space is, of course, β-reduction. Using the subscripted form $app_{t,s}$ for the application of the operator app to the types t, s, this is described by the equation between terms

$$app_{t,s}\ (\lambda_{t,s}\ f)\ a = f\ a$$

Since f is a meta-function, that is an element of type

$$El(t) \rightarrow El(s)$$

substitution in the object language is thus described by β-reduction in the meta-language. A similar approach is equally effective with the other variable-binding operations.

The origins of this approach seem to lie in Martin-Löf's theory of *arities* [Martin-Löf, 1985] and his work on *categories* of the philosophical and not the mathematical sort, reported in [Martin-Löf, 1983]. Explicit discussions of the presentation of type theory in this form are to be found in [Dybjer, 1988] and in Part III of [Nordström *et al.*, 1990].

This approach has been used in the Edinburgh Logical Framework, which provides a machine environment for general logical reasoning, [Harper *et al.*, 1987], and has shown itself capable of expressing a variety of different logics [Avron *et al.*, 1987]. A consequence of descriptions of this sort is that the complexity of logics such as Hoare's logic for imperative languages such as Pascal is greater than might at first be thought; the effect is similar to the complexity of languages revealed by their complete denotational semantic definition.

8.4   The inversion principle

When describing a type in TT we give four kinds of rules. First we give the formation rule which introduces the new type expression, building a new type from constituent parts. An example is

$$\frac{A \text{ is a formula} \quad B \text{ is a formula}}{(A \vee B) \text{ is a formula}}(\vee F)$$

The elements of the type are then described by a number of introduction rules, such as

$$\frac{q \,:\, A}{inl\ q \,:\, (A \vee B)}(\vee I_1) \qquad \frac{r \,:\, B}{inr\ r \,:\, (A \vee B)}(\vee I_2)$$

Now, the elimination and computation rules are needed to characterize the fact that the elements of the type are *only* those given by the introduction rules. These are the closure or *induction* rules. It appears that no more information about the type need be supplied to characterize these rules, as the elements exhausting the type have already been specified, so the closure rules should be definable by **inversion**.

This idea, which can be traced back to Gentzen and [Prawitz, 1965], has been pursued by a number of investigators. The first of these is Schroeder-Heister who investigated the problem of generating the elimination rules from the introduction rules in first-order intuitionistic logic; see [Schroeder-Heister, 1983a; Schroeder-Heister, 1983b].

Concentrating for the present on the example of '∨', how do we summarize the fact that a proof of $A \vee B$ is either a proof of A or a proof of B? We do it thus: given hypothetical proofs of C from A and from B, we can deduce C from $A \vee B$. This means that any proof of $A \vee B$ must have been a proof either of A or of B. This gives us the logical rule

$$\frac{(A \vee B) \quad \overset{[A]}{\underset{\vdots}{C}} \quad \overset{[B]}{\underset{\vdots}{C}}}{C} (\vee E')$$

How do we lift this to type theory, in which we have explicit *proof objects* which inhabit the propositions?

$$\frac{p:(A \vee B) \quad \overset{[x:A]}{\underset{\vdots}{u:C}} \quad \overset{[y:B]}{\underset{\vdots}{v:C}}}{vcases'_{x,y} \ p \ u \ v \ : \ C} (\vee E')$$

Given proof objects, p, u, v, of the appropriate type we form the new proof object

$$vcases'_{x,y} \ p \ u \ v$$

binding the variables x and y in u and v respectively, since the logical rule discharges these assumptions. This is a new expression form, but we can see how it may be simplified. A proof of $A \vee B$ is either *inl a* or *inr b*. In the former case, we can get a proof of C by substituting a for x in u; in the latter we substitute b for y in v, giving the familiar computation rules

$$vcases'_{x,y} \ (inl \ a) \ u \ v \quad \longrightarrow \quad u[a/x]$$
$$vcases'_{x,y} \ (inr \ b) \ u \ v \quad \longrightarrow \quad v[b/y]$$

We can generalize this inversion thus. If the n introduction rules for the connective θ take the form

$$\frac{H_{i,1} \ \ldots \ H_{i,m_i}}{\theta \ A_1 \ \ldots \ A_k} (\theta I_i)$$

for $i = 1, \ldots, n$ then there are n and only n different ways of introducing the formula $\theta \ A_1 \ldots A_k$ (which we shall write as ϕ). If we can deduce a formula C from each of the sets of hypotheses

$$H_{i,1} \ \ldots \ H_{i,m_i}$$

then this exhausts all the ways in which we could have introduced ϕ and so we can deduce C from ϕ itself. This is written as a rule

$$\frac{\phi \qquad \overset{\displaystyle [H_{1,1} \ldots H_{1,m_1}]}{\overset{\vdots}{C}} \qquad \ldots \qquad \overset{\displaystyle [H_{n,1} \ldots H_{n,m_n}]}{\overset{\vdots}{C}}}{C}(\theta E)$$

If we now look at the situation in type theory, each of the introduction rules introduces a constructor K_i for elements of the type ϕ, depending upon the appropriate elements of the hypothesis types,

$$\frac{y_{i,1} : H_{i,1} \ \ldots \ y_{i,m_i} : H_{i,m_i}}{K_i \ y_{i,1} \ \ldots \ y_{i,m_i} \ : \ \phi}(\theta I_i)$$

We define a new elimination object $\theta-elim$, which will bind the variables $y_{i,j}$ in the hypothetical proofs p_i:

$$\frac{p : \phi \ \ldots \qquad \overset{\displaystyle [y_{i,1} : H_{i,1} \ \ldots \ y_{i,m_i} : H_{i,m_i}]}{\overset{\vdots}{p_i : C}} \qquad \ldots}{\theta-elim \ p \ p_1 \ \ldots \ p_n \ : \ C}(\theta E)$$

Given a proof $K_i \ a_1 \ \ldots \ a_{m_i}$ of ϕ, we can simplify the proof of C given by (θE) by substituting the objects a_j for the hypotheses $y_{i,j}$, thus,

$$\theta-elim \ (K_i \ a_1 \ \ldots \ a_{m_i}) \ p_1 \ \ldots \ p_n \quad \rightarrow \quad p_i[a_1/y_{i,1}, \ldots, a_{m_i}/y_{i,m_i}]$$

Let us now consider an example of another connective, conjunction. The introduction rule is

$$\frac{a : A \quad b : B}{(a,b) : A \wedge B}(\wedge I)$$

As we have a single introduction rule, the above scheme gives the elimination rule

$$\frac{p : A \wedge B \qquad \overset{\displaystyle [x : A, y : B]}{\overset{\vdots}{c : C}}}{\wedge-elim_{x,y} \ p \ c \ : \ C}(\wedge E')$$

where we give the subscript in $\wedge\!-\!elim_{x,y}$ to make plain which variables are bound in c by the conjunction elimination. The computation rule reads

$$\wedge\!-\!elim_{x,y}\,(a,b)\,c \;\rightarrow\; c[a/x,b/y]$$

How does this rule relate to the usual ones? If we take $c:C$ to be $x:A$, we have

$$\wedge\!-\!elim_{x,y}\,(a,b)\,x \;\rightarrow\; a\,:\,A$$

so that fst is recovered as $\lambda p\,.\,(\wedge - elim_{x,y}\,p\,x)$; snd is recovered in a similar way. The rule $(\wedge E')$ is no stronger than the usual rules, as given $c:C$ depending upon $x:A, y:B$, and the element $p:A \wedge B$, we can build the object

$$c[fst\,p/x, snd\,p/y] \;:\; C$$

which behaves exactly like the object $\wedge - elim_{x,y}\,p\,c$ when p is a pair.

The inversion principle applies to the rules for the existential quantifier, and also to the rules for finite types, N_n, the natural numbers and all well-founded types such as lists and trees. It does not, however, apply to the naïve rule $(SetE)$ for subset elimination.

There is a difficulty in inverting the rules for implication and universal quantification, because the introduction rules for these constructs discharge a hypothesis. Taking the example of implication,

$$\frac{\begin{array}{c}[A]\\ \vdots \\ B\end{array}}{A \Rightarrow B}(\Rightarrow I)$$

To perform our inversion successfully, we need to introduce hypothetical hypotheses, which we first saw in Section 7.7.2. These are introduced in [Schroeder-Heister, 1983a] and [Backhouse, 1986], which seems to have been developed independently of the earlier paper.

We add to our system terms of the form

$$\{\,\Gamma \rhd J\,\} \tag{8.2}$$

where Γ is a context and J is a judgement. This is intended to mean that the statement 8.2 is **introduced** by giving a derivation of the judgement

J in the context Γ, that is

$$\frac{\begin{array}{c}[\Gamma]\\ \vdots\\ J\end{array}}{\{\,\Gamma \rhd J\,\}}(\rhd I)$$

To eliminate such a hypothetical hypothesis we have the rule

$$\frac{\{\,\Gamma \rhd J\,\}\quad \Gamma[t_1/x_1,\ldots,t_n/x_n]}{J[t_1/x_1,\ldots,t_n/x_n]}(\rhd E)$$

where a derivation of an instance of a context is taken to be a collection of derivations of the instances of the constituent judgements. How do we use these hypothetical hypotheses in the inversion of the rule for implication? Following the inversion procedure, we have

$$\frac{A \Rightarrow B \qquad \begin{array}{c}[\{\,A \rhd B\,\}]\\ \vdots\\ C\end{array}}{C}(\Rightarrow E')$$

which gives the rule of *modus ponens* thus:

$$\frac{A \Rightarrow B \quad \dfrac{[\{\,A \rhd B\,\}]\quad A}{B}(\rhd E)}{B}(\Rightarrow E')$$

In order to state correctly the rule for $\Rightarrow$ elimination in this form, we need to be careful about how variables are bound in expressions. The most perspicacious statement can be made if we assume a binding operation Λ in the meta-language, with the object language λ acting as a constant as we explained above. Under this discipline the informal abstraction $\lambda x \,.\, e$ will be written $\lambda(\Lambda x.x)$.

If we denote meta-theoretic application by an infix '$\cdot$', we have

$$\frac{f\!:\!A \Rightarrow B \qquad \begin{array}{c}[\{\,x\!:\!A \rhd (e \cdot x)\!:\!B\,\}]\\ \vdots\\ (c \cdot e)\;:\;C\end{array}}{expand\,f\,c\;:\;C}(\Rightarrow E')$$

with the associated computation rule

$$expand\,(\lambda\,g)\,c \;\rightarrow\; c \cdot g$$

Backhouse gave a number of principles for the inversion, but there are difficulties of deciding when his method produces a consistent system, especially when recursive types are involved. In [Dybjer, 1989] a more general inversion principle is presented, which is based on the observation that all the types of type theory, apart from the universes, can be seen as arising from systems of inductive definitions in the appropriate logical framework. He shows that the type forming operations may be parametrized, and can also permit simultaneous definition of types.

Such a system also has semantic implications: if a proposed type can be presented as a positive inductive definition then consistent rules for its elimination and computation can be deduced automatically. It would appear that this sanctions additions such as [Dyckhoff, 1985], though not the subset or quotient constructions.

A final remark is in order. It is well known that in classical logic, various sets of connectives such as $\neg, \Rightarrow$ and $\neg, \wedge$ are complete, in being able to express all possible propositional functions; what is the situation for intuitionistic logic? It is shown in [Schroeder-Heister, 1983b] that the set $\wedge, \vee, \Rightarrow, \neg, \exists, \forall$ is sufficient to define all the connectives defined by the *standard* forms of introduction and elimination rules, where by this is meant rules which abide by the inversion principle described above.

Exercises

8.1 Show that the inversion principle fails to apply to the rule $(SetE)$ introduced in the previous chapter.

8.2 Check that the inversion principle applies to the rules for the finite types, the natural numbers and to the rules for the type of finite lists.

8.3 Does the inversion principle apply to the rules for the inductive and co-inductive types of Sections 7.10 and 7.11? Does it apply to the definitions of general recursion given in the previous chapter?

Chapter 9
Conclusions

This chapter gives a survey of a number of approaches related to some degree to constructive type theory; we have tried to stress the major points of difference between these systems and type theory itself, but to do complete justice to them would require another book of this size.

9.1   Related work

This section examines various systems, implemented or theoretical, which are related to Martin-Löf's type theory. Rather than give exhaustive descriptions, the chapter contains brief introductions to the systems, bibliographic references and finally a discussion of points of similarity and difference between the systems. Throughout our exposition we have concentrated on the intensional version of type theory [Martin-Löf, 1975b]; we have discussed differences between this and the extensional version as we have gone along.

9.1.1   The Nuprl system

For the past 15 years there has been an active research group in the Computer Science Department of Cornell, lead by Constable and Bates, interested in the implementation of logics. In particular interest has focused upon logics for the formalization of mathematics and program development, and this research has culminated in the development of the Nuprl system, described in the book [Constable and others, 1986]. Nuprl consists of an implementation of a type theory related to the extensional version of

TT, [Martin-Löf, 1985], but modified and augmented in a number of ways, which we discuss presently. Constable's book provides the comprehensive reference on the system; shorter accounts of the underlying ideas can be found in [Bates and Constable, 1985; Constable *et al.*, 1984].

More importantly, the orientation of the system is different from our treatment of type theory in this book, which we have viewed principally as a functional programming system. The emphasis of Nuprl is logical, in that it is designed to support the top-down construction of derivations of propositions in a natural deduction system. The proof objects of type theory are called 'extract terms', the idea being that these are extracted *post hoc* from derivations in which they appear only implicitly.

Proofs are constructed in a top-down way, using the *tactics* and *tacticals* much in the same way as the LCF system [Paulson, 1987]. Indeed the logic is embedded in the ML meta-language, exactly as LCF.

We mentioned earlier that the system differed somewhat from [Martin-Löf, 1985]. In particular it features the strong elimination rules of Section 7.7.2, as well as the liberal notion of *direct computation rules* [Constable and others, 1986], Appendix C, which allow the rewriting of terms without demanding the usual attendant proofs of well-formedness, which are necessitated by the interlinking of syntax and derivation in type-theoretic systems.

It is also augmented in a number of ways, including as it does subsets (see Section 7.2), quotient types (Section 7.5), partial function types (Section 7.12) and so forth. It should be said that many of the additional constructs are introduced with the aim of eliminating computationally irrelevant information from the objects extracted, as we discussed in Section 7.1.2. This is in part due to the implicit nature of the proof objects in many of the derivations.

9.1.2 TK: a theory of types and kinds

The system TK is introduced in the paper [Henson and Turner, 1988] which contains a useful comparison between TT and TK; the topic of program development in TK is discussed in [Henson, 1989]. TK is a theory of constructive sets 'designed with program development as the major desideratum'.

The principle of complete presentation together with the identification of types and propositions are central to type theory as we have introduced it here, and Henson and Turner argue that they leads to a number of its shortcomings, including the unsatisfactory treatment of subsets and general recursion. They propose instead that the system TK should separate the two, with a simpler collection of types (or sets) and a separate collection of logical assertions. The principal set formation operations are *separation* and *induction*. Separation allows definitions such as

$$\{x|\Phi(x)\}$$

which contains precisely those x which have the property Φ. Inductive constructions are performed along lines similar to Section 7.10. To increase expressibility, a hierarchy of universes or *kinds* are also added to the set theory – hence the name TK.

Another difference betweem TK and TT is that terms in the former theory can be partial or undefined, whereas in TT they are, of course, total. The merits of the two approaches can be argued; note that since the logic and the types are no longer identified the presence of partial objects does not make the logic inconsistent.

Reasoning about the sets is performed in a rich logical language, and since the logic is constructive, there are realizability models for it. Using the techniques outlined in Section 8.1.2 programs can be extracted from constructive proofs, and it is this technique for program development which the authors stress, especially in [Henson, 1989]. The realizability approach allows a lot of flexibility in the choice of realizing operations: for example, a conditional assertion can be added to the language and its realizers can be made quite distinct from those of its usual logical definition, for example.

Another advantage of the realizability approach is that computationally irrelevant parts of functions need not appear, a topic we discussed earlier and which is examined in [Henson, 1991].

On the other hand, we have seen that in TT *both* the options of program extraction and explicit functional programming are available and can be combined within a single development – whether they can be combined so well in TK is not clear.

Work on the theoretical foundations of TK and on an implementation both proceed, and it seems certain that our understanding of TT will be enriched by these. It remains to be seen which, if either, of the two systems is the superior for practical program development purposes.

9.1.3 *PX*: a computational logic

It is not only from a type theory that proofs can be extracted; realizability models of intuitionistic formal systems allow the extraction of computations from the system. A markedly different system, called PX, has been built at the Research Institute of Mathematical Sciences at Kyoto University, and is introduced in [Hayashi, 1990] and described in detail in the monograph [Hayashi and Nakano, 1988].

PX is a logic for a type-free theory of computations, based on Feferman's T_0 [Feferman, 1979], from which LISP programs are extracted by a notion of realizability called **px**-realizability. Hayashi argues the requirement that a theory such as TT be total is too restrictive for practical program development, in justification of his logic being based around a system of possibly non-terminating computations. Because of this possibility he incorporates two sorts of variables in the system, one kind ranging over terminating objects, the other over all objects, together with a definedness predicate, E, much as in [Scott, 1979].

Crucial to the logic is the principle of **CIG** (for conditional inductive generation). This is the means by which sub-classes of the domain are defined, by which recursions proceed and by which inductive proofs, including proofs of termination over a domain, are given. In this respect it is analogous to the recursive definitions given by well-founded recursion in Section 7.9, as well as the inductive types of Section 7.10.

Hayashi defines a subset of the language consisting of the formulas which contain no $\vee$ or $\exists$ and which are said to be of *Rank 0*. No realizing terms are needed for rank zero formulas, as they have no computational content. An example of a formula of rank zero is the inclusion $A \subseteq B$; an instance of such a formula might be an assertion of termination: the set A is contained in the domain of definition, B, of the function f. It is shown that such formulas can be proved using classical logic without risking the consistency or computational interpretation of the system, manifesting the flexibility we discussed in the previous section.

9.1.4   AUTOMATH

The AUTOMATH project was begun at Eindhoven University under the direction of Nicolaas de Bruijn in 1966, with the aim

> to develop a system of writing entire mathematical theories in such a precise fashion that verification of the correctness can be carried out by formal operations on the text.

The quotation comes from [de Bruijn, 1980] which gives a survey of the project; examples of the style of presentation of mathematics in the system can be found in [de Bruijn, 1973]. A pinnacle in the achievements of the group is the complete formalization of Landau's *Grundlagen*, a text on analysis.

The system itself uses a form of type theory, based on the notion of propositions as types, to represent logics of either classical or constructive mathematics. Amongst its technical innovations are a discussion of the **irrelevance** of proofs when working in a classical context, which is one of the reasons advanced by de Bruijn for the separation between the notions of **type** and **prop** in the system, an idea anticipating by some years discussions in the computing science community, reported in Section 7.1.2.

In the course of implementing the system, the problem of identifying λ-expressions which agree up to a change of bound variable names (α-conversion) was found to be a considerable overhead. [de Bruijn, 1972] introduces a most useful method of circumventing the problem. Variable names are replaced by numerical indexes; an occurrence of a variable x is replaced by the number of λs which lie between the occurrence and the λx binding it, so that for example the λ-expression

$$\lambda a \,.\, \lambda b \,.\, \lambda c \,.\, (ac)(bc)$$

is replaced by

$$\lambda.\lambda.\lambda.(20)(10)$$

This technique has found application in the implementation of functional programming languages as well as logics; see [Huet, 1990a], Part I.

9.1.5 Type theories

The systems TT_0 and TT can be seen as extensions of the simply typed λ-calculus, as explored in Chapter 2. Other extensions exist, and we examine the two most important here. The first is the **second-order** or *polymorphic* λ-calculus, invented independently by [Reynolds, 1974] and [Girard, 1972], the latter calling the calculus 'System F'. A short yet comprehensive introduction is provided by [Reynolds, 1990].

The calculus extends the first-order lambda calculus by allowing type variables $\alpha, \beta, \ldots$ so that a function such as

$$K \equiv_{df} \lambda x \,.\, \lambda y \,.\, x$$

can be given the type $\alpha \Rightarrow \beta \Rightarrow \alpha$, just as is possible in polymorphic languages such as SML and Miranda. The variables in the expression above can be thought of as being implicitly universally quantified, the function K having the type $\alpha \Rightarrow \beta \Rightarrow \alpha$ for all *instances* of α and β. This implicit quantification is made explicit in the second-order λ-calculus with the introduction of the type abstraction operator Λ and the type forming Π. Given

$$K_{\alpha,\beta} \equiv_{df} \lambda x_\alpha \,.\, \lambda y_\beta \,.\, x \; : \; \alpha \Rightarrow \beta \Rightarrow \alpha$$

we can form

$$K \equiv_{df} \Lambda\alpha.\, \Lambda\beta.\, \lambda x_\alpha \,.\, \lambda y_\beta \,.\, x \; : \; \Pi\alpha.\, \Pi\beta.\, (\alpha \Rightarrow \beta \Rightarrow \alpha)$$

In general, if

$$e \; : \; t$$

then the expression $\Lambda\alpha.\,e$ is parametrized over the type variable α, giving it the type $\Pi\alpha.\,t$. Type abstractions are applied just as ordinary ones, and

$$(\Lambda\alpha.\,e)\,\xi \;:\; t[\xi/\alpha]$$

where ξ is an arbitrary type expression. The system is stronger than the Milner type system, as types can contain embedded universal quantifiers, such as

$$(\Pi\alpha.(\alpha \Rightarrow \alpha)) \Rightarrow (\Pi\alpha.(\alpha \Rightarrow \alpha))$$

but here lies a twist: this type is in the domain of the $\Pi\alpha\ldots$ quantification, so that there is a circularity in the definition of the type. Contrast this with the TT type

$$((\forall\alpha\!:\!U_0).(\alpha \Rightarrow \alpha)) \Rightarrow ((\forall\alpha\!:\!U_0).(\alpha \Rightarrow \alpha))$$

whose definition is not circular – the type lies in U_1 and not U_0 and so is outside the range of the quantifier $(\forall\alpha\!:\!U_0)\ldots\ldots$.

We are used to circularities in definitions of recursive functions and types, so we should not abandon hope about the system. Indeed, it can be shown consistent and strongly normalizing, having the proof-theoretic strength of second-order arithmetic, thus making it more expressive than TT_0. These results can be found in [Girard *et al.*, 1989], and a number of papers on the semantics of the second-order λ-calculus can be found in [Huet, 1990a], Part II.

The Curry–Howard isomorphism extends to this situation, with quantification over types having the equivalent of **quantifying over all propositions**. This has the interesting corollary that we can define many of the propositional connectives from Π. For instance, recalling the simple rule for disjunction elimination, we have

$$\frac{(A \vee B) \quad (A \Rightarrow C) \quad (B \Rightarrow C)}{C}(\vee E)$$

From $A \vee B$ we can infer $(A \Rightarrow C) \Rightarrow (B \Rightarrow C) \Rightarrow C$ for all propositions C, so that in the terminology of the second-order λ-calculus, we have

$$\Pi C.\,(\,(A \Rightarrow C) \Rightarrow (B \Rightarrow C) \Rightarrow C\,)$$

Given an element $a\!:\!A$ we can form an object of this type,

$$\Lambda C.\,\lambda f\,.\,\lambda g\,.\,(f\,a)$$

and of course we can do the same with $b : B$. Are all elements of the type of this form? This question revolves around quite subtle issues in the semantics of the calculus, discussed in [Huet, 1990a], Part II.

The second-order calculus provides no means of defining the type transformation

$$A, B \mapsto \Pi C. \left(\left(A \Rightarrow C \right) \Rightarrow \left(B \Rightarrow C \right) \Rightarrow C \right)$$

as an operation of the calculus itself. This extension of the system is provided by the **calculus of constructions** of Coquand and Huet, to which we turn now. The system was introduced in [Coquand and Huet, 1985], and is discussed in the context of other type theories in [Huet, 1990b], and it allows direct definition of such operators. One means of so doing is the addition of a new type **Prop** of propositions, but we have seen earlier that this leads to logical inconsistency [Girard, 1972]. Without allowing this, the theory of constructions allows the definition of these type operators, and thus a large portion of mathematics is developed in a very simple foundational theory. One point to note is the apparent undefinability of a strong existential type in the language; the definition which embodies the equivalence between

$$(\forall x : A) . \left(C(x) \Rightarrow B \right) \quad \text{and} \quad \left((\exists x : A) . C(x) \right) \Rightarrow B$$

(when x is not free in B) defines a weak equality. The difficulty is the way in which the proof objects and types are mingled in the elimination rule for the strong existential type.

A realizability semantics for the calculus of constructions is discussed in [Huet, 1990a], Part III.

9.2   Concluding remarks

It can be seen from the contents of the last two Chapters that research into type theory is still in flux; despite this, the core of the system has been shown to be a sound and elegant combination of logic and functional programming, and I hope that the reader can share my enthusiasm for the subject. One of the keenest intellectual pleasures is to see connections in the hitherto unconnected, and I can still remember the thrill on discovering that the proof of the deduction theorem for a Hilbert-style logic, learned as a beginning graduate student in logic, is exactly the same as the bracket abstraction algorithm in the λ-calculus, a result used in the implementation of functional programming languages, and which I came upon in a computing context, years later.

Reflecting on the material in Chapter 7, one negative conclusion seems inescapable: additions to the system are quite possible, but each of them seems to extract a price, either by increasing the complexity of the system or by changing some of its meta-mathematical properties. We should therefore be quite certain that we need to add a feature before doing so.

This conclusion is obvious to anyone familiar with the majority of programming languages, in which a jumble of features co-exist in a most precarious fashion; perhaps it is something we have to learn for ourselves.

Nonetheless, the plight of imperative programming seems to get ever more hopeless. Although it is in theory quite possible to develop proofs for programs written in Pascal and C, it simply does not happen. Functional languages offer a much brighter prospect, as their clean semantics makes proofs shorter and higher level. The next step seems to be to move to a system such as type theory, which can provide a single foundation for activities of program development, transformation and verification, just as a LISP Machine supports integrated debugging, profiling and the like. There is still much to be done in making type theory a usable and attractive system which supports programming in the large, but I am certain that languages based on type theory will be as popular in a few years' time as contemporary functional languages such as Miranda and ML based on the simply typed λ-calculus.

References

[Abramsky, 1990] Samson Abramsky. The lazy lambda calculus. In David A. Turner, editor, *Research Topics in Functional Programming*. Addison-Wesley, 1990.

[Aczel, 1980] Peter Aczel. Frege structures and the notions of proposition, truth and set. In *The Kleene Symposium*. North-Holland, 1980.

[Allen, 1987a] Stuart Allen. A non-type-theoretic definition of Martin-Löf's types. In *Proceedings of the Second Annual Symposium on Logic in Computer Science*. IEEE, 1987.

[Allen, 1987b] Stuart Allen. *A Non-Type-Theoretic Semantics for Type-Theoretic Language*. PhD thesis, Cornell University, 1987. Available as technical report TR 87-866 from the Department of Computer Science, Cornell University.

[Andrews, 1965] Peter Bruce Andrews. *A transfinite type theory with type variables*. Studies in logic and the foundations of mathematics. North-Holland, 1965.

[Avron *et al.*, 1987] Arnon Avron, Furio A. Honsell, and Ian A. Mason. Using typed lambda calculus to implement formal systems on a machine. Technical Report ECS-LFCS-87-31, LFCS, Department of Computer Science, University of Edinburgh, 1987.

[Backhouse *et al.*, 1989] Roland Backhouse, Paul Chisholm, Grant Malcolm, and Erik Saaman. Do-it-yourself type theory. *Formal Aspects of Computing*, 1, 1989.

[Backhouse, 1986] Roland Backhouse. On the meaning and construction of the rules in Martin-Löf's theory of types. Technical Report CS 8606, Department of Mathematics and Computing Science, University of Groningen, 1986.

[Backhouse, 1987a] Roland Backhouse. Notes on Martin-Löf's theory of types. *FACS FACTS*, 9(3), October 1987. Newsletter of the BCS Formal Aspects of Computing Science Special Interest Group.

[Backhouse, 1987b] Roland Backhouse. Overcoming the mismatch between programs and proofs. In Peter Dybjer *et al.*, editors, *Proceedings of the Workshop on Programming Logic*. Programming Methodology Group, University of Goteborg and Chalmers University of Technology, 1987. Technical Report, number 37.

[Barendregt, 1984] Henk P. Barendregt. *The lambda calculus – its syntax and semantics*, volume 103 of *Studies in Logic and Foundations of Mathematics*. North-Holland, 1984.

[Basin and del Vecchio, 1989] David A. Basin and Peter del Vecchio. Verification of computational logic in Nuprl. Technical Report TR 89-1018, Department of Computer Science, Cornell University, 1989.

[Bates and Constable, 1985] Joseph L. Bates and Robert L. Constable. Proofs as programs. *ACM Transactions on Programming Languages and Systems*, 7, 1985.

[Beeson, 1985] Michael J. Beeson. *Foundations of Constructive Mathematics*. Springer Verlag, 1985.

[Bentley, 1986] Jon Bentley. *Programming Pearls*. Addison-Wesley, 1986.

[Bird and Wadler, 1988] Richard Bird and Philip Wadler. *An Introduction to Functional Programming*. Prentice-Hall, 1988.

[Bishop and Bridges, 1985] Errett Bishop and Douglas Bridges. *Constructive Mathematics*, volume 279 of *Grundlehren der Mathematischen Wissenschaften*. Springer Verlag, 1985.

[Burstall *et al.*, 1980] Robert M. Burstall, David B. MacQueen, and Donald T. Sanella. HOPE: An experimental applicative language. Technical report, Department of Computer Science, University of Edinburgh, 1980.

[Cardelli and Wegner, 1985] Luca Cardelli and Peter Wegner. On understanding types, data abstraction and polymorphism. *Computing Surveys*, 17, 1985.

[Chisholm, 1987] Paul Chisholm. Derivation of a parsing algorithm in Martin-Löf's theory of types. *Science of Computer Programming*, 8, 1987.

[Chisholm, 1988a] Paul Chisholm. On the relationship between the subset and sigma types in Martin-Löf's 1979 type theory. Technical Report CS 8802, Department of Mathematics and Computing Science, University of Groningen, 1988.

[Chisholm, 1988b] Paul Chisholm. Reducing the proof burden when reasoning with congruence types. Technical Report CS 8807, Department of Mathematics and Computing Science, University of Groningen, 1988.

[Cohn and Milner, 1982] Avra Cohn and Robin Milner. On using Edinburgh LCF to prove the correctness of a parsing algorithm. Technical Report CSR-113-82, Computer Science Department, Edinburgh University, 1982.

[Constable and others, 1986] Robert L. Constable *et al.* *Implementing Mathematics with the Nuprl Proof Development System*. Prentice-Hall Inc., 1986.

[Constable and Smith, 1987] Robert L. Constable and Scott Fraser Smith. Partial objects in constructive type theory. In *Proceedings of the Second Annual Symposium on Logic in Computer Science*. IEEE, 1987.

[Constable *et al.*, 1984] Robert L. Constable, Todd Knoblock, and Joseph L. Bates. Writing programs that construct proofs. *Journal of Automated Reasoning*, 1, 1984.

[Coquand and Huet, 1985] Thierry Coquand and Gérard Huet. A theory of constructions. In *Semantics of Data Types*. Springer Verlag, 1985.

[Coquand, 1986] Thierry Coquand. An analysis of Girard's paradox. In *Proceedings of the First Annual Symposium on Logic in Computer Science*. IEEE, 1986.

[Curry and Feys, 1958] Haskell B. Curry and Robert Feys. *Combinatory Logic*, volume I. North-Holland, 1958.

[Cutland, 1981] Nigel J. Cutland. *Computability*. Cambridge University Press, 1981.

[de Bruijn, 1972] Nicolaas G. de Bruijn. Lambda calculus notation with nameless dummies, a tool for automatic formula manipulation, with an application to the Church–Rosser theorem. *Indag. Math.*, 34, 1972.

[de Bruijn, 1973] Nicolaas G. de Bruijn. AUTOMATH, a language for mathematics. Technical report, Les Presses de l'Université de Montréal, 1973.

[de Bruijn, 1980] Nicolaas G. de Bruijn. A survey of the project AUTOMATH. In Jonathan P. Seldin and J. Roger Hindley, editors, *To H. B. Curry: Essays on combinatory logic, lambda calculus and formalism*. Academic Press, 1980.

[Dijkstra, 1976] Edsger W. Dijkstra. *A Discipline of Programming*. Prentice-Hall International, 1976.

[Diller and Troelstra, 1984] Justus Diller and Anne S. Troelstra. Realizability and intuitionistic logic. *Synthese*, 60, 1984.

[Diller, 1980] Justus Diller. Modified realization and the formulae-as-types notion. In Jonathan P. Seldin and J. Roger Hindley, editors, *To H. B. Curry: Essays on combinatory logic, lambda calculus and formalism*. Academic Press, 1980. A reprint of an unpublished manuscript from 1969.

[Dummett, 1977] Michael Dummett. *Elements of Intuitionism*. Oxford University Press, 1977.

[Dybjer, 1987] Peter Dybjer. From type theory to LCF – a case study in program verification (draft). In Peter Dybjer *et al.*, editors, *Proceedings of the Workshop on Programming Logic*. Programming Methodology

Group, University of Goteborg and Chalmers University of Technology, 1987. Technical Report, number 37.

[Dybjer, 1988] Peter Dybjer. Inductively defined sets in Martin-Löf's type theory. In *Proceedings of the Workshop on General Logic, Edinburgh, February 1897*, 1988. Report ECS-LFCS-88-52, Laboratory for the Foundations of Computer Science, Edinburgh University.

[Dybjer, 1989] Peter Dybjer. An inversion principle for Martin-Löf's type theory. In Peter Dybjer *et al.*, editors, *Proceedings of the Workshop on Programming Logic*. Programming Methodology Group, University of Goteborg and Chalmers University of Technology, 1989. Technical Report, number 54.

[Dyckhoff, 1985] Roy Dyckhoff. Category theory as an extension of Martin-Löf type theory. Technical Report CS/85/3, Department of Computational Science, University of St Andrews, 1985.

[Dyckhoff, 1987] Roy Dyckhoff. Strong elimination rules in type theory. In Peter Dybjer *et al.*, editors, *Proceedings of the Workshop on Programming Logic*. Programming Methodology Group, University of Goteborg and Chalmers University of Technology, 1987. Technical Report, number 37.

[Enderton, 1977] Herbert B. Enderton. *Elements of Set Theory*. Academic Press, 1977.

[Feferman, 1979] Solomon Feferman. Constructive theories of functions and classes. In M. Boffa, D. van Dalen, and K. MacAloon, editors, *Logic Colloquium '78*. North-Holland, 1979.

[Fortune *et al.*, 1983] Steven Fortune, Daniel Leviant, and Michael O'Donnell. The expressiveness of simple and second-order type structures. *Journal of the ACM*, 30(1):151–185, 1983.

[Girard *et al.*, 1989] Jean-Yves Girard, Yves Lafont, and Paul Taylor. *Proofs and Types*, volume 7 of *Cambridge Tracts in Theoretical Computer Science*. Cambridge University Press, 1989.

[Girard, 1972] Jean-Yves Girard. Intérpretation fonctionelle et élimination des coupres dans l'arithmétique d'ordre supérieure. Thèse d'Etat, Université Paris VII, 1972.

[Girard, 1980] Jean-Yves Girard. The system F of variable types, fifteen years later. *Theoretical Computer Science*, 45, 1980.

[Gödel, 1958] Kurt Gödel. Über eine bisher noch nicht benütze Erweiterung des finiten Standpunktes. *Dialectica*, 12, 1958.

[Harper *et al.*, 1987] Robert Harper, Furio Honsell, and Gordon Plotkin. A framework for defining logics. In *Proceedings of the Symposium on Logic in Computer Science*. IEEE, 1987.

[Harper, 1986] Robert Harper. Introduction to Standard ML. Technical Report ECS-LFCS-86-14, Laboratory for Foundations of Computer

Science, Department of Computer Science, University of Edinburgh, November 1986.

[Harrop, 1960] Ronald Harrop. Concerning formulas of the types $A \rightarrow B \vee C$, $A \rightarrow (\exists x)B(x)$ in intuitionistic formal systems. *Journal of Symbolic Logic*, 25, 1960.

[Hayashi and Nakano, 1988] Susumu Hayashi and Hiroshi Nakano. *PX: A Computational Logic*. The MIT Press, 1988.

[Hayashi, 1990] Susumu Hayashi. An introduction to PX. In Gérard Huet, editor, *Logical Foundations of Functional Programming*. Addison-Wesley, 1990.

[Henson and Turner, 1988] Martin C. Henson and Raymond Turner. A constructive set theory for program development. In *Proceedings of the 8th Conference on FST and TCS*, volume 338 of *Lecture Notes in Computer Science*. Springer Verlag, 1988.

[Henson, 1989] Martin C. Henson. Program development in the constructive set theory TK. *Formal Aspects of Computing*, 1, 1989.

[Henson, 1991] Martin C. Henson. Information loss in the programming logic TK. In *Proceedings of the IFIP TC2 Working Conference on Programming Concepts and Methods*. Elsevier, 1991.

[Hodges, 1977] Wilfrid Hodges. *Logic*. Penguin Books, 1977.

[Howard, 1980] William A. Howard. The formulae-as-types notion of construction. In Jonathan P. Seldin and J. Roger Hindley, editors, *To H. B. Curry: Essays on combinatory logic, lambda calculus and formalism*. Academic Press, 1980. A reprint of an unpublished manuscript from 1969.

[Howe, 1988] Douglas J. Howe. *Automating Reasoning in an Implementation of Constructive Type Theory*. PhD thesis, Cornell University, 1988. Available as technical report TR 88-925 from the Department of Computer Science, Cornell University.

[Hudak and Wadler, 1990] Paul Hudak and Philip Wadler. Report on the functional programming language Haskell. Draft proposed standard for the functional programming language, designed by the authors and twelve others, 1990.

[Huet, 1990a] Gérard Huet, editor. *Logical Foundations of Functional Programming*. Addison-Wesley, 1990.

[Huet, 1990b] Gérard Huet. A uniform approach to type theory. In Gérard Huet, editor, *Logical Foundations of Functional Programming*. Addison-Wesley, 1990.

[Hughes, 1983] John Hughes. *The Design and Implementation of Programming Languages*. PhD thesis, University of Oxford, 1983.

[Hughes, 1990] John Hughes. Why functional programming matters. In David A. Turner, editor, *Research Topics in Functional Programming*.

Addison-Wesley, 1990. First published in The Computer Journal, April 1989.

[Jacobs, 1989] Bart Jacobs. The inconsistency of higher order extensions of Martin-Löf's type theory. *Journal of Philosophical Logic*, 18, 1989.

[Johnsson, 1985] Thomas Johnsson. Lambda lifting – transforming programs to recursive equations. In J. P. Jouannaud, editor, *Functional Programming Languages and Computer Architecture*, volume 201 of *Lecture Notes in Computer Science*. Springer Verlag, 1985.

[Kleene, 1945] Stephen C. Kleene. On the interpretation of intuitionistic number theory. *Journal of Symbolic Logic*, 10, 1945.

[Knoblock and Constable, 1986] Todd B. Knoblock and Robert L. Constable. Formalized metareasoning in type theory. Technical Report TR 86-742, Department of Computer Science, Cornell University, 1986.

[Lambek and Scott, 1986] J. Lambek and P. J. Scott. *Introduction to higher order categorical logic*. Cambridge University Press, 1986.

[Lemmon, 1965] E. J. Lemmon. *Beginning Logic*. Thomas Nelson and Sons Limited, 1965.

[MacQueen, 1986] David MacQueen. Using dependent types to express modular structure. In *Proceedings of the 13th ACM Symposium on Principles of Programming Languages*. ACM Press, 1986.

[MacQueen, 1990] David MacQueen. A higher-order type system for functional programming. In David A. Turner, editor, *Research Topics in Functional Programming*. Addison-Wesley, 1990.

[Malcolm and Chisholm, 1988] Grant Malcolm and Paul Chisholm. Polymorphism and information loss in Martin-Löf's type theory. Technical Report CS 8814, Department of Mathematics and Computing Science, University of Groningen, 1988.

[Martin-Löf, 1970] Per Martin-Löf. *Notes on Constructive Mathematics*. Almqvist & Wiksell, Stockholm, 1970.

[Martin-Löf, 1971] Per Martin-Löf. A theory of types. Technical Report 71-3, Department of Mathematics, University of Stockholm, 1971.

[Martin-Löf, 1975a] Per Martin-Löf. About models for intuitionistic type theories and the notion of definitional equality. In Stig Kanger, editor, *Proceedings of the Third Scandinavian Logic Symposium*, Studies in Logic and the Foundations of Mathematics. North-Holland, 1975.

[Martin-Löf, 1975b] Per Martin-Löf. An intuitionistic theory of types: Predicative part. In H. Rose and J. C. Shepherdson, editors, *Logic Colloquium 1973*. North-Holland, 1975.

[Martin-Löf, 1983] Per Martin-Löf. On the meanings of the logical constants and the justifications of the logical laws. Notes taken by Giovanni Sambin and Aldo Ursini of a short course given at the meeting Teoria della Dimostrazione e Filosofia della Logica, Siena, April, 1983.

[Martin-Löf, 1984] Per Martin-Löf. *Intuitionistic Type Theory*. Bibliopolis, Naples, 1984. Based on a set of notes taken by Giovanni Sambin of a series of lectures given in Padova, June 1980.

[Martin-Löf, 1985] Per Martin-Löf. Constructive mathematics and computer programming. In C. A. R. Hoare, editor, *Mathematical Logic and Programming Languages*. Prentice-Hall, 1985.

[Mendelson, 1987] Elliott Mendelson. *Introduction to Mathematical Logic*. Wadsworth, third edition, 1987.

[Mendler, 1987] Paul Francis Mendler. *Inductive Definition in Type Theory*. PhD thesis, Cornell University, 1987. Available as technical report TR 87-870 from the Department of Computer Science, Cornell University.

[Meyer and Reinhold, 1986] Albert R. Meyer and M. B. Reinhold. Type is not a type. In *Proceedings of the 13th ACM Symposium on Principles of Programming Languages*. ACM Press, 1986.

[Milner, 1978] Robin Milner. A theory of type polymorphism in programming. *Journal of Computer and System Sciences*, 17, 1978.

[Moschovakis, 1974] Yiannis N. Moschovakis. *Elementary Induction on Abstract Structures*, volume 77 of *Studies in Logic and Foundations of Mathematics*. North-Holland, 1974.

[Nordström and Petersson, 1983] Bengt Nordström and Kent Petersson. Types and specifications. In *IFIP'83*. Elsevier, 1983.

[Nordström and Petersson, 1985] Bengt Nordström and Kent Petersson. The semantics of module specifications in Martin-Löf's type theory. Technical Report 36, Programming Methodology Group, University of Goteborg and Chalmers University of Technology, 1985.

[Nordström et al., 1990] Bengt Nordström, Kent Petersson, and Jan M. Smith. *Programming in Martin-Löf's Type Theory – An Introduction*, volume 7 of *International Series of Monographs on Computer Science*. Oxford University Press, 1990.

[Nordström, 1985] Bengt Nordström. Multilevel functions in Martin-Löf's type theory. In *Programs as Data Objects*, volume 217 of *Lecture Notes in Computer Science*. Springer Verlag, 1985.

[Nordström, 1988] Bengt Nordström. Terminating general recursion. *BIT*, 28, 1988.

[Paulin-Mohring, 1987] Christine Paulin-Mohring. An example of algorithm development in the calculus of constructions: Binary search for the calculation of the lambo function. In Peter Dybjer et al., editors, *Proceedings of the Workshop on Programming Logic*. Programming Methodology Group, University of Goteborg and Chalmers University of Technology, 1987. Technical Report, number 37.

[Paulin-Mohring, 1989] Christine Paulin-Mohring. Extracting F_ω's programs from proofs in the calculus of constructions. In *Proceedings of the 16th ACM Symposium on Principles of Programming Languages*. ACM Press, 1989.

[Paulson, 1986] Lawrence C. Paulson. Constructing recursion operators in intuitionistic type theory. *Journal of Symbolic Computation*, 2, 1986.

[Paulson, 1987] Lawrence C. Paulson. *Logic and Computation – Interactive proof with Cambridge LCF*. Cambridge University Press, 1987.

[Perry, 1989] Nigel Perry. Hope+. Technical report, Department of Computing, Imperial College, London, 1989. Version 6.

[Péter, 1967] Rosa Péter. *Recursive Functions*. Academic Press, 1967.

[Petersson and Smith, 1985] Kent Petersson and Jan Smith. Program derivation in type theory: The Polish flag problem. In Peter Dybjer *et al.*, editors, *Proceedings of the Workshop on Specification and Derivation of Programs*. Programming Methodology Group, University of Goteborg and Chalmers University of Technology, 1985. Technical Report, number 18.

[Petersson and Synek, 1987] Kent Petersson and Dan Synek. A set constructor for inductive sets in Martin-Löf's type theory. Technical Report 48, Programming Methodology Group, University of Goteborg and Chalmers University of Technology, 1987.

[Peyton Jones, 1987] Simon Peyton Jones. *The Implementation of Functional Programming Languages*. Prentice-Hall International, 1987.

[Prawitz, 1965] Dag Prawitz. *Natural Deduction – A Proof-Theoretical Study*. Almqvist & Wiksell, 1965.

[Reade, 1989] Chris Reade. *Elements of Functional Programming*. Addison-Wesley, 1989.

[Reynolds, 1974] John C. Reynolds. Towards a theory of type structure. In *Colloque sur la Programmation*, volume 19 of *Lecture Notes in Computer Science*. Springer Verlag, 1974.

[Reynolds, 1990] John C. Reynolds. Polymorphic lambda calculus – introduction to part II. In Gérard Huet, editor, *Logical Foundations of Functional Programming*. Addison-Wesley, 1990.

[Rogers, 1967] Hartley Rogers. *Theory of Recursive Functions and Effective Operations*. McGraw-Hill, 1967.

[Russell and Whitehead, 1910] Bertrand Russell and Alfred North Whitehead. *Principia Mathematica*. Cambridge University Press, 1910.

[Saaman and Malcolm, 1987] Erik Saaman and Grant Malcolm. Wellfounded recursion in type theory. Technical Report CS 8710, Department of Mathematics and Computing Science, University of Groningen, 1987.

[Salvesen and Smith, 1989] Anne Salvesen and Jan Smith. The strength of the subset type in Martin-Löf's type theory. In *Proceedings of the Third Annual Symposium on Logic in Computer Science*. IEEE Computer Society Press, 1989.

[Salvesen, 1989a] Anne Salvesen. On specifications, subset types and interpretation of propositions in type theory. In Peter Dybjer *et al.*, editors, *Proceedings of the Workshop on Programming Logic*. Programming Methodology Group, University of Goteborg and Chalmers University of Technology, 1989. Technical Report, number 54.

[Salvesen, 1989b] Anne Salvesen. Polymorphism and monomorphism in Martin-Löf's type theory. Updated version of a Technical Report from the Norwegian Computing Centre, 1989.

[Schmidt, 1986] David A. Schmidt. *Denotational Semantics*. Allyn and Bacon, 1986.

[Schroeder-Heister, 1983a] Peter Schroeder-Heister. The completeness of intuitionistic logic with respect to a validity concept based on an inversion principle. *Journal of Philosophical Logic*, 12, 1983.

[Schroeder-Heister, 1983b] Peter Schroeder-Heister. Generalized rules for quantifiers and the completeness of the intuitionistic operators $\&, \vee, \supset, \perp, \forall, \exists$. In *Computation and Proof Theory, Proceedings of Logic Colloquium Aachen*. Springer Verlag, 1983.

[Schütte, 1977] Kurt Schütte. *Proof Theory*. Springer Verlag, 1977.

[Scott, 1979] Dana S. Scott. Identity and existence in intuitionistic logic. In M. P. Fourman, C. S. Mulvey, and D. S. Scott, editors, *Applications of Sheaves*. Springer Verlag, 1979.

[Scott, 1980] Dana S. Scott. Relating theories of the lambda calculus. In Jonathan P. Seldin and J. Roger Hindley, editors, *To H. B. Curry: Essays on combinatory logic, lambda calculus and formalism*. Academic Press, 1980.

[Smith, 1984] Jan M. Smith. An interpretation of Martin-Löf's type theory in a type-free theory of propositions. *Journal of Symbolic Logic*, 49, 1984.

[Smith, 1987] Jan M. Smith. The independence of Peano's fourth axiom from Martin-Löf's type theory without universes. Technical Report 31, Programming Methodology Group, University of Goteborg and Chalmers University of Technology, 1987.

[Smith, 1988] Scott Fraser Smith. *Partial Objects in Type Theory*. PhD thesis, Cornell University, 1988. Available as technical report TR 88-938 from the Department of Computer Science, Cornell University.

[Stoy, 1977] Joseph E. Stoy. *Denotational Semantics: The Scott-Strachey approach to programming language theory*. MIT Press, 1977.

[Strachey, 1967] Christopher Strachey. Fundamental concepts in programming languages. In *Proceedings of International Summer School in Computer Programming*, 1967.

[Swaen, 1989] Marco D. G. Swaen. *Weak and Strong Sum-Elimination in Intuitionistic Type Theory.* PhD thesis, University of Amsterdam, 1989.

[Tait, 1967] William W. Tait. Intensional interpretation of functionals of finite type, I. *Journal of Symbolic Logic*, 32, 1967.

[Tennent, 1979] Robert D. Tennent. *Principles of Programming Languages.* Prentice-Hall, 1979.

[Thompson, 1986] Simon J. Thompson. Laws in Miranda. In *Proceedings of the ACM Conference on LISP and Functional Programming.* ACM Press, 1986.

[Thompson, 1989a] Simon J. Thompson. Functional programming: Executable specifications and program transformation. In *Proceedings of Fifth International Workshop on Software Specification and Design.* IEEE Press, 1989.

[Thompson, 1989b] Simon J. Thompson. A logic for Miranda. *Formal Aspects of Computing*, 1, 1989.

[Thompson, 1990] Simon J. Thompson. Lawful functions and program verification in Miranda. *Science of Computer Programming*, 13, 1990.

[Troelstra and van Dalen, 1988] Anne S. Troelstra and D. van Dalen. *Constructivism in Mathematics, An Introduction*, volume I and II. North-Holland, 1988.

[Troelstra, 1973] Anne S. Troelstra, editor. *Metamathematical Investigation of Intuitionistic Arithmetic and Analysis*, volume 344 of *Lecture Notes in Mathematics.* Springer Verlag, 1973.

[Troelstra, 1986] Anne S. Troelstra. Strong normalization for typed terms with surjective pairing. *Notre Dame Journal of Formal Logic*, 27, 1986.

[Troelstra, 1987] Anne S. Troelstra. On the syntax of Martin-Löf's type theories. *Theoretical Computer Science*, 51, 1987.

[Turner, 1985] David A. Turner. Miranda: a non-strict functional language with polymorphic types. In J. P. Jouannaud, editor, *Functional Programming Languages and Computer Architecture.* Springer Verlag, 1985.

[Turner, 1989] David A. Turner. A new formulation of constructive type theory. In Peter Dybjer *et al.*, editors, *Proceedings of the Workshop on Programming Logic.* Programming Methodology Group, University of Goteborg and Chalmers University of Technology, 1989. Technical Report, number 54.

[Turner, 1990] David A. Turner. *Research Topics in Functional Programming.* Addison-Wesley, 1990.

[Wadler and Blott, 1989] Philip Wadler and Stephen Blott. Making *ad hoc* polymorphism less *ad hoc*. In *Proceedings of the 16th ACM Symposium on Principles of Programming Languages*. ACM Press, 1989.

[Wikström, 1987] Åke Wikström. *Functional Programming in Standard ML*. Prentice-Hall, 1987.

Rule Tables

Formation, introduction and elimination rules

$$\frac{A \text{ is a type} \quad B \text{ is a type}}{(A \wedge B) \text{ is a type}}(\wedge F) \qquad \frac{p \,:\, A \quad q \,:\, B}{(p,q) \,:\, (A \wedge B)}(\wedge I)$$

$$\frac{r \,:\, (A \wedge B)}{\mathit{fst}\ r \,:\, A}(\wedge E_1) \qquad\qquad \frac{r \,:\, (A \wedge B)}{\mathit{snd}\ r \,:\, B}(\wedge E_2)$$

$$\frac{A \text{ is a type} \quad B \text{ is a type}}{(A \Rightarrow B) \text{ is a type}}(\Rightarrow F) \qquad \frac{\begin{array}{c}[x:A]\\ \vdots\\ e \,:\, B\end{array}}{(\lambda x{:}A)\,.\,e \,:\, (A \Rightarrow B)}(\Rightarrow I)$$

$$\frac{q \,:\, (A \Rightarrow B) \quad a \,:\, A}{(q\ a) \,:\, B}(\Rightarrow E)$$

$$\frac{A \text{ is a type} \quad B \text{ is a type}}{(A \vee B) \text{ is a type}}(\vee F)$$

$$\frac{q \,:\, A}{\mathit{inl}\ q \,:\, (A \vee B)}(\vee I_1) \qquad\qquad \frac{r \,:\, B}{\mathit{inr}\ r \,:\, (A \vee B)}(\vee I_2)$$

$$\frac{p \,:\, (A \vee B) \quad f \,:\, (A \Rightarrow C) \quad g \,:\, (B \Rightarrow C)}{\mathit{cases}\ p\ f\ g \,:\, C}(\vee E)$$

$$\frac{p{:}(A \vee B) \quad \begin{array}{c}[x:A]\\ \vdots\\ u{:}C\end{array} \quad \begin{array}{c}[y:B]\\ \vdots\\ v{:}C\end{array}}{\mathit{vcases}'_{x,y}\ p\ u\ v \,:\, C}(\vee E')$$

$$\frac{[x:A] \qquad\qquad [y:B]}{}$$

$$\frac{p:(A\vee B) \quad u:C[inl\ x/z] \quad v:C[inr\ y/z]}{vcases''_{x,y}\ p\ u\ v\ :\ C[p/z]}(\vee E'')$$

$$\frac{p:(A\vee B) \quad q:(\forall x:A).C[inl\ x/z] \quad r:(\forall y:B).C[inr\ y/z]}{cases^\dagger\ p\ q\ r\ :\ C[p/z]}(\vee E^\dagger)$$

$$\frac{}{\bot\ is\ a\ type}(\bot F) \qquad\qquad \frac{p\ :\ \bot}{abort_A\ p\ :\ A}(\bot E)$$

$$\frac{A\ is\ a\ type}{x:A}(AS)$$

$$\frac{[x:A]}{\vdots}$$

$$\frac{A\ is\ a\ type \quad P\ is\ a\ type}{(\forall x:A).P\ is\ a\ type}(\forall F) \qquad \frac{p\ :\ P}{(\lambda x:A).p\ :\ (\forall x:A).P}(\forall I)$$

$$\frac{a\ :\ A \quad f\ :\ (\forall x:A).P}{f\ a\ :\ P[a/x]}(\forall E)$$

$$[x:A]$$
$$\vdots$$

$$\frac{A\ is\ a\ type \quad P\ is\ a\ type}{(\exists x:A).P\ is\ a\ type}(\exists F) \qquad \frac{a\ :\ A \quad p\ :\ P[a/x]}{(a,p)\ :\ (\exists x:A).P}(\exists I)$$

$$\frac{p\ :\ (\exists x:A).P}{Fst\ p\ :\ A}(\exists E'_1) \qquad\qquad \frac{p\ :\ (\exists x:A).P}{Snd\ p\ :\ P[Fst\ p/x]}(\exists E'_2)$$

$$[x:A;y:B]$$
$$\vdots$$

$$\frac{p\ :\ (\exists x:A).B \qquad c:C}{Cases_{x,y}\ p\ c\ :\ C}(\exists E')$$

$$[x:A;y:B]$$
$$\vdots$$

$$\frac{p:(\exists x:A).B \quad c:C[(x,y)/z]}{Cases_{x,y}\ p\ c\ :\ C[p/z]}(\exists E)$$

$$\frac{a\leftrightarrow b \quad B(a)\ is\ a\ type}{B(b)\ is\ a\ type}(S_1) \qquad \frac{a\leftrightarrow b \quad p(a):B(a)}{p(b):B(b)}(S_2)$$

$$\frac{A\leftrightarrow B \quad A\ is\ a\ type}{B\ is\ a\ type}(S_3) \qquad \frac{A\leftrightarrow B \quad p:A}{p:B}(S_4)$$

$$[x:A]$$
$$\vdots$$

$$\frac{a:A \quad B \text{ is a type}}{B[a/x] \text{ is a type}}(S_5)$$

$$[x:A]$$
$$\vdots$$

$$\frac{a:A \quad b:B}{b[a/x]:B[a/x]}(S_6)$$

$$\frac{}{bool \text{ is a type}}(bool\ F) \qquad \frac{}{True\ :\ bool}(bool\ I_1) \qquad \frac{}{False\ :\ bool}(bool\ I_2)$$

$$\frac{tr\ :\ bool \quad l\ :\ C[True/x] \quad d\ :\ C[False/x]}{if\ tr\ then\ l\ else\ d\ :\ C[tr/x]}(bool\ E)$$

$$\frac{}{N_n \text{ is a type}}(N_n F) \qquad \frac{}{1_n\ :\ N_n}(N_n I) \quad \cdots \quad \frac{}{n_n\ :\ N_n}(N_n I)$$

$$\frac{e:N_n \quad l_1:C[c_1/x] \ \ldots\ l_n:C[c_n/x]}{cases_n\ e\ c_1 \ldots c_n\ :\ C[e/x]}(N_n E)$$

$$\frac{}{\top \text{ is a type}}(\top F) \qquad\qquad \frac{}{Triv\ :\ \top}(\top I)$$

$$\frac{x:\top \quad l:C(Triv)}{case\ x\ c\ :\ C(x)}(\top E)$$

$$\frac{}{N \text{ is a type}}(N F) \qquad\qquad \frac{}{0\ :\ N}(N I_1) \qquad \frac{n\ :\ N}{(succ\ n)\ :\ N}(N I_2)$$

$$\frac{n\ :\ N \quad l\ :\ C[0/x] \quad f\ :\ (\forall n:N).(C[n/x] \Rightarrow C[succ\ n/x])}{prim\ n\ c\ f\ :\ C[n/x]}(N E)$$

$$\frac{}{tree \text{ is a type}}(tree\ F) \qquad\qquad \frac{}{Null\ :\ tree}(tree\ I_1)$$

$$\frac{n:N \quad u:tree \quad v:tree}{(Bnode\ n\ u\ v):tree}(tree\ I_2)$$

$$\frac{\begin{array}{l} t:tree \\ l:C[Null/x] \\ f:(\forall n:N).(\forall u:tree).(\forall v:tree).(C[u/x] \Rightarrow C[v/x] \Rightarrow C[(Bnode\ n\ u\ v)/x]) \end{array}}{trec\ t\ c\ f\ :\ C[t/x]}(tree\ E)$$

$$\frac{A \text{ is a type} \quad a:A \quad b:A}{I(A,a,b) \text{ is a type}}(IF) \qquad \frac{a:A}{r(a)\ :\ I(A,a,a)}(II)$$

$$\frac{a \leftrightarrow b \quad a:A \quad b:A}{r(a):I(A,a,b)}(II') \qquad \frac{l\ :\ I(A,a,b) \quad d\ :\ C(a,a,r(a))}{J(c,d)\ :\ C(a,b,c)}(IE)$$

$$\frac{A \text{ is a type}}{[A] \text{ is a type}}(list\ F)$$

$$\frac{}{[\ ] \ : \ [A]}(list \ I_1)$$

$$\frac{a:A \quad l:[A]}{(a::l) \ : \ [A]}(list \ I_2)$$

$$\frac{\begin{array}{l} l:[A] \\ s:C[[\ ]/x] \\ f:(\forall a:A).(\forall l:[A]).(C[l/x] \Rightarrow C[(a::l)/x]) \end{array}}{lrec \ l \ s \ f \ : \ C[l/x]}(list \ E)$$

$$[x \ : \ A]$$
$$\vdots$$
$$\frac{A \ is \ a \ type \quad B(x) \ is \ a \ type}{(W \ x:A).B(x) \ is \ a \ type}(WF)$$

$$\frac{a \ : \ A \quad f \ : \ (B(a) \Rightarrow (W \ x:A).B(x))}{node \ a \ f \ : \ (W \ x:A).B(x)}(WI)$$

$$\frac{w:(W \ x:A).B(x) \quad R:Ind(A,B,C)}{(Rec \ w \ R) \ : \ C(w)}(WE)$$

$$[x:A]$$
$$\vdots$$
$$\frac{A \ is \ a \ type \quad B \ is \ a \ type}{\{\,x:A \mid B\,\} \ is \ a \ type}(SetF) \qquad \frac{a:A \quad p:B[a/x]}{a \ : \ \{\,x:A \mid B\,\}}(SetI)$$

$$[x:A; y:B]$$
$$\vdots$$
$$\frac{a:\{\,x:A \mid B\,\} \quad c(x):C(x)}{c(a) \ : \ C(a)}(SetE)$$

$$\frac{\begin{array}{l} A \ is \ a \ type \\ x:A \ , \ y:A \vdash E \ is \ a \ type \\ x:A \vdash r \ : \ E[x/x, x/y] \\ x:A \ , \ y:A \ , \ r:E \vdash s:E[y/x, x/y] \\ x:A \ , \ y:A \ , \ z:A \ , \\ \quad r:E \ , \ s:E[y/x, z/y] \vdash t:E[x/x, z/y] \end{array}}{A/\!/E_{x,y} \ is \ a \ type}(QF)$$

$$\frac{a:A}{a:A/\!/E_{x,y}}(QI)$$

$$\frac{\begin{array}{c}[x:A]\\\vdots\\a:A/\!/E_{x,y}\end{array}\quad\begin{array}{c}\\\\c(x):C(x)\end{array}\quad\begin{array}{c}[x:A\,,\,y:A\,,\,p:E]\\\vdots\\t:I(C(x),c(x),c(y))\end{array}}{c(a)\ :\ C(a)}(QE)$$

$$\frac{a:A\quad b:A\quad p:E[a/x,b/y]}{r(a)\ :\ I(A/\!/E_{x,y},a,b)}(Q\!=)$$

$$\frac{\begin{array}{cc}&[x:A,y:A]\\&\vdots\\A\ is\ a\ type&(x\prec y)\ is\ a\ type\end{array}}{Acc(A,\prec)\ is\ a\ type}(AccF)$$

$$\frac{\begin{array}{cc}&[y:A,y\prec a]\\&\vdots\\a:A&y:Acc(A,\prec)\end{array}}{a:Acc(A,\prec)}(AccI)$$

$$\frac{\begin{array}{cc}&\left[\begin{array}{c}x:Acc(A,\prec)\\z:A,z\prec x\quad\triangleright\quad(f\,z):C(z)\end{array}\right]\\&\vdots\\p\ :\ Acc(A,\prec)&(e\,x\,f):C(x)\end{array}}{rec\,e\,p\ :\ C(p)}(AccE)$$

$$\frac{\Theta\ monotonic}{Fix\ \Theta\ is\ a\ type}(IndF)$$

$$\frac{\begin{array}{c}[\,T\subseteq Fix\ \Theta\,]\\\vdots\\g\ :\ (\forall x:T).C\Rightarrow(\forall y:\Theta\,T).C[y/x]\end{array}}{fix\ g\ :\ (\forall z:Fix\ \Theta).C[z/x]}(IndE)$$

$$\frac{\Psi\ monotonic}{(Xif\ \Psi)\ is\ a\ type}(CoinF)$$

$$\frac{\begin{array}{cc}&[y:D\,,\,z:D\Rightarrow T]\\&\vdots\\d\ :\ D&b\ :\ \Psi\,T\end{array}}{xif_{y,z}\ b\,d\ :\ Xif\ \Psi}(CoinI)$$

Computation rules

$$fst\ (p,q)\ \rightarrow\ p$$
$$snd\ (p,q)\ \rightarrow\ q$$
$$((\lambda x:A)\,.\,p)\ a\ \rightarrow\ p[a/x]$$
$$cases\ (inl\ q)\ f\ g\ \rightarrow\ f\ q$$
$$cases\ (inr\ r)\ f\ g\ \rightarrow\ g\ r$$
$$vcases_{x,y}\ (inl\ a)\ u\ v\ \rightarrow\ u[a/x]$$
$$vcases_{x,y}\ (inr\ b)\ u\ v\ \rightarrow\ v[b/y]$$
$$Fst\ (p,q)\ \rightarrow\ p$$
$$Snd\ (p,q)\ \rightarrow\ q$$
$$Cases_{x,y}\ (a,b)\ c\ \rightarrow\ c[a/x,b/y]$$
$$if\ True\ then\ c\ else\ d\ \rightarrow\ c$$
$$if\ False\ then\ c\ else\ d\ \rightarrow\ d$$
$$cases_n\ 1_n\ c_1 \ldots c_n\ \rightarrow\ c_1$$
$$cases_n\ 2_n\ c_1 \ldots c_n\ \rightarrow\ c_2$$
$$\ldots$$
$$cases_n\ n_n\ c_1 \ldots c_n\ \rightarrow\ c_n$$
$$case\ x\ c\ \rightarrow\ c$$
$$prim\ 0\ c\ f\ \rightarrow\ c$$
$$prim\ (succ\ n)\ c\ f\ \rightarrow\ f\ n\ (prim\ n\ c\ f)$$
$$trec\ Null\ c\ f\ \rightarrow\ c$$
$$trec\ (Bnode\ n\ u\ v)\ c\ f\ \rightarrow\ f\ n\ u\ v\ (trec\ u\ c\ f)\ (trec\ v\ c\ f)$$
$$J(r(a),d)\ \rightarrow\ d$$
$$lrec\ [\,]\ s\ f\ \rightarrow\ s$$
$$lrec\ (a::l)\ s\ f\ \rightarrow\ f\ a\ l\ (lrec\ l\ s\ f)$$
$$Rec\ (node\ a\ f)\ R\ \rightarrow\ R\ a\ f\ (\lambda x\,.\,Rec\ (f\ x)\ R)$$
$$rec\ e\ p\ \rightarrow\ e\ p\ (rec\ e)$$
$$Fix\ \Theta\ \rightarrow\ \Theta\ (Fix\ \Theta)$$
$$fix\ g\ \rightarrow\ g\ (fix\ g)$$
$$xif_{y,z}\ b\ d\ \rightarrow\ b[d/y\,,\ \lambda w\,.\,(xif_{y,z}\ b\ w)/z]$$

Index